Tax Design and Administration in a Post-BEPS Era:

A Study of Key Reform Measures in 18 Jurisdictions

Tax Design and Administration in a Post-BEPS Era:

A Study of Key Reform Measures in 18 Jurisdictions

Kerrie Sadiq, Adrian Sawyer and Bronwyn McCredie

Editors

Tax Design and Administration in a Post-BEPS Era.

Fiscal Publications, Unit 100, The Guildhall Edgbaston Park Road, Birmingham, B15 2TU, UK.

For more information, contact info@ fiscalpublications.com
or visit: http://www. fiscalpublications.com

ISBN: 978-1-906201-48-7

Typesetting by P.K. McBride.

Cover design by Filter Design Ltd.

Printed in Great Britain by CPI Antony Rowe, Cheltenham.

Contents

For Lily, Erin, Anna, Andrew, Arnika, and Jorja. May our work on tax reform make the world a better place for your future.

Preface and Acknowledgements

With the initial stages of the G20/OECD BEPS program complete, many participating jurisdictions have incorporated significant reforms into their domestic tax policy. While there is high level support for international reform, each jurisdiction has designed its reforms in light of local social and economic goals. As a result, the type of international tax reform introduced at a domestic level will vary between capital importing and capital exporting jurisdictions, developed and developing jurisdictions, and those jurisdictions with a sophisticated tax administrative system compared to those without.

Tax changes made in response to the BEPS project and the 15 Actions it sets out will impact business models and operating structures and taxpayer responses will necessarily vary across the spectrum of approaches taken by different jurisdictions. This volume is the outcome of a project seeking to understand and reconcile the positions that different jurisdictions are taking. A case study method based on representative reports from 18 jurisdictions that responded to the call for international tax reform as part of the OECD's BEPS initiative provided the basis for the study.

The 18 jurisdictions reported in this volume reflect a diverse range of tax jurisdictions to provide a picture of the different approaches to BEPS implementation at a domestic level. The jurisdictions represent a mix of OECD member and non-member jurisdictions, G20 member and non-member jurisdictions, and jurisdictions with different levels of capital import and export. As the chapters reveal, each jurisdiction is unique, each has had different experiences adopting BEPS measures, and some have gone beyond the 15 Actions to also introduce unilateral measures designed to enhance the integrity and transparency of tax regimes. Each chapter commences with an overview of the relevant jurisdiction and its unique attributes. Discussion centres on the political system, tax system, OECD and G20 membership status, regional affiliation and industries. An analysis follows of that jurisdiction's response to BEPS. The body of each chapter highlights the extent to which and how the recommendations in the 15 Actions are reflected in local law. Unilateral measures are also discussed, with chapters concluding with a review of local tax administration systems and prospects for the future of international tax reform.

A project of this magnitude would not be possible without the support of many people. First and foremost, we wish to thank CPA Australia for a 2017 Global Perspectives Research Grant. This project was made possible with their support and funding. We specifically thank Jan Haverfield, Gavan Ord, and Paul Drum, for their support. Thanks, too, are due to Andy Lymer of Fiscal Publications for working with us to ensure the project came to fruition.

Research assistance for this project was provided by Dr Peter Mellor and Dr Melinda Jone. We thank them both. Completing this project in 12 months was only made possible with their assistance. Melinda undertook early work on the project scoping out jurisdictions and providing the foundations for each chapter – the authors were incredibly grateful for her work. Peter undertook a multitude of tasks including database searches, proofreading, editing, and writing. Each and every author has expressed their gratitude to Peter for the research work he carried out and the suggestions he offered for their work. The project is unique because of their contributions and the unique perspectives they bring. Finally, we thank Professor Richard Krever for being our Principal Adviser on the project and providing us with his expert guidance from start to finish. The hours he willingly and graciously devoted to this project are too many to count. His passion for tax and deep knowledge of its workings is evident in this project.

We would also like to formally express our thanks to the chapter contributors to this volume, a mix of academics, practitioners and revenue authority personnel. A total of 32 people were involved in this project with everyone committing to our deadlines and delivering this final product. The speed and magnitude of changes to the international tax system in the past decade is unprecedented. Reflections on where we now stand and how we got there can provide helpful insights into where we may be heading next. We are grateful to all whose inputs helped bring the project to fruition.

Kerrie Sadiq

Adrian Sawyer

Bronwyn McCredie

The Editors

Kerrie Sadiq

Kerrie is a Professor of Taxation in the School of Accountancy at the QUT Business School, Queensland University of Technology. She holds a B Com (UQ), LLB (Hons) (UQ), LLM (QUT), and PhD (Deakin). Kerrie is a Chartered Tax Adviser as designated by the Taxation Institute of Australia and a Graduate of the Australian Institute of Company Directors. Kerrie primarily researches in international tax, tax expenditures and capital gains tax. She is author of numerous publications in both Australian and International journals and edited books and is a co-author of taxation texts. She is co-editor of *Australian Tax Review*, one of Australia's leading tax journals. Recent work has been specifically on issues in international tax, such as transfer pricing, the OECD's approach to base erosion and profit shifting (BEPS), Australia's role in the G20 and the BEPS project, automatic exchange of tax information and country-by-country reporting. Prior to joining Queensland University of Technology in 2012, Kerrie spent 20 years at The University of Queensland, as a member of both their Law School and Business School.

Adrian Sawyer

Adrian Sawyer is a Professor of Taxation at the University of Canterbury (UC) Business School. He has just completed a five-year period as the Research Director for the UC Business School. He holds a BCom, LLB and MCom(Hons) (all from UC) and an SJD (Virginia). He is a CA (Chartered Accountants Australia and New Zealand) and CPA (CPA Australia), and Barrister and Solicitor of the High Court of New Zealand. He has an extensive publication record, with articles appearing in scholarly and professional journals and chapters in books published in Asia, Australasia, Europe and North America. He is on numerous editorial boards and is Chair of the Editors of the *New Zealand Journal of Taxation Law and Policy*. His recent work has encompassed aspects of international tax, including both the OECD's and New Zealand's approaches to the BEPS project, automatic exchange of tax information and country-by-country reporting. His other research interests include numerous issues within tax administration and taxpayer compliance. Adrian has been at UC since 1991, and before that was an investigating accountant at the New Zealand Inland Revenue.

Bronwyn McCredie

Bronwyn McCredie is a lecturer in the School of Accountancy at the QUT Business School, Queensland University of Technology. She holds a Bachelor of Commerce with first class honours in Finance and the University medal (BCom Hons Class 1) from the University of Newcastle, a PhD in Finance from the University of

Newcastle and a Postgraduate Certificate in Academic Practice from Queensland University of Technology. She is also a fellow of the Higher Education Academy (HEA). Dr McCredie primarily researches in financial law, taxation and regulation. Her current research focuses on the efficacy of the OECD BEPS program and resultant tax transparency legislation and corporate social responsibility reporting.

1 Actions to Counter Base Erosion and Profit Shifting: A General Report

Kerrie Sadiq* **and Richard Krever****

Abstract

World events in the first decade of this century led many to question the state of the international tax regime and the role it could play in solving national fiscal problems. In 2012, leaders of the Group of 20 (G20) set the OECD an ambitious agenda of working out how tax base erosion and profit shifting could be addressed. The OECD responded with a BEPS (base erosion and profit shifting) plan including 15 distinct Actions. Following a decision by G20 leaders to extend the BEPS project to all countries, under the guidance of the OECD the project evolved into a blueprint for the reform of international tax regimes around the world. By October 2018, 118 jurisdictions had joined the BEPS Inclusive Framework, as the project was labelled. This chapter reviews the 15 Actions and summarises the 18 case studies included in this volume to show how jurisdictions are responding to the obligations set out in the Actions. The case studies indicate countries are taking two paths to combat international tax avoidance – multilateral cooperation through the BEPS program, along with its associated multilateral instrument, and unilateral moves through the adoption of new taxes imposed on multinational enterprises. It remains to be seen which approach will prevail in the long term and whether the multilateral path might someday lead to an international treaty on the allocation of multinational income.

1.1 Setting the Agenda

For the past half decade, much of the attention of tax practitioners, scholars and officials has been focused on the Base Erosion and Profit Shifting (BEPS) initiative of the Organisation for Economic Co-operation and Development (OECD) and government responses to the 15 "Actions" advocated by that body to reduce international tax avoidance. Undertaken at the behest of and with full endorsement by leaders of the Group of 20 (G20), the most powerful and influential nations on the globe, the OECD's program envisages a sweeping rewrite and alignment of international tax norms.

* QUT Business School, Queensland University of Technology.

** Law School, University of Western Australia.

The BEPS project is commonly traced to work commenced by the OECD starting in the mid-1990s at the request of its member states on what it terms "harmful tax competition", a euphemism for uncooperative tax havens that refused to cooperate with tax authorities in OECD member states. As the organisational terminology shifted from harmful tax *competition* to harmful tax *practices,* in 2000 the OECD released a controversial list of harmful tax havens. Following the election of George W. Bush to the US presidency late that year and with pressure from various quarters in the country that viewed tax competition and the tax havens as useful instruments to inhibit the government's taxing powers, the US announced a re-evaluation of its participation in the OECD program. Following the terrorist attacks on the United States in September 2001 there was an appreciation by some that financial secrecy facilitated the financing of terrorist bodies and in November 2008 at the inaugural leaders summit of the G20, the US joined with other leaders in calling on the OECD to continue efforts to promote tax information exchange.

The G20 leaders meeting took place two months after the collapse of financial services firm Lehman Brothers that triggered a global financial crisis. With the crisis deepening substantially by the time the leaders met again in April 2009, the second leaders meeting called on the OECD to continue efforts to eliminate tax secrecy, prompting the OECD to expand its tax initiative to a "Global Forum on Transparency and Exchange of Information for Tax Purposes". The OECD's work expanded to include studies on base erosion and profit shifting, a development endorsed by the G20 leaders at their 2012 summit, which had specifically identified combating avoidance by way of transfer pricing as a policy priority. In early 2013 the OECD released a report on how base erosion and profit shifting could be tackled (OECD, 2013a) which was followed mid-year by an Action Plan setting out the areas to be addressed (OECD, 2013b). Fifteen Actions were developed and presented to G20 finance ministers in October 2015. A month later the G20 leaders endorsed the package of 15 Actions and called on the OECD to open the BEPS program to all interested countries, including developing countries. In response, the OECD developed an "inclusive framework" to open the BEPS program to non-OECD members, which was established early in 2016 and immediately endorsed by a meeting of G20 finance ministers.

While the program is based on 15 Actions, the BEPS framework has developed into a broader project that includes regular meetings between participants and, for countries joining the framework, agreement that they will adopt "mandatory" elements of the project, most notably four minimum standards: addressing harmful tax practices as set out in Action 5, addressing tax treaty abuse as set out in Action 6, adopting a country-by-country reporting system for transfer pricing as set out in Action 13, and implementing improvements in cross-border tax dispute resolution as set out in Action 14. As of end-September 2018, 118 countries had joined the BEPS inclusive framework agreement.

As the jurisdiction reports in this volume indicate, adoption of other BEPS Actions has been inconsistent in single countries let alone between countries. In some jurisdictions, political impetus has even gone beyond the introduction of the BEPS Actions to include unilateral measures. Perhaps the most notable of these are the UK with its diverted profits tax and Australia with its own later version of that tax, described in the closing part of this chapter. In one key respect, however, the project has arguably upended international tax. In the early decades of the 20th century, particularly shortly before and during the First World War, income taxes were adopted in almost all Western countries that had not previously enacted these taxes. Competition for primary taxing rights was inevitable in a period of growing cross-border investment and business activity as tax bases evolved to assess residents on global income and non-residents on income sourced in the jurisdiction. A group of experts commissioned by the League of Nations to resolve disputes over primary taxing rights concluded the optimal answer was a multilateral treaty dividing taxing rights between residence and source nations. When it became apparent that the optimal solution was not politically attainable, the fall back of bilateral tax treaties based on a common model was proposed.

The prospects for a multilateral treaty on taxation remained dim for half a century but were revived by the OECD and Council of Europe in the early 1980s when a Convention on Mutual Administrative Assistance in Tax Matters was developed. Signed in 1988, the convention became effective in 1995. Prior to the BEPS project, however, the implementation of further multilateral tax agreements outside economic or political communities still seemed unlikely. A proposal for a single multilateral agreement that would be amended by individual signatories through bilateral deviations from the multilateral agreement failed to gain traction (Thuronyi, 2010). The Global Financial Crisis and elevation of the OECD's anti-tax haven program into a full-blown assault on international tax avoidance proved to be a game changer, however. In mid-2017, four years after the release of the BEPS Actions, a Multilateral Convention to Implement Tax Treaty Related Measures to Prevent Base Erosion and Profit Shifting (Multilateral Instrument or MLI), a key Action in the BEPS program, was signed initially by 67 jurisdictions. As of July 2018, when the convention came into effect, 83 jurisdictions were signatories, with Saudi Arabia signing in September 2018 taking the current number to 84.

The shift of global support from unilateral and bilateral solutions to a multilateral approach to tax through joint "actions" and, more significantly, a multilateral tax treaty, may be the most important legacy of the BEPS experience. The world's mindset has changed. With the exception of the United States, always an outlier on global tax matters, multilateralism is no longer anathema to most nations. The door may have opened just slightly to an eventual solution to other global tax issues, most significantly finding an alternative to transfer pricing rules to allocate the income of multinational enterprises, by means of a multilateral agreement.

1.2 Action 1: Addressing Tax Challenges of the Digital Economy

The digital economy poses challenges to both income tax and value added tax (VAT)/goods and services tax (GST) systems. On the income tax side, digital communication makes it possible to provide from a remote location services that previously required a permanent establishment or presence by individual service providers. In some cases, a local server might still be helpful but increasingly cloud computing makes it possible to provide services from servers in any location. On the VAT/GST side, services and products that once had to be stored on media – movies, music, software, games, etc. – and cross customs borders when entering the country can now be sold in digital format and delivered from a location outside the country via the internet, bypassing entirely a customs collection point. At the same time, internet sales platforms provide the means for any number of small suppliers to offer their goods to foreign buyers, leading to a flood of low value items purchased from abroad.

The Action 1 report addressed both income tax and VAT/GST issues related to the digital economy, but unequally. The final report acknowledged that it would be difficult to ring-fence the digital economy from the rest of the economy for income tax purposes. Consequently, while the Action 1 report discussed key features of digital transactions that exacerbate BEPS risks, it did not propose digital specific responses and instead suggested that measures should be adopted in conjunction with general reforms described under the other Action items. The primary solution to income tax issues, it suggested, was a modification of the definition of a permanent establishment to address digital economy enterprises, an option explored further in Action 7, which dealt with other permanent establishment issues as well. It was eventually concluded that the optimal approach would be a modification of the definition of permanent establishment by way of a multilateral treaty, the subject of Action 15.

The primary focus of the Action 1 report was on GST/VAT issues with consideration of a supplier registration system for digital supplies and four alternative collection models for imposing tax on imports of low value tangible goods. The report discussed the merits of and problems with each proposal but made no firm recommendations.

Measures to require foreign vendors of digital services to register when supplies exceed the registration threshold have been adopted or are in the process of being adopted in many developed countries.[1] In the case of the EU, vendors register centrally through a "Mini One-Stop-Shop" (MOSS) system that provides a single central clearing house registration for merchants selling to any number of EU

1 Australia, Japan, Korea, New Zealand, Singapore, South Africa, and Thailand. The United States has no VAT and is generally not supportive of consumption taxes on cross-border digital services.

member states.[2] The story is very different in less developed countries, however. Limited measures such as an equalisation levy on electronic advertisements,[3] a withholding tax on some e-transactions[4] and formal recognition of e-commerce as an industry with no proposed accompanying tax measures[5] have been adopted or proposed but it is clear that less developed countries have made far less progress than wealthier nations on extending the VAT effectively to imported digital supplies.

1.3 Action 2: Neutralising the Effects of Hybrid Mismatch Arrangements

Hybrid mismatch arrangements exploiting differences in tax treatment of business structures in different jurisdictions are widespread. An example of a hybrid mismatch is a partnership treated as a flow-through entity in one jurisdiction and separate legal entity in another. Exploiting the different treatments can cause substantial tax base erosion or may equally lead to overtaxation. If, for example, the business is viewed as a transparent entity in the jurisdiction in which it carries on business and a legal entity in the home jurisdiction, the entity may be unable to claim foreign tax credits for the operating jurisdiction tax borne by the individual partners, persons different from the legal entity seeking a credit.

The problem has long been recognised in international tax circles. Previously, the OECD attempted to address the issue through suggested "interpretations" of existing provisions in the OECD model treaty, with the hope that these interpretations would be applied by countries when interpreting their own bilateral treaties. The limitations of this approach were obvious, however, as the wording in the model treaty and bilateral treaties clearly did not anticipate the problem, making a solution by way of interpretation inconsistent with the actual treaties and underlying domestic legislation. In its plan for Action 2, the OECD suggests a dual prong solution to address the problem, based on modification of treaties by way of the MLI combined with explicit domestic legislation by treaty partners to ensure their domestic laws can accommodate the suggested changes.

A number of OECD countries surveyed in this volume have adopted or are in the process of adopting explicit measures in local law to deal with hybrid mismatches[6] or modifying earlier rules.[7] Complementary assent to the MLI is discussed below, in Action Plan 15. Significantly, jurisdictions surveyed that have entered into the MLI have all, apart from New Zealand, incorporated reservations of some sort to the hybrid mismatch rules. Taking the dissent one step further, the United States on

2 Used by the Netherlands and the UK in this survey.
3 India.
4 Indonesia.
5 Vietnam.
6 Australia, Canada, Japan, Korea, the Netherlands, New Zealand.
7 United Kingdom.

principle does not accept the logic of a need for local action. The problem and need for local responses seems not to be recognised by non-OECD members surveyed,[8] while the view in one jurisdiction, China, appears to be that local law precludes the possibility that a hybrid arrangement could be subject to different legal characterisations inside and out of the country.

1.4 Action 3: Designing Effective Controlled Foreign Company (CFC) Rules

Action 3 recommendations address tax deferral associated with investments through companies in low tax jurisdictions. It has long been recognised that tax law's respect for separate entities offers many opportunities for tax deferral – income could be accumulated in a controlled foreign company located in a tax haven with the owners incurring no tax liability until the funds were repatriated to them. In the interim, the tax haven entity could invest in any asset that its owners might otherwise buy directly.

The world's first comprehensive anti-deferral regime was adopted in 1962 in the United States. Since then, the US "Subpart F" rules, as they are known from their location in the Internal Revenue Code, have served as a loose model for comparable anti-deferral regimes across the globe. The spread of anti-deferral rules accelerated significantly from the 1980s as countries loosened or removed currency controls, making it possible for taxpayers to hold investments through foreign holding companies.

While the mechanics vary from country to country, all anti-deferral systems raise the same issues. The operational heart of the regimes is the attribution of income derived by a controlled foreign company (CFC) to its shareholders. Where the shareholders are unable to prove the actual income of the subsidiary, a deemed rate of return is used, much higher than the prevailing home country government bond rate on the assumption that rational investors are unlikely to put capital in a foreign company with allegedly no way of knowing what income that company is deriving unless it is far greater than the guaranteed income safely available in the home jurisdiction.

Four refinements commonly complete a CFC regime. First, the attribution rules generally only apply to shareholders with interests greater than an attribution threshold and only when the company is a "controlled" foreign company, usually meaning at least a designated number of residents have a controlling voting or dividend entitlement in the company. Ownership is normally traced through any number of intermediary interests that have direct or indirect interests in the CFC.

Second, attribution is usually limited to income derived by CFCs located in tax havens or low tax jurisdictions. A variety of mechanisms are used to identify these

8 See, for example, Nigeria and Thailand.

countries including a number of lists and various definitions of low effective tax rates. Third, it is common to attribute only "passive" income derived by a CFC, on the assumption that passive investments have been diverted to a low tax jurisdiction for tax minimisation purposes only while investment in active business operations has been made to exploit location specific features of the jurisdiction. Fourth, a mechanism such as foreign tax credits is needed to prevent double taxation when attributed income is subject to some taxation. Devising measures to prevent double taxation of income earned through CFCs may be far more challenging than designing comparable rules for resident companies. This is because the foreign tax may be payable in a third country, not the country in which the CFC is resident. For example, if a resident investor has an indirect interest in a tax haven CFC via a subsidiary in a comparable tax jurisdiction, the income of the CFC may be attributed to both the intermediary subsidiary and the shareholders at the top of the ownership chain in another country.

The OECD's Action 3 report views an effective CFC regime as a requisite element of an anti-avoidance armoury and indicates the issues that must be addressed for a CFC rule to work efficiently. The Plan provides little in the way of prescriptive or even suggestive guidance, however, noting that a variety of responses to each issue is possible and the actual path chosen will depend on other design elements of a CFC system.

The impact of Action Plan 3 has been limited. Most advanced economies and some middle income jurisdictions had CFC regimes in place prior to the BEPS project and generally believe their systems are both adequate and compliant with the BEPS Action Plan.[9] One country surveyed adopted a CFC regime in 2017, after the commencement of the BEPS project,[10] and a number of countries amended their CFC rules in the same year.[11] There is, however, no indication the changes have been in response to the BEPS Action Plan.

Several jurisdictions have territorial income tax systems and so do not regard it as avoidance for residents to derive and accumulate income through CFCs.[12] They therefore have neither CFC regimes in place nor plans to adopt them. For other countries that apply tax on a worldwide basis, existing regimes may be in need of improvement[13] and lower income countries with no regimes in place may be particularly vulnerable to deferral avoidance through CFCs.[14]

It seems likely that the impact of Action Plan 3 in the short term will continue to be limited. Jurisdictions with CFC systems in place will tinker with them from time to time but for the most part have sorted out operational issues. Jurisdictions with

9 Australia, the Netherlands, New Zealand and the UK.
10 Indonesia.
11 The United States, South Africa, and Japan.
12 Hong Kong, Singapore, and Malaysia.
13 China.
14 India and Vietnam.

territorial tax systems have no interest in the regimes and countries that arguably would benefit most from adoption of CFC rules to date have not taken the initiative to add anti-deferral rules to their tax laws.

1.5 Action 4: Limiting Base Erosion Involving Interest Deductions and Other Financial Payments

Action 4 recommendations address the problem of base erosion resulting from the use of excessive debt to capitalise subsidiaries in higher tax jurisdictions. Almost all company income tax systems allow companies to deduct interest payments when calculating taxable income but not dividends. As a result, even if dividends are subject to lower withholding tax rates than interest, or even no withholding tax, profits repatriated as dividends will have borne company tax in the source country that is likely to be higher than the withholding tax only imposed on interest payments. The different treatment of interest and dividends has led to thin capitalisation arrangements in which subsidiaries in higher tax jurisdictions are funded with small amounts of capital and larger amounts of debt to shift profits from the higher tax jurisdictions. The problem has been long recognised and the widespread response has been the adoption of thin capitalisation rules that deny a company deductions for interest paid on intragroup loans to the extent a company's debt exceeds a designated ratio to equity. Action 4 suggests an alternative approach, denying deductions for interest expenses to the extent that interest exceeds a prescribed percentage of a company's earnings before interest, taxes, depreciation and amortisation (EBITDA). The proposal anticipates adjustment of the percentage where appropriate if the group as a whole has a higher percentage of interest expenses payable to third parties.

The approach taken in Action 4 has not been widely embraced by those jurisdictions that appear to be satisfied with existing limitations based on a debt-equity ratio rather than the percentage of income system.[15] Australia coincidentally is in the process of adjusting existing rules but has retained the debt-equity ratio basis for its thin capitalisation rule[16] and Korea has also retained a debt-equity ratio thin capitalisation rule applying to financial institutions but supplemented it with an income ratio limitation. Indonesia has recently adopted an interest deduction limitation based on the debt-equity approach. The income percentage approach advocated in Action 4 is used in some jurisdictions,[17] including EU member states that have been required to ensure local laws conform to an EU-wide anti-avoidance

15 China uses a debt-equity ratio rule and no plans to shift have been announced.

16 Australia, for example, intends to modify its rules for valuing assets when applying the debt-equity ratio.

17 India (since 2017), Japan, South Africa (since 2015), and Vietnam (since 2017), for example. Vietnam has indicated it will adopt thin capitalisation rules in addition to the interest deduction limitation rules.

Directive,[18] and the income percentage is under consideration in other cases.[19] As is often the case, the United States has taken a unique path, retaining its current thin capitalisation rules for interest paid to related parties and adopting in 2017 a rule that limits interest deductions on debt between unrelated parties to a maximum of business interest income and 30 per cent of adjusted taxable income. Neither Hong Kong nor Thailand have interest deduction limitation rules, though in the case of Hong Kong it may be possible to use anti-avoidance rules to limit deductions.

1.6 Action 5: Countering Harmful Tax Practices More Effectively, Taking into Account Transparency and Substance

Action 5 looks beyond specific anti-avoidance measures to the role of transparency and modification of tax regimes so they apply to the true underlying substance of arrangements. In a sense, the work is a continuation from the starting point for the OECD's work in the area, a report on *Harmful Tax Competition: An Emerging Global Issue* published in 1998. Action 5 builds on that work and specifically allocates responsibility for progressing the work under the Action to the body that grew out of the earlier initiative, the Forum on Harmful Tax Practices (FHTP).

There are two parts to Action 5: the identification of preferential regimes and obtaining a commitment by countries to transparency through compulsory spontaneous exchange of information of preferential rulings provided to taxpayers. The recommendations respond to concerns that preferential tax regimes are being exploited by way of artificial profit shifting, a process facilitated by the secrecy surrounding preferential rulings provided to taxpayers. Arrangements taking advantage of these situations benefit one jurisdiction while eroding the tax base of other jurisdictions. While the goal of Action 5 is not to harmonise countries' systems for taxing multinationals, it is designed to reduce the distortionary effects of taxation on the location of mobile activities.

As the work to be undertaken under Action 5 was effectively a revamp of the work of the FHTP, the criteria used to identify a harmful tax regime under the first part of Action 5 had already been established. The Final Report on Action 5 adopted four key factors used in the original work and added eight other factors to determine if the tax system in a jurisdiction should be considered a preferential regime. The four key factors are: (1) the regime imposes no or low effective tax rates on income from geographically mobile financial and other service activities; (2) the regime is ring-fenced from the domestic economy; (3) the regime lacks transparency, and (4) there is no effective exchange of information with respect to the regime. In addition, a "substantial activity" requirement was elevated from one of the "other factors" to a key factor with this requirement aligning taxation

18 Applying to the Netherlands and the United Kingdom, in this survey.

19 For example, Malaysia and Nigeria.

with substance by ensuring that taxable profits are not artificially shifted from the location where value is created. The approach agreed on to determine whether there is substantial activity is known as the "nexus approach" where expenditure is used as a proxy for activity.

Contained in the final report were the findings of a review of 43 preferential regimes, including 16 intellectual property (IP) regimes. Of the jurisdictions reported in this volume, China, the Netherlands, and the UK all had their IP regimes reviewed and all were found to be inconsistent with the nexus approach. Australia, China, India, Japan, and South Africa all had non-IP regimes reviewed which were found to be not harmful, while four of Indonesia's special regimes were originally placed under review but found to be outside the scope of the OECD's work in 2017. Several of Korea's regimes were also found to be outside the scope of the work. Most recently, Singapore's IP development incentive was reported as not harmful while Vietnam still has several regimes, such as its IP benefits and economic zones regimes, under review. Thailand is in the process of amending several of its regimes including its international headquarters regime and regional operating headquarters regime, both of which were found to be potentially harmful. Hong Kong is also in the process of amending several of its regimes, including its profits tax concessions for corporate treasuries and captive insurers, to comply with Action 5. Another Asian jurisdiction, Malaysia, is also in the process of amending various miscellaneous regimes such as its biotechnology industry regime and pioneer status regime.

The second part of Action 5 requires countries that are members of the inclusive framework to agree to the compulsory spontaneous exchange of certain tax rulings. Five types of rulings are covered: (1) rulings relating to certain preferential regimes; (2) unilateral advance pricing arrangements (APAs) or other cross-border unilateral rulings in respect of transfer pricing; (3) rulings providing for a downward adjustment of taxable profits; (4) permanent establishment (PE) rulings, and (5) related party conduit rulings. On 4 December 2017 the OECD released its report on the outcome of the first peer review of the implementation of this standard. This report covers 44 jurisdictions, of which 12[20] are the subjects of reports contained in this volume. More than 10,000 rulings issued in the period 1 January 2010 to 31 December 2016 were found to be within the scope of the transparency framework and almost 6500 exchanges took place in the year of review, 1 January 2016 to 31 December 2016. Recommendations for improvement were made for China, India, Korea, the Netherlands, and the UK. The peer review process is continuing.

20 Australia, Canada, China, India, Indonesia, Japan, Korea, Netherlands, New Zealand, South Africa, UK, US.

1.7 Action 6: Preventing the Granting of Treaty Benefits in Inappropriate Circumstances

Recommendations set out in the Action 6 report target a wide range of arrangements that share the common feature of taxpayers relying on treaty provisions to shelter income from taxation in "inappropriate circumstances". Although the report does not directly define when arrangements are inappropriate, the examples it provides show the intention is to target arrangements that technically fit within the protection against taxation in a treaty or achieve other treaty benefits such as lower rates but which were not intended to apply to the taxpayer seeking to benefit from the treaty. The primary example explored in the Action 6 report is treaty shopping – taxpayers that operate through another country to take advantage of a treaty between that country and the place in which they wish to invest or conduct business. The report refers to two arrangements commonly discussed in international tax planning, a "conduit" company and a "base" company. While there is no universal understanding of these terms, the former is often used to describe an entity established in a third country to receive passive income (interest, dividends, or royalties) from enterprises in the target country and a "base" company is used to describe an entity established in a third country that is responsible for active business operations in the target jurisdiction.

The report also identifies a number of secondary methods used to exploit the benefits of treaties inappropriately, some of which are also discussed in other Action reports. One of these is splitting contracts so each separate contract lasts less than a threshold designated in a treaty as giving rise to a deemed permanent establishment. A second technique is described as a "dividend transfer" arrangement where a dominant shareholder acquires shares temporarily from other shareholders to pull its shareholding over a threshold that entitles it to a lower dividend withholding tax rate under a treaty. A third technique, often referred to as "dividend stripping" in domestic tax planning literature, exploits differences in transaction characterisation rules to extract profits from a company as a capital gain, shielded from tax under a treaty, rather than a dividend, which could be subject to withholding tax under the treaty. A fourth technique is the use of partnerships or trusts to hold real property to avoid the look-through provisions in treaties that allow source countries to retain the right to tax gains realised indirectly on the sale of real property by selling interests in companies whose value is attributable mostly to real property in the source country.

The Action 6 report offers a host of different solutions to these problems. It recommends a response to transactions to avoid the characterisation of profit distributions as dividends be deferred until a non-designated future time. Most of the other issues, apart from treaty shopping, it suggests can be addressed through changes to the OECD model treaty or the commentary to that model.

The Action 6 report offers a tri-track solution to the main problem of treaty shopping via domestic anti-abuse rules, a "limitation-on-benefits" rule to be added to the OECD model treaty and, through that route, eventually incorporated into bilateral treaties, and a "principal purpose test" incorporated into the MLI. The report points out that a "limitation-on-benefits" or "LOB" rule has long been a feature of US tax treaties and is now found in select treaties of other countries. The report suggests a new LOB Article be added to the OECD model. The "principal purpose test" or "PPT", as it is sometimes called, added to the MLI as Article 7(1) will deny treaty benefits to income if it can be concluded having regard to all relevant facts and circumstances that obtaining the benefit was one of the principle drivers of the transaction giving rise to the income. The PPT will not apply, however, if the taxpayer can establish that granting relief in its case would be consistent with the purpose of the relevant treaty Article.

Signatories to the MLI have effectively added the PPT to all their existing bilateral treaties with other signatories to the MLI. In addition, some countries are including analogous wording into the preamble of new treaties[21] and some are also adding LOB Articles to treaties.[22]

1.8 Action 7: Preventing the Artificial Avoidance of Permanent Establishment Status

The measure in double tax treaties with the most significant impact in terms of allocation of taxing rights over income from cross-border activities is the business income article, commonly based on Article 7 of the OECD model treaty. Article 7 removes, subject to later Articles in the treaty, the right of the source country to apply its domestic income tax provisions to business income derived by a non-resident unless the non-resident operates through a permanent establishment in the source jurisdiction. The later Articles that might override Article 7 allow source countries to retain limited taxing rights over dividends, interest and royalties and full taxing rights over capital gains realised on the disposal of real property.

The reach of Article 7 depends entirely on the definition of a permanent establishment in Article 5. The core components in Article 5 deal with physical presence – factories, offices, mines, etc. – and these are supplemented by a range of deeming provisions. A further deeming rule found in the UN model treaty explicitly and, via the commentary in the OECD treaty implicitly, treats the provision of employees providing services as a permanent establishment of the non-resident employer.

The final Action 7 report detailed a number of techniques identified by tax administrations (and often litigated) that are used by non-resident enterprises to effectively operate in another jurisdiction without having a permanent establishment in the jurisdiction. The technique that receives most attention is the use of *commissionnaire* arrangements by foreign enterprises selling directly

21 See, for example, Australia.

22 For example, China and India.

to customers in the foreign jurisdiction through local facilities. Instead of using a subsidiary (which would be resident in the jurisdiction) or a branch (which would constitute a permanent establishment), the non-resident enterprise sells through another person who is paid on a commission basis for each sale. The person selling on behalf of the non-resident enterprise merely acts as a sales intermediary and never acquires title to the items sold. These remain the property of the non-resident enterprise until sold and all profits from the sale, apart from the commission paid to sales person in the *commissionnaire* arrangement, are sheltered from tax in the source country because the actual seller has no permanent establishment. Action 7 addresses the problem through the MLI, which modifies existing treaties to ensure *commissionnaire* arrangements will be treated as permanent establishments of the non-resident seller and profits from the sales can thus be subject to taxation in the source country (the country in which the items are sold).

The Action report also describes a number of other techniques used by non-resident businesses to avoid operations in another country being characterised as a permanent establishment. One method is the fragmentation of the operations of a business so each fragmented part fits into one of the exemptions in the definition of a permanent establishment, particularly those for "preparatory or auxiliary" activities. Again, the proposed solution is a modification of the definition of permanent establishment in the MLI.

Another technique used by non-resident enterprises to avoid having a permanent establishment that is based on a temporal presence in the jurisdiction such as the deemed permanent establishment for construction projects or the deemed permanent establishment for extended personal services provided through employees is "splitting-up of contracts". Under this technique, a project appears to be carried out by a number of different enterprises, with each part lasting for a time less than that required for a permanent establishment though in fact the contractors are commonly owned. Action 7 suggests this problem can be addressed partly through changes to the model treaty and accompanying commentary but indicates domestic anti-avoidance rules may deal more directly with the problem.

For the most part, jurisdictions surveyed in this volume have addressed these issues through the MLI, although many have entered reservations to some aspects of the MLI as it applies to permanent establishments. In many cases, moreover, jurisdictions have not endorsed the full MLI suite of measures. Australia, for example, has not accepted the *commissionnaire* rules, the UK is only adopting the anti-fragmentation rules, and the Netherlands has lodged a reservation to avoid application of the contract splitting rules as they apply to mining exploration and exploitation to avoid conflict with the specific rules on mining permanent establishments set out in its existing treaties. A number of jurisdictions have complemented the MLI with domestic legislation.[23]

23 For example, Hong Kong, India, Japan, and Korea.

1.9 Actions 8-10: Aligning Transfer Pricing Outcomes with Value Creation (Intangibles, Risks & Capital, and High Risk Transactions)

Actions 8-10 are collectively known as the transfer pricing Actions, which contain recommendations designed to assure that transfer pricing outcomes are in line with value creation in relation to intangibles (Action 8), risk allocation taking into account contractual arrangements between related parties (Action 9), and to other high-risk transactions including intragroup management fees and head office expenses (Action 10). Intragroup transactions have grown exponentially since the arm's length requirement for transfer pricing was first introduced in the 1920s. The arm's length principle is found in both tax treaties and domestic legislation and is adopted almost universally. The overarching objective of Actions 8-10 is to ensure income is taxed in the location of economic activity generating value. Subsequent to the release of final Action reports, the OECD's Transfer Pricing Guidelines for Multinational Enterprises and Tax Administrations were amended, and updates are now reflected in the 2017 edition of those Guidelines. While significant work has been done in relation to transfer pricing and revised guidelines do mean that there is an improvement in terms of getting closer to allocation principles relating to economic activity, some have regarded the refusal by the OECD to consider alternative methods of allocating profit, such as formulary apportionment, as disappointing.

Many of the jurisdictions surveyed in this volume have adopted the new Guidelines by means of legislation that incorporates the Guidelines into domestic transfer pricing methodology or practices,[24] indicated that their revenue authority can and will follow the updated Guidelines without the need for further legislation or regulations[25] or suggested that the Guidelines are already in line with (some of) the practices and policies of the revenue authority.[26] Other countries are expected to follow the new Guidelines but are yet to confirm.[27] The work on transfer pricing is ongoing with further work mandated by the G20 Development Working Group.

1.10 Action 11: Measuring and Monitoring BEPS

Action 11 sets out a program for the provision of data to national governments by the OECD to improve monitoring of responses to the BEPS agenda and to allow governments to consider national responses in light of observable trends globally. The Action is concerned with the availability of information to national governments and does not contemplate direct engagement by those governments for the Action to be carried out. As part of this initiative, the OECD will, in the future, release a Corporate Tax Statistics dataset that will report on a range of data

24 Australia, Hong Kong, New Zealand, Singapore, UK, Nigeria.
25 Canada.
26 China, India, Netherlands, US.
27 Indonesia, Japan.

in an internationally consistent format. Beyond country use of the data, findings will also enable the OECD to measure and monitor the impact of the BEPS package.

1.11 Action 12: Mandatory Disclosure Rules

Many of the Actions set out in the OECD's BEPS agenda deal with specific tax minimisation arrangements by multinational entities such as transfer pricing, excessive debt loading, hybrid mismatches and treaty abuse. Action 12 is part of the package of transparency measures designed to support the substantive reform measures by assisting revenue authorities to detect aggressive tax planning strategies and respond to the risks associated with such behaviour through measures such as risk assessments, audits, and, where needed, changes to domestic legislation. Action 12 was seen as necessary because many of the existing domestic disclosure regimes focus on schemes that are mass marketed by promoters and affect small to medium-sized entities as well as wealthy individuals. Schemes entered into by multinational entities that result in base erosion and profit shifting tend to be bespoke arrangements that often fall outside the scope of existing disclosure regimes.

Action 12 is not a minimum standard but rather is described as "guidance based on best practices for countries which seek to strengthen their domestic legislation relating to mandatory disclosure by taxpayers of aggressive or abusive transactions, arrangements, or structures". The report itself covers four key areas: an overview of mandatory disclosure, options for model mandatory disclosure rules, international tax schemes, and information sharing. Action 12 took the form of what the OECD describes as a modular framework that allows countries to design a disclosure framework tailored to their own needs.

Amongst the OECD and G20 countries, mandatory disclosure rules existed prior to the BEPS initiative in the United States, Canada, South Africa, the United Kingdom, Portugal, Ireland, Israel, and Korea, as reports on five of those countries included in this volume indicate.[28] These regimes are either transaction-based or promoter-based and the OECD Action builds upon these systems with recommendations on possible definitions of "promoter" and "adviser". Many of the hallmarks used to identify arrangements that must be reported under current disclosure rules relate to domestic schemes and the Action supplements these with further wider indicators that can extend disclosure triggers to international schemes. Suggested hallmarks for international schemes include transactions with cross-border consequences that have material impacts in the reporting country.

To date, despite the intended focus of the BEPS project on attacking international tax minimisation schemes, the response to Action 12 has been underwhelming. Two trends are apparent: jurisdictions either suggest that they already have some sort of mandatory disclosure regime in place or that there are no plans to

28 United States, Canada, South Africa, United Kingdom, and Korea.

implement such a regime. The lack of response may be due to the nature of the report on Action 12 which, while comprehensive and easily understood, is little more than a summary of existing regimes packaged as recommendations for best practice. The very general recommendations set out in Action 12 contrast with the detailed and prescriptive minimum standard set out in Action 13, which deals with transfer pricing documentation and what is labelled country-by-country reporting. Discussion on the future direction of mandatory disclosure has tended to focus on the specific country-by-country reporting rules in Action 13 and whether countries would agree to embrace a mandatory publicly available country-by-country reporting regime, diverting attention from the more general issues covered by Action 12. Taxpayers have expressed their concern over additional compliance costs in relation to country-by-country reporting and any suggestion of further mandatory reporting requirements that are viewed as optional BEPS initiatives are likely to be strongly resisted. To this end, countries considering further mandatory reporting are likely to be faced with competing policy priorities. Vietnam is one such country concerned about the impact of such rules.

Action 12 recommendations, if implemented, operate as both a compliance tool for revenue authorities and a deterrence measure for taxpayers and promoters engaging in aggressive tax planning arrangements. To this extent, pressure for mandatory reporting regimes is likely to be politically driven and at a national rather than international level. This is especially the case where data is collected, and questions are asked around its analysis and subsequent use to alter taxpayer behaviour and lead to regulatory change. While country responses to Action 12 have been limited, political impetus for such measures can be seen. The European Commission appears to support the initiative with a draft Directive published on 30 June 2017 requiring taxpayers or lead intermediaries within the EU to report on certain cross-border tax planning arrangements. This draft Directive broadly reflects the sentiment of the OECD report on Action 12. This is consistent with other EU measures around transparency and countries have committed to the EU proposed Directive for cross-border reportable arrangements.[29]

1.12 Action 13: Transfer Pricing Documentation and Country-by-Country Reporting

Action 13, dealing with transfer pricing documentation and Country-by-Country Reporting, is one of the most controversial BEPS Actions. This is likely due to its impact on taxpayers and the tax profession not only in terms of additional compliance costs but concerns around exposure to additional risk assessments and revenue authority audit activities. Like Action 12, Action 13 is also part of the BEPS program centred on increased transparency, but unlike Action 12, it is part of the minimum standards in the BEPS Inclusive Framework which means it is a mandatory Action for countries which have signed to that framework. All

29 For example, The Netherlands.

jurisdictions included in this volume have agreed to implement Country-by-Country Reporting (CbCR).

The origins of CbCR are commonly attributed to a proposal by Richard Murphy in 2003 that transnational companies should be required to publicly account for their tax payments (Murphy, 2003). His suggestion was made in the context of a proposed accounting standard rather than a legislative requirement, with the aim of providing "information that will assist those seeking to appraise the organisation with regard to: its corporate social responsibility; investment risk; tax risk; its contribution by way of value added to the societies in which it operates; [and] its contribution to national well-being by way of tax payment within those locations" (Murphy, 2003, pp. 20-21). Murphy's proposal was adopted by civil society groups and the notion of CbCR became a popular concept in the call for greater transparency of multinational entity tax practices. Two years after Murphy's proposal, the European Union Joint Transfer Pricing Forum's Scheme recommended another version of CbCR that could be used by revenue authorities as a risk assessment tool in transfer pricing cases. Subsequent consideration of the issue by the OECD led to that organisation adopting what appears to be a combination of the proposals by Murphy and the European Union but with a focus on an underlying goal of increased transfer pricing documentation and confidentiality (revenue authority access only) rather than public disclosure.

The final report on Action 13 provides a template for CbCR of income, taxes paid, and certain measures of economic activity. It is a three-tiered standardised approach to transfer pricing documentation with a high level master file outlining business operations and transfer pricing policies, detailed transactional transfer pricing documentation known as the local file, and a country-by-country report which provides annually, and for each tax jurisdiction in which a multinational entity does business, the amount of revenue, profit before income tax and income tax paid and accrued. The threshold for reporting has been set at group revenue of EUR 750 million with jurisdictions converting the threshold amount to the equivalent in their own currency for the purposes of domestic legislation.

One of the biggest challenges facing multinational entities is the collection and collation of data required for the CbC Report. Many taxpayers were underprepared for the reporting requirements. As the chapters in this volume reveal, most countries were quick to act on the recommendations contained in Action 13 with many enacting legislation in 2016.[30] As a result, some taxpayers were faced with a reporting deadline as early as 2017. While many jurisdictions passed legislation mandating CbCR, other jurisdictions concluded that their existing laws were sufficient to support CbCR.[31] Different domestic approaches have been adopted in Australia, Canada, China, Hong Kong, India, Indonesia, Japan, Korea, Malaysia, the Netherlands, Nigeria, New Zealand, Singapore, South Africa, the UK, the US,

30 For example, Australia, Canada, China, Japan, the Netherlands, South Africa and the UK.

31 For example, Indonesia.

and Vietnam, all of which have domestic legislation in place that supports CbCR. Thailand is the only jurisdiction with a report in this volume that does not yet comply with Action 13. Thailand still needs to implement transfer pricing legislation that allows the revenue authority to require transfer pricing documentation and CbCR.

CbCR information can be exchanged between revenue authorities either under the *Multilateral Competent Authority Agreement on the Exchange of Country-by-Country Reports* (MCAA) or a specific bilateral Competent Authority Agreement such as a tax treaty. As at 8 August 2018, 72 countries had signed the MCAA, of which 15 are surveyed in this volume. As Thailand does not have the necessary legislative regime to require the documentation, it has not signed. In addition, the US has not signed but has been rated as largely compliant with the OECD requirements on exchange of information based on its bilateral network of treaties. To date, Vietnam has not signed and currently has no way to exchange information.

Taxpayers have expressed concern about two aspects of CbCR (in addition to the compliance costs involved). First, they are apprehensive that revenue authorities may use CbCR for purposes other than transfer pricing assessments and, second, they are disquieted by the possibility that in the future mandatory reports will become publicly available. In light of developments in the EU, corporate social reporting requirements, and a drive by civil society groups to move towards publicly available CbCR, the latter possibility may not be remote.[32]

1.13 Action 14: Dispute Resolution

Action 14 of the BEPS program sets out a prescription for more effective international tax dispute resolution mechanisms. It is designated as a minimum standard for BEPS inclusive framework members meaning all 118 jurisdictions joining the framework are committed to adopting the standard to resolve treaty-related disputes in a timely, effective and efficient manner.

Where tax authorities in two jurisdictions sharing a bilateral tax treaty disagree on the possible application of a treaty provision, income derived by a taxpayer in one of the treaty jurisdictions may be subject to double taxation on the same income. The problem could arise, for example, if both authorities agree a receipt by a person with no permanent establishment in the source country is business income but disagree on the character of the income, with the source country viewing it as royalty income and the residence country characterising it as commission income. The source country will claim a taxing right over the royalty and the residence country will tax the same amount as commission with no credit for any source country withholding tax as it does not recognise the source country's right to tax the income. In circumstances similar to this, taxpayers can ask the two tax authorities to invoke what is known as a "mutual agreement procedure" (MAP) included in

32 For further analysis of CbCR, see Johnston and Sadiq (2017); Longhorn, Rahim and Sadiq (2016).

all bilateral tax treaties. The MAP provides a process for the two tax authorities to resolve the potential double taxation by coming to an agreement on a common approach to the problem.

The MAP process has often been subject to criticism. In many cases it is inordinately slow and cumbersome, with disputes sometimes taking years to resolve. In some cases, the dispute is never resolved; in treaties that do not provide for compulsory arbitration in the event of non-agreement, there are no sanctions for simply giving up on efforts to reach an agreement.

Prior to commencement of the BEPS program, much of the focus of the OECD's tax agenda was directed at dividing taxing rights between source and residence countries and requiring signatories to bilateral treaties to adopt credit or exemption rules to prevent double taxation where the treaty divides taxing rights between the parties to the treaty. One significant feature of the BEPS program has been a change in concern by the OECD with preventing double taxation to preventing less than single taxation. Evidence of this shift is the requirement for countries which have agreed to the minimum standards to include in their tax treaties an express statement that their common intention is to eliminate double taxation without creating opportunities for non-taxation or reduced taxation through tax evasion or avoidance (Action 6).

By its very nature, the BEPS program seeks to prevent less than single taxation, leaving Action 14 as the only Action item that focuses on the prevention of double taxation. This Action has generally been welcomed by taxpayers who see this measure as recognition of the importance of tax certainty in light of increased scrutiny, but it is seen as creating additional administrative requirements for revenue authorities.

The Action Report contains four parts, consisting of the Terms of Reference, Assessment Methodology, MAP Statistics Reporting Framework, and Guidance on Specific Information and Documentation Required to be Submitted with a Request for MAP Assistance. The Terms of Reference allow for the assessment of a framework member's legal and administrative framework, including the practical implementation of this framework to determine how its MAP regime performs relative to certain criteria in four key areas: the prevention of disputes; the availability and ease of access to MAP; the resolution of MAP cases; and the implementation of MAP agreements. The Terms of Reference contain 21 elements and 12 best practices and form the basis of a peer review used to monitor each member's progress on implementing the Action.

The most onerous part of Action 14 falls on revenue authorities who are required to provide documentation on their MAP procedures when subject to a MAP peer review and monitoring process. This process is conducted by a sub-group of the Forum on Tax Administration, a body sponsored by the OECD and comprising tax commissioners from 50 jurisdictions, with the oddly repetitive title of Forum on Tax Administration MAP Forum. Specifically, Action 14 requires members to provide timely and complete reporting of MAP data based on the new MAP statistics reporting framework and publish their MAP profiles in the agreed template. Peer review reports are released to the public upon completion. As at 30 August 2018, the OECD has conducted four rounds of its stage 1 peer reviews, assessing the implementation of Action 14 reporting in 28 countries.

The peer review process commenced in December 2016. Of the jurisdictions with reports in this volume, Canada, the Netherlands, the UK and the US were in the first batch of peer reviews, Korea and Singapore in the third batch and Australia, Japan, and New Zealand were in the fourth batch. The reviews of the remaining nine jurisdictions are yet to be finalised, with India and South Africa in the sixth batch, and China, Hong Kong and Indonesia in the seventh batch. Peer reviews have been deferred until 2020 for some countries including Malaysia and Nigeria.

The Action on improving treaty dispute resolution has not been universally applauded. Countries such as Australia, Canada, Japan, the Netherlands, New Zealand, the UK and the US, with what would be regarded as sophisticated tax regimes, have generally embraced Action 14. However, it has become clear that other countries, despite their size and relative sophistication, are finding it difficult to embrace this minimum standard. All three "BRICS" countries reported in this volume indicate that they are either facing resource constraints (China), are opposed to MAP (India) or have not yet committed to MAP (South Africa). Other less developed countries have been slow to embrace Action 14. For example, Vietnam is working on developing recommendations while Indonesia has some local rules with a further review being undertaken.

1.14 Action 15: Multilateral Convention to Implement Tax Treaty Related Measures to Prevent BEPS

The BEPS program contemplated completion of Actions in three ways: through direct actions by participating jurisdictions, by the OECD overseeing the process (primarily in respect of collecting data on implementation and reporting back to all framework members), and by adoption of a multilateral treaty, the "Multilateral Convention to Implement Tax Treaty Related Measures to Prevent BEPS". Action 15 was designed to analyse the tax and public international law issues related to the development of a multilateral agreement and on the basis of that analysis develop a multilateral instrument (MLI) that could be entered into by willing countries to easily implement many of the BEPS recommendations, particularly those related to existing tax treaties. The text of the MLI and its accompanying Explanatory Statement was accepted by the BEPS framework participants in November 2016 with the first signing taking place in June 2017. The instrument was not made a minimum standard for BEPS framework members and it was thus not compulsory for countries who are part of the BEPS Inclusive Framework to sign it.

While tax treaties are based on a common set of principles, each is negotiated bilaterally. Changes to the principles, usually reflected in changes to the model treaty that acts as the starting point for the design of bilateral treaties, do not automatically flow through to treaties already concluded and put into effect. These can only be amended on an individual basis following separate renegotiation, signing and ratification. Renegotiating all of the globe's tax treaties would be an almost impossible task. One object of the MLI was to short-circuit the impossible time burden by modifying in one instrument all bilateral treaties signed by signatories to the multilateral instrument.

It was anticipated that not all signatories would wish to modify all of their bilateral treaties in the manner set out in the MLI. To accommodate this, only three elements of the MLI are mandatory for parties signing the instrument and countries are able to opt out of the remainder of the agreement either entirely or by placing reservations on their adoption of the MLI. The MLI itself has 39 Articles, 24 of which relate to potential substantive changes to relevant treaties in the areas of hybrid mismatches, treaty abuse, permanent establishments and dispute resolution. The three areas that are mandatory are a new treaty preamble, a measure for the prevention of treaty abuse, and changes to the mutual agreement procedure. All other elements of the MLI are optional and registering reservations to some Articles of the MLI is a common trend, with all of the countries reported in this volume placing at least some reservations on the adoption of the standard MLI Articles.

1.15 A Fork in the Tax Road

A pair of cataclysmic events in the first decade of the 21st century – unprecedented global terrorist attacks and a global financial crisis – led to an extraordinary shift in attitudes to long-accepted international tax norms. Previously sacrosanct notions such as the inevitability of tax havens and tax secrecy as elements of tax competition and the appropriateness of profit shifting via transfer pricing within limits were swept away as the global community came together for the first time and agreed to pursue a united quest against international tax avoidance. The result of this resolve was the BEPS project. As the reports in this volume show, a commitment to multilateral or cooperative approaches to confronting international tax avoidance took hold, even if there were disagreements on some details or local shortcomings that make implementation of particular measures problematic.

As the BEPS project unfolded, jurisdictions that were in the process of reforming local legislation continued their domestic initiatives. In most cases the changes they made, including updates to Australia's transfer pricing regime and amendments to the Japanese and the US CFC regimes, complemented commitments later agreed to in the BEPS program. The same is true of unilateral anti-avoidance rule reforms adopted by some jurisdictions. Examples include Australia's extension of its general anti-avoidance rule to apply to international arrangements of concern and analogous initiatives in China and India to strengthen their anti-avoidance rules.

While technically unilateral rules, these amendments largely resonated with the goals of the BEPS agenda. So, too, did additional transparency measures that were introduced by some countries. Shortly before the BEPS project commenced, Australia adopted rules that require the revenue authority to publish specified information about the tax affairs of large corporate taxpayers. Large taxpayers are also now encouraged to disclose tax information under the Tax Transparency Code in a voluntary tax transparency report. While few countries have gone this far, jurisdictions such as Hong Kong and Korea have focused on ensuring greater transparency through existing regimes, also consistent with the BEPS objectives.

Multilateralism complemented by parallel domestic rules that support BEPS objectives has not been the only response to the events that led to BEPS, however. Some nations participating in the BEPS framework also pursued a parallel path of unilateral action untied to, and sometimes markedly diverging from, BEPS principles. The important precedent for alternative unilateral action was the enactment by the United States in 2010, shortly before the commencement of BEPS, of its controversial Foreign Account Tax Compliance Act (FATCA) measure. FATCA imposed on all banks worldwide an obligation to report to US authorities information on the assets and income of depositors with "US-person" status, a characteristic attributed to a person satisfying any one of a variety of designated indicators of ties with the US. The measure could be unilaterally enforced on foreign banks by the threat of cutting their ties with the international banking system operated from the US in the event of non-compliance.

In some cases, unilateral actions continued after the commencement of the BEPS project without apparent regard to the OECD's request that BEPS participants refrain from unilateral measures beyond the apparent scope and intention of the BEPS initiatives. The best known of the recently adopted unilateral rules is the UK's diverted profits tax (DPT), colloquially known as the Google tax, first announced in December 2014 and passed into law the following year, with effect from April 2015. Adopted in response to domestic political pressure, as reported in the UK chapter in this volume, the UK DPT imposes an income tax at a rate higher than the UK company tax rate on profits deemed to have been diverted from the UK. The legislation defines diverted profits in terms of companies with global supply chains making substantial sales into the UK using methods other than a UK subsidiary or branch and companies that have a UK operation that incurred expenses to foreign affiliates where the impugned acquisitions lack economic substance. A high turnover trigger threshold (GBP 10 million) ensures the tax is limited to large multinational firms.

A second example is the Australian DPT, announced a few weeks after the UK tax went into effect and operating since January 2016. The Australian legislation is aimed at multinationals effectively operating in Australia but avoiding arrangements that would constitute a permanent establishment. Like its UK counterpart, the Australian DPT has a high trigger threshold and was reportedly aimed at about 30 large multinational enterprises.

The international tax system thus finds itself at a fork in the road. At the same time they have embraced the cooperative and multilateral principles of BEPS, some jurisdictions have ventured down the unilateral move fork, equating tax sovereignty with wholly independent actions. In parallel with their BEPS activities, these countries have bolstered their participation in the international cooperative program with national rules that appear to extend domestic tax bases beyond prevailing international norms. These moves may turn out to be the start of a shift towards *ad hoc* individual country base broadening responses to international tax avoidance or they may simply be the first forays into what eventually become generally accepted principles of the international tax system.

The alternative fork is the multilateral path based on international agreement and multilateral tax treaties. This approach sees cooperation not as a ceding of tax sovereignty but rather an exercise of that sovereignty, reaching compromises that benefit each signatory even as others enjoy positive outcomes from the agreement. Endorsement of the inclusive framework, which at the time of writing has a membership of 118 countries, and the MLI, which currently has 84 signatures, is evidence of global support for multilateral solutions to the problem of international tax avoidance.

Is it possible that international cooperation might some day extend to a multinational solution to the still untouched elephant in the room problem, the current allocation of multinational enterprise income on the basis of notional artificial "arm's length" transactions between parts of the same business? A multilateral agreement on the global division of taxing rights over income of multinational firms would, to be sure, appear to be a large step from the MLI that in effect embraces and reinforces the impact of bilateral tax agreements by updating these treaties to reflect contemporary and widely held values. At the same time, however, it could be said that a treaty imposing common rules and standards on aspects of most of the world's bilateral treaties marks a shift from bilateral to multilateral solutions and the next step, an international agreement on the allocation of taxing rights, is no longer unimaginable. Moving from procedural measures and assertions of treaty purpose changes to agreement on the division of taxing rights on a global scale is a significant step, but arguably it is just that, a step, and not a revolution. The world is already telling countries how their agreements to divide taxing rights between each other should look. A logical progression would be agreement on how all signatories should divide taxing rights in supply chains involving multiple countries.

The BEPS project has been one of the most important developments in international tax in decades. The question that flows from the reports that follow in this volume is whether it is the end of a process or the start of a new one. The answer remains elusive.

References

Johnston, Andrew and Kerrie Sadiq (2017), "Beyond country-by-country reporting: A modest proposal to enhance corporate accountability", 27(3) *New Zealand Universities Law Review* 569-600.

Longhorn, Monique, Mia Rahim and Kerrie Sadiq (2016), "Country-by-country reporting: An assessment of its objective and scope", 14(1) *eJournal of Tax Research* 4-33.

Murphy, Richard, on behalf of the Association for Accountancy and Business Affairs (2003), *A Proposed International Accounting Standard - Reporting Turnover and Tax by Location*, Ely and Basildon, UK, https://www.taxjustice.net/cms/upload/pdf/new_int._Account_Standard.pdf.

Organisation for Economic Co-operation and Development (OECD) (2013a), *Addressing Base Erosion and Profit Shifting*, February (Paris: OECD).

Organisation for Economic Co-operation and Development (OECD) (2013b), *Action Plan on Base Erosion and Profit Shifting*, July (Paris: OECD).

Thuronyi, Victor (2010), "Tax Treaty Templates", in Arthur Cockfield (ed.), *Globalization and its Tax Discontents: Tax Policy and International Investments, Essays in Honour of Alex Easson* (Toronto: University of Toronto Press, 2010), 239-254.

2 The Adoption of BEPS in Australia

Kerrie Sadiq[*] and Peter Mellor[**]

Abstract

Australia was part of the initial group of countries agreeing to adopt the Inclusive Framework minimum standards contained in Actions 5, 6, 13 and 14. To date, Australia has been proactive in adopting these Actions and has made substantial progress in this regard, passing domestic legislation, signing multilateral agreements and negotiating tax treaties based on the minimum requirements. More broadly, Australia already had initiatives to deal with multinational tax avoidance in progress at the time of announcement of the BEPS project in October 2015 and very quickly signalled its commitment to implement the wider measures. Steps have been taken in all areas as at August 2018 apart from Action 3 (Controlled Foreign Companies), where efforts from some years ago (subsequently abandoned) to update the provisions have not to date been reinstituted, and Action 11 (BEPS data) which is the subject of ongoing monitoring. As in the case of the UK, Australia has also taken the significant unilateral step of imposing a Diverted Profits Tax, at the rate of 40 per cent.

2.1 Introduction

With a population of a little over 24 million people, 28.5 per cent of whom were born overseas (Organisation for Economic Co-operation and Development (OECD), 2018, p. 15), Australia operates as a democracy[1] within the framework of a federal parliamentary constitutional monarchy. There are three levels of government; the Commonwealth Government, governments of six States and two self-governing Territories, and local government. The tax system is predominantly legislated by the Commonwealth Parliament (also known as the Federal Parliament), which consists of the House of Representatives, the Senate, and the Monarchy, although State, Territory and local governments also impose a limited range of taxes. At the federal level, to become law, legislation must pass through both houses of Parliament and then be given royal assent by the Governor-General as the monarch's representative. The Australian Treasury, as part of the executive branch of govern-

* Professor, QUT Business School, Queensland University of Technology

** Research Fellow, Department of Business Law and Taxation, Monash University.

1 Since Federation in 1901 Australia has become the world's sixth oldest continuous democracy: International Business Publications (2013, p. 31).

ment, provides advice on the design of Australia's tax system, although tax policy development is influenced by numerous sources such as political parties, Senate inquiries, economic think tanks, academics and lobby groups (Heferen, Mitchell and Amalo, 2013). Tax proposals are then typically proposed by the Federal Treasurer, often through the annual Budget process. Within the tax context, Treasury undertakes its role in conjunction with the Australian Taxation Office (ATO), which administers the tax laws and is the main revenue collection agency. The Treasury and ATO have been described as the joint stewards of Australia's tax system with an official Protocol in place to provide a framework for the working arrangements and collaborative approach adopted between the two.[2]

Income tax is the main form of taxation in Australia with individual income tax representing approximately 52 per cent of federal tax revenue collected and company income tax representing approximately 19 per cent. This is followed by a consumption tax known as the goods and services tax (GST) contributing approximately 16 per cent of tax revenue collected (ATO, 2018). For individual income tax, the health care and social assistance industry contributes the most, followed by professional, scientific and technical services, construction, and agriculture, forestry, and fishing (ATO, 2018). The highest industry contributor of company tax is financial and insurance services followed by mining, wholesale trade, manufacturing and construction (ATO, 2018). Australia is regarded as a developed country which is prosperous, currently having achieved 26 years of continuous economic growth. Its GDP per capita is well above the OECD average as are average earnings, and public debt and government spending remain low (OECD, 2018). Australia's company income tax as a proportion of GDP is higher than the OECD average suggesting that the country is more vulnerable to corporate tax base erosion than other OECD countries.

Australia has had full member status of the OECD since 1971, making it the 23rd member (Department of Foreign Affairs and Trade, 2011). It is seen as having a strong voice on the global stage and positions itself to influence global co-operation (OECD, 2018). It is supportive of OECD efforts to engage with countries beyond membership and is particularly active in the South-East Asia region.[3] Australia is also a member of the G20 and has been involved since its inception at a finance ministers meeting. It held the G20 Presidency in 2014 and the Brisbane Summit in November of 2014. It was at this summit that the OECD presented seven of the 15 elements of its BEPS Action Plan to the G20 Leaders Summit.

Geographically, Australia belongs to the Asia-Pacific, South-East Asia and Australia and Oceania regions. Indonesia is its largest near-neighbouring country, fol-

2 ATO, "Treasury and Australian Taxation Office – Tax and Superannuation Protocol" (27 April 2012), https://www.ato.gov.au/General/New-legislation/In-detail/ATO---Treasury-protocols/ATO---Treasury-protocol/.

3 Department of Foreign Affairs and Trade, Australia, "The OECD", http://dfat.gov.au/trade/organisations/oecd/Pages/oecd.aspx.

lowed by Papua New Guinea and New Zealand. Being a member of these regions as well as institutions such as APEC, the G20, World Trade Organization and the OECD means that Australia has numerous free trade agreements with neighbouring countries. Australia has traditionally been largely dependent on the agricultural industry, but this has declined over the years with mining representing a large part of the export market. Australia is the 22nd largest export economy in the world, with China, Japan and South Korea being the top three export destinations, and is ranked 69th for economic complexity.[4]

2.2 Australia's Response to Base Erosion and Profit Shifting

Australia has generally been regarded as having a robust tax regime in place. Key elements of its international tax regime are found in the *Income Tax Assessment Act 1936* (Cth), *Income Tax Assessment Act 1997* (Cth) and relevant double tax agreements to which Australia is a party. Australia has 44 comprehensive double tax agreements in place: 26 with OECD countries and 18 with non-OECD countries. These treaties are incorporated into domestic law through the *International Tax Agreements Act 1953* which specifies that the terms of these treaties take priority over domestic tax law except for the general anti-avoidance provisions. Australia also currently has 36 Tax Information Exchange Agreements (TIEAs) along with numerous other minor agreements.[5] Domestic law provides the basic principles of residence and source, along with international tax rules such as transfer pricing, thin capitalisation (excessive debt loading), controlled foreign corporation rules, and general anti-avoidance rules.

In terms of the historical underpinnings of these rules, it can be noted that Australia has generally placed a strong emphasis on source taxation in the international sphere, perhaps due to its position generally as a substantial capital importer. Australia only moved to add residence-based taxation to its income tax law as late as 1930, in the course of development of the country's independence from the UK. At different times prior to the emergence of the post-World War II arm's length consensus, Australia's international tax regime has included approaches such as formula apportionment rules, specific source rules for certain industries such as mining and mineral processing, presumptive domestic income calculation rules and regimes to assess overseas principals in agency transactions (Krever and Mellor, 2016, pp. 48-49).

In recent times, it has been suggested that Australia's international tax and treaty policy has moved more to a residence-based approach (Vann, 2009). Nevertheless, reform initiatives and reviews in recent years have continued to include consideration of rent taxes on natural resource extraction (such taxes have been enacted in

4 Observatory of Economic Complexity, "Australia", https://atlas.media.mit.edu/en/profile/country/aus/ (accessed on 23 August 2018).

5 For a full and up to date list, see Australian Treasury, "Tax Treaties", https://treasury.gov.au/tax-treaties/.

the case of the petroleum and gas industries) and approaches such as destination-based calculation of the corporate income tax,[6] while formula apportionment also continues to receive substantial attention and commentary as a reform option (see, e.g., Sadiq, 2017). The question has been noted as to whether the BEPS project led to new tax reform initiatives in Australia or merely gave further impetus to moves that were already being developed (Cooper, 2017, p. 172), but in any event it is clear that source taxation has a strong ongoing significance in Australia's international tax policy.

It should also be noted that, while the BEPS project can be seen as seeking to protect the classical corporate income tax model (Vann, 2014), it has not diminished debate in Australia about the need at least for its headline corporate tax rate to be set at a level which is "internationally competitive". Australia currently has a dual rate corporate income tax with a lower rate (at present 27.5 per cent) for relevantly defined small businesses and a standard rate of 30 per cent for all other businesses. Moves to lower this standard rate were rejected by the Parliament in August 2018.

2.2.1 Transfer Pricing

Australia has had transfer pricing rules in various forms for many decades. Following a court decision in 1980 which took a strict view of the provision at the time allowing the Commissioner in certain circumstances to determine an appropriate taxable income of Australian businesses controlled abroad,[7] a more detailed transfer pricing regime broadly adopting the OECD's approach to the arm's length requirement was enacted in 1981.[8] Australia adopts Business Profits and Associated Enterprises Articles in its double tax agreements which also deal with transfer pricing matters (for detailed analysis of Australia's tax treaty provisions, see Bain, Krever and van der Westhuysen, 2011). A review into the 1981 transfer pricing regime commenced in 2011 with new provisions enacted in 2012 and having retrospective application to 1 July 2004.[9] These provisions were introduced to deal with a deficiency in the existing laws to ensure that where a double tax agreement was in place, the determination of transfer prices under the domestic regime would function along the same lines as the powers under the DTA and so expressly take into account the OECD's transfer pricing guidelines (Krever and Zhang, 2011, p. 208). From 29 June 2013, the 1981 transfer pricing provisions were entirely repealed and the 2012 provisions were terminated from the 2013-14 year and replaced with new transfer pricing rules.[10] The current transfer pricing rules ensure that the amounts

6 This was one reform discussed publicly in the lead-up to the finalisation of the report of the Henry Review in December 2009 (Australia's Future Tax System Review Panel, 2009).

7 *Federal Commissioner of Taxation v Commonwealth Aluminium Corporation Ltd* (1980) 143 CLR 646.

8 *Income Tax Assessment Act 1936*, new Div 13 of Pt III, ss 136AA-136AG.

9 *Income Tax Assessment Act 1997*, Div 815-A and *Income Tax (Transitional Provisions) Act 1997*, s 815-1, enacted by *Tax Laws Amendment (Cross-Border Transfer Pricing) Act (No. 1) 2012*.

10 *Income Tax Assessment Act 1997*, Divs 815-B, 815-C, 815-D and 815-E, enacted by *Tax Laws Amendment (Countering Tax Avoidance and Multinational Profit Shifting) Act 2013*.

brought to tax in Australia from cross-border transactions between related parties are at an arm's length price. For the purposes of determining the effect of the provisions, the OECD Transfer Pricing Guidelines for Multinational Enterprises and Tax Administrations as at 2010 (or a later version that may be prescribed) are to be specifically referred to, meaning that Australia's transfer pricing regime is broadly consistent with the OECD guidelines (though the 2017 update is yet to be incorporated into Australian law).

A thin capitalisation (excessive debt loading) regime was first introduced in Australia in 1987 with a new regime replacing the original one in 2001. The current rules, contained in Division 820 of the *Income Tax Assessment Act 1997*, apply to Australian entities investing overseas and foreign entities investing in Australia. The rules operate by disallowing a proportion of the otherwise allowable interest expense where certain limits are exceeded. There are three tests which may apply: (i) the safe harbour debt amount; (ii) an arm's length debt amount, and (iii) a worldwide gearing amount. The safe harbour debt amount, generally referred to as the allowable debt to equity ratio, is the most relied upon and is currently legislated at a ratio of 1.5:1.

2.2.2 Further Provisions

Australia's controlled foreign company (CFC) rules, which largely follow the models already in place in comparable jurisdictions, were introduced with effect from 1 July 1990. While the focus of various reviews, the CFC rules have not tended to be a topic of discussion in the same way as have the transfer pricing and thin capitalisation regimes. In addition to the above specific rules which target international transactions, Australia has had its current general anti-avoidance regime (GAAR), known as Part IVA of the *Income Tax Assessment Act 1936*, in place since 1981 when it replaced a limited and arguably ineffective regime. Despite the broad nature of Australia's GAAR, it has more recently been considered to be potentially insufficient to deal with international tax avoidance and as a result amendments to the GAAR itself and further provisions, such as most notably a Diverted Profits Tax as discussed below (section 2.5.4), have now been introduced.

The consequence of the above provisions prior to the announcement of the OECD/G20 BEPS project was that Australia considered itself to already have in place a robust international tax regime to deal with base erosion and profit shifting, but recognised the need for reform in certain areas as well as a requirement for international cooperation to address the challenges being faced globally. In May 2013, the Australian Treasury released an issues paper for public consultation which outlined the challenges that the international tax system was facing due to changes in the global economy (Australian Treasury, 2013a). In July 2013, the Australian Treasury released a scoping paper entitled *Risks to the Sustainability of Australia's Corporate Tax Base* (Australian Treasury, 2013b) which made it clear that it was concerned about multinational profit shifting and aggressive tax minimisation and was prepared to update rules where it was deemed necessary.

2.3 Australia's Adoption of the BEPS Inclusive Framework Minimum Standards

Australia was part of a group of 48 countries which were initial BEPS associates agreeing to adopt the minimum standards contained in Actions 5, 6, 13 and 14. To date, Australia has been proactive in adopting these Actions and has made substantial progress in this regard, passing domestic legislation, signing multilateral agreements and negotiating tax treaties based on the minimum requirements.

2.3.1 Multilateral Instrument

On 7 June 2017, Australia signed the *Multilateral Convention to Implement Tax Treaty Related Measures to Prevent Base Erosion and Profit Shifting* (the Multilateral Instrument) which covers 35 of Australia's bilateral tax treaty partners. The Multilateral Instrument will enable implementation of some of the BEPS measures through the simplified modification of tax treaties. Domestic legislation has been enacted to give force to the Multilateral Instrument and Australia ratified the Convention on 26 September 2018, so that it will enter into force for the country on 1 January 2019.

2.3.2 Action 5: Peer Review and Monitoring

Action 5, Peer Review and Monitoring, consists of two elements. The first element involves the identification of preferential regimes through peer review, while the second requires a commitment to transparency through compulsory spontaneous exchange of information of taxpayer rulings. To date, no preferential regimes have formally been identified in the Australian tax system and Australia does not have any intellectual property regimes for which transparency requirements were imposed, although its Offshore Banking Units regime and the Conduit Foreign Income regime have been recognised as falling within the scope of the exchange of information requirements of Action 5. Australia was also part of the first annual peer review of the transparency network which covered the year 2016 and was published by the OECD in December 2017 (OECD, 2017). Australia was reported as having met all aspects of the terms of reference for the year in review and no recommendations were made. Of the five types of rulings which must be exchanged, Australia has four within the scope of the transparency framework: (i) preferential regimes; (ii) cross-border unilateral advance pricing agreements and any other cross-border unilateral tax rulings covering transfer pricing issues; (iii) permanent establishment rulings, and (iv) related party conduit rulings. Statistics reported by the ATO to the OECD reveal that Australia has issued 208 past rulings and from 1 April 2016 to 31 December 2016 it has issued nine future rulings. Australia has domestic legislation in place for the spontaneous exchange of information, is a party to the Convention on Mutual Administrative Assistance in Tax Matters[11] and

11 OECD, "Convention on Mutual Administrative Assistance in Tax Matters" (last updated July 2018), http://www.oecd.org/tax/exchange-of-tax-information/convention-on-mutual-administrative-assistance-in-tax-matters.htm.

has bilateral agreements with 45 jurisdictions taking the network of agreements to a total of 109 jurisdictions (OECD, 2017).

2.3.3 Action 6: Preventing Treaty Abuse

Action 6, Preventing Treaty Abuse, requires countries which have agreed to the minimum standards to include in their tax treaties an express statement that their common intention is to eliminate double taxation without creating opportunities for non-taxation or reduced taxation through tax evasion or avoidance, including through treaty-shopping arrangements. They will also be required to include anti-abuse provisions in their tax treaties to counter treaty-shopping.

To date, Australia has met its requirements under Action 6 by both signing the Multilateral Instrument and by including a new clause in its renegotiated tax treaties. Through the Multilateral Instrument it has agreed to include the additional preamble text into its treaties and has adopted the principal purpose test (PPT) to counter treaty abuse. Countries have the choice to adopt the PPT and/or the Limitation-on-Benefits (LOB) test to address treaty abuse but, consistent with most countries, Australia has adopted the PPT which is in line with a broader anti-abuse rule and denies treaty benefits where one of the principal purposes of the transactions or arrangements is to obtain treaty benefits unless it is established that the granting of the benefits is in accordance with the object and purpose of the provisions of the treaty. The newly ratified Australia-Germany tax treaty, which was signed on 13 November 2015 and came into force on 7 December 2016 replacing the 1972 treaty, is the first of Australia's treaties to include the new preamble specifically stating that the purpose is also to address tax avoidance and to include the new PPT test to deny certain tax treaty benefits (Markham, 2017). The Federal Treasurer announced in a media release on 6 October 2015 that prevention of treaty shopping articles will be adopted in any new or updated tax treaty that Australia enters into (Morrison, 2015).

2.3.4 Action 13: Country-by-Country Reporting

Australia has been particularly proactive in its implementation of Action 13, Country-by-Country Reporting (CbCR). Domestic legislation to implement CbCR was passed in December 2015 and was effective from 1 January 2016, requiring significant global entities to lodge a CbC report, master file and local file.[12] Significant global entities can be Australian headquartered entities or the local operations of foreign headquartered multinationals and are defined as a global parent entity with annual global income of AUD 1 billion or more or a member of a group of consolidated entities where the global parent entity has an annual global income of AUD 1 billion or more.

12 *Tax Laws Amendment (Combating Multinational Tax Avoidance) Act 2015*, introducing new Div. 815-E into the transfer pricing regime of the *Income Tax Assessment Act 1997*.

The CbC report is to be lodged using the OECD's XML Schema while the ATO has developed a combined XML Schema for the master file and local file which may be lodged simultaneously or separately using the same file. Generally, the Australian reporting entity will be responsible for the master file and the local file while the CbC report will usually be lodged by the head entity. There are two types of local file, the short form local file and the detailed local file. The short form local file applies to entities which have a limited amount of related party international dealings. Australia will exchange CbC reports under the *Multilateral Competent Authority Agreement on the Exchange of Country-by-Country Reports* which was signed on 27 January 2016, or a specific bilateral Competent Authority Agreement, such as a tax treaty, signed with another jurisdiction.

2.3.5 Action 14: Tax Treaty Dispute Resolution

Action 14 requires countries to implement rules on a mutual agreement procedure (MAP) so that business has a more effective tax treaty-based dispute resolution procedure. The new MAP rules are being implemented through the MLI (Article 16) with the aim of ensuring that other BEPS measures do not result in double taxation. The MLI modifies existing MAP rules to ensure taxpayers, within three years from notification of action, have an option to present a case to a competent authority of either treaty jurisdiction, and require the competent authorities to endeavour to resolve the case by mutual agreement. Australia's approach to this recommendation is to adopt it without reservation. To this end, the new Australia-Germany tax treaty includes the best practice recommendations of Action 14.

2.4 Australia's Adoption of the BEPS Package

Australia was quick to respond to the OECD BEPS recommendations released on 5 October 2015 as, on 6 October 2015, the Federal Treasurer released a media statement suggesting that Australia had already implemented some of the measures and that it was "firmly on the right track when it comes to ensuring multinationals pay their fair share of tax" in Australia (Morrison, 2015). In the same media release it was stated that the "Australian Government is proud to have led the way globally in this fight against tax avoidance during its G20 Presidency in 2014 and we now have some of the strongest tax integrity rules in the world".

2.4.1 Action 1: Digital Economy

Action 1 of the BEPS project specifically dealt with the tax challenges of the digital economy with the OECD ultimately recommending that Action 1 digital economy issues be dealt with by other Action items. Despite the OECD approach to Action 1, at the time of writing there was a suggestion that Australia may introduce a digital levy or a digital economy tax. Such a possibility was signalled by the Federal Treasurer in March 2018 when he said that "we've got a new economy which tax systems were not built for and the new economy shouldn't be some sort of a tax-free environment" (Morrison, 2018). If Australia does introduce such a tax, it would be a unilateral measure and outside the scope of the OECD's recommendations. It has been suggested that the tax would be on turnover, not income, and would be a flat rate percentage similar to the current European Union proposal to introduce a 3 per cent turnover tax on digital products. Australia has also amended its goods and services tax (GST) to add the GST to digital services. Dubbed the "Netflix Tax", from 1 July 2017 foreign businesses supplying imported services and digital products to Australian consumers are liable to charge a flat rate of 10 per cent GST.

2.4.2 Action 2: Hybrid Mismatch Arrangements

The Federal Government, in the 2016-17 Budget, announced that it would implement the OECD's Action 2 recommendations on neutralising the effects of hybrid mismatch arrangements. The rules[13] are broadly consistent with the OECD recommendations in that entities that are liable to income tax in Australia will be prevented from being able to avoid income taxation, or obtain a double non-taxation benefit, by exploiting differences between the tax treatment of entities and instruments across difference countries. The new rules, if applicable, will either deny a deduction or include amounts in assessable income. In particular, the measures:

i deny imputation benefits on franked distributions made by an Australian corporate tax entity under Australia's dividend imputation system if all or part of the distribution gives rise to a foreign income deduction;

ii prevent certain foreign equity distributions received by an Australian corporate tax entity from being non-assessable non-exempt income if all or part of the distribution gives rise to a foreign income tax deduction;

iii limit the scope of the exemption for foreign branch income and prevent a deduction from arising for payments made by an Australian branch of a foreign bank to its head office in certain circumstances.

The rules also go beyond the OECD recommendations by including a targeted integrity provision which applies where there are financing arrangements through interposed entities in zero tax countries which reduce Australian profits without those profits being subject to foreign tax. The ATO has issued draft Practical Compliance Guideline PCG 2018/D4[14] to assist taxpayers who are affected by the rules.

2.4.3 Action 3: Controlled Foreign Companies

To date, Australia's view on the Action 3 recommendations for best practice in relation to CFC rules is to suggest that the current regime already meets OECD best

13 The *Treasury Laws Amendment (Tax Integrity and Other Measures No. 2) Act 2018* giving effect to the measures was enacted on 24 August 2018.

14 ATO, "Part IVA of the Income Tax Assessment Act 1936 and restructures of hybrid mismatch arrangements", Draft Practical Compliance Guideline PCG 2018/D4 (21 June 2018), https://www.ato.gov.au/law/view/document?docid=COG/PCG2018D4/NAT/ATO.

practice guidance (Morrison, 2015). Australia's CFC rules were introduced in 1990 with a modernisation of the rules announced in 2009. This was formally abandoned in 2013 and, while most suggest that the rules are outdated, there are no proposals to amend them due to their containing almost all of the OECD's recommended building blocks (Greenwoods and Herbert Smith Freehills, 2015).

2.4.4 Action 4: Interest Deductions and Other Financial Payments

The OECD recommendations on Action 4, limiting base erosion involving interest deductions and other financial payments, involve a series of options for countries to use. To this extent, the Australian government was initially of the view that Australia's thin capitalisation regime was sufficiently robust and did not need amending. This is despite the OECD recommendations on a fixed ratio rule and worldwide group ratio rule which Australia does not currently have. Australia's stated position was based on 2014 amendments to the domestic regime tightening the safe harbour debt limit from 3:1 to 1.5:1 on a debt to equity basis and the introduction of a worldwide gearing debt limit.

Despite the initial announcement that the thin capitalisation regime would not be amended to take into account any of the OECD's recommendations, the federal government, in their 2018 Budget, did announce amendments to tighten the rules. The proposed change will require the valuation of assets to be based on the value in accordance with financial statement disclosures. Currently, taxpayers can use market value for assets regardless of the financial statement disclosures.

2.4.5 Action 7: Permanent Establishment Status

The Action 7 recommendations of the OECD BEPS program, dealing with permanent establishment (PE) status, set out changes to the definition of a PE in the OECD model tax treaty to lower the threshold used to determine whether a PE exists. At the date of the release of the BEPS recommendations, Australia's Multinational Anti-Avoidance Law (MAAL) (discussed in section 2.5.3 below) was already before Parliament[15] and the government considered this law to be consistent with OECD recommendations. Further, it was proposed that other recommendations were in line with Australia's treaty practice. However, it is likely that the precise language used in future treaties will change to align with the revised OECD model treaty. To this extent, Australia included all of the OECD recommended revisions in relation to PE status in its newly renegotiated treaty with Germany. Australia has adopted the changes through the MLI but preserves existing corresponding bilateral rules.

2.4.6 Actions 8-10: Transfer Pricing

The OECD's transfer pricing recommendations are contained in Actions 8-10. Most of the work of the OECD has involved changes to the Transfer Pricing Guidelines

15 *Tax Laws Amendment (Combating Multinational Tax Avoidance) Act 2015*, the Bill for which was introduced into the Parliament on 16 September 2015.

for Multinational Enterprises and Tax Administrations (Transfer Pricing Guidelines) and is centred on difficult areas of transfer pricing such as intangibles, risk and capital, and other high risk transactions. Australia's domestic transfer pricing regime incorporates the OECD's Transfer Pricing Guidelines but initially referred to the 2010 Guidelines. The Australian Government is of the view that no substantive changes are required to the current transfer pricing regime. However, legislation was passed in 2017 to ensure that the income tax law was updated to reflect a reference to the OECD's Actions 8-10 2015 Final Reports.[16]

2.4.7 Action 11: BEPS Data

In response to Action 11, dealing with methodologies to collect and analyse BEPS data, the Australian Government has recognised that further work needs to be done to measure progress of the BEPS initiatives. To date, there has been no official Australian response to Action 11.

2.4.8 Action 12: Disclosure of Aggressive Tax Planning Practices

The Action 12 recommendations provide a best practice approach to the disclosure of aggressive tax planning practices. While countries such as the US, UK, Korea, Canada and South Africa have mandatory reporting regimes in place, Australia has previously not had such a regime *per se*, but rather some of the elements of one. For example, since 2011 Australia has required certain corporate taxpayers to lodge a reportable tax position (RTP) schedule disclosing its most contestable and material tax positions. The list of taxpayers affected was expanded for years after 30 June 2018 to include economic groups with a turnover greater than AUD 250 million. Taxpayers are required to provide information in three categories: tax uncertainties in the tax return, tax uncertainties in the financial statements, and reportable arrangements as identified in ATO guidance material. In 2016, the Government sought community input on the OECD's mandatory disclosure rules proposal. To date, the outcome of that consultation has not been made publicly available. Should Australia choose to introduce mandatory disclosure rules, it could do so by adapting the current promoter penalty regime to clarify who should report.

2.4.9 Action 15: Multilateral Instrument

Action 15 provides a multilateral instrument to implement many of the BEPS recommendations into relevant double tax agreements. As noted in section 2.3.1, Australia signed the MLI on 7 June 2017. Legislation to provide for incorporation of the MLI into Australia's domestic law was enacted on 24 August 2018,[17] and Australia ratified the MLI on 26 September 2018 so that it will enter into force for the country on 1 January 2019. The MLI will ensure that any tax treaty to which both parties are signatories of the MLI, does not need to be individually renegotiated. As of

16 *Treasury Laws Amendment (Combating Multinational Tax Avoidance) Act 2017.*

17 *Treasury Laws Amendment (OECD Multilateral Instrument) Act 2018.*

23 July 2018, eight countries with which Australia has DTAs have decided not to become signatories to the MLI. These countries are the US, the Philippines, Thailand, Vietnam, Taiwan, Sri Lanka, Papua New Guinea and Kiribati. There are four additional countries, Austria, Korea, Sweden and Switzerland, which have chosen not to nominate their DTA with Australia as a Covered Tax Agreement. The effect of this is that for the relevant DTA it is as if the MLI has not been signed.

Australia has not adopted the MLI without reservations. Rather, it has not adopted MLI Article 10 – "Anti-abuse rule for permanent establishments situated in third jurisdictions", or Article 12 – "Artificial avoidance of permanent establishment status through commissionaire arrangements and similar strategies". It has also made a reservation to the mandatory binding arbitration provisions to exclude their application to disputes involving the domestic anti-avoidance rules (including the MAAL and DPT) (MacInnes and Watkins, 2018). The rationale for formulating a reservation in relation to the anti-abuse provision is that none of Australia's tax treaties have similar provisions. It is also unclear as to the economic impact of this provision on Australia. It is also necessary to look at the partner country reservations on the MLI in each case as this will affect Australia's position as well.

2.5 Unilateral Measures

2.5.1 Transfer Pricing Rules

Australia is seen as one of the most proactive countries in terms of introducing unilateral measures. In fact, the breadth and speed at which Australia has done so has caused some alarm. As previously stated, Australia was already in the process of amending its transfer pricing regime in response to the 2011 Full Federal Court decision in *Federal Commissioner of Taxation v SNF Australia Pty Ltd.*[18] Those changes, which were introduced in 2013 in subdivisions 815-B to 815-D of the *Income Tax Assessment Act 1997*, resulted in the ATO having broader reconstruction powers and a requirement that they be applied so as best to achieve consistency with the OECD Transfer Pricing Guidelines. The overarching rationale for the reform was to modernise Australia's transfer pricing regime to bring the rules into line with international standards and best practice. The most significant change has been the shift in focus from the old laws on the arm's length consideration of transactions to the arm's length profit and profit allocation.[19]

2.5.2 Political Climate

The political climate in Australia has also been a significant driver of a great deal of change. In 2014, the Senate Economics References Committee commenced an inquiry into corporate tax avoidance. The proceedings ran for four years reflecting

18 *Federal Commissioner of Taxation v SNF Australia Pty Ltd* [2011] FCAFC 74; 2011 ATC 20-265; 193 FCR 149.

19 For a comprehensive analysis of the new transfer pricing laws, see Preshaw and Sadiq (2017).

the significance of both the evidence deduced and its findings, and was extended eight times to 30 May 2018. It culminated in three Senate reports: *You cannot tax what you cannot see* (August 2015), *Gaming the system* (April 2016), and *Much heat, little light so far* (May 2018). These reports provided recommendations to the Australian Government and reaffirmed the importance of addressing corporate tax practices to combat tax avoidance and minimisation, protect Australia's revenue base, and collect corporate taxes. Witnesses before the Senate inquiry included a number of multinational enterprises as well as the "big end of town" accounting and advisory firms.

2.5.3 Multinational Anti-Avoidance Law

One of the most significant unilateral measures introduced by Australia since the OECD's BEPS program is what is known as the multinational anti-avoidance law or MAAL, which is based on the first limb of the UK's diverted profits tax. The MAAL, designed to tackle the artificial avoidance of Australian permanent establishments, came into effect on 11 December 2015 and applies to certain entities and schemes on or after 1 January 2016. It is contained in section 177DA as an extension of the existing general anti-avoidance provisions in Part IVA of the *Income Tax Assessment Act 1936*.[20] Where the MAAL applies, the date the scheme was entered into is irrelevant. The MAAL applies to significant global entities (SGEs) which are either global parent entities with annual global income of AUD 1 billion or more, or a member of a group of entities consolidated (for accounting purposes) where the global parent entity has an annual global income of AUD 1 billion or more. This means that both Australian headquartered entities and the local operations of foreign headquartered multinationals are included. The Government indicated that the MAAL was targeted at 30 large multinationals, however currently, there are more than 1,600 multinational entities operating in Australia with revenue over AUD 1 billion indicating that the reach may be broader than first thought.

For the MAAL to apply, the scheme must be entered into for a principal purpose of obtaining a tax benefit. This threshold is lower than the general anti-avoidance rule which requires the scheme to have a sole or dominant purpose of obtaining a tax benefit. In broad terms, it applies where: (i) there is a scheme entered into for a principal purpose of obtaining a tax benefit and a foreign entity derives income by making a supply to an Australian customer of the foreign entity; (ii) activities are undertaken in Australia directly in connection with the supply by an Australian entity which is an associate of, or is commercially dependent on, the foreign entity, and (iii) some or all of that income is not attributable to an Australian permanent establishment of the foreign entity. Where the MAAL applies, the foreign entity will be taxed as if the income had not been avoided with penalties of up to 120 per cent applied.

20 Part IVA is expressed to prevail over the terms of Australia's DTAs: *International Tax Agreements Act 1953*, s. 4(2).

In the 2017-18 Budget, the Federal Government announced that the MAAL would be strengthened even further by preventing SGEs from using foreign trusts and partnerships in corporate structures to avoid the application of the MAAL. Legislation to effect this change is yet to be passed through Parliament. A further amendment was also proposed in the 2018-19 Budget to extend the definition of significant global entities to include groups headed by entities other than listed public companies (e.g. private companies, trusts and investment entities).

2.5.4 Diverted Profits Tax

Subsequent to the MAAL, in the 2016-17 Federal Budget, the Government announced that it would also introduce a diverted profits tax (DPT) of 40 per cent. The DPT, which came into effect from 1 July 2017, is designed to ensure that the tax paid by SGEs (as defined in section 2.5.3 above) properly reflects the economic substance of their activities in Australia by preventing the diversion of profits offshore through arrangements involving related parties (Nguyen, 2017). While the DPT applies to tax years after 1 July 2017, it can apply to schemes entered into before that date. Again, a principal purpose test is applied to determine whether a scheme was entered into or carried out, between a taxpayer and a foreign entity that is an associate of the taxpayer, to obtain an Australian tax benefit or to obtain an Australian and foreign tax benefit.

There are three exceptions to the DPT rules applying: (i) the Australian income of the taxpayer and its associates does not exceed AUD 25 million; (ii) it is reasonable to conclude that sufficient foreign tax has been paid (at least 80 per cent of the reduced Australian tax), and (iii) the profit made by each entity reasonably reflects the economic substance of the entity's activities in connection with the scheme.

2.5.5 Transparency Measures

In addition to the substantive law changes outlined above, Australia has also adopted unilateral measures to deal with transparency concerns around the tax practices of multinational entities.

The first of these measures, introduced prior to the OECD's BEPS program and recommendations, requires the ATO to publish certain information about the tax affairs of large corporate taxpayers. Australia is one of the first jurisdictions in the current environment to legislate mandatory disclosure of taxpayer information by a revenue authority. The *Tax Laws Amendment (2013 Measures No. 2) Act 2013* requires the Commissioner of Taxation to publish an annual corporate tax transparency report. Specifically, where an Australian public or foreign-owned company returns a total income of AUD 100 million or more for an income year, section 3C of the *Taxation Administration Act 1953* now requires the Commissioner of Taxation to publish an entity's name and ABN, total income, taxable income, and tax payable, as reported in its company tax return for the year. The Commissioner is also required to disclose the same information for Australian-owned resident private companies with total income of AUD 200 million or more, entities that have petroleum resource rent tax (PRRT) payable, and entities that have minerals resource rent tax (MRRT) payable for the years it was in place. The first publication of Australian public and foreign owned company information, entitled *The Report of Entity Tax Information* (Australian Taxation Office, 2015) was released on 17 December 2015. This report disclosed what was previously considered sensitive tax information in relation to approximately 1,500 of Australia's top public companies, including their total income, taxable income and tax paid. To date, the ATO has published three tax years' worth of such data: 2013-14, 2014-15 and 2015-16. It is expected that the effects of the MAAL and DPT may be seen through an analysis of future figures. The effects of the MAAL may be apparent in the 2016-17 data where companies have restructured as a response to the legislation implemented from 1 January 2016. Where this has occurred, the ATO expects to see percentage increases in gross income along with increases in taxable income and tax payable. The effects of the DPT are likely to be seen in the 2017-18 data through an increase in profits allocated to Australia.

Additionally, as part of the 2015 Budget, the Federal Treasurer requested that the Board of Taxation, an independent Government appointed body, develop a code on the public disclosure of tax information by businesses. On 3 May 2016, the Government released the Board of Taxation's final report endorsing its recommendations on what is now known as the Tax Transparency Code (TTC) (Board of Taxation, 2016). The TTC provides a set of principles and "minimum standards" to guide disclosure of tax information by businesses, particularly large multinationals. It is claimed that the TTC is currently the most advanced and comprehensive tax transparency measure in the world. The intended audience for the TTC data is broad and includes "interested users" (such as social justice groups, media, analysts and shareholders) and general users (the "person in the street"), rather than the ATO which already has access to extensive data. It is recommended that, as a minimum, large businesses provide a reconciliation of accounting profit to tax expense and to income tax paid or income tax payable, identify material temporary and non-temporary differences, provide the accounting effective company tax rates for Australian and global operations, provide their approach to tax strategy and governance, list a tax contribution summary for corporate taxes paid, and provide information about international related party dealings. "Large businesses" for the purposes of the TTC are defined as businesses with aggregated TTC Australian turnover of AUD 500 million or more, although businesses with an annual turnover of AUD 100 million or more are encouraged to publish information about their tax affairs.

2.6 Tax Administration and BEPS

Australia has a sophisticated tax administration body and has publicly stated that it believes it is leading the global fight against multinational tax avoidance.[21] Additional funding has recently been provided to enforce the existing international tax regime as well as any new measures discussed above. Given this fact, it is likely that information collected through measures such as country-by-country reporting, and from the expanding process of automatic exchange of information, will be increasingly acted on to assess the practices of multinational entities operating in Australia.

Australia also has a strong track record of investigating tax avoidance. In particular, in 2006, what was known as the Project Wickenby compliance program was established to focus on international tax evasion. It raised AUD 2.3 billion in tax liabilities through over 4,500 audits and resulted in 46 convictions. As a response to the current problem of BEPS, in 2016, an ATO Tax Avoidance Taskforce was established to specifically investigate the tax affairs of multinationals, large public and private groups as well as wealthy individuals operating in Australia. The ATO estimates that by June 2020 the Taskforce will have reviewed the tax practices of the top 1,000 public groups and top 320 private groups.

To complement the various government initiatives, it was announced as part of the 2016 Federal Budget that new whistleblower protections would be introduced to protect people who disclose information about tax misconduct to the ATO (Sadiq, 2018). Legislation is yet to pass through Parliament,[22] but the proposed reform of whistleblower protection is seen as a significant step in ensuring there is a comprehensive regime for the protection of individuals who report breaches or suspected breaches of the tax law and/or tax misconduct. Rewards are not part of the scheme; however, the identity of the whistleblower will be protected as will their liability from criminal, civil and administrative liability. It is also expected that new rules will be developed to further require tax and financial advisers to report potentially aggressive tax planning schemes.[23]

As part of a tax integrity package, administrative penalties for breaching reporting obligations have also been increased. The increased penalties, which operate from 1 July 2017, apply to SGEs as defined in section 2.5.3 above. Penalties apply to such behaviour as failing to lodge on time, making a false or misleading statement, making a statement which treats a law as applying in a way that was not reasonably arguable, and failing to provide a document as required. These changes increase the maximum penalty from AUD 5,250 to AUD 525,000 together with a specified percentage of any tax shortfall (ranging up to 150 per cent) resulting from the breach.

21 See, for example, Australian Treasury, "Tax evasion and multinational tax avoidance", https://treasury.gov.au/tax-evasion/.

22 Treasury Laws Amendment (Enhancing Whistleblower Protections) Bill 2017.

23 Australian Treasury, "Tax evasion and multinational tax avoidance", above n. 21.

2.7 The Future of International Tax Reform for Australia

There is little doubt that Australia's international tax regime and administrative practices will remain closely aligned with the OECD's guidelines and recommendations and likely continue to go beyond the recommended globally accepted common approach to include adoption of unilateral measures. Perhaps the biggest danger in specific terms to Australia's international tax regime is its complexity especially given administrative resource constraints and the country's political stance against base erosion and profit shifting by multinationals (on tax compliance challenges and responses in Australia, see Evans, 2018).

More generally, Australia's international tax policy steps in coming years probably depend at least as much as, if not more than, that of other countries on the future of the institutions of international tax governance themselves. It suffices merely to note here that the future prospects of these institutions is a matter that many commentators are quite cautious about (see, e.g., Eccleston and Smith, 2016, p. 191). In this context, any unfavourable developments in the arena of global tax governance might leave Australia confronting a policy choice, namely, whether to persevere with policies similar to those of the OECD/G20 BEPS project, or alternatively turn to significantly different policies drawn from its own history in the field, such as, for example, formulary apportionment or presumptive taxation methods. Such a choice would need to be informed by broader conditions in the global economic and geopolitical spheres prevailing at the time.

References

Australian Taxation Office (ATO) (2018), *Taxation Statistics 2015-16*, Canberra.

Australian Treasury (2013a), "Implications of the Modern Global Economy for the Taxation of Multinational Enterprises: Issues Paper", May, https://treasury.gov.au/consultation/implications-of-the-modern-global-economy-for-the-taxation-of-multinational-enterprises/.

Australian Treasury (2013b), "Risks to the Sustainability of Australia's Corporate Tax Base: Scoping Paper", July, https://static.treasury.gov.au/uploads/sites/1/2017/06/BEPSscoping_paper.pdf.

Australia's Future Tax System Review Panel (Dr Ken Henry, chair) (2009), *Australia's Future Tax System: Report to the Treasurer*, December (Henry Review).

Bain, Kathrin, Richard Krever and Anthony van der Westhuysen (2011), "The Influence of Alternative Model Tax Treaties on Australian Treaties", 26(1) *Australian Tax Forum* 31-49.

Board of Taxation, Australia (2016), *A Tax Transparency Code: A Report to the Treasurer*, Canberra, February, http://taxboard.gov.au/files/2016/05/BoT_TransparencyCode_Final-report.pdf.

Cooper, Graeme (2017), "Implementing BEPS, or Maybe Not – the Australian Experience One Year On", 2 *New Zealand Law Review* 145-174.

Department of Foreign Affairs and Trade, Australia (2011), "Australia and the OECD", https://dfat.gov.au/about-us/publications/Documents/australia-and-the-oecd.pdf.

Eccleston, Richard and Helen Smith (2016), "The G20, BEPS and the Future of International Tax Governance", in Peter Dietsch and Thomas Rixen (eds.), *Global Tax Governance: What is Wrong With It and How to Fix It* (Colchester: ECPR Press), 175-197.

Evans, Chris (2018), "Australia", in Chris Evans, Michael Lang, Alexander Rust, Josef Schuch, Claus Staringer and Pasquale Pistone (eds.), *Improving Tax Compliance in a Globalized World* (Amsterdam: IBFD), 79-108.

Greenwoods and Herbert Smith Freehills (2015), "G20/OECD deliver BEPS project but it's not over", *Tax Brief*, 9 October, http://www.greenwoods.com.au/media/1706/g20-oecd-deliver-beps-project-but-its-not-over.pdf.

Heferen, Rob, Nicole Mitchell and Ian Amalo (2013), "Tax policy formulation in Australia", 2 *Economic Roundup* 1-13, https://treasury.gov.au/publication/economic-roundup-issue-2-2013-2/economic-roundup-issue-2-2013/tax-policy-formulation-in-australia/.

International Business Publications (2013), *Australia Country Study Guide, Vol. 1: Strategic Information and Developments* (Washington, DC: International Business Publications).

Krever, Richard and Peter Mellor (2016), "Australia", in Michael Lang, Jeffrey Owens, Pasquale Pistone, Alexander Rust, Josef Schuch and Claus Staringer (eds.), *GAARs – A Key Element of Tax Systems in the Post-BEPS World* (Amsterdam: IBFD), 45-64.

Krever, Richard and Jiaying Zhang (2011), "Australia: Resolving the Application of Competing Treaty and Domestic Law Transfer Pricing Rules", in Michael Lang, Pasquale Pistone, Josef Schuch, Claus Staringer, Alfred Storck, Luc De Broe, Peter Essers, Eric C. C. M. Kemmeren and Frans Vanistendael (eds.), *Tax Treaty Case Law around the Globe - 2011* (Vienna: Linde), 197-213.

MacInnes, Isabelle and David Watkins (2018), "OECD BEPS Multilateral Instrument: One Step Closer", *Weekly Tax Bulletin*, Issue 36 (24 August) [1158].

Markham, Michelle (2017), "The New Australia-Germany Income and Capital Tax Treaty (2015): A Tax Treaty for the Era of the OECD/G20 BEPS Initiative?", 71(8) *Bulletin for International Taxation* 410-423.

Morrison, Hon. Scott (Treasurer) (2015), "OECD report supports Australian Government action on multinational tax avoidance", Media Release, 6 October, http://sjm.ministers.treasury.gov.au/media-release/003-2015/.

Morrison, Hon. Scott (Treasurer) (2018), "Transcript of Interview with Michael McKee, Bloomberg", 19 March, http://sjm.ministers.treasury.gov.au/transcript/031-2018/.

Nguyen, H. Khiem (Jonathan) (2017), "Australia's New Diverted Profits Tax: The Rationale, the Expectations and the Unknowns", 71(9) *Bulletin for International Taxation* 513-522.

Organisation for Economic Co-operation and Development (OECD) (2017), *Inclusive Framework on BEPS, Action 5: Harmful Tax Practices – Peer Review Reports on the Exchange of Information on Tax Rulings*, December (Paris: OECD), https://www.oecd-ilibrary.org/taxation/harmful-tax-practices-peer-review-reports-on-the-exchange-of-information-on-tax-rulings_9789264285675-en.

Organisation for Economic Co-operation and Development (OECD) (2018), *OECD Development Co-operation Peer Reviews: Australia 2018* (Paris: OECD), https://doi.org/10.1787/9789264293366-en.

Preshaw, Damian and Kerrie Sadiq (2017), "The Future of Transfer Pricing: Australia", *Cahiers de Droit Fiscal International Vol. 102B: The Future of Transfer Pricing* 111-134.

Sadiq, Kerrie (2017), "Unitary Taxation of the Finance Sector", in Sol Picciotto (ed.), *Taxing Multinational Enterprises as Unitary Firms* (Brighton: Institute of Development Studies), 119-129.

Sadiq, Kerrie (2018), "Tax and Whistle-Blower Protection: Part of a Commitment to Tackling Tax Misconduct in Australia", 46(5) *Intertax* 429-433.

Vann, Richard (2009), "Australia's Future Tax Treaty Policy", in Chris Evans and Richard Krever (eds.), *Australian Business Tax Reform in Retrospect and Prospect* (Sydney: Thomson), 401-414.

Vann, Richard (2014), "Policy Forum: The Policy Underpinnings of the BEPS Project – Preserving the International Corporate Income Tax?", 62(2) *Canadian Tax Journal* 433-441.

3 The Adoption of BEPS in Canada

Vokhid Urinov*

Abstract

Canada has been actively engaged in addressing aggressive cross-border tax avoidance arrangements through legislation and administrative measures for many years. However, the country was also aware that this work could not be achieved in isolation from other countries. In this context, the OECD/G20 BEPS initiative has emerged as a critical opportunity. The initiative allowed many countries to come together to develop a common framework to address many pressing global tax problems. The chapter below highlights Canada's implementation of the OECD/G20 initiative and recommendations on base erosion and profit shifting, and the interaction of these recommendations with the country's existing rules on similar issues.

3.1 Introduction

Canada is the world's second largest country by area. It is a federal parliamentary democracy and is divided into ten provinces and three territories. Canada has two constitutional levels of government – federal and provincial/territorial, each having its own legislative powers and tax system.[1] Consequently, personal and corporate income are taxed at two levels: at the federal level by applying the federal *Income Tax Act* of 1972 and at provincial or territorial levels by applying their corresponding income tax legislation.

The federal income tax legislation and its corresponding regulations are administered and enforced by the Canada Revenue Agency (CRA). The CRA administers and collects income taxes both on behalf of the federal as well as the provincial and territorial governments except the provinces of Quebec and Alberta which admin-

* Assistant Professor, Faculty of Law, University of New Brunswick, Canada. This report was supported by my research assistant Samer Alam, a Juris Doctor student at the Faculty of Law, University of New Brunswick. His assistance in collecting data and editorial support have greatly improved the quality of this work.

1 See Government of Canada, "The constitutional distribution of legislative powers", https://www.canada.ca/en/intergovernmental-affairs/services/federation/distribution-legislative-powers.html.

ister or partially administer their own tax systems.[2] The CRA also oversees social benefit and economic incentive programs delivered through the tax system, registration of charities, and tax credit programs in Canada.[3]

A major review of Canada's modern income tax system was conducted from 1962 by the Royal Commission on Taxation chaired by Kenneth Carter (the Carter Commission) to comprehensively study the country's tax system. In 1967, the Carter Commission finalised its seven volume report as a result of its study, recommending fundamental changes to the country's tax system.[4] Drawing on these recommendations, the government issued a White Paper on Tax Reform in 1969.[5] These resulted in what is now known as the *Income Tax Act of 1972* (ITA).[6] Since then the ITA has grown to a little more than 3,000 pages and 269 sections undergoing additions and revisions with every federal budget but its policy rationales remain largely the same as those that were proposed by the Carter Commission.

Since the institution of its federal income tax system in 1917, Canada has had a special judicial body which has resolved tax-specific disputes between the taxpayer and the government. It carried out this mandate with different levels of independence and under various names until 1983, when it was then named the Tax Court of Canada (Campbell, 2016, pp. 547-557). As an alternative to its general procedure, Tax Court cases may proceed by way of a simplified informal procedure where the total tax and penalties at issue are below CAD 25,000 or the amount of the loss at issue is less than CAD 50,000.[7]

Finally, Canada is a developed country with a nominal GDP of approximately USD 1.52 trillion.[8] This makes Canada the 11th largest economy in the world by nominal GDP. The country's economy is primarily based on the service industry, the production and export of food, natural resource products, such as minerals, oil and gas, and forest products. In 2017, the country's exports totalled CAD 549.8 billion, while its imports of goods were worth CAD 573.5 billion.[9] Thus, last year Canada incurred a trade deficit of around CAD 23.7 billion.[10] The country

2 Canada Revenue Agency, "About the Canada Revenue Agency (CRA)", https://www.canada.ca/en/revenue-agency/corporate/about-canada-revenue-agency-cra.html.

3 Canada Revenue Agency, "Structure and Operational Framework", https://www.canada.ca/en/revenue-agency/corporate/about-canada-revenue-agency-cra/canada-revenue-agency-structure-operational-framework.html.

4 Royal Commission on Taxation (Kenneth Carter, chair), *Recommendations of the Royal Commission on Taxation* (1967) (Carter Commission).

5 Department of Finance, Canada, "Proposals for Tax Reform - White Paper on Taxation" (1969).

6 RSC 1985, c. 1 (5th Supplement) as amended.

7 *Tax Court of Canada Act* (RSC 1985, c. T-2), ss 17-18.

8 International Monetary Fund, "World Economic Outlook Database" (July 2017), http://www.imf.org/external/pubs/ft/weo/2017/01/weodata/index.aspx.

9 Statistics Canada, "International merchandise trade for all countries and by Principal Trading Partners", https://www.statcan.gc.ca/tables-tableaux/sum-som/l01/cst01/gblec02a-eng.htm (accessed on 18 June 2018).

10 Statista, "Canada: Trade balance of goods from 2007 to 2017", https://www.statista.com/statistics/262851/trade-balance-of-goods-in-canada (accessed on 18 June 2018).

is a member of the Organisation for Economic Co-operation and Development (OECD), the Group of 20 (G20), and the Group of Seven (G7).

3.2 Canada's Response to the G20/OECD BEPS Project

In June 2012, the OECD launched the project against base erosion and profit shifting (BEPS) in cooperation with the G20.[11] The project was aimed at exploring international tax planning strategies used by multinational enterprises to inappropriately shift their profits away from the jurisdictions where their true economic activity takes place to countries where they have no significant economic activity but where they pay a low tax or no tax. As a result of this project, the OECD prepared the report *Addressing Base Erosion and Profit Shifting* released on 12 February 2013 (OECD, 2013a). The report presented the base erosion and profit shifting activities as a serious risk to the integrity and fairness of national tax law and tax sovereignty of countries. It also showed that current tax standards may not have kept pace with changes in global business practices and urged that a more holistic approach is necessary to address the BEPS issues. The G20 Finance Ministers welcomed and expressed strong support for the report and asked the OECD to develop an action plan to address the BEPS problems, possibly before their July 2013 meeting. The purpose of the Action Plan was to identify actions necessary to address BEPS issues.

Consistent with these expectations, on 19 July 2013 the OECD released its initial action plan (BEPS Action Plan) and presented it at the G20 Finance Ministers' meeting in Moscow.[12] In essence, the BEPS Action Plan labelled the base erosion and profit shifting activities as harmful to governments, individual taxpayers, and businesses (OECD. 2013b, p. 8). It proposed that the interested countries implement 15 Action items to eradicate or significantly limit such activities. Action items 1 to 10 provide guidance on substantive BEPS issues, while Action items 11-14 are procedural in nature. Action item 15 envisages the development of a multilateral instrument to facilitate the implementation of BEPS.

The G20 leaders endorsed the BEPS Action Plan and encouraged all interested countries to participate in the initiative.[13] The G20 also called on member countries to examine how their own domestic laws contribute to BEPS. A more comprehensive action plan was to be delivered within two years by the joint OECD/G20 BEPS Project. Finally, on 5 October 2015 the OECD released 13 final reports together with an explanatory statement (2015 BEPS Reports).[14] The recommendations contained in the reports reflect varying degrees of consensus among the OECD and the G20 countries and they can be grouped into three broad categories:

---

11 "We reiterate the need to prevent base erosion and profit shifting and we will follow with attention the ongoing work of the OECD in this area": G20 Leaders Declaration signed in Los Cabos, Mexico (19 June 2012), [48], www.g20.utoronto.ca/2012/2012-0619-loscabos.html.

12 Communiqué, G20 Meeting of Finance Ministers and Central Bank Governors, Moscow (20 July 2013), http://www.g20.utoronto.ca/2013/2013-0720-finance.html.

13 Ibid.

14 OECD, "BEPS 2015 Final Reports", www.oecd.org/ctp/aggressive/beps-2015-final-reports.htm.

a) minimum standards;
b) reinforced standards, and
c) best practices.

Following the release of the BEPS recommendations in October 2015, G20 leaders urged their "timely implementation" and called on the OECD "to develop an inclusive framework by early 2016 with the involvement of interested non-G20 countries and jurisdictions", including developing economies.[15] The Inclusive Framework was established in January 2016 and brought together over 110 interested jurisdictions to collaborate on the implementation of the BEPS Project globally.[16] The framework also contemplates establishing mechanisms to peer review and monitor the implementation of the whole BEPS Package.

In the meantime, the OECD also developed the Multilateral Convention to Implement Tax Treaty Related Measures to Prevent Base Erosion and Profit Shifting (MLI) to implement certain tax treaty measures contained in the OECD/G20 BEPS Project in an expedient and predictable manner. As of 23 July 2018, the number of signatory countries of the MLI had reached 83.[17]

As a member of the OECD and the G20, Canada has been at the forefront of the BEPS project from its inception.[18] Moreover, the Canadian government has reiterated its support for and commitment to the BEPS initiative in each of its annual federal budget reports since 2014 (see, e.g., Department of Finance, 2014, p 257; Department of Finance, 2015, pp. 471-472; Department of Finance, 2016a, pp. 217-219). In fact, the 2016 federal budget introduced concrete steps to implement some of the BEPS recommendations. These include new Canadian legislation on the Country-by-Country reporting for large multinational enterprises and commencement of the spontaneous international exchange of tax rulings that could potentially give rise to BEPS concerns.[19] Finally, Canada has become party to the Inclusive Framework, signed the MLI and expressed its commitment to implementing all of the minimum BEPS standards.[20]

15 G20 Leaders' Communique, Antalya Summit (15-16 November 2015), [15], http://www.consilium.europa.eu/media/23729/g20-antalya-leaders-summit-communique.pdf.

16 OECD, "Members of the Inclusive Framework on BEPS" (May 2018), http://www.oecd.org/tax/beps/inclusive-framework-on-beps-composition.pdf.

17 OECD, "Signatories and Parties to the Multilateral Convention to Implement Tax Treaty Related Measures to Prevent Base Erosion and Profit Shifting, Status as of 23 July 2018", http://www.oecd.org/tax/treaties/beps-mli-signatories-and-parties.pdf (accessed on 7 August 2018).

18 Department of Finance Update by Brian Ernewein (General Director of the Department of Finance Tax Policy Branch) at the 68th CTF Annual Tax Conference (29 November 2016), https://taxinterpretations.com/content/392451.

19 Department of Finance (2016, pp. 217-219); see also Canada Revenue Agency, "Guidance on Country-By-Country Reporting in Canada", RC4651 (24 March 2017), https://www.canada.ca/en/revenue-agency/services/forms-publications/publications/rc4651.html.

20 Department of Finance, Canada, "Canada Signs Agreement to Combat International Tax Avoidance", Press Release (7 June 2017), https://www.fin.gc.ca/n17/17-054-eng.asp; see also the 2017 Budget: Department of Finance (2017, pp. 202-203).

The reasons for Canada to support the BEPS Project are very comprehensible. On the one hand, the country already had in its domestic laws some of the anti-abuse provisions proposed by the BEPS Action Plan. For example, Canada has had Controlled Foreign Corporation rules since 1976 (ITA, s. 95(1); (i.e., the Action 3 item), General Anti-Avoidance Rules since 1988 (ITA, s. 245), Transfer Pricing Rules based on the arm's length principle since 1997 (ITA, s. 247; i.e., the Actions 8-10 items). The BEPS Project confirms and acknowledges the validity of Canada's long-established position on these tax issues and may encourage the country to advance these regimes.

On the other hand, Canada did not have all the anti-abuse provisions as proposed in the BEPS final report and its approaches in addressing certain international tax avoidance issues differed from international practice. For example, for many years Canada has tried to address the problem of treaty shopping on an ad hoc basis. However, the Canadian government was not very successful in challenging such cases through this approach. In fact, it has lost almost all alleged treaty shopping cases.[21] Thus, the practice has continued to pose significant risks to the country's tax base (Department of Finance, 2013a, p. 373). The BEPS project, especially through the MLI, has provided Canada with the opportunity to revisit the issue and resolve it in an internationally coordinated manner by swiftly implementing anti-treaty shopping measures.

3.3 Canada's Adoption of the Four Minimum Standards in the BEPS Inclusive Framework

Consistent with the government's expressed intentions when Canada signed the Inclusive Framework and the MLI, the country proposes to adopt the BEPS minimum standards on countering harmful tax practices (Action 5), treaty abuse (Action 6), transfer pricing documentation and country-by-country reporting (Action 13), as well as improving dispute resolution in relation to tax treaty disputes (Action 14). These minimum standards were agreed to tackle issues in cases where no action by some countries or jurisdictions would have created negative spillovers on others.

3.3.1 Action 5: Countering Harmful Tax Practices More Effectively, Taking into Account Transparency and Substance

BEPS Action 5 urges countries to refrain from harmful tax practices with a priority on improving transparency, including compulsory spontaneous exchange of rulings related to preferential regimes. Canada's responses to these two broad requirements are examined in turn below.

21 *MIL (Investments) SA v. The Queen*, 2007 FCA 236.

3.3.1.1 Compulsory Spontaneous Exchange of Tax Rulings

The CRA has two service divisions that issue rulings: the Competent Authority Services Division on advance pricing agreements and the Income Tax Rulings Directorate on other tax ruling categories. Consistent with the BEPS recommendation to improve transparency, the CRA announced in March 2016 that the exchange initiative for binding advance income tax rulings would go into full force on 1 April 2016.[22] On 22 April 2016, Canada released Information Circular 70-6R7 and Technical Interpretations to outline the types of tax rulings that Canada intends to spontaneously share with other jurisdictions.[23]

The process enables the spontaneous exchange of information on cross-border tax rulings with participating countries in five areas: a) rulings relating to preferential regimes; b) rulings related to transfer pricing advance pricing agreements; c) rulings relating to a downward adjustment to taxpayer's taxable profits not directly reflected in the taxpayer's accounts; d) Permanent Establishment rulings, and e) related party conduit rulings. The Circular specifies that:

> [i]f a ruling falls into one of the above categories, a summary of its contents may be exchanged with the countries of residence of the immediate parent company, the ultimate parent company and certain other parties. These countries may then ask to receive relevant portions of the ruling in further detail.[24]

This provides participating countries with timely information on rulings that have been granted to a foreign related party of their resident taxpayers. They can use such information in conducting risk assessments, which in the absence of exchange may give rise to BEPS concerns.

Currently, Canada has the necessary legal framework and administrative process for exchanging information on rulings as contemplated under Action 5 (OECD, 2017a, para. 6). All of Canada's double tax treaties permits spontaneous exchange of information with treaty partners. In addition, the income tax rulings may be exchanged under the Multilateral Convention on Mutual Administrative Assistance in Tax Matters (Multilateral Convention) as amended by the protocol and under some Tax Information Exchange Agreements (TIEAs). Canada ratified the Multilateral Convention in November 2013.[25]

---

22 Canada Revenue Agency, Internal Tax Interpretation T.I. 2016-0632941I7 - BEPS exchange of tax rulings, 22 March 2016, https://taxinterpretations.com/cra/severed-letters/2016-0632941i7.

23 Canada Revenue Agency, "Advance Income Tax Rulings and Technical Interpretations", Income Tax Information Circular IC70-6R7 (22 April 2016), https://www.canada.ca/en/revenue-agency/services/forms-publications/publications/ic70-6r7/ic70-6r7-advance-income-tax-rulings-technical-interpretations.html.

24 Ibid, [55].

25 Department of Finance, "Ratification of the Convention on Mutual Administrative Assistance in Tax Matters", Press Release (23 November 2013), https://www.fin.gc.ca/treaties-conventions/notices/maatm-aammf-eng.asp.

3.3.1.2 Harmful Tax Practices

Canada currently does not have known harmful tax regimes, and thus no changes are required regarding the minimum standard in this area. One potentially harmful tax regime in Canada involved the international banking centre rules (ITA, s. 33.1). The rules were introduced in 1987 to facilitate the development of certain banking activities that would otherwise be carried on offshore (Bhattacharya, 1989, p. 133). Such banking business essentially accepted deposits from non-residents of Canada and made loans to non-residents of Canada. However, the international banking centre regime was abolished in 2013.[26]

Another harmful tax practice that the OECD BEPS project is particularly concerned with relates to "patent box" regimes. The concern is that multinational enterprises have the potential to shift the location of patents and other forms of intellectual property and the income accruing to them to low-tax countries for tax planning purposes. Therefore, the BEPS program urges countries not to maintain patent box regimes unless the patent was the result of domestic research and development expenditures. Canada currently does not have a patent box regime at the federal level, and therefore no changes are required in this area.

3.3.2 Action 6: Preventing the Granting of Treaty Benefits in Inappropriate Circumstances

Canada recognises treaty shopping as a significant risk to the country's tax base (Department of Finance, 2013a, p. 373). Until now the country has taken mainly an ad hoc approach in trying to address treaty shopping cases through the courts. When challenging treaty shopping cases, the CRA has most often relied on the domestic general anti-avoidance rule under section 245 of the ITA.[27] Alternatively, the CRA has also tried to argue that Canada's tax treaties have an inherent anti-abuse rule designed to address treaty shopping.[28] Occasionally, the CRA has also attempted to challenge certain treaty shopping cases through the treaty beneficial ownership test.[29]

However, these claims have not been very successful. In fact, the government has lost almost all cases of alleged treaty shopping. Canadian courts have generally concluded that even if treaty shopping has occurred there has not been a sufficiently clear policy intention in the legislation or terms of the relevant tax treaty

26 See Senate of Canada, Evidence to Standing Senate Committee on National Finance (7 May 2013), sencanada.ca/en/Content/Sen/committee/411/nffn/50146-e (accessed on 18 June 2018).

27 *Crown Forest Industries v. Canada*, [1995] 2 SCR 802; *RMM Canadian Enterprises Inc. v. Canada*, 97 DTC 302 (TCC); *MIL (Investments) SA v. The Queen*, 2006 TCC 460, *aff'd* 2007 DTC 5437; *Antle v. Canada*, 2009 TCC 465.

28 "Even if the GAAR does not apply to deny the treaty benefit in this case, it is still possible to deny the treaty based on the anti-abuse rule inherent within the Treaty itself": *MIL (Investments) SA v. The Queen*, 2006 TCC 460, *aff'd* 2007 DTC 5437, para. 76.

29 *Prévost Car v. MNR*, 2008 TCC 231, *aff'd* 2009 FCA 57; *Velcro Canada Inc. v. Canada*, 2012 TCC 57. See Department of Finance (2013b).

to deny the benefit. Therefore, the Canadian federal Budget of 2013 stressed the importance of developing safeguards and announced public consultations to seek the views of interested parties regarding possible approaches to address treaty shopping (Department of Finance, 2013a, p. 373). On 12 August 2013, a consultation paper was released to serve as the basis for a discussion aimed at reaching a workable solution to this issue (Department of Finance, 2013b). After engaging in consultations, however, Canada decided to await further work from the OECD/G20 on the BEPS Project (Department of Finance, 2014, pp. 249-252).

When the BEPS Action 6 Final Report came out, it recommended a minimum standard to prevent treaty shopping. The minimum standard set out in Action 6 included an amendment to the preamble of the relevant tax treaties, which refers to the purpose of a tax treaty as the elimination of double taxation without creating opportunities for non-taxation or reduced taxation through tax evasion or avoidance. Additionally, countries are also expected to implement either the integration of the "limitation-on-benefits rule" and the "principal purpose rule" under relevant tax treaties. In fact, these rules were already known to Canada, as the country has had them under some of its tax treaties.[30]

Canada's Department of Finance has confirmed that Canada would opt for the "principal purpose test" as a substantive technical anti-treaty shopping rule (Department of Finance, 2017b). It also implied that the country would, over the longer term, seek to negotiate, on a bilateral basis, a detailed "limitation of benefits provision" that would also meet the minimum standard. Canada has also decided to adopt the new preamble in its tax treaties covered under the MLI. This means that all Canadian treaties covered by the MLI will be modified by the addition of the new preamble, except those treaties with respect to which the other country has not signed the MLI.

On 28 May 2018, the Department of Finance tabled the draft legislation, the Multilateral Instrument in Respect of Tax Conventions Bill, in the House of Commons for consideration, formalising Canada's intention to introduce legislation to enact the MLI into Canadian law.[31] Article 7 (Prevention of Treaty Abuse) of the draft legislation includes the relevant anti-treaty shopping rules.

One matter that remains unclear is the interaction of the principal purpose test with Canada's existing general anti-avoidance rule (GAAR) under section 245 of the ITA. Although not limited to treaty abuse, the GAAR may apply to treaty shopping cases, in accordance with section 4.1 of the *Income Tax Conventions Inter-*

30 Department of Finance (2013b). Choudhury and Rodrigues (2017, p. 1259) provide a detailed discussion of the limitation-on-benefits and the principal purpose rules under Canadian tax treaties using the Canada – United States tax treaty (XXIXA), Canada – UK tax treaty (Articles 10(8), 11(9), 12(8)), Canada – Hong Kong tax treaty (Articles 10(7), 11(7), 12(7)) as examples.

31 Department of Finance, "Notice of Ways and Means Motion to introduce an Act to implement a multilateral convention to implement tax treaty related measures to prevent base erosion and profit shifting", Press Release (28 May 2018).

pretation Act.[32] These two instruments also appear to have very similar language even though one of them is specifically designed to apply in a treaty context. The CRA has recently implied that it might use both the principal purpose test and the GAAR as alternative tools to assess treaty shopping cases (Thomson and Carruthers, 2017). It is yet to be seen what issues and challenges this dual approach to addressing the same issue would entail.

3.3.3 Action 13: Transfer Pricing Documentation and Country-by-Country Reporting

The OECD's three-tiered approach to transfer pricing documentation proposed under the Action 13 Report represents a fundamental shift in the common transfer pricing documentation practices of multinational enterprises that extends far beyond mere transfer-pricing reporting. The standard provides for a Master File, a Local File, and Country-by-country reporting. The master file contains high level business information of an MNE that will be available to all relevant tax administrations (OECD, 2015e, p. 14). MNEs also need to maintain detailed transactional transfer pricing documentation by way of a local file specific to each country (OECD, 2015e, p. 15). Large multinational enterprises will be required to file annually a country-by-country report for each tax jurisdiction in which they do business containing the amount of revenue, profit before income tax, income tax paid and accrued, and some other information (OECD, 2015e, p. 16). Such reports are intended to be automatically exchanged with the tax administrators in each jurisdiction in which the MNE group conducts business.

3.3.3.1 Transfer Pricing Documentation

Canada has robust transfer pricing rules under section 247 of the ITA. This provision applies to transactions between a taxpayer and a non-resident person with whom the taxpayer does not deal at arm's length. A taxpayer includes an individual, corporation, trust as well as partnership. One of the main requirements of the transfer pricing rules is contemporaneous documentation described under section 247(4). Under this provision the taxpayer is generally not deemed to have made reasonable efforts ("the reasonable effort test") to determine an arm's length transfer price unless the taxpayer's records or documents are complete and accurate in all material respects as to: a) the property or service to which the transaction relates; b) the terms and conditions of the transaction and their relationship, if any, to the terms and conditions of other transactions between the participants; c) the identity of the participants, and their relationship at the time the transaction was entered into; d) the functions performed, the property used or contributed, and the risks assumed by the participants in the transaction; e) the data and methods

32 Osler, Hoskin & Harcourt LLP, "New PPT rule in the OECD's Multilateral Instrument to displace Canadian GAAR?", Update (27 November 2017), https://www.osler.com/en/resources/regulations/2017/new-ppt-rule-in-the-oecd-s-multilateral-instrument (accessed on 18 June 2018).

considered and the analysis performed to determine the transfer prices, and f) the assumptions, strategies and policies, if any, that influenced the determination of the transfer prices.

The transfer pricing documentation required under Action 13 appears to exceed by far what is currently required under section 247(4) of the ITA and the CRA administrative guidance. However, Canada has not yet announced any new specific requirements on transfer pricing documentation based on the BEPS guidelines other than the rules regarding country-by-country reporting. Thus, for the time being Canadian transfer pricing documentation requirements as stipulated in subsection 247(4) of the ITA will continue to apply.

3.3.3.2 Country-by-Country Reporting

On 22 March 2016, through its federal Budget, the Canadian federal government announced that it would introduce legislation to strengthen transfer pricing documentation by introducing country-by-country reporting. Canada enacted the country-by-country rules on 15 December 2016, which started applying to fiscal years of multinational enterprises that began on or after 1 January 2017.[33] The rules are contained in section 233.8 of the ITA. Canada also signed the Multilateral Competent Authority Agreement on the Exchange of Country-by-Country Reports on 11 May 2016.[34] Thus, country-by-country reports filed with the Canada Revenue Agency will be automatically exchanged with other jurisdictions in which the multinational group operates. First exchanges between jurisdictions of country-by-country reports were expected to have occurred by June 2018.[35]

The Canadian country-by-country reporting legislation generally conforms to the OECD model legislation (Eyitayo, 2018, p. 110). The country-by-country report will be required to be filed with the Canada Revenue Agency by ultimate parent entities of MNCs resident in Canada with a consolidated group revenue of no less than EUR 750 million by using Form RC4649 within one year of the end of the fiscal year to which it relates. In 2017, the CRA released "RC4649 Country-by-Country Report" and "RC4651 Guidance on Country-By-Country Reporting in Canada" which are the current guidelines on country-by-country reporting. Finally, the CRA has made it clear that wherever there are differences between the OECD model legislation and the Canadian country-by-country reporting legislation, the Canadian legislation takes precedence.[36]

33 Canada Revenue Agency, "Guidance on Country-By-Country Reporting in Canada", above n. 19, p. 4.

34 OECD, "Signatories of the Multilateral Competent Authority Agreement on the Exchange of Country-by-Country Reports (CbC MCAA) and Signing Dates" (15 June 2018), www.oecd.org/tax/automatic-exchange/about-automatic-exchange/CbC-MCAA-Signatories.pdf.

35 Canada Revenue Agency, "Guidance on Country-By-Country Reporting in Canada", above n. 19, p. 3.

36 Ibid, p. 4.

3.3.4 Has Canada Started Complying with Action 14?

Canada has a reasonably comprehensive mutual agreement procedure (MAP) program and extensive experience in resolving MAP cases. The CRA has the practice of publishing a report describing the country's MAP procedures and statistics annually (Canada Revenue Agency, 2018). The country is also committed to the effective and timely resolution of tax treaty-related disputes by improving the MAP in Canada's tax treaties under the BEPS initiative (Department of Finance, 2017a). Canada is also a party to the optional mandatory binding arbitration provisions of the MLI to resolve treaty-related disputes (Department of Finance, 2018b). The country is committed to meeting the Action 14 minimum standard through a combination of the signing of the MLI and bilateral negotiations.

Canada was also among the first batch of countries to have undergone the MAP peer review in 2017. The peer review confirms that Canada meets most of the elements of the Action 14 minimum standard (OECD, 2017b, p. 9). The country resolves a significant number of MAP cases every year (e.g., 160 cases in 2016) with the approximate resolution time being less than 24 months (OECD, 2017b, p. 10). The report also found that Canada actively monitors the implementation process and is able to identify why the implementation of some MAP agreements may have been delayed.

In terms of deficiencies, the peer review found that all Canadian tax treaties have a provision on MAP which generally follows Article 25 of the OECD Model Tax Convention except for the fact that: (a) 75 per cent of the country's tax treaties include a time limit for the submission of MAP requests that is less than 3 years, and (b) almost 40 per cent of Canada's tax treaties do not provide that mutual agreement should be implemented notwithstanding any domestic law time limits (OECD, 2017b, p. 10). Therefore, the peer review concludes that in order to be fully compliant with the Action 14 minimum standard, Canada needs to amend most of its tax treaties. This also requires the CRA to change its relevant administrative practices. Currently, the country is working to address the deficiencies identified in the peer review reports.

3.4 Canada's Response to the Other BEPS Recommendations

3.4.1 MLI

In addition to the minimum standards, Canada proposes to adopt a number of the optional provisions in the MLI upon its ratification (Department of Finance, 2018b).

3.4.2 Action 1: Addressing the Tax Challenges of the Digital Economy

Currently non-resident persons carrying on e-commerce businesses in Canada often do not pay income tax in the country. This is due to the fact that the OECD

Model Tax Convention does not generally allow the source jurisdiction to tax the business income of a non-resident enterprise unless that enterprise has a fixed place of business (i.e., permanent establishment) in the source jurisdiction through which the business is wholly or partially carried on or has a dependent agent who solicits orders or offers anything for sale on behalf of the enterprise in the source country.[37] A company may carry on an online retail business in Canada but have nothing more there than a storage facility to deliver goods to the customers. Canadian tax treaties which are based largely on the OECD Model Convention explicitly exclude storage facilities from the definition of permanent establishment. Moreover, most online retail businesses do not need to have an agent in the country. As a result, non-resident persons carrying on e-commerce businesses in Canada often do not pay income tax in the country even though they derive substantial business income from the country.

On 26 April 2018, Canada's House of Commons released a Report of the Standing Committee on International Trade, *E-Commerce: Certain Trade-Related Priorities of Canada's Firms* (Parliament of Canada, House of Commons Standing Committee on International Trade, 2018). The report recommends that the Canadian government work with other countries in ensuring that online sales, and the profits earned by firms making such sales, are taxed in the country where the products are consumed and where the economic activities that created the income occur, which would be consistent with relevant recommendations made by the OECD. However, to this date there has not been any specific Canadian legislative change on these matters.

3.4.2.1 Implications for Indirect Tax

Action 1 also identifies indirect tax issues in cross-border digital transactions. It notes some difficulties in the collection of VAT/GST on products and services provided in the source country by non-residents using e-commerce. The BEPS program concludes that VAT revenue should accrue to the destination territory, with the relevant issue being the enforcement of this requirement through collection of tax from a digital vendor. Every non-resident person, other than a small supplier,[38] who is carrying on business in Canada[39] and is making taxable supplies in Canada,

37 OECD, *OECD Model Tax Convention on Income and on Capital 2010* (2010), p. 130.

38 A person is a small supplier when the total value of the consideration for worldwide taxable supplies, including zero-rated supplies, made by the person (or an associate of the person at the beginning of the particular calendar quarter) that became due, or was paid without becoming due, in the previous four calendar quarters does not exceed CAD 30,000 or, in the case of a person who is a public service body, CAD 50,000: *Excise Tax Act* (RSC, 1985, c. E-15), s. 148(1). See also Canada Revenue Agency, "Small suppliers", GST/HST Memorandum 2.2 (revised 13 October 2000), https://www.canada.ca/en/revenue-agency/services/forms-publications/publications/2-2/small-suppliers.html.

39 A facts and circumstances test is used to determine whether a business is being carried on in Canada. A non-resident person with a significant presence in Canada is considered to be carrying on business in Canada. For further discussion on the topic, see Canada Revenue Agency, "Carrying on Business in Canada", GST/HST Policy Statement P-051R2 (28 April 2005),

including supplies made by electronic means, is required to register for VAT (GST/HST) purposes and to charge GST/HST on its taxable (other than zero-rated) supplies made in Canada.[40] Also, a non-resident person who has a permanent establishment in Canada (which could include a server) is subject to the same GST/HST obligations as a domestic supplier in respect of activities carried on through the permanent establishment. The permanent establishment test for these purposes is analogous to the permanent establishment definition found under Canadian tax treaties[41] and is meant to capture dependent agents with fixed places of business who work on behalf of the GST registrant. Foreign-based digital vendors with no physical presence in Canada are generally not required to collect GST/HST on their sales in Canada (though unregistered importers and consumers are liable to remit tax on such imported services). In the case of physical goods that are purchased online and shipped to Canada by post or courier, customs duties and GST/HST would generally be collected by the Canada Border Services Agency at the time of importation. However, in certain cases non-residents without a physical presence in Canada may be required to register and act as the collection agent for GST purposes pursuant to section 240(4) of the *Excise Tax Act* (ETA) which applies to non-residents who solicit orders in Canada to supply prescribed publications such as books, magazines or newspapers.

The Canadian government has also been exploring the possibility of extending GST/HST to foreign-based digital services such as Netflix.[42] While to date there has not been any national legislative change on this matter, in March 2018 the Quebec government announced its budget plan according to which companies in the rest of Canada and foreign companies that sell digital services to Quebec residents will be required to register with the government and pay provincial sales tax once they pass CAD 30,000 per year in revenue from such sales (Department of Finance, Quebec, 2018). This tax regime is reportedly intended to level the playing field between foreign providers of digital content that are currently not obligated to charge sales taxes on consumers and local competitors who have to collect such tax. This tax regime is scheduled to enter into force in 2019.

3.4.3 Action 2: Neutralising the Effects of Hybrid Mismatch Arrangements

A hybrid mismatch arrangement is a cross-border tax avoidance strategy that is designed to exploit differences in the tax treatment of an entity or a financial instrument under the law of two or more tax jurisdictions to achieve double non-taxation, including long-term deferral (OECD, 2015a). Such an arrangement can arise

www.canada.ca/en/revenue-agency/services/forms-publications/publications/p-051r2.html.

40 *Excise Tax Act*, s. 240(1).

41 *Excise Tax Act*, s. 123(1).

42 Michael Geist, "Not Exactly a Netflix Tax: Where Canada Stands on a Digital Sales Tax" (18 January 2017), http://www.michaelgeist.ca/2017/01/not-exactly-a-netflix-tax-where-canada-stands-on-a-digital-sales-tax/ (accessed on 19 June 2018).

either from a hybrid financial instrument or a hybrid entity.

BEPS Action 1 regards such hybrid mismatch arrangements as undesirable and recommends that countries develop domestic law and treaty rules to neutralise their effects through conditioning the tax treatment of an instrument or entity in one jurisdiction to their proper tax treatment in another jurisdiction. The OECD has also proposed to add a new provision to Article 1 of the OECD Model Treaty to address tax mismatches arising from dual resident entities and transparent entities.

Canada has certain anti-hybrid mismatch measures to combat perceived abuses from the use of hybrid instruments or entities. One such anti-hybrid mismatch rule is found in Article IV (7) of the Canada-US Tax Treaty.[43] Under this provision, a US limited liability company (LLC) is not entitled to treaty benefits on the basis of not being residents of the US for treaty purposes on the ground that LLCs are flow-through entities for US tax purposes. Another anti-hybrid mismatch measure involves the foreign tax credit generator rules introduced to the ITA in 2010.[44] Foreign tax credit generators involve complex transactions or structures that are designed to generate foreign tax credits out of proportion to the economic profits earned and actual foreign taxes paid. The rules limit foreign tax credits where a taxpayer is considered to have a smaller interest in the foreign income under the source country tax provisions than otherwise would be under the Canadian tax provisions.

On 28 May 2018 the Canadian government tabled in Parliament draft legislation to give effect to the MLI that is designed to amend about 75 of Canada's tax treaties with other countries.[45] The law includes in its Part II all main recommendations made on the BEPS Action 2.

3.4.4 Action 3: Designing Effective Controlled Foreign Company Rules

BEPS Action 3 stresses the importance of Controlled Foreign Corporation (CFC) rules in countering base erosion and profit shifting and makes several recommendations regarding the design of domestic CFC rules. It sets out six "building blocks" necessary for the implementation of a robust CFC regime (OECD, 2015b, pp. 9-10).

Canada has a sophisticated CFC regime in the form of the foreign accrual property income (FAPI) rules found in section 91 of the ITA. When these rules apply, the specified income of a foreign corporation ("foreign affiliate") controlled by the Canadian corporation is taxable in the hands of the Canadian corporation on an accrual basis.[46] The rules apply to controlled foreign affiliates (CFAs), including

43 *Convention between Canada and the United States of America with Respect to Taxes on Income and on Capital* (signed 26 September 1980) entered into force 1 January 1985.

44 See ITA, ss 91(4.1)-(4.5) and 126(4.11)-(4.13).

45 Department of Finance, "Notice of Ways and Means Motion to introduce an Act to implement a multilateral convention to implement tax treaty related measures to prevent base erosion and profit shifting" (May 2018), https://www.fin.gc.ca/drleg-apl/2018/adtpfe-edipef-eng.asp.

46 ITA, s. 91(1): "In computing the income for a taxation year of a taxpayer resident in Canada,

where there are partnerships or foreign PEs. The concept of control under the FAPI regime is direct or indirect *de jure* control.[47]

The FAPI regime is probably one of the most complex and unique forms of CFC regime in that while recognising the problem with resident corporations shifting their income to a low tax jurisdiction, the rules also recognise the importance of Canadian corporate investments and businesses abroad. Thus, the FAPI regime attempts to classify the income of a Canadian controlled foreign corporation into two broad categories and apply the anti-deferral provisions only with respect to one of these categories, namely the category comprising "income from property", "income from business other than active business", and some capital gains of a CFA. Income from property for this purpose generally includes rents, royalties, interest and non-foreign affiliate dividends and income from investment business. The FAPI also includes certain Canadian source sales income, income from insuring Canadian risks, certain Canadian source financial income, licencing income and service income.[48] When the income of a CFA is subject to the FAPI rules, this income is subject to tax in Canada on an accrual basis.[49]

The FAPI regime does not apply to "active" income of such entities. An active business of a CFA is defined to mean any business carried on by the affiliate other than an investment business.[50] In certain cases, income that would otherwise be

there shall be included, in respect of each share owned by the taxpayer of the capital stock of a controlled foreign affiliate of the taxpayer, as income from the share, the percentage of the foreign accrual property income of any controlled foreign affiliate of the taxpayer, for each taxation year of the affiliate ending in the taxation year of the taxpayer, equal to that share's participating percentage in respect of the affiliate, determined at the end of each such taxation year of the affiliate".

47 The ITA sets two separate tests for the control: 1) the taxpayer itself controls the foreign affiliate (here the focus is on whether the taxpayer owns sufficient shares to elect the majority of the board of directors of the foreign affiliate; this suggests the ownership of 51 per cent of the shares), or 2) the taxpayer and up to four other Canadian residents, being a person or persons with whom the taxpayer does not deal at arm's length, control the foreign affiliate. See s. 95(1) for the definition of "controlled foreign affiliate".

48 See ITA, ss 95(2)(a.1), 95(2)(a.2), 95(2)(a.3) and 95(2)(b). There are essentially two cases where service income of a CFA is considered FAPI:

(1) the service fee is deductible in computing: (a) the Canadian business income of a taxpayer for whom the affiliate is an FA or of any non-arm's length person in relation to that taxpayer of the FA; or (b) the FAPI of a foreign affiliate or of any taxpayer who does not deal at arm's length with the foreign affiliate; and

(2) the service is provided by: (a) a taxpayer for which the affiliate is a FA; (b) certain Canadian residents that do not deal with at arm's length with the affiliate but excluding non-residents whose services are performed outside Canada; or (c) partnerships including persons from those other categories.

These types of income are included in the FAPI as they have the potential of eroding Canadian-source income to a foreign corporation resident in a low-tax jurisdiction.

49 See ITA, s. 91(1). The computation is done separately for each year of the foreign affiliate. If the computed amount is negative, the negative amount cannot be attributed to Canada.

50 See ITA, s. 95(1). The investment business is deemed to be an active business if throughout the period in the year during which the business was carried on by the affiliate: a) the business,

FAPI in the nature of interest, rents, royalties is deemed to be active business income of the CFA if it is received from another member of a corporate group that deducts the payments from its active business income.[51] These are commonly known as "character preservation" rules.

If the income is not subject to the FAPI rules, it is either exempt or is not taxable in Canada until it is distributed to the Canadian parent. The exemption applies to dividends received by Canadian corporations from their foreign affiliates if they are situated in a country with which Canada has a tax information exchange agreement or tax treaty (such jurisdictions are commonly called "designated treaty countries") and earn the income from active business.[52] Thus, the FAPI rules seek to strike a balance between preventing deferral of tax on passive income while at the same time not hindering the competitiveness of Canadian multinational enterprises' foreign active businesses and direct investments.

It is worthwhile to note some of the main differences between the Canadian CFC rules and the CFC rules recommended under the BEPS program. BEPS Action 3 recommends that CFC rules should apply both a legal and an economic control test so that the satisfaction of either test results in control (OECD, 2015b, p. 21). However, the control test under the Canadian FAPI regime is legal control. Action 3 also recommends that a CFC system should include a tax rate exemption that would allow companies that are subject to an effective tax rate above a particular threshold to be exempt from accrual taxation (OECD, 2015b, p. 9). However, under the FAPI rules there is no such exemption. The FAPI regime does however have a *de minimis* threshold of CAD 5,000 which is relatively low compared to that of other countries.

Overall, except for some differences the Canadian FAPI (CFC) rules are largely consistent with the BEPS Action 3 recommendations. The government notes that it

---

other than any business conducted principally with non-arm's length persons, is a foreign bank, insurer, trader, or other such financial entity the activities of which are regulated in that foreign country, or is the development of real estate for sale, the lending of money, the leasing or licensing of property or the insurance or reinsurance of risks, and b) there are more than five (5) employees full time in the active conduct of the business. In order to qualify for the investment business exception, some taxpayers have pooled investment assets in a single foreign affiliate but with each taxpayer receiving a return that tracks the performance of the assets contributed by that taxpayer to the foreign affiliate ("tracking arrangements"). The 2018 federal Budget proposes to eliminate this planning opportunity by treating specific activities carried out by a foreign affiliate that accrues to the benefit of a specific taxpayer under a tracking arrangement as a separate business, which must separately satisfy the six-employee test and other requirements to the exception to investment business status.

51 See ITA, s. 95(2).

52 See the "exempt surplus" under subsection 113(1) of the ITA. "Where in a taxation year a corporation resident in Canada has received a dividend on a share owned by it of the capital stock of a foreign affiliate of the corporation, there may be deducted from the income for the year of the corporation for the purpose of computing its taxable income for the year, an amount equal to the total of (a) an amount equal to such portion of the dividend as is prescribed to have been paid out of the exempt surplus, as defined by regulation (in this Part referred to as 'exempt surplus') of the affiliate [...]".

will continue to monitor the effectiveness of the FAPI rules and to amend them as needed (Department of Finance, 2018a). However, Canada has not yet taken any concrete steps to amend its FAPI rules in response to the BEPS Action 3 item.

3.4.5 Action 4: Limiting Base Erosion Involving Interest Deductions and Other Financial Payments

The use of excessive related-party or intra-group debt and interest expense is perhaps one of the simplest and most prevalent techniques of base erosion available in international tax planning. BEPS Action 4 makes recommendations for the design of domestic rules to prevent tax base erosion through the use of interest expense and other financial payments. It describes best practices to restrict interest deductibility both in general and through certain targeted measures (OECD, 2016). As a general best practice, Action 4 recommends adoption of a "fixed-ratio rule". The rule limits an entity's net interest deductions to a set percentage of its tax-Earnings Before Interest, Taxes, Depreciation and Amortization (EBITDA). Action 4 also recommends an optional supplementary "group-ratio rule" that would allow an entity to deduct interest up to the level of the net interest, which would be the EBITDA ratio of its worldwide group in circumstances where it exceeded the fixed benchmark ratio (OECD, 2016). Action 4 also encourages countries to allow the carry forward of disallowed interest capacity. Finally, the report notes that countries may continue to apply withholding tax alongside the best practice (OECD, 2016, p. 24).

Canada is not among the countries that currently use either the fixed ratio rule or the group ratio rule. It also does not use carry forward rules with respect to the denied interest deduction. Instead, Canada currently employs thin capitalisation rules to address excessive interest deductions. The Canadian thin capitalisation regime, enacted under section 18(4) of the ITA in 1972, is probably one of the oldest in the world. Under these rules, until 2012, interest paid by a Canadian corporation on loans received from "specified non-resident persons"[53] or non-resident persons that do not deal at arm's length with specified shareholders was not deductible to the extent that such loans exceeded twice the equity of that corporation (i.e., a debt-to-equity ratio of 2:1).[54] The disallowed interest will be recharacterised as a

53 Specified non-resident shareholders are non-resident shareholders who, either alone or together with persons with whom the shareholder is not dealing at arm's length, own shares of the Canadian corporation representing 25 per cent or more of its votes or value.

54 There were several problems with this regime: a) the rule applied only to Canadian corporations owned by non-residents; foreign companies that carried on business in Canada through partnerships, trusts or branches were not subject to the same limitation; b) the rules prevented foreign businesses from circumventing the rules by financing their Canadian subsidiaries through "back-to-back" loans but the rule that addressed back-to-back loans was quite narrow; c) the existing the maximum debt-to-equity ratio of 2:1 was found still too generous, and d) the interest expense that was not deductible under the thin capitalisation rules maintained its character as interest for both domestic and tax treaty purposes. This allowed non-resident creditors to benefit from a lower withholding tax rate applicable to

dividend to which Canadian non-resident dividend withholding tax will apply at a 25 per cent rate. This general withholding tax rate is subject to reduction under an applicable tax treaty.

Budget 2012 extended the thin capitalisation rules to apply to partnerships of which a Canadian-resident corporation is a member. The Budget also reduced the debt-to-equity ratio from 2:1 to 1.5:1 and provided for treatment of disallowed interest expense under the thin capitalisation rules as dividends for Part XIII withholding tax purposes.[55] As of March 2012, the Canadian government also had rules to limit debt dumping or pushdown arrangements, through a somewhat broader anti-avoidance rule intended to counter foreign affiliate dumping more generally.[56] Budget 2013 further improved the integrity of the thin capitalisation rules by extending the scope of their application to Canadian resident trusts (Department of Finance, 2013a, p. 370). In the case of a trust, the thin capitalisation rules apply to debts owing to a specified beneficiary that is not resident in Canada and to debts owing to any other non-resident that does not deal at arm's length with a specified beneficiary. Budget 2014 introduced a new line of rules to limit the use of back-to-back loan arrangements in the context of Canada's thin capitalisation and withholding rules (Department of Finance, 2014; see also Suarez, 2014). These rules were intended to prevent non-residents avoiding Canadian withholding tax[57] or the thin capitalisation rules by entering into back-to-back loan arrangements[58] with third-party financial intermediaries to effectively make indirect loans to their Canadian subsidiaries. Finally, in 2016 Canada expanded the back-to-back loan rules in the context of Canada's withholding tax regime (Kandev, 2017, p. 1088). If the back-to-back conditions are satisfied, these rules essentially disregard the intermediary and deem interest to be paid to the ultimate funder.

Given the difference between what has been proposed under BEPS Action 4 and the Canadian practice to limit interest deductions, the adoption of the BEPS best practices on this item would require a significant reformulation of the Canadian rules. There are no specific legislative changes to date as a result of BEPS Action 4.

---

interest as opposed to dividends. See Advisory Panel on Canada's System of International Taxation (2008, pp. 65-67).

55 Department of Finance (2012, pp. 418-420). See also ITA, s. 214(16)-(17).

56 See ITA, s. 212.3.

57 Section 212(1)(b) of the ITA imposes interest withholding tax on interest paid to a non-resident person not dealing at arm's length with the payer, or participating debt interest. Thus, Canadian interest withholding tax is generally relevant only in a non-arm's-length context. Absent the back-to-back loan rules, such third-party loans could be used fairly easily to get around the limitations of the interest withholding tax.

58 Back-to-back arrangements generally involve interposing a third party (e.g., a foreign bank) between two related taxpayers in an attempt to avoid the application of thin capitalisation rules that would apply if a loan were made, and interest paid, directly between the two taxpayers.

3.4.6 Action 7: Preventing the Artificial Avoidance of Permanent Establishment Status

A non-resident enterprise carrying on business in Canada is liable to pay income tax on its Canadian source income.[59] The ITA sets a very low threshold for determining whether a non-resident is carrying on business in Canada thereby triggering taxable presence. According to the general criteria, a non-resident entity will be deemed to be carrying on business in Canada, among other things, if it produces, grows, mines, creates, manufactures, fabricates, improves, packs, preserves or constructs, in whole or in part, anything in Canada.[60] This threshold is met also when the non-resident has no fixed place of business but solicits orders or offers anything for sale in Canada through an agent or servant, whether the contract or transaction is to be completed inside or outside Canada. Overall, non-residents earning business income from a Canadian source cannot easily avoid the Canadian income tax.

However, this robust regime for non-residents earning business income from Canada is often overruled by Canadian tax treaties. Consistent with the OECD Model Tax Convention, they offer a much-relaxed threshold for "carrying on business in Canada" known as "permanent establishment" or "PE" under these treaties. The threshold of activity that results in the creation of a PE in Canada is determined by two forms of presence:

1 an enterprise maintains a fixed place of business in Canada through which it carries on its business. This is subject to a number of specific exemptions (e.g., the maintenance of facilities only for storage, display, delivery, or processing, purchasing of goods or merchandise, collection of information; carrying on supervisory activities in Canada for less than 12 months in connection with a building site, or a construction, installation or assembly project which is being undertaken in that State);

2 an enterprise has a dependent agent in Canada acting on its behalf and who habitually exercises an authority to conclude contracts in its name. This is also subject to some exceptions (e.g., the agent's activities are limited to the purchase of goods or merchandise for the enterprise).

Unfortunately, the PE criteria, as defined under the tax treaties, could be easily avoided.

BEPS Action 7 proposes to redefine the thresholds for PE status under the OECD Model Tax Convention (OECD, 2015c, pp. 23-25). In particular, this Action proposes three major changes to the existing PE rules: changes to the specific activity exemptions; introducing provisions against splitting-up contracts, and excluding persons closely related to the enterprise from the definition of independent agent for the purpose of a PE. These changes were incorporated in the MLI as optional provisions for countries to consider.

59 See ITA, ss 2(3) and 150(1)(a)(i)(B).

60 See ITA, s. 253. See also *Maya Forestales SA v. Canada*, 2006 FCA 35; *Zhu v. R*, 2016 FCA 113; *Standard Life v. R*, 2015 TCC 97.

Canada reserved its rights for the entirety of these expansions of the PE thresholds as stipulated under the MLI not to apply to its Covered Tax Agreements.[61] However, these preliminary positions may change prior to or after completing the domestic ratification process of the MLI.

3.4.7 Actions 8-10: Aligning Transfer Pricing Outcomes with Value Creation

Entities within a multinational corporate group often trade goods or provide services to each other. Since the prices of such goods and services are determined in the absence of market competition, the multinational enterprises may manipulate these prices to shift their profits from high tax jurisdictions to low or no tax jurisdictions. However, as a foundational principle of international law, income ought to be taxed in the country or countries where value is created (Christians and van Apeldoorn, 2018, p. 5).

To achieve this goal, Canada has adopted transfer pricing rules. The main source of transfer pricing rules in Canada is section 247 of the ITA, introduced in 1998 to replace the transfer pricing provisions under sections 69(2) and (3) of the ITA to harmonise them with the OECD transfer pricing guidelines and arm's length principles recommended by the OECD at that time (it must be noted that the old Canadian transfer pricing rules followed the "reasonable amount" standard rather than an arm's-length standard).[62] The ITA also introduced penalties in respect of transfer pricing adjustments proposed by tax authorities.[63] Finally, the new rules introduced formal transfer pricing documentation requirements.[64]

Overall, the arm's length principle has become the principle mandated by the ITA to deal with transfer pricing issues in Canada. However, the ITA does not specify how the principle is to be applied or interpreted. Thus, although the OECD Transfer Pricing Guidelines are not explicitly incorporated into Canada's legislation, currently they are used by taxpayers, the CRA and the courts in interpreting and applying the transfer pricing rules under section 247 of the ITA.[65] However, Canadian courts have repeatedly made it clear that the Guidelines are not law in Canada; ultimately, if there is an inconsistency between the domestic law and the

61 Department of Foreign Affairs, Trade and Development, Canada, "Status of List of Reservations and Notifications at the Time of Signature by Canada of the OECD's Multilateral Convention to Implement Tax Treaty Related Measures to Prevent Base Erosion and Profit Shifting pursuant to Articles 28(7) and 29(4) of the Convention" (30 May 2017), pp. 16-17, http://www.oecd.org/tax/treaties/beps-mli-position-canada.pdf.

62 The former transfer pricing rules (i.e., under s. 69(2)) were based on a "reasonable standard" for determining transfer prices. See Department of Finance, "Draft Legislation and Information Circular on Transfer Pricing Released", News Release (11 September 1997); OECD, *OECD Transfer Pricing Guidelines for Multinational Enterprises and Tax Administrations* (1995).

63 See ITA, s. 247(3).

64 See ITA, s. 233.1.

65 Canada Revenue Agency, "International Transfer Pricing", Information Circular 87-2R (1999).

Guidelines, the issue must be resolved according to the ITA.[66]

In October 2015, the OECD released the BEPS Actions 8-10 reports which seek to set out a number of significant revisions to the existing OECD transfer pricing guidelines (OECD, 2015d). The Action 8 report relates to intangibles, Action 9 to risk and capital, and Action 10 to high-risk transactions. They propose significant amendments to Chapters I (General principles), II (Commodity transactions), VI (Intangibles), VII (Low value-adding intra-group services), and VIII (Cost contribution arrangements) of the existing OECD Guidelines. The proposed changes seek to ensure that the companies performing important functions, incurring economically significant risks and contributing assets derive income reflecting an appropriate return for the value of their contribution.

The Canadian government announced in its 2016 Budget that the revisions "generally support the CRA's current interpretation and application of the arm's length principle, as reflected in its audit and assessing practices" and it would be applying the revised OECD guidelines on the arm's-length principle (Department of Finance, 2016a, p. 218). However, the Canadian government noted that where the revisions to the Transfer Pricing Guidelines were not yet complete, the CRA would not be adjusting its administrative practices, especially on low value-adding services, and risk-free and risk-adjusted returns for minimally functional entities. Canada would decide on a course of action on these measures after the OECD's ongoing work is complete (Department of Finance, 2016b).

The OECD released its renewed Transfer Pricing Guidelines for Multinational Enterprises and Tax Administrations on 10 July 2017.[67] In its 2018 federal Budget, without further details, the Canadian government reiterated its adoption of the revised OECD Transfer Pricing Guidelines (Department of Finance, 2018a, p. 71). This may entail some changes in the existing transfer pricing rules, especially on transfer pricing documentation requirements. Thus, more detailed guidance such as additional or revised CRA information circulars and transfer pricing memoranda series is expected to be issued by the government.

3.4.8 Action 12: Mandatory Disclosure Rules

BEPS Action 12 proposes a general framework that is aimed at enabling countries and their tax authorities to identify potentially abusive tax avoidance transactions at an early stage through adopting mandatory disclosure requirements and to some extent to deter the use of such schemes.

Canada already has such a disclosure regime. In order to identify potentially abusive tax avoidance transactions in an efficient and timely manner so that they can be properly reviewed, monitored and, if appropriate, challenged, in June 2013 Canada introduced a new information reporting regime and enacted it under sec-

66 *GlaxoSmithKline Inc. v. R*, 2012 DTC 5147 (SCC).

67 OECD, *OECD Transfer Pricing Guidelines for Multinational Enterprises and Tax Administrations* (2017), https://doi.org/10.1787/tpg-2017-en.

tion 237.3 of the ITA. This reporting regime is intended to assist the CRA in monitoring tax avoidance transactions in the light of the Canadian General Anti Avoidance Rule (GAAR).

This reporting regime applies to certain "reportable transactions" entered into after 2010. Reportable transactions are transactions that meet two requirements: first, the transaction meets the conditions of being an "avoidance transaction" within the terms of the Canadian GAAR (i.e. section 245(3)); second, at any time the transaction must meet two of any of the following three hallmarks in respect of that avoidance transaction:[68]

1 the tax advisor is remunerated with a "fee" based, at least in part, on the dollar value of the tax benefit resulting from the transaction or is contingent upon the obtaining of a tax benefit that results, or would result but for the GAAR, from the avoidance transaction;
2 the tax advisor requires that the transaction remain confidential. This is generally evidenced by the existence of an agreement that prohibits the participant from disclosing the details or structure of the transaction to any person;
3 the taxpayer or the advisor obtains "contractual protection".

Even though these conditions are not themselves evidence of aggressive tax avoidance, their presence often indicates that the underlying transactions carry a higher risk of abuse of the ITA.

The information reporting obligation is imposed on: (a) the person for whom a tax benefit could result from an avoidance transaction; (b) any person who enters into an avoidance transaction for the benefit of another person (i.e., a nominee or agent); (c) any advisor or promoter who is entitled to a "fee" in circumstances described in the definition of "reportable transactions", and (d) any person not dealing at arm's length with an advisor or promoter with respect to the transaction and who is entitled to the fee described in (c) above.[69] Since the reporting obligation is imposed on multiple parties to the same transaction, a full and accurate disclosure of the reportable transaction by one of these parties is generally deemed to be the filing by every other party required to report the same transaction.[70]

Non-compliance with the reporting obligations may entail strict penalties.[71] However, the provision includes a due diligence defence for a person who has exercised the degree of care, diligence and skill to prevent the failure to file.[72]

Since Canada already has this reporting regime which is substantially consist-

68 ITA, s. 237.3(1).
69 ITA, s. 237.3(2).
70 ITA, s. 237.3(4) (If full and accurate disclosure is not made, ITA also imposes a penalty equal to the total of all fees that have been received by anyone in respect of the transaction).
71 ITA, ss 237.3(6) and 237.3(8).
72 ITA, s. 237.3(11).

ent with the Action 12 recommendations, it has not announced any specific action in relation to this BEPS action item.

3.4.9 Developing a Multilateral Instrument to Modify Bilateral Tax Treaties

As discussed in the OECD materials, abuse of tax treaties is an important source of base erosion and profit shifting. Therefore, the BEPS initiative recommends several changes to the prevailing treaty rules in order to combat the use of tax treaties for purposes of base erosion and profit shifting described in the BEPS reports. The main problem with implementation of these changes was that it would take decades for countries to renegotiate their bilateral tax treaties to implement the changes. Currently, there are thousands of such bilateral treaties across the global treaty network. Consideration of this challenge gave rise to the idea of the *Multilateral Convention to Implement Tax Treaty Related Measures to Prevent Base Erosion and Profit Shifting* (MLI). The MLI's objective, as a multilateral framework, is to modify existing bilateral tax treaties in a coordinated manner in order to swiftly, predictably, and consistently implement the series of tax treaty measures that were contained in the OECD/G20 Base Erosion and Profit Shifting (BEPS) Project. These measures relate to neutralising the effects of hybrid mismatch arrangements, treaty abuse, the artificial avoidance of permanent establishment status, improving resolution of disputes arising from tax treaties, and the use of arbitration in resolving such disputes.

The MLI does not operate as an independent tax treaty on its own, but rather modifies the relevant provisions of existing bilateral tax treaties of states which have ratified the MLI, where the treaty has been nominated by the parties as one to which the MLI applies (Covered Tax Agreements). The parties may also reserve the application of the MLI in respect of any of its provisions other than the specified minimum standards. Thus, the MLI was developed by a group of over 100 countries including developed countries and was presented for interested countries in 2016. To enter into force for any treaty, the MLI required that five signatories deposit their instruments of ratification.[73] As at 23 July 2018, nine countries had deposited their ratification instruments.[74] The MLI entered into force on 1 July 2018.

Canada signed the MLI on 7 June 2017 and has listed 75 of its 93 tax treaties as Covered Tax Agreements.[75] Canada has registered provisional reservations on all of the provisions of the MLI, other than the minimum standards. The country took

73 MLI, Article 34(1).

74 OECD, "List of Signatories and Parties to the Multilateral Convention to Implement Tax Treaty Related Measures to Prevent Base Erosion and Profit Shifting, Status as of 23 July 2018", above n. 17.

75 Department of Foreign Affairs, Trade and Development, Canada, "Status of List of Reservations and Notifications at the Time of Signature of the OECD's Multilateral Convention to Implement Tax Treaty Related Measures to Prevent Base Erosion and Profit Shifting pursuant to Articles 28(7) and 29(4) of the Convention", above n. 61.

this "minimalistic" approach largely to allow itself as much flexibility as possible to take a gradual approach to adoption of the optional provisions in the MLI. This is because the terms of the MLI allow reservations to be withdrawn in the future but generally would not permit new reservations to be added following ratification.[76]

The Canadian Department of Finance has recently indicated that the government intends to adopt a number of the MLI's optional provisions upon its ratification. These provisions include Article 4 (Dual Resident Entities), Article 5 (Application of Methods for Elimination of Double Taxation), Article 8 (Dividend Transfer Transactions) and Article 9 (Capital Gains from the Alienation of Shares or Interests of Entities Deriving their Value Principally from Immovable Property) (Department of Finance, 2018b; Abitbol, 2018).

As noted in section 3.3.2 above, on 28 May 2018 the Canadian Department of Finance tabled the draft legislation "An Act to Implement a Multilateral Convention to Implement Tax Treaty Related Measures to Prevent Base Erosion and Profit Shifting" in the House of Commons for consideration (Department of Finance, 2018b). On 20 June 2018, the draft legislation to enact the MLI ("Bill C-82") received first reading in the House of Commons.[77] According to some commentators, the MLI could come into force in Canada by early 2019.[78] If this legislation is enacted, Canada would go beyond the required minimum standards to adopt the three abovementioned optional provisions of the MLI.

3.5 Tax Administration in relation to International Tax Reform in Canada

Canada's implementation of the BEPS minimum standards on tax dispute resolution, country-by-country reporting, and the exchange of tax rulings has had an inevitable impact on the CRA's existing tax administrative practices where it had to adopt new rules and practices.

For example, Canada's enactment of the country-by-country rules under section 233.8 of the ITA and signing the Multilateral Competent Authority Agreement on the Exchange of Country-by-Country Reports have some significant administrative implications. These required the CRA to introduce new administrative practices; in 2017, the CRA released "RC4651 Guidance on Country-By-Country Reporting in Canada" setting out compliance requirements under this new regime. Under BEPS Action Plan 5, Canada has also committed to spontaneous exchange of certain tax rulings. On 22 April 2016, the CRA released Information Circular 70-6R7 and Technical Interpretations outlining the procedure and types of tax rulings that Canada

76 MLI, Article 28.

77 Parliament of Canada, House of Commons Progress Report on Bill C-82, 42nd Parliament, 1st Session. https://www.parl.ca/LegisInfo/BillDetails.aspx?billId=9898204.

78 Osler, Hoskin & Harcourt LLP, "Canada tables NWMM to ratify MLI; Updates MLI reservations" (29 May 2018), https://www.osler.com/en/resources/cross-border/2018/canada-tables-nwmm-to-ratify-mli-updates-mli-reservations.

intends to spontaneously share with other jurisdictions.[79] Even though not exclusively for these purposes, in 2018 the Canadian government also pledged to invest CAD 90.6 million over five years to further address tax evasion and tax avoidance, both domestically and internationally (Department of Finance, 2018a, p. 69).

3.6 Conclusion

The international tax system is undergoing a substantial reform as a result of the OECD/G20 BEPS Project. It is one of the first internationally coordinated efforts in many years to address the multitude of issues prevailing in relation to the taxation of multinational corporations.

Canada is one of the countries which already had some robust rules designed to tackle most international tax problems that the BEPS initiative aims to address. However, the effectiveness of the Canadian rules was often limited due to their unilateral character or being overridden by its tax treaties. As far as the treaty-related BEPS measures are concerned, it was also doubtful whether Canada would have been able to achieve as many tax treaty changes as achieved by the MLI through its traditional bilateral negotiations without many years of negotiations. In this sense, the BEPS measures build on actions that the Canadian government has already taken to enhance the integrity of its tax system.

Yet, it is too early to judge the results of the BEPS project at this stage. Some commentary has emphasised the need for Canada to ensure that in determining its stance on BEPS-related measures it also protects the competitiveness of Canadian-owned foreign businesses and the attractiveness of Canada for inbound investment. These factors will necessarily include close attention to the direction of tax policy in the US and the measures to deal with BEPS enacted there.

References

Abitbol, Reuben (2018), "Canada Goes Beyond the MLI's Minimum Standards", 8(3) *Canadian Tax Focus*.

Advisory Panel on Canada's System of International Taxation (Peter C Godsoe, chair) (2008), *Final Report: Enhancing Canada's International Tax Advantage*, Ottawa, December, https://www.fin.gc.ca/access/tt-it/apcsit-gcrcfi/pdf/apcsit-report-rapport-gcrcfi-eng.pdf.

Bhattacharya, Anindya K (1989), "The Costs and Benefits of Establishing an International Banking Center", in Yoon S. Park and Musa Essayyad (eds.), *International Banking and Financial Centers* (Dordrecht: Springer Publishing), 131-142.

Campbell, Colin (2016), *Administration of Income Tax 2016* (Toronto: Thomson Reuters).

79 Canada Revenue Agency, "Advance Income Tax Rulings and Technical Interpretations", above n. 23.

Canada Revenue Agency (2018), *Mutual Agreement Procedure Program Report 2016*, Ottawa, https://www.canada.ca/content/dam/cra-arc/serv-info/tax/non-res/map/mp_rprt_2016-en.pdf.

Choudhury, Ron and Victoria Rodrigues (2017), "Canada and Treaty Shopping – From Then to Now", 87 *Tax Notes International* 1259-1271.

Christians, Allison and Laurens Van Apeldoorn (2018), "Taxing Income Where Value is Created", *Florida Tax Review* forthcoming, https://papers.ssrn.com/sol3/papers.cfm?abstract_id=3132538.

Department of Finance, Canada (2012), *Jobs, Growth and Long-Term Prosperity: 2012 Budget Economic Action Plan*, 29 March, https://www.budget.gc.ca/2012/plan/pdf/Plan2012-eng.pdf.

Department of Finance, Canada (2013a), *Jobs, Growth and Long-Term Prosperity: 2013 Budget Economic Action Plan*, 21 March, https://www.budget.gc.ca/2013/doc/plan/budget2013-eng.pdf.

Department of Finance, Canada (2013b), "Consultation Paper on Treaty Shopping – The Problem and Possible Solutions", 12 August, https://www.fin.gc.ca/activty/consult/ts-cf-eng.asp#a1.

Department of Finance, Canada (2014), *The Road to Balance: Creating Jobs and Opportunities: 2014 Budget Plan*, 11 February, https://www.budget.gc.ca/2014/docs/plan/pdf/budget2014-eng.pdf.

Department of Finance, Canada (2015), *Strong Leadership: A Balanced-Budget, Low-Tax Plan for Jobs, Growth and Security: 2015 Budget Plan*, 21 April, https://budget.gc.ca/2015/docs/plan/budget2015-eng.pdf.

Department of Finance, Canada (2016a), *Growing the Middle Class: 2016 Budget Plan*, 22 March, https://www.budget.gc.ca/2016/docs/plan/budget2016-en.pdf.

Department of Finance, Canada (2016b), *Budget 2016: Tax Measures. Supplementary Information*, https://www.budget.gc.ca/2016/docs/plan/toc-tdm-en.html.

Department of Finance, Canada (2017a), *Building a Strong Middle Class: 2017 Budget Plan*, 22 March, https://www.budget.gc.ca/2017/docs/plan/budget-2017-en.pdf.

Department of Finance, Canada (2017b), "Backgrounder: Impact of Multilateral Convention to Implement Tax Treaty Related Measures to Prevent Base Erosion and Profit Shifting", 7 June, www.fin.gc.ca/n17/data/17-054_1-eng.asp.

Department of Finance, Canada (2018a), *Equality + Growth, A Strong Middle Class: 2018 Budget Plan*, 27 February, www.budget.gc.ca/2018/docs/plan/budget-2018-en.pdf.

Department of Finance, Canada (2018b), "Backgrounder: The Next Step in the Fight Against Aggressive International Tax Avoidance", 28 May, https://www.fin.gc.ca/n18/data/18-037_1-eng.asp.

Department of Finance, Quebec (2018), *Budget 2018-2019: Additional Information Part B, Plan to Ensure Tax Fairness*, Quebec City, March, http://www.budget.finances.gouv.qc.ca/budget/2018-2019/en/index.asp.

Eyitayo, Oladiwura Ayeyemi (2018), "Profit Shifting by Canadian Multinational Corporations: Prospects of Reversal under Canada's Country-by-Country Reporting Rules, 26 *Dalhousie Journal of Legal Studies* 79-111.

Kandev, Michael (2017), "Canada Expands Back-to-Back Regime: Examining the Character Substitution Rules", 86 *Tax Notes International* 1087-1092.

Organisation for Economic Co-operation and Development (OECD) (2013a), *Addressing Base Erosion and Profit Shifting*, February (Paris: OECD).

Organisation for Economic Co-operation and Development (OECD) (2013b), *Action Plan on Base Erosion and Profit Shifting*, July (Paris: OECD).

Organisation for Economic Co-operation and Development (OECD) (2015a), *Action 2 - 2015 Final Report: Neutralising the Effects of Hybrid Mismatch Arrangements* (Paris: OECD).

Organisation for Economic Co-operation and Development (OECD) (2015b), *Action 3 - 2015 Final Report: Designing Effective Controlled Foreign Company Rules* (Paris: OECD).

Organisation for Economic Co-operation and Development (OECD) (2015c), *Action 7 - 2015 Final Report: Preventing the Artificial Avoidance of Permanent Establishment Status* (Paris: OECD).

Organisation for Economic Co-operation and Development (OECD) (2015d), *Actions 8-10 - 2015 Final Reports: Aligning Transfer Pricing Outcomes with Value Creation* (Paris: OECD).

Organisation for Economic Co-operation and Development (OECD) (2015e), *Action 13 - 2015 Final Report: Transfer Pricing Documentation and Country-by-Country Reporting* (Paris: OECD).

Organisation for Economic Co-operation and Development (OECD) (2016), *Inclusive Framework on BEPS, Action 4 – 2016 Update: Limiting Base Erosion Involving Interest Deductions and Other Financial Payments* (Paris: OECD).

Organisation for Economic Co-operation and Development (OECD) (2017a), *Inclusive Framework on BEPS, Action 5: Harmful Tax Practices – Peer Review Reports on the Exchange of Information on Tax Rulings* (Paris: OECD).

Organisation for Economic Co-operation and Development (OECD) (2017b), *Inclusive Framework on BEPS, Action 14: Making Dispute Resolution More Effective – MAP Peer Review Report, Canada (Stage 1)* (Paris: OECD).

Parliament of Canada, House of Commons Standing Committee on International Trade (2018), *E-Commerce: Certain Trade-Related Priorities of Canada's Firms*, Report of the Standing Committee on International Trade, Ottawa, April, http://www.ourcommons.ca/Content/Committee/421/CIIT/Reports/RP9795758/ciitrp09/ciitrp09-e.pdf.

Suarez, Steve (2014), "Canada's Problematic Proposed New Loan Rules", *Tax Notes International*, 441-449.

Thomson, Sherry & Lori Carruthers (2017), "Application of the Principal Purpose Test in Article 7 of the MLI", Materials of the Canadian Tax Foundation's Annual Conference, 21 November, members.videotax.com/technical-interpretations/2017-0724151C6-2017-ctf-q8-principal-purpose-test (accessed 18 June 2018).

4 The Adoption of BEPS in China

Na Li*

Abstract

China has been actively involved in the BEPS project. In implementing the BEPS actions, China has not created any new tax, but has made efforts in issuing new measures to enforce its existing anti-tax avoidance regime and to improve tax transparency. China has taken actions in compliance with all four minimum standards under the BEPS project's Inclusive Framework. As for the remaining BEPS actions, China has made significant efforts to address transfer pricing issues, with the clear intention of enhancing the Chinese government's argument for inclusion of location specific advantages in transfer pricing determinations.

4.1 Introduction

The People's Republic of China is a unitary state located in Asia. China has four autonomous municipalities, five autonomous regions, two special administrative regions and 23 provinces.[1] Since the two special administrative regions (i.e., Hong Kong and Macau) and Taiwan province apply different tax systems separately from the mainland part of China, this chapter addresses only the key tax reform measures of the mainland part of China.

China is not an Organisation for Economic Co-operation and Development (OECD) member state but is a member of the G20. Since 2011, China has become the second largest economy in the world, but the Chinese government still declares China as a developing country. For most of the last three decades, China was one of the largest capital importers in the world. But since 2014 it has become a net exporter of capital (i.e., capital exported is greater than capital imported), and accordingly China is changing its international tax policy from that of a pure source state to a mixed position of being both a residence state and a source state. China's main export products in 2017 were electronic equipment, textiles, steel products, furniture and plastic products; and its main import products in 2017 were electronic equipment, high-tech products, oil, iron sand, cars and soy products.[2]

* Lecturer, East China University of Political Science and Law, Shanghai, China. The author can be contacted at na.li@wu.ac.at.

1 State Council of China, "Administrative division of the People's Republic of China", http://www.gov.cn/guoqing/2005-09/13/content_5043917.htm (accessed on 22 June 2018).

2 Data published by the National Bureau of Statistics of China, http://data.stats.gov.cn/easyquery.htm?cn=C01 (accessed on 20 May 2018).

At present, there are 18 types of taxes in China, which can be divided into three categories: goods and services taxes, income taxes, and property and behaviour taxes. In 2017 China was ranked seventh of all 94 countries on the Financial Complexity Index Ranking.[3] The Chinese government agency in charge of tax policy is the Ministry of Finance (MOF), while the agency in charge of tax administration is the State Administration of Taxation (SAT). The MOF and the SAT, both ministry-level agencies under the State Council, are authorised to issue circulars with regard to interpretation and implementation of domestic laws and tax treaties including enacting and implementing new measures relating to the BEPS project.[4]

4.2 China's Response to the BEPS Project

China, despite not being an OECD member country, has been actively involved in the BEPS project. For instance, China was nominated as an "associate" with the same standing as the OECD member countries with regard to the discussions on the BEPS initiatives, and China also held the vice-chair of the Ad Hoc Group for developing multilateral instruments. The SAT, being the highest level Chinese tax authority, has played a key role in China's involvement in the BEPS project, including (but not being limited to) attendance at the various meetings and conferences on behalf of China regarding the BEPS project, enactment of new tax measures, instruction and supervision of local tax authorities in China in undertaking anti-tax avoidance measures, and addition of new anti-treaty abuse provisions to tax treaties when negotiating bilateral tax treaties and multilateral agreements.

China's active role in BEPS project is due to the fact that China has over a long period suffered from tax avoidance arrangements, in particular transfer pricing, treaty abuse and offshore indirect transfers of shares (Qiu, 2014a). Especially since 2008, when China abolished its foreign-oriented tax incentive policies in the form of tax holidays, reduced tax rates and tax exemptions, many multinational enterprises (MNEs) have entered into tax avoidance arrangements more aggressively for the purpose of shifting their profits out of China.[5]

3 TMF Group, Financial Complexity Index Ranking, https://www.tmf-group.com/en/news-insights/publications/2017/financial-complexity-index-2017 (accessed on 20 May 2018).

4 The framework of Chinese domestic tax law can be regarded as a pyramid with three tiers. At the top of the pyramid, there are the four tax laws promulgated by the National People's Congress (NPC) and its Standing Committee, which are the legislative organs of China. At the second tier of the pyramid, there are approximately 30 tax regulations enacted by the State Council, which is the highest executive organ in China. The State Council derives its legislation power partially from the legislation and partially from the delegation of legislative power from the NPC. Finally, at the bottom of the pyramid, there are more than 5,000 ministerial rules and tax circulars enacted by the MOF and SAT under the legislative power delegated from the State Council to enact such measures to implement the tax laws.

5 SAT, Notice on Conducting Anti-Tax Avoidance Investigation on Excessive Payment to Abroad (Circular 146 [2014]), issued by the SAT on 29 July 2014, and SAT, Announcement on Issues concerning Enterprise Income Tax on Expenses Paid by Enterprises to Their Overseas Affiliates (Announcement No. 16 [2015]), enacted by the SAT on 18 March 2015.

In fact, before the BEPS project was launched by the OECD/G20 in 2013, China already had its own tax avoidance regime, consisting of both specific anti-tax avoidance rules (SAARs) and a general anti-avoidance rule (GAAR). The first transfer pricing rule was introduced as part of China's enterprise income tax law applicable to foreign companies and foreign investment companies enacted in 1991,[6] and was also introduced into the Law on the Administration of Tax Collection of China in 1993.[7] In 2008 a whole regime of tax avoidance measures was introduced as part of China's enterprise income tax, including four SAARs and one GAAR.[8] The four SAARs relate to transfer pricing rules, cost-sharing arrangement rules, controlled foreign company (CFC) rules and thin capitalisation rules. The GAAR is designed as the Chinese tax authorities' last resort which tests whether transactions have a "reasonable business purpose".[9] If taxpayers fail to demonstrate such a purpose, the Chinese authorities may disregard the legal form of a transaction and tax the transaction according to its economic substance.[10]

However, these SAARs and GAAR were not effectively implemented in China to invalidate MNEs' base erosion and profit shifting arrangements, and China's corporate income tax revenue loss in 2011 as a result of MNEs' tax avoidance practices reached RMB 10.637 billion.[11] Therefore, active involvement in the BEPS project is one necessary approach (as well as an opportunity) for the Chinese government to enhance its tax avoidance regime. In implementing the BEPS actions, China has not created any new tax (such as the diverted profits tax), but has made efforts in issuing new measures to enforce its existing anti-tax avoidance regime and to improve tax transparency.

4.3 China Implements the Four Minimum Standards under the BEPS Inclusive Framework

China has taken actions in compliance with all four minimum standards under the BEPS project's Inclusive Framework, namely Action 5 (Countering Harmful Tax Practices), Action 6 (Prevention of Treaty Benefits in Inappropriate Circumstances), Action 13 (Transfer Pricing Documentation and Country-by-Country Reporting) and Action 14 (More Effective Dispute Resolution Mechanisms).

6 Income Tax Law for Foreign-Invested Enterprises and Foreign Enterprises (Tax Law in 1991), Art. 13.

7 Law on the Administration of Tax Collection of China, Art. 24.

8 Enterprise Income Tax Law (EITL) 2008, promulgated by the NPC on 16 March 2007 with effect from 1 January 2008.

9 EITL, Ch. 6.

10 Measures for the Administration of General Anti-Tax Avoidance (for Trial) (SAT Order 32), enacted by the SAT on 25 November 2014 with effect from 1 February 2015.

11 Yang and Zhuang (2014, p. 46). The total of RMB 10.637 billion represented approximately USD 1.668 billion at the USD/RMB exchange rate of 6.3763 as at 31 December 2011 published by the Bank of China: see Bank of China, http://srh.bankofchina.com/search/whpj/search.jsp (accessed on 20 May 2018).

4.3.1 Compliance with Action 5

Harmful tax practices under Action 5 were no longer concerns for China, even before the BEPS project was launched. From as early as 1 January 2008, China had already abolished all foreign-oriented tax incentive measures which may be interpreted as harmful tax practices as defined in the 1998 OECD report (OECD, 1998).[12] Nowadays all Chinese tax resident enterprises, whether foreign-invested or domestically-owned, are subject to the same income tax at a standard tax rate of 25 per cent, with a few tax incentives designed for certain industry sectors or rural areas rather than for attracting geographically-mobile activities. Industry sectors benefiting from these tax incentives are agriculture, forestry and fishery industries, public infrastructure projects, environmental protection projects, energy and water saving projects, etc. These tax incentives are also clearly provided through tax laws and the process for taxpayers to become entitled to these incentives is transparent too, as China has so far not provided any advance rulings to taxpayers.

In 2015, the OECD Forum placed China's tax incentives provided to high-tech enterprises under review, as such tax incentives in the form of lower tax rates, additional deductions and tax exemptions applied to all income of qualified high-tech enterprises, rather than solely to their intellectual property-related income. The Forum in the first three peer reviews in May 2015, November 2016 and March 2017 decided that these tax incentives did not satisfy the nexus approach for intellectual property tax incentives, but it subsequently changed its decision after the SAT proved that the criteria for enterprises to qualify as high-tech enterprises eligible for these tax incentives are of a more comprehensive nature and of a higher threshold than needed under the nexus approach, and also that a finding of qualification should be reviewed and approved by the Ministry of Science and the SAT for each high-tech enterprise on a case by case basis. Thus, the Forum finally decided in May 2017 that China's tax incentives to high-tech enterprises are "not harmful".[13]

4.3.2 Compliance with Action 6

Countering treaty abuse under Action 6 is in line with Chinese tax authorities' practice. Given that China has a large treaty network which by the end of May 2018 already consisted of 106 bilateral tax treaties, treaty-shopping issues exist in both inbound investment into China and Chinese outbound investment (Qiu, 2014a). In order to counter treaty abuse, the SAT has issued circulars narrowing down

12 Prior to 1 January 2008, China provided tremendous tax incentives to attract foreign investment, including but not limited to tax holidays, lower income tax rates, accelerated depreciation, and refunds of tax paid when reinvestment took place. Chinese domestic investment however barely received any tax incentive. When its new EITL came into force on 1 January 2008, China abolished all these foreign-oriented incentives.

13 SAT, "Report on the development of rule of law by the State Administration of Taxation in 2017" (27 April 2018), http://www.chinatax.gov.cn/n810214/n2897183/c3427202/content.html (accessed on 29 June 2018).

the scope of eligible "beneficial ownership"[14] and has also extended the list of the documentation which taxpayers must provide for the purpose of benefiting from treaty entitlement.[15]

The SAT has also added anti-avoidance provisions into some newly concluded bilateral tax treaties. For instance, the Belgium-China Income Tax Treaty (2009) clearly provides that the application of the domestic anti-tax avoidance rules of Belgium or China should not be overridden by the tax treaty.[16] In 2015, for the first time, China included both a principal purpose test (PPT) clause and a limitation on benefits (LOB) clause into one of its bilateral tax treaties, namely the Chile-China Income Tax Treaty.[17] The LOB clause provides that the entitlement to treaty benefits should be solely to "qualified persons",[18] while the PPT clause requires

14 SAT, Notice on Administration Method for Non-Residents to Benefit from Tax Treaties (Circular 124 [2009]), with effect from 1 October 2009; SAT, Notice of the State Administration of Taxation on How to Understand and Determine the "Beneficial Owners" in Tax Treaties (Circular 601 [2009]), with effect from 27 October 2009; SAT, Bulletin on the Recognition of Beneficial Owners in Tax Treaties (Notice [2012]), with effect from 29 June 2012; SAT, Supplementary Rules on "Beneficial Owners" (Notice 24 [2014], with effect from 1 June 2014.

15 SAT, Administrative Method for Non-Tax Residents to Benefit from Tax Treaties (Announcement No. 60 [2015]), issued on 27 August 2015 with effect from that date.

16 *Agreement between the Government of the Kingdom of Belgium and the Government of the People's Republic of China for the Avoidance of Double Taxation and the Prevention of Fiscal Evasion with Respect to Taxes on Income*, art. 23 (signed 7 October 2009), which provides that "[n]othing in this Agreement shall prejudice the right of each Contracting State to apply its domestic laws and measures concerning the prevention of tax evasion and avoidance, whether or not described as such, insofar as they do not give rise to taxation contrary to this Agreement".

17 *Agreement between the Government of the People's Republic of China and the Government of the Republic of Chile for the Elimination of Double Taxation and the Prevention of Tax Evasion and Avoidance with Respect to Taxes on Income* (signed 25 May 2015) (Chile-PRC Income Tax Treaty (2015)).

18 Article 26(2) of the Chile-PRC Income Tax Treaty (2015) defines a "qualified person" as follows: "A resident of a Contracting State shall be a qualified person at a time when a benefit would otherwise be accorded by the Agreement if, at that time, the resident is:
   a) an individual;
   b) a Contracting State, or local authority thereof, or a person that is wholly-owned by such State or local authority;
   c) a person other than an individual, if
      i) A) more than 50 per cent of the beneficial interest in such person (or in the case of a company more than 50 per cent of the number of shares of each class of the company's shares) is owned, directly or indirectly, by any combination of one or more of:
         (a) individuals who are residents of one of the Contracting States;
         (b) companies as described in subparagraph 2 c) ii); and
         (c) one of the Contracting States or local authorities; and
      B) less than 50 per cent of the gross income of such person, as determined in the person's Contracting State of residence, for the taxable period that includes that time is paid or accrued, directly or indirectly, to persons who are other than persons described in clauses (a) through (c) of subparagraph c) i) A) in the form of payments that are deductible for purpose of the taxes covered by this Agreement in the

consideration of taxpayers' principal purpose in conducting transactions.[19] In addition, the Chile-China Income Tax Treaty (2015) in the preamble paragraph also states that the purpose of the tax treaty includes the prevention of double non-taxation.[20] China and Chile included such multiple anti-treaty abuse provisions into their tax treaty in part due to the influence of Action 6 (OECD, 2015), and due to the fact that a low withholding tax rate (only 4 per cent) is provided in this treaty in respect of interest derived from loans granted by banks, insurance companies and other financial institutions, which is much lower than the tax rate suggested by the OECD Model Convention or UN Model Convention (10 per cent). Thus, the contracting states inevitably have greater concerns in this case about treaty abuse.

However, this practice of using the multiple anti-abuse clauses in one tax treaty probably will not become a common practice in China's future tax treaties, given that China in June 2017 made a notification of intending to use only the PPT clause in its covered tax agreements when it signed the Multilateral Instrument (MLI). Therefore, it is likely that contracting states will need to negotiate with China case by case if intending to include the LOB clause or the double non-taxation provisions into their tax treaties with China.

4.3.3 Compliance with Action 13

China signed the Multilateral Competent Authority Agreement for the Automatic Exchange of Country-by-Country (CbC) Reports in May 2016;[21] and the SAT introduced the CbC reporting regime into China in July 2016 through issuing Bulletin [2016] No. 42,[22] which sets out certain requirements for taxpayers to maintain and submit contemporaneous transfer pricing documentation including a master file, local file and special issues file. This CbC reporting regime can help Chinese tax

person's Contracting State of residence (but not including arm's length payments in the ordinary course of business for services or tangible property); or

ii) it is a company which is a resident of a Contracting State and in whose principal class of shares there is substantial and regular trading on a recognized stock exchange."

19 Chile-PRC Income Tax Treaty (2015), art. 26(5), which provides that "[n]otwithstanding the other provisions of this Agreement, a benefit under this Agreement shall not be granted in respect of an item of income if it is reasonable to conclude, having regard to all relevant facts and circumstances, that obtaining that benefit was one of the principal purposes of any arrangement or transaction that resulted directly or indirectly in that benefit, unless it is established that granting that benefit in these circumstances would be in accordance with the object and purpose of the relevant provisions of this Agreement".

20 The preamble to the Chile-PRC Income Tax Treaty (2015) states that the tax treaty should not give rise to "opportunities for non-taxation or reduced taxation through tax evasion or avoidance (including through treaty-shopping arrangements aimed at obtaining reliefs provided in this Agreement for the indirect benefit of residents of third States)".

21 See SAT, "Bulletin on the 10th Tax Administration Forum, Beijing, 13 May 2016", www.chinatax.gov.cn/n810219/n810744/n2128547/n2128559/c2140587/content.html (accessed on 20 May 2018).

22 SAT, Bulletin on Refining the Filing of Related Party Transactions and Administration of Contemporaneous Transfer Pricing Documentation (SAT Bulletin [2016] No. 42).

authorities to assess the data about the whole picture of MNEs' business activities around the world as well as the value chain (including the location specific advantage factors) in China, which Chinese tax authorities previously had very great difficulty assessing. Concerns on the part of MNEs include the cost for preparing and submitting the CbC reports and how the tax authorities (both of China and of other countries) will use these reports.

The definition of "associated enterprises" China adopts under the CbC reporting regime is broad, taking into account factors in shareholding control, loan control, franchise control, procurement, sales and acceptance of services control, personnel control and all other common interests. This CbC reporting regime also covers a broad range of transactions amongst associated enterprises, including financial asset transfers, intangible asset transactions, service transactions, and includes cash pooling in financing transactions, etc. MNEs in China having total consolidated revenue of more than RMB 5.5 billion must file CbC reports with Chinese tax authorities containing details of their overall operations and information regarding transactions with affiliates, the restructuring of business or functions, the MNEs' value chains and, in particular, the location specific advantage factors that the MNEs have taken into account in locating profits in China. For example, where an enterprise engages in a single manufacturing business such as processing-on-order, processing of imported materials etc. for its overseas related parties, or engages in distribution, contracted research and development business, Chinese tax authorities request that such an enterprise in principle maintains a reasonable profit level in China. Where such an enterprise incurs losses, regardless of whether it attains the standards for preparation of contemporaneous documentation, it still needs to prepare local files for contemporaneous documentation with respect to the loss-making year. Chinese tax authorities then focus on examination of the local files of the enterprise in question and strengthen monitoring and administration.

This CbC reporting regime also provides MNEs with a self-assessment opportunity. The SAT in Bulletin [2016] No. 42 listed nine risk indicators for tax audits, including where an MNE's business involves: (i) related-party transactions in large transaction amounts, or varied types of related-party transactions; (ii) incurring of long-term losses, low profits or non-linear profits; (iii) profit lower than the industry's level; (iv) a profit level that does not match the functional risks borne, or earnings shared which do not match the costs shared; (v) carrying out of related-party transactions where the related parties are located in low tax countries (regions); (vi) failure to declare related-party transactions or prepare contemporaneous documentation pursuant to the provisions; (vii) ratios of debt investments and equity investments accepted from related parties which exceed the stipulated standards; (viii) a group structure containing an enterprise controlled by a resident enterprise or by a resident enterprise and a Chinese resident, which is established in a country (region) with an actual tax burden lower than 12.5 per cent, which does not distribute profit or reduces profit distribution and such non-distribution or reduced distribution is not due to reasonable business needs; and finally (ix) implementation of other tax planning or arrangements which do not have a reasonable business objective.

These risk indicators may assist MNEs in self-assessing their risk as well as in providing simplicity and certainty to both the MNEs and Chinese tax authorities.

4.3.4 Compliance with Action 14

Action 14 addresses concerns which the Chinese government also holds. A greater number of tax disputes arose following the Chinese tax authorities' strengthening of enforcement of anti-tax avoidance measures and the increase in Chinese outbound investment. However, China's bilateral tax treaties all provide only for the mutual agreement procedures (MAPs), without any mediation or arbitration options. Given that the MAPs are inefficient for resolving tax disputes between contracting states, Chinese residents are encountering a substantial risk of double taxation.

China's approach is to enhance the MAP process through provision of a more detailed indication of the procedure for taxpayers when filing MAP applications involving treaty-related disputes[23] or transfer pricing related disputes.[24] The challenge however is that the SAT has very limited human resources to handle the MAPs at this point in time. Given China's refusal to adopt the arbitration option under the MLI,[25] it is likely that the SAT will have to increase its MAP team staffing levels for the purpose of increasing the efficiency of resolution of disputes.

4.4 China's Response to Other BEPS Actions

4.4.1 Response to Action 1

Determining how to tax the digital economy is a major challenge for the Chinese government. As at the end of May 2018, the Chinese government had not enacted any new income tax measures in this area. With regard to value-added tax (VAT), China has already included electronic commerce activities within the taxable scope of VAT, but the challenge remains as to how to collect the VAT due from business-to-customer (B2C) suppliers. With regard to income tax, despite the fact that non-Chinese residents are subject to tax in China in respect of the income sourced in China, China's domestic laws do not contain a source rule with regard to the digital economy. However, China will need to reform its tax system and/or tax treaties to deal with digital economy activities, as China on the one hand is one of the largest consumption markets for digital products and services, while on the other hand, many Chinese MNEs engage in electronic commerce throughout the world.

23 SAT, Implementation Method of the Mutual Agreement Procedure in Tax Treaties (*Gong Gao* [2013] No. 56), issued by the SAT on 24 September 2013 with effect from 1 November 2013.

24 SAT, Bulletin on Administrative Measures for Special Tax Investigations and Adjustments and the Mutual Agreement Procedure (SAT Bulletin [2017] No. 6).

25 See OECD, People's Republic of China - Status of List of Reservations and Notifications at the Time of Signature, http://www.oecd.org/tax/treaties/beps-mli-position-china.pdf (accessed on 20 May 2018).

4.4.2 Response to Action 2

Not applicable in China, as Chinese company laws do not allow hybrid mismatch arrangements.

4.4.3 Response to Action 3

The CFC rules were for the first time introduced in China in 2008 as part of the Enterprise Income Tax Law of that year. The Chinese CFC rules provide that, where an enterprise is located in a tax jurisdiction where the actual tax burden is clearly lower than the normal 25 per cent enterprise income tax rate, and the enterprise is controlled by one or more Chinese resident enterprises or jointly by Chinese resident enterprise(s) and individual(s), the profits of the enterprise that are not distributed or are insufficiently distributed without reasonable business needs shall be included in the income of the current period of the controlling Chinese resident enterprise(s), to the extent that those profits are attributable to the Chinese controlling enterprise(s). The key provision in this rule, "the actual tax burden is clearly lower than normal 25 per cent enterprise income tax rate", refers to a situation where the actual tax burden is more than 50 per cent lower than the normal 25 per cent enterprise income tax rate.[26] Following implementation of the rule, the SAT in 2014 issued a circular requesting that Chinese companies report their overseas investments.[27] Then in 2015, the Chinese tax authorities reported their first CFC investigation, in respect of which a wholly-owned subsidiary in Hong Kong of a Chinese company was held by the Chinese tax authorities to be a CFC.[28]

However, when compared with the suggestions in Action 3, the Chinese CFC rules may be found to have been drafted in a very limited and ambiguous way. First, the "control test" in China's CFC rules mainly addresses shareholding control, as management control is only for supplementary purposes;[29] second, although an exemption is provided with respect to the profits derived from an "active business operation", the law has not defined what constitutes such an active business operation; third, only CFCs in a form of corporations are subject to the rules, while look-through entities and permanent establishments are not covered; fourth, in order to

26 See Regulation on Implementing the Enterprise Income Tax Law, Art. 118.

27 SAT, Announcement on Resident Enterprises Reporting Information about their Overseas Investment and Income (*Gong Gao* [2014] No. 38), enacted on 30 June 2014 and effective on 1 September 2014.

28 See SAT Beijing, http://www.bjsat.gov.cn/bjsat/qxfj/zsefj/zcqqy/ssfx/201509/t20150910_236608.html (accessed on 20 May 2018).

29 See Regulation on Implementing the Enterprise Income Tax Law, Art. 117. The term "controlled by one or more Chinese resident enterprises or jointly by Chinese resident enterprise(s) and individual(s)" refers to two circumstances: (1) more than 10 per cent of the equity with voting rights of a foreign enterprise is directly or indirectly held by each such Chinese resident enterprise or individual and more than 50 per cent of the equity is held by all Chinese resident enterprise(s) and individual(s) jointly; (2) with respect to equity, capital, business management, sale or purchase, a foreign enterprise is effectively controlled by one or more Chinese resident enterprises or jointly by Chinese resident enterprise(s) and individual(s), where the equity holding ratios in (1) are not reached.

reduce the tax administrative burden and taxpayer compliance costs and increase certainty, the SAT issued a "white list" carveout of some high-tax jurisdictions (as determined by the SAT) from the application of the CFC rules.[30] However, after almost ten years so far, this list has never been updated and some jurisdictions can no longer be considered high-tax jurisdictions (Li, 2014). The Chinese government has not amended these defects yet, but they are becoming concerns to the Chinese government with the rapid increase in Chinese outbound investment.

4.4.4 Response to Action 4

Thin capitalisation rules were also introduced in China as part of the Enterprise Income Tax Law of 2008. In contrast to the suggestions in Action 4, the Chinese rules only apply to interest paid to related parties and concern only the debt-to-equity ratio, i.e., that the ratio of the loan capital received from affiliated parties to the equity capital received from affiliated parties in an enterprise is in excess of a stipulated criterion. This debt-to-equity ratio is 5:1 for a financial enterprise and 2:1 for any other type of enterprise.[31] Taxpayers are not allowed to deduct interest expenses relating to excess loan capital received from affiliated parties when computing the taxable income of that enterprise. The Chinese government has not to date amended its thin capitalisation rules.

4.4.5 Response to Action 7

China has reserved its right in the MLI not to apply the permanent establishment (PE) provisions.

4.4.6 Response to Actions 8-10

The recommendations in the Actions 8-10 reports are in line with long-standing practices in China. The arm's length principle for transfer pricing is expressly stated in both Chinese domestic laws and all bilateral double tax treaties China has concluded, although Chinese tax authorities have criticised this principle as being in numerous circumstances too vague and requiring a process of locating an appropriate comparable which is too difficult in practice. This explains why certain deviations from the OECD approach are found in China's transfer pricing rules. For example, no preference is specified in relation to the transfer pricing methods to be applied, and methods such as the comparable uncontrolled price method, resale price method, cost-plus method, transactional net margin method and profit split method are all of the same importance when analysing transfer pricing amongst associated enterprises. In addition, other methods, such as the cost method, market method and income method and so forth are also applicable,

30 These jurisdictions include the US, the UK, France, Germany, Japan, Italy, Canada, Australia, India, South Africa and Norway; see the Circular on Simplified Determination of Actual Tax Burden of Foreign Enterprises Controlled by Chinese Resident Shareholders (*Guoshuihan* [2009] No. 37).

31 Regulation on Implementing the Enterprise Income Tax Law, Art. 119.

as long as they comply with the independent transaction principle.

The BEPS project has influenced China in enacting transfer pricing rules as well as conducting tax adjustments. The SAT has issued Bulletin [2017] No. 6[32] which reflects the result of the BEPS report that "the place where profit and economic activities occur matches the place of value creation", and also reshapes China's transfer pricing rules on "location-specific advantages" (LSAs) and intra-group services. This is most significant with regard to assessing the value of, and payments arising from, intangibles, as follows:

- first, the Bulletin extends the definition of intangibles in China to include both application intangibles (e.g., local efforts to make technological improvements to the production process) and marketing intangibles (related to local marketing activities) which are treated as intangibles for tax purposes;
- second, it clarifies that legal ownership of intangibles alone no longer determines entitlement to a return on the intangible, and thus having legal ownership alone of intangibles is not accepted as giving rise to a right to all (or indeed any) of the return that is generated by the exploitation of the intangibles. In order to assess the value of the intangible, a full analysis must be conducted of the global operational process of the enterprise's group, that fully considers the value contribution of each party to the development, value increase, maintenance, protection, application and promotion of the intangible assets, and methods for realisation of the value of the intangible assets, as well as the interaction between the intangible assets and the functions, risks and assets of other businesses within the group. For those enterprises owning only the intangible assets but not contributing to the value of the intangible assets, they are not allowed to participate in profit distribution of the intangible assets; and for those enterprises only providing funding in the process of formation and use of the intangible assets but not actually performing the relevant functions and bearing the corresponding risks, they are allowed to receive only a reasonable return on the cost of capital. In other words, royalty payments must match the economic benefits brought by the intangible assets to the payor;
- third, it affirms again that LSAs in China are considered by the Chinese tax authorities as being amongst the most important elements in the value creation chain. This is in accordance with China's consistently maintained position that MNEs must allocate to China "reasonable profits" reflecting their LSAs generating benefits from China, a position which China has taken steps to ensure is expressly stated in both the 2013 (1st Ed.) and 2017 (2nd Ed.) UN Transfer Pricing Manual (United Nations, 2013; 2017). Tax audits in recent years have particularly paid attention to the question of whether MNEs have attributed such "reasonable profits" to China when their Chinese subsidiar-

32 SAT, Bulletin on Administrative Measures for Special Tax Investigations and Adjustments and the Mutual Agreement Procedure (Bulletin [2017] No. 6), issued in March 2017.

ies have paid their foreign affiliates in respect of interest, service charges, management and technical fees, and royalties.[33] One further important but still outstanding issue is then how to determine whether the profits being allocated to China are reasonable and sufficient to reflect the LSA factors. Chinese laws have not provided any apportionment formula or safe harbour for this issue, and thus significant uncertainty remains for both Chinese tax authorities and taxpayers in practice. Thus, the challenge China is facing at this point in time is how to provide simplicity and certainty when applying the transfer pricing rules.

4.4.7 Response to Action 11

This is an OECD measure, not for country implementation.

4.4.8 Response to Action 12

A mandatory disclosure regime is still not imposed on tax advisors in China at present, although there is no constraint under Chinese constitutional laws on introducing such a regime. In May 2017, the SAT issued a circular specifying that all tax advisors, and tax planning and filing agents must register with tax authorities and also receive supervision from China's Tax Agent Association;[34] however this circular did not impose any disclosure obligation on tax advisors and agents.

4.4.9 Response to Action 15

On 7 June 2017, China signed the Multilateral Convention,[35] as China needs the multilateral instrument to change its tax treaties with contracting states. It is obviously infeasible for China to negotiate individually with its more than 100 contracting jurisdictions to amend each of their bilateral treaties respectively. However, what China has committed to so far are the minimum standards.[36] At the same time, it is clear that China may opt to enact certain provisions such as the principal purpose test (PPT) for preventing treaty abuse and the requirement for the full implementation of the mutual agreement procedure. However, the signing of the Convention only indicates a provisional position for supporting the multilateral instrument approach and such a position is still subject to change before being ratified by the National People's Congress.

---

33 SAT, Notice on Conducting Anti-Tax Avoidance Investigation on Excessive Payment to Abroad (Circular 146 [2014]), issued by the SAT on 29 July 2014; SAT, Announcement on Issues concerning Enterprise Income Tax on Expenses Paid by Enterprises to Their Overseas Affiliates (Announcement No. 16 [2015]), enacted by the SAT on 18 March 2015.

34 Bulletin 2017 No. 13, Supervision Method on Tax Related Professional Service (Trial), issued by the SAT on 5 May 2017 and entering into force on 1 September 2017.

35 The tax arrangements China (Mainland China) has concluded with Hong Kong, Macau and Taiwan are not covered by the MLI.

36 See OECD, People's Republic of China - Status of List of Reservations and Notifications at the Time of Signature, www.oecd.org/tax/treaties/beps-mli-position-china.pdf (accessed on 20 May 2018).

4.5 Unilateral BEPS Measures Adopted by China

One notable measure is that the Chinese tax authorities have strengthened the application of the general anti-avoidance rule (GAAR) in recent years, in particular on indirect share transfer arrangements. This form of share transfer is often carried out by foreign investors selling the shares that they hold in a company located outside China. In the SAT's opinion, the capital gains derived from such offshore share transfers should be taxed in China if the transfer of shares in respect of the foreign company gives rise, in substance, to a similar effect of selling an interest in its Chinese subsidiaries. The test that the Chinese tax authorities apply to such share transfers is the "reasonable business purpose" test under the Chinese GAAR, the burden of proof of which lies with the sellers in the offshore share transfers.[37] Since 2009, the SAT has issued several circulars in an attempt to guide taxpayers as to what circumstances would be deemed to have "no reasonable business purpose": for instance, whether the transaction is an artificial scheme with a primary purpose of obtaining tax benefits, whether 75 per cent or more of the value of the shares in the foreign target company is derived, directly or indirectly, from Chinese taxable assets, whether 90 per cent or more of the income of the foreign target company is derived from investments in China at any time within one year prior to the indirect transfer, and so forth.[38] It is, however, not possible for the SAT to list all relevant circumstances. Consequently, as long as the sole test with regard to such offshore indirect shares transfer is subjective, i.e., the business purpose of the seller, uncertainty will remain in carrying out such transfers.

Another notable measure involves China's efforts to implement its commitment for exchange of information under the Model Competent Authority Agreement (CAA) which China signed in 2015. On 19 May 2017, the SAT, MOF and other relevant governmental agencies issued a circular requiring financial institutions in mainland China to carry out due diligence in checking and collecting tax-related information relating to financial accounts owned by non-residents and then sub-

37 Qiu (2014b, p. 77); de Goede (2012); Qiu (2010). The Chinese tax authorities have often published articles in newspapers sponsored by the Chinese government regarding their successfully investigating such indirect offshore share transfer transactions and having collected tax revenue from the foreign sellers. However, these articles are usually very brief with regard to the facts of the transactions and the information in respect of the relevant taxpayers is kept confidential. It is, therefore, difficult for readers to understand the investigation or to contact the taxpayers for the purposes of verification.

38 SAT, Notice on Issuing the Measures for the Implementation of Special Tax Adjustments (Trial) (*Guoshuifa* [2009] No. 2), issued by the SAT on 8 January 2009 but with retrospective effect from 1 January 2008; SAT, Circular of the State Administration of Taxation on Strengthening the Administration of Enterprise Income Tax on Incomes from Non-resident Enterprises' Equity Transfers (*Guoshuihan* [2009] No. 698), enacted on 10 December 2009 but with retrospective effect from 1 January 2008; SAT, Notice on Several Issues on Administration of Non-Residents Income Taxes (Notice 24[2011]), enacted by the SAT on 28 March 2011 with effect from 1 April 2011; SAT, Announcement on Several Issues concerning the Enterprise Income Tax on Income from the Indirect Transfer of Assets by Non-Resident Enterprises (Announcement No. 7 [2015]), enacted by the SAT on 3 February 2015 with effect from the same date.

mitting them to Chinese tax authorities for information exchange in compliance with the Common Reporting Standard (CRS) starting from September 2018.[39]

4.6 China's Tax Administration Reform relating to the BEPS Project

The Chinese parliament, i.e., the National People's Congress, decided in March 2018 to terminate China's 24-year experiment with dual central and provincial tax administrations and to mandate the absorption of provincial tax administrations into the central tax authority.[40] This reform caps a process of shifting control over both China's tax revenue and administrative power to the central government (Li and Krever, 2018). One factor behind the decision to merge the administrations may be a response to the BEPS project, as a bifurcated tax administrative structure involving incompatible data systems was clearly detrimental to effective tax administration. After the merger, the unified tax team could be more efficient in collecting the data required and combating tax avoidance.

4.7 Future of China's International Tax Reform

The future of China's international tax reform involves both opportunities and challenges. Participation in the development of the BEPS project measures and their implementation is an opportunity for China to establish a more important role in the international community in terms of the making of international tax rules. So China has been quite active in engaging in the BEPS project action relating to development of the Multilateral Instrument. For example, China participates in the Ad Hoc Group, and Mr. Liao Tizhong, the General Director of the International Tax Department of the SAT, also serves as one of the Vice-Chairs in the Group developing Final Reports of the Actions for BEPS project, in particular in relation to location specific advantage factors and aligning profits with value creation and economic activities (Liao, 2014). Beyond the BEPS project, China has also participated in various other relevant projects, committees and forums on international tax coordination, such as the UN Committee of Experts on International Cooperation in Tax Matters, OECD/G20 Global Forum on Transparency and Exchange of Information for Tax Purposes, as well as the OECD Forum on Tax Administration. Thus, China's contribution to the enactment and enforcement of international tax rules is on a trend of inevitable increase.

However, challenges are unavoidable as well. With China's position changing from a pure source state to a mixed role of being both a source state and a residence

39 Due Diligence of Tax-Related Information of Financial Accounts Owned by Non-Residents (*Gong Gao* [2017] 14), issued by the SAT, MOF, People's Bank of China, China Banking Supervision and Management Committee, China Securities Supervision and Management Committee and China Insurance Supervision and Management Committee on 9 May 2017.

40 Plan for Deepening the Institutional Restructuring of the Communist Party and of the Country, approved by the first session of the 13th National People's Congress (20 March 2018), para. 46.

state, conflicts of interest now arise when deciding China's domestic tax policy as well as treaty policies. One example in point is that China is very cautious and has still not enacted rules for taxing the digital economy, because the country on the one hand is one of the largest economies consuming digital products and services, and on the other hand it is also a residence state having a significant number of residents engaging in digital business outside China. Thus, any aggressive rules for taxing the digital economy might also result in an increasing tax cost for Chinese residents, which consequently may harm their competitiveness in other countries' markets. Another example is the location-specific advantages argument which the Chinese tax authorities impose to tax MNEs. With increasing Chinese outbound investment, this LSA rule actually will benefit those source states rather than China, being in the position of the residence state. These source states where Chinese tax residents invest might argue for a higher level of taxation based on such LSA arguments too. How the Chinese tax authorities would respond to such disputes arising for Chinese investors in source states would then be of interest to observers worldwide.

References

De Goede, Jan J. P. (2012), "Allocation of Taxing Rights on Income from Cross-Border (Indirect) Sale of Shares", 18(3) *Asia-Pacific Tax Bulletin* 211-220.

Li, Na (2014), "China's CFC Regime: Existing Rules and Improvement Suggestions", 68(10) *Bulletin for International Taxation* 536-540.

Li, Na and Richard Krever (2018), "24 Years Later - China Finally Centralizes Its Tax Administration", 90(5) *Tax Notes International* 539-544.

Liao, Tizhong (2014), "Impact of BEPS Project and China's Reaction", 20(7) *International Taxation in China* 13-15.

Organisation for Economic Co-operation and Development (OECD) (1998), *Harmful Tax Competition: An Emerging Global Issue* (Paris: OECD).

Organisation for Economic Co-operation and Development (OECD) (2015), *Action 6 – 2015 Final Report: Preventing the Granting of Treaty Benefits in Inappropriate Circumstances* (Paris: OECD).

Qiu, Dongmei (2010), "China's Capital Gains Taxation of Nonresidents and the Legitimate Use of Tax Treaties", 60(8) *Tax Notes International* 593-621.

Qiu, Dongmei (2014a), "Collecting Unpaid Tax Offshore: Caribbean Tax Havens and Foreign Direct Investment in China", 68(12) *Bulletin for International Taxation* 648-659.

Qiu, Dongmei (2014b), "Legal Interpretation of Tax Law: China", in Robert F. van Brederode and Richard Krever (eds.), *Legal Interpretation of Tax Law* (Alphen aan den Rijn: Kluwer Law International), 73-106.

United Nations (2013), *United Nations Practical Manual on Transfer Pricing for Developing Countries*, ST/ESA/347 (New York: United Nations).

United Nations (2017), *United Nations Practical Manual on Transfer Pricing for Developing Countries*, ST/ESA/ (New York: United Nations).

Yang, Haiyan and Xuying Zhuang (2014), "Tax Evasion Scale and Features of Foreign-funded Enterprises in China", 35(10) *Finance & Trade Economics* 41-49.

5 The Adoption of BEPS in Hong Kong Special Administrative Region

Yan Xu*

Abstract

As one of the world's major international financial centres, Hong Kong has actively responded in a number of ways to the OECD and G20 initiatives on combating tax avoidance, well-known as the anti-BEPS action plans, while leveraging the reform to consolidate its competitive edge in the global economy through tax policies. This chapter sheds light on the key reform measures on tax design and administration in Hong Kong as a response to the implementation of the four minimum standards introduced by the OECD's BEPS package. The chapter further elucidates Hong Kong's unilateral reform measures, involving revamping the tax legislative framework to implement other actions in the anti-BEPS package, and its efforts to enable the application of the multilateral agreements on tax cooperation in the post-BEPS era.

5.1 Introduction

As a special administrative region (SAR) of the People's Republic of China (PRC), Hong Kong has enjoyed a high degree of autonomy. The "one country two systems" principle established in the Basic Law of the Hong Kong SAR allows Hong Kong to have legislative, executive and judicial systems separate from the PRC. Influenced by the British Westminster system and inherited from the colonial regime, the SAR operates an executive-led parliamentary government system.[1]

In economic terms, Hong Kong is categorised as an advanced economy by international standards, and its GDP per capita is higher than that of many advanced economies including Canada, France, Japan and the United Kingdom.[2] The city

---

* Associate Professor, Faculty of Law, The Chinese University of Hong Kong.

1 The Basic Law of the Hong Kong Special Administrative Region of the People's Republic of China (National People's Congress, adopted April 4, 1990, effective July 1, 1997), Ch. 2 (Basic Law). See also Gagnon-Bélanger (2016); Chen (2004, p. 221).

2 World Bank, "GDP Per Capita, PPP (Current International $)" (2016 data), data.worldbank.org/indicator/ NY.GDP.PCAP.PP.CD (accessed on 7 June 2018). See also International Monetary Fund, "GDP Per Capita, Current Prices" (2018 data), www.imf.org/external/datamapper/NGDPDPC@WEO/OEMDC/ADVEC/ WEOWORLD (accessed on 7 June 2018).

has long had a free market economy and that economy has been highly dependent on international trade and finance.[3] The services sector has been the most important industrial sector in the SAR: in 2016, it constitutes about 92 per cent of total GDP according to the government.[4] As a free port, there are no tariffs on imported goods, nor are there quotas or dumping laws[5] or foreign exchange controls.[6]

As a result of the "one country two systems" principle, the SAR maintains a separate fiscal and tax system which is independent of the rest of the country. The specific provisions regarding taxation issues under the Basic Law have the effect of continuation of the system of tax statutes and case law and the continuation of tax legislation and amendments.[7] Specifically, the tax statutes and case law that were applicable prior to the handover of Hong Kong sovereignty to the PRC on 1 July 1997 continue to apply after the handover, and the legislative power continues to be exercised by the local legislature.[8] The final arbiter of appeals on tax matters, however, has changed to the Court of Final Appeal from the Privy Council in the UK as was the case previously.[9] The Inland Revenue Ordinance is the most fundamental tax law in Hong Kong, which governs the levy of the three income-based taxes, namely the Salaries Tax, the Profits Tax and the Property Tax. Most essentially, the low tax policy and simple tax system adopted prior to the handover continues to apply as the key taxation principle in the SAR after the handover.[10]

The tax system in Hong Kong has been considered attractive to international investors due to a number of notable features. First, taxation in Hong Kong is based on the territorial source principle, which means only income arising in or derived from Hong Kong is taxable in Hong Kong. Second, there is no comprehensive income tax system. Any income other than salaries, (business) profits and property rental income will not be taxable. Third, tax rates are internationally competitively low: the profits tax on corporations is 16.5 per cent and on non-incorporated bodies 15 per cent. A reduced half tax rate has recently been made available under the profits tax system in the circumstances which a corporation or non-incorporated body has annual assessable profits below a certain threshold.[11] No tax is charged in relation to capital gains, nor is withholding tax imposed on dividends and interest.

3 See the Census and Statistics Department, Government of the Hong Kong SAR, "National Income" (2016 data), https://www.censtatd.gov.hk/hkstat/sub/sp250.jsp?tableID=036&ID=0&productType=8 (accessed on 7 June 2018).

4 Ibid.

5 US Central Intelligence Agency, "East & Southeast Asia: Hong Kong", The World Factbook, 1 May 2018, https:// www.cia.gov/library/publications/the-world-factbook/geos/hk.html.

6 US International Trade Administration, "Hong Kong Country Commercial Guide", http://www.export.gov/article?id=Hong-Kong-Macau-foreign-exchange-controls (accessed on 7 June 2018).

7 Basic Law, Arts 8, 106-108.

8 Basic Law, Arts 18, 66, 73.

9 Basic Law, Art. 82.

10 Basic Law, Art. 108.

11 Inland Revenue Ordinance (Cap. 112), Schedules 8A-8B.

Only a limited scope of payments, notably royalties received by non-residents, is subject to tax similar to withholding tax.[12] As a whole, the taxation system in Hong Kong has been regarded as simple, efficient and straightforward among jurisdictions in the world.[13]

Internationally, although not an official member of the Organisation for Economic Co-operation and Development (OECD), Hong Kong has been an observer to the OECD trade and finance committees.[14] For international conventions or multilateral instruments, Hong Kong in general does not have the right to sign or join. With regard to the BEPS project, Hong Kong's signing of the OECD Multilateral Convention to Implement Tax Treaty Related Measures to Prevent Base Erosion and Profit Shifting (MLI) on 7 June 2017 was effected by the PRC Central Government on the SAR's behalf.[15] As a result, Hong Kong has become a signatory and a party to the MLI, which facilitates its implementation of the BEPS package in the SAR.[16]

5.2 Hong Kong SAR and BEPS

5.2.1 The Government Response in General

The BEPS project is having a significant impact on Hong Kong SAR. The government officially indicated its commitment to implementing the OECD BEPS action plans in July 2016.[17] To fulfil this commitment, it launched a public consultation on legislative proposals in late 2016 which focused on the four minimum standards of the BEPS package while aiming to maintain Hong Kong's simple and low tax

12 Inland Revenue Ordinance, ss 50A, 20B. See also PricewaterhouseCoopers (PwC), "Hong Kong: Corporate - Withholding Taxes", Worldwide Tax Summaries, 1 December 2017, taxsummaries.pwc.com/ID/Hong-Kong-Corporate-Withholding-taxes (accessed 7 June 2018).

13 InvestHK, Government of the Hong Kong SAR, "Low, Simple and Competitive Tax System", https://www.investhk.gov.hk/en/why-hong-kong/low-simple-and-competitive-tax-system.html (accessed on 7 June 2018).

14 Trade and Industry Department, Government of the Hong Kong SAR, "International Trade Organisations", www.tid.gov.hk/english/ito/oecd/index.html (accessed on 7 June 2018).

15 State Administration of Taxation, PRC, "Hong Kong SAR of the PRC (Submitted by the People's Republic of China) - Status of List of Reservations and Notifications at the Time of Signature [of the MLI]", http://www.oecd.org/ tax/treaties/beps-mli-position-hong-kong.pdf (accessed on 7 June 2018); OECD, "Signatories and Parties to the Multilateral Convention to Implement Tax Treaty Related Measures to Prevent Base Erosion and Profit Shifting: Status as of 5 June 2018", http://www.oecd.org/tax/treaties/beps-mli-signatories-and-parties.pdf (accessed on 7 June 2018).

16 OECD, "Signatories and Parties to the Multilateral Convention to Implement Tax Treaty Related Measures to Prevent Base Erosion and Profit Shifting: Status as of 5 June 2018", above n. 15.

17 Information Services Department, Government of the Hong Kong SAR, "Hong Kong to Join Inclusive Framework for Implementation of Package against Base Erosion and Profit Shifting", press release (20 June 2016), www.info.gov.hk/gia/general/201606/20/P201606200520.htm. See also Inland Revenue Department, Government of the Hong Kong SAR (IRD), "Government Releases Consultation Report on Measures to Counter Base Erosion and Profit Shifting by Enterprises", press release (31 July 2017), www.ird.gov.hk/eng/ppr/archives/ 17073101.htm.

regime.[18] The comments received from the consultation led to various adjustments in the legislative proposals and an amendment bill based on the revised proposals, Inland Revenue (Amendment) (No. 6) Bill 2017 (Amendment Bill No. 6), was officially introduced to the legislature for adoption in January 2018. This Amendment Bill was passed into law on 4 July 2018 and has come into effect following its publication in the Gazette on 13 July 2018. In specific terms, the majority of the provisions relating to transfer pricing, consequential relief on transfer pricing adjustments, advance pricing arrangements, tax credits and profits tax concessions will apply in relation to tax payable for a year of assessment beginning on or after 1 April 2018. The provisions relating to Country-by-Country reporting will apply in relation to an accounting period beginning on or after 1 January 2018, whilst those relating to master file and local file will apply in relation to an accounting period beginning on or after 1 April 2018.[19]

To increase tax transparency and compliance and also to meet the new international standard on information exchange, the government introduced a separate amendment bill to the legislature, Inland Revenue (Amendment) (No. 5) Bill 2017,[20] which was passed as the Inland Revenue (Amendment) Ordinance 2018 in January 2018.[21] The Ordinance provides a necessary legal framework for Hong Kong to move from a bilateral basis to a multilateral approach to implementing the arrangements relating to the automatic exchange of information (AEOI) and Country-by-Country (CbC) reports through participating in the Multilateral Convention on Mutual Administrative Assistance in Tax Matters (OECD and Council of Europe, 2011).[22] Hong Kong has been given approval in principle from the PRC Central Government for territorial extension of the Multilateral Convention to the

18 Government of the Hong Kong SAR, "Consultation on Measures to Counter Base Erosion and Profit Shifting Launched", press release (26 October 2016), http://www.info.gov.hk/gia/general/201610/26/P2016102500716.htm; Financial Services and the Treasury Bureau and Inland Revenue Department (2017, p. 2) (Consultation Report). It is stated in the Consultation Report that a pragmatic approach shall be adopted to minimise compliance costs and the burden on business.

19 Legislative Council, Hong Kong SAR, "Bills Committee on Inland Revenue (Amendment) (No. 6) Bill 2017 - Background Brief", LC Paper No. CB(1)509/17-18(01 (22 January 2018), 2, available at https://www.legco.gov.hk/ yr17-18/english/bc/bc02/papers/bc0220180123cb1-509-1-e.pdf. See also Ng (2016, p. 3); Legislative Council, Hong Kong SAR, "Voting Results of the Council meeting: 04 - 05.07.2018" (4 July 2018), 1, https://www.legco.gov.hk/yr17-18/chinese/counmtg/voting/v20180704.pdf. See also PricewaterhouseCoopers Hong Kong (PwC), "The New BEPS and Transfer Pricing Law Passed in Hong Kong" (July 2018), available at https://www.pwccn.com/en/hk-tax-news/2018q3/hongkongtax-news-jul2018-9.pdf; Government of the Hong Kong SAR, "Inland Revenue (Amendment) (No. 6) Ordinance 2018 Gazetted", Press Release (13 July 2018), http://www.info.gov.hk/gia/general/201807/13/P2018071100388.htm.

20 See Legislative Council, Hong Kong SAR, https://www.legco.gov.hk/yr17-18/english/bc/bc01/general/bc01.htm.

21 IRD, "Inland Revenue (Amendment) Ordinance 2018 Gazetted", press release (2 February 2018), https://www.ird. gov.hk/eng/ppr/archives/18020201.htm.

22 Ibid; for the provisions of the legislation as gazetted, see https://www.gld.gov.hk/egazette/pdf/20182205/es 1201822055.pdf.

SAR.[23] Ever since all the legislative procedures were completed, including an issuance of a declaration order by Hong Kong's Chief Executive and a scrutiny of the order by the legislature, the Multilateral Convention has come into legal effect in Hong Kong from 1 September 2018. The Multilateral Convention is the first major multilateral tax agreement in the SAR. The legislative move indicates that the SAR government is eager to become a "cooperative tax jurisdiction" in the current round of international tax reform.[24]

Prior to the OECD and G20 initiatives on combating tax avoidance, base erosion and profit shifting seems not to have been a substantial concern for Hong Kong. The most recent legislative actions relating to the anti-BEPS measures by the government reflect more of a pragmatic policy than an urgent need to fight serious BEPS problems in the region.[25] As stated in the 2017 Consultation Paper, the purpose of introducing reforms relating to the BEPS package in Hong Kong is to provide legal certainty for taxpayers and to align Hong Kong tax practices with international standards while keeping the simple tax policy and the well-established territorial source principle intact.[26]

Indeed, given the special features of Hong Kong's taxation system and the sound rule of law system, tax avoidance has been dealt with comparatively effectively by the tax authority and also the courts. The Inland Revenue Ordinance includes some specific anti-tax avoidance provisions, such as limitation of the utilisation of losses by limited partners in limited partnerships and prevention of trafficking in loss companies,[27] and general anti-tax avoidance rules (GAARs).[28] The statutory GAARs apply to any transaction entered into for the sole or dominant purpose of enabling a person to obtain a tax benefit.[29] The GAARs have an overriding effect, empowering the tax authority to make appropriate adjustments to counteract the tax benefit.[30] In respect of transfer pricing (TP), one of the most significant areas of concern in the

23 Legislative Council, Hong Kong SAR, Panel on Financial Affairs, "Application of the Multilateral Convention on Mutual Administrative Assistance in Tax Matters in Hong Kong", LC Paper No. CB(1)1030/16-17(08) (5 June 2017), para. 13, https://www.legco.gov.hk/yr16-17/english/panels/fa/papers/fa20170605cb1-1030-8-e.pdf.

24 IRD, "Inland Revenue (Amendment) Ordinance 2018 Gazetted", above n. 21. The last paragraph of the press release states: "[t]o allow Hong Kong to implement the new initiatives on international tax co-operation more effectively and reduce the risk of Hong Kong being identified as a 'non-cooperative tax jurisdiction', the Government will strive to complete the procedures for participating in the Multilateral Convention as soon as practicable". See OECD, "Jurisdictions Participating in the Convention on Mutual Administrative Assistance in Tax Matters, Status – 28 August 2018", http://www.oecd.org/ctp/exchange-of-tax-information/Status_of_convention.pdf.

25 Consultation Report, para. 1.3.

26 Ibid., para. 2.3.

27 Inland Revenue Ordinance, ss 22B, 61B.

28 Inland Revenue Ordinance, ss 61, 61A.

29 Inland Revenue Ordinance, ss 61, 61A. See also IRD, Departmental Interpretation and Practice Notes (DIPN) No. 15, "General Anti-Avoidance Provision" (and other matters) (Revised) (January 2006), https:// www.ird.gov.hk/eng/pdf/e_dipn15.pdf.

30 Inland Revenue Ordinance, s. 61A(2)(b).

BEPS project, the legislation in Hong Kong prior to the most recent passage of the Amendment Bill No. 6 into Amendment (No. 6) Ordinance 2018 only has very limited TP provision.[31] The then Inland Revenue Ordinance did not contain statutory TP rules addressing non-arm's length transactions between associated enterprises. The tax authority, the Inland Revenue Department (IRD), had relied on the general tax provisions and case law to handle TP issues, but such an approach had a limited effect on addressing non-arm's length pricing in certain circumstances (Ng, 2016, paras 3.1, 3.3, 3.4). Such limitations will be overcome after the Amendment (No. 6) Ordinance 2018 commences operation since the new legislation codifies a TP regulatory regime, providing necessary tax provisions on TP documentation, CbC reporting and other related taxation matters. The codification of TP rules is part of the government's effort to comply with the four minimum standards of the BEPS package.

5.2.2 The Four Minimum Standards

Hong Kong has joined the BEPS Inclusive Framework as an Associate.[32] As noted above, it has started implementing the four minimum standards.

5.2.2.1 Action 5: Harmful Tax Practices

Action 5 revamps the work on harmful tax practices with a focus on improving transparency, including compulsory spontaneous exchange of rulings related to preferential regimes and requirement of substantial activity for preferential regimes such as the intellectual property (IP) regimes.

The OECD has conducted peer review in assessing whether selected preferential tax regimes of members of the BEPS Inclusive Framework are harmful or not. A number of factors are taken into account in the assessment, among which the two key factors are whether "the regime is ring-fenced from the domestic economy" and whether "it meets the substantial activities requirement".[33] Ring-fencing would lead to the base erosion of the jurisdictions from which the geographically mobile activities are attracted whilst the domestic tax base of the jurisdiction providing the regime will not be affected.

The Hong Kong government has taken steps to remove any ring-fencing features that are regarded as harmful. Specifically, the government has extended the tax regime for offshore aircraft leasing activities to onshore aircraft leasing activi-

31 Inland Revenue Ordinance, s. 20; see also IRD, DIPN No. 45, "Relief from Double Taxation Due to Transfer Pricing or Profit Reallocation Adjustments" (April 2009), https://www.ird.gov.hk/eng/pdf/e_dipn45.pdf; IRD, DIPN No. 46, "Transfer Pricing Guidelines – Methodologies and Related Issues" (December 2009), https://www.ird.gov.hk/eng/pdf/e_dipn46.pdf; IRD, DIPN No. 48, "Advance Pricing Arrangement" (March 2012), https://www.ird.gov.hk/eng/pdf/e_dipn48.pdf.

32 Information Services Department, Government of the Hong Kong SAR, "Hong Kong to Join Inclusive Framework for Implementation of Package against Base Erosion and Profit Shifting", above n. 17.

33 OECD (2015a, p. 20). See also PricewaterhouseCoopers Hong Kong (PwC) (2018a).

ties in order to avoid any possible perception of ring-fencing through the Inland Revenue (Amendment) (No. 2) Ordinance 2017, which has come into effect from 28 June 2017.[34]

As for the concessionary tax regimes for corporate treasury centres (CTCs), professional reinsurance and captive insurance, Amendment (No. 6) Ordinance 2018 contains amendment provisions to extend the half-rate concession, namely 8.25 per cent, to profits derived from domestic transactions, and to extend the provisions for preventing abusive activities to the concessionary tax regimes.[35] Moreover, to satisfy the OECD's substantial activity requirement, Amendment (No. 6) Ordinance includes provisions to the effect that the concessionary treatment will be available only if specified threshold requirements for determining whether profit-producing activities are carried out in Hong Kong are met.[36] All of these measures show that the three concessionary tax regimes are in the process of being amended by the legislature (OECD, 2017b, p. 19).

The efforts made by the Hong Kong government have been acknowledged by the OECD. A good example is that the profits tax exemptions for ship operators and aircraft leasing business in Hong Kong are confirmed by the OECD not to be harmful (OECD, 2017b, pp. 19, 21). Meanwhile, spontaneous exchange of information on tax rulings under BEPS Action 5 is being advanced through Hong Kong's participating in the Multilateral Convention.[37]

5.2.2.2 Action 6: Treaty Abuse

Abuse of tax treaties is identified as an important source of base erosion and profit shifting in the OECD final reports of the anti-BEPS project. Action 6 develops model treaty provisions and recommendations regarding the design of domestic rules to prevent treaty abuse. The MLI is adopted as a multilateral instrument to enable jurisdictions to efficiently and synchronously modify the existing bilateral tax treaties, in particular treaty provisions on hybrid instruments and entities, dual resident entities and the granting of treaty benefits.[38]

As a signatory and also a party to the MLI, Hong Kong has taken measures to comply with Action 6. It submitted to the OECD, through the PRC Central Government, that all its comprehensive double taxation agreements (CDTAs), except for the ones with PRC, India (pending) and Finland (pending), are to be covered by

34 Consultation Report, p. 24, para. 5.15.

35 Ibid. Inland Revenue Ordinance, s. 16(1A).

36 Inland Revenue (Amendment) (No.6) Ordinance 2018, s. 26AB.

37 See above n. 24; Multilateral Convention on Mutual Administrative Assistance in Tax Matters, Art. 7.

38 OECD, Explanatory Statement to the Multilateral Convention to Implement Tax Treaty Related Measures to Prevent Base Erosion and Profit Shifting, November 2016, 1, http://www.oecd.org/tax/treaties/explanatory-statement-multilateral-convention-to-implement-tax-treaty-related-measures-to-prevent-BEPS.pdf.

and amended through the MLI.[39]

Hong Kong also proposes to adopt a "principal purpose test" (PPT) rule in future CDTAs and it would accept symmetrical application if the treaty partners do not adopt the "PPT only" rule.[40] From Hong Kong's perspective, the PPT rule is considered sufficient to prevent treaty abuse, while the "limitation on benefits" (LOB) rule would be unnecessarily restrictive as it might result in some funds (including those set up in Hong Kong) not being able to enjoy the treaty benefits under the CDTAs.[41]

Another way to prevent treaty abuses in Hong Kong is to tighten the issuance of a Certificate of Resident Status, which is the prerequisite (but not assurance) for the claim of treaty benefits.[42] Essentially, the IRD will consider whether the applicant is truly a beneficial owner under the tests of place of residence, place of incorporation, or place of central management and control. It is impossible for an applicant to obtain such certificate without satisfying the substance requirements.[43]

5.2.2.3 Action 13: Transfer Pricing Documentation

Action 13 introduces revised guidance on TP documentation, including the template for CbC reporting, with the aim to enhance tax transparency across the jurisdictions. The OECD has most recently published an updated version of the Transfer Pricing Guidelines for Multinational Enterprises and Tax Administrations (TP Guidelines) as a response to the changes made to the TP rules by the BEPS project (OECD, 2017a).

The arm's length principle for setting transfer prices remains unaltered in Action 13 and also the TP Guidelines. Hong Kong has long been following the

39 MLI, Art. 2(1)(a)(ii); see State Administration of Taxation, PRC, "Hong Kong SAR of the PRC (Submitted by the People's Republic of China) - Status of List of Reservations and Notifications at the Time of Signature", above n. 15; IRD, "Comprehensive Double Taxation Agreements concluded", https://www.ird.gov.hk/eng/tax/dta_inc.htm.

40 This is because investment funds generally could not meet the requirement of "qualified person" and thus would be denied treaty benefits, even where such funds do not lead to treaty-shopping concerns. See Consultation Report, para. 4.2.

41 Ibid., pp. 17-18.

42 IRD, "Certificate of Resident Status", https://www.ird.gov.hk/eng/tax/dta_cor.htm (accessed on 7 June 2018).

43 There is no specific DIPN dealing with the issuance of such certificate. However, DIPN No. 54, "Taxation of Aircraft Leasing Activities", October 2017, https://www.ird.gov.hk/eng/pdf/e_dipn54.pdf, states that such certificate is required for aircraft leasing business, and DIPN No. 44 (Revised), "Arrangement between the Mainland of China and the Hong Kong Special Administrative Region for the Avoidance of Double Taxation and the Prevention of Fiscal Evasion with respect to Taxes on Income", August 2008, mentions that when the IRD is unable to ascertain if a person is a resident of PRC, that person will be referred to the PRC tax authorities for determination. The IRD has recommended that applicants refer to the relevant CDTA provisions and protocol to check whether they qualify as a Hong Kong resident for the purpose of that CDTA. The specific requirements on issuance of tax-residence certificate may thus vary under CDTAs.

principle, but the principle was not codified in the Inland Revenue Ordinance until the recent enactment of Amendment (No. 6) Ordinance. Before the enactment, the Hong Kong tax authority merely adopted the principle in the department notes on transfer pricing.[44] The newly passed Ordinance provides that all transactions between associated enterprises in Hong Kong are taxed on the arm's length basis, and the TP rules require an adjustment of the profits or losses of an enterprise where the transactions between two associated persons depart from those between independent persons and thereby have created a tax advantage.[45]

Importantly, the new Ordinance provides a necessary legal basis for the interpretation of transfer pricing principles by reference to the OECD TP Guidelines, and it incorporates the OECD guidance on development, enhancement, maintenance, protection or exploitation (DEMPE) functions related to the use or transfer of intangibles. The Ordinance is also domestic legislation for CbC reporting, compliant with Action 13. The recent passage of tax legislation on giving effect to the Multilateral Convention in Hong Kong will help Hong Kong to conduct automatic exchange of CbC reports.[46]

As provided in Amendment (No. 6) Ordinance 2018, Hong Kong will follow the OECD three-tier standardised approach on transfer pricing documentation, namely master file, local file, and CbC report, to require the relevant Hong Kong enterprises to prepare the respective documentation, proposed for the fiscal year starting on or after 1 April 2018.[47]

For master file and local file, all enterprises which carry on trade or business in Hong Kong and which have engaged in transactions with associated enterprises will be mandated to prepare the two types of files.[48] Exemption may be granted if the size of business or value of related party transactions satisfies certain conditions, which is to minimise the compliance burden on the business sector. As a result, an enterprise is not required to prepare both the master and local files if it satisfies any two of the following conditions:

i) total annual revenue not more than HKD 200 million;

ii) total assets not more than HKD 200 million;

iii) not more than 100 employees.

An enterprise will also be exempted from preparing a local file for a particular category of transactions if the amount of that category of transactions for the relevant accounting period is below the following threshold in each case:

44 Legislative Council, Hong Kong SAR, Legislative Council Brief - Inland Revenue (Amendment) (No. 6) Bill 2017, 27 December 2017, p. 2, para. 4, https://www.legco.gov.hk/yr17-18/english/bills/brief/b201712291_brf.pdf.

45 Inland Revenue (Amendment) (No. 6) Ordinance 2018, ss 50AAC-50AAW.

46 For detailed information about the tax legislation, see above nn. 20 and 21.

47 Inland Revenue (Amendment) (No. 6) Ordinance 2018, ss 58B-58M.

48 Inland Revenue (Amendment) (No. 6) Ordinance 2018, s. 58C.

i) transfers of properties (other than financial assets and intangibles): HKD 220 million;

ii) transactions in respect of financial assets: HKD 110 million;

iii) transfers of intangibles: HKD 110 million;

iv) any other transactions (e.g., service income and royalty income): HKD 44 million.

Moreover, Hong Kong follows the PRC practice to exempt the enterprise which is fully exempted from preparing a local file from preparing a master file.[49]

For CbC reporting, Hong Kong will adopt the filing threshold prescribed by the OECD. That is, multinational enterprises (MNEs) with annual consolidated group revenue equal to or more than EUR 750 million (HKD 6.8 billion) would be required to file CbC reports (OECD, 2018, p. 19). The primary obligation of report filing falls on the ultimate parent entity of the MNE group that is resident in Hong Kong.[50] Amendment (No. 6) Ordinance 2018 also includes a "secondary" and "surrogate" filling mechanism, which follows the OECD approach.[51] Under this mechanism, if the ultimate parent entity of an MNE group is in a jurisdiction that does not require CbC reporting or does not exchange such reports with Hong Kong, the constituent entities of the group in Hong Kong would be subject to a secondary filing obligation. A constituent entity of the group may be authorised to file CbC reports to the IRD on behalf of the group for exchange of the reports with other jurisdictions, which is called surrogate filing.[52]

Meanwhile, even if the abovementioned conditions are met, the Hong Kong constituent entity may not be required to file CbC reports if the reports have been filed by the reportable group's surrogate parent entity in another tax jurisdiction which has adequate information exchange mechanisms in place with Hong Kong.[53]

The government is also introducing a voluntary filing arrangement, in which the ultimate parent entity of an MNE group that is resident in Hong Kong could voluntarily submit its CbC reports regarding an accounting period between 1 January 2016 and 31 December 2017 for exchange with other jurisdictions, as the CbC reporting requirement in Hong Kong applies to an accounting period commencing on or after 1 January 2018. This arrangement would relieve the constituent entities of the MNE group in overseas jurisdictions of the secondary filing obligation for that accounting period.[54]

49 See Legislative Council, Hong Kong SAR, Legislative Council Brief - Inland Revenue (Amendment) (No. 6) Bill 2017, above n. 44, p. 4.

50 Ibid., p. 5.

51 Inland Revenue (Amendment) (No. 6) Ordinance 2018, Schedule 17I.

52 See Legislative Council, Hong Kong SAR, Legislative Council Brief - Inland Revenue (Amendment) (No. 6) Bill 2017, above n. 44, p. 5.

53 Ibid.

54 Ibid. Inland Revenue (Amendment) (No. 6) Ordinance 2018, Part 2, Div. 3, Note 6.

5.2.2.4 Action 14: Dispute Resolution

To fulfil the minimum standard on improving the cross-border disputes resolution mechanism, Hong Kong has proposed to adopt a statutory resolution mechanism, including mutual agreement procedures (MAP) and arbitration, which is reflected in Amendment (No. 6) Ordinance 2018.[55]

Key features of the proposed statutory mechanism include:[56]

i) a taxpayer may present a case for MAP and/or arbitration under the relevant CDTA;

ii) the Commissioner of Inland Revenue may give a notice requiring the taxpayer to provide information regarding the case;

iii) the Commissioner may request the taxpayer to reimburse or pay any costs and reasonable expenses incurred in the course of the MAP and arbitration; and

iv) the Commissioner must give effect to any solution unilaterally arrived at by the Commissioner or agreement reached with the other tax authority concerned in the course of the MAP or arbitration, and any decision delivered by arbitrators in the case of arbitration.

5.2.3 Other BEPS Actions

At the same time as fulfilling the four minimum standards under the BEPS package, the Hong Kong government has responded to the other BEPS Actions.

For Action 1, the IRD indicates that it intends to propose an amendment to the Inland Revenue Ordinance or issue a practice note on the digital economy based on the existing department note on e-commerce,[57] but the specific plan is yet to be announced.[58] As regards Action 2, the government introduced legislation on 26 May 2016 to clarify that regulatory capital securities comprising certain hybrid instruments would be treated as debt.[59] Although the IRD has issued a department note on taxation of financial instruments that deals with tax treatment of hybrid instruments, the relevant note does not deal with double non-taxation on those instruments with a treaty partner. It is proposed that the IRD will enact rules to address hybrid mismatch arrangements, but again the expected time for doing so is not clear.[60] As Hong Kong applies the territorial source principle and dividends are

55 Inland Revenue (Amendment) (No.6) Ordinance 2018, s. 50AAB.

56 Ibid.

57 IRD, DIPN No. 39, "Profits Tax: Treatment of Electronic Commerce" (July 2001), https://www.ird.gov.hk/eng/pdf/e_dipn39.pdf.

58 See discussion on the need for such a review in Taxation Institute of Hong Kong (2016, p. 18). See also Sawyer (2017), citing Deloitte (2016).

59 Inland Revenue (Amendment) (No. 4) Bill 2015, Div. 3, cl. 17B, which is now in force as the Inland Revenue Ordinance, Part 2, Schedule 16.

60 This is however never mentioned in any government publication, press release or speech. But as an international financial centre, Hong Kong may take action to further align with international best practice on the matter.

not subject to tax, the controlled foreign company rules that are commonly applied in a worldwide tax system or jurisdictions taxing dividends do not exist in the tax statutes in Hong Kong. Accordingly, Action 3 has no real relevance to the jurisdiction. Action 4 relates to interest deduction. While Hong Kong does not have the thin capitalisation rules that are adopted in many jurisdictions for the purposes of preventing excessive borrowing deductions, it has in place specific anti-avoidance provisions that limit interest deductions in certain circumstances, in particular those relating to interest paid to non-residents.[61] The IRD might review the interest deduction rules in Hong Kong, but this seems not to be urgent in the jurisdiction.

In relation to Action 7, the standard for determination of permanent establishment (PE) status has been modified in the OECD final reports and also the most updated version of the OECD Model Tax Convention to reflect the changes of the economic environment in an increasingly globalised and digitalised era (OECD 2015b). The legislative measure to follow the modified PE rules has already been put in provisions introduced by Amendment (No. 6) Ordinance 2018, which completely adopt Action 7 on PE thresholds.[62] The IRD also indicates it will issue a department note to provide guidelines on the application of the modified PE rules in Hong Kong.

Actions 8-10 clarify and revise transfer pricing rules to reflect transfer pricing outcomes aligning with value creation. Hong Kong has very recently codified the arm's length principle as noted above, and it has generally followed the OECD TP Guidelines in tax administration and practices. The government has attached significant importance to transfer pricing, and the newly passed Amendment (No. 6) Ordinance 2018 includes formal transfer pricing rules, rules for empowering the IRD to make adjustments in non-arm's length situations, rules for relieving double taxation with a tax treaty partner, penalty provisions, statutory advance pricing agreement (APA) rules, and rules on the three-tiered transfer pricing documentation regime.[63] It is clear that the government intends to have a comprehensive regulatory transfer pricing framework in place since the Amendment Bill for introducing the Ordinance, to the public's surprise, contains 162 pages. It is the largest tax amendment bill in Hong Kong and it introduces a strict approach to determining the arm's length price (PwC, 2018b).

For Action 12 on disclosure of aggressive tax planning, the IRD indicates it will consider the question of how disclosure rules can be developed and transformed into domestic legislation. The relevant legislative or administrative measures are not yet known, however. Finally, Action 15 on the Multilateral Instrument has been effectively translated to Hong Kong. As noted earlier, Hong Kong has signed the MLI and become a party to it by way of the PRC Central Government extension

61 IRD, DIPN No. 13A, "Profits Tax: Deductibility of Interest Expense" (December 2004), https://www.ird.gov.hk/eng/pdf/e_dipn13a.pdf.

62 Inland Revenue (Amendment) (No.6) Ordinance 2018, s.50AAK.

63 Inland Revenue (Amendment) (No.6) Ordinance 2018, ss 50AAC-AAW, 58B-58O.

and declaration. It has also provided a list of reservations and notifications to be made for its existing CDTAs at the time of signing the MLI on 7 June 2017.[64]

5.2.4 Unilateral Measures

Hong Kong has been active in enhancing tax transparency. It is viewed by the OECD Global Forum as largely compliant with international standards on information exchange (OECD, 2016, p. 16; OECD, 2013). The government has enacted tax provisions to align with the international standard on automatic exchange of financial account information in tax matters.[65] The relevant legislation has come into effect from 30 June 2016 and the first exchanges will start by the end of 2018.

All financial institutions in Hong Kong are required to identify financial accounts held by tax residents of reportable jurisdictions or by passive non-financial entities whose controlling persons are tax residents of reportable jurisdictions in accordance with due diligence procedures. Required information of these accounts must be collected and furnished to the IRD, and such information will be exchanged on an annual basis.[66]

Currently, Hong Kong has concluded 40 CDTAs and seven Tax Information Exchange Agreements (TIEAs), which provide a necessary legal basis for the government to exchange information for determining and addressing harmful tax practices.[67] Most significantly, the translation of the Multilateral Convention in Hong Kong will help further the exchange of information in an efficient way.[68]

For the APA regime related to transfer pricing, Amendment (No. 6) Ordinance has responded to the taxpayers' demand to extend the scope to unilateral APAs. As such, taxpayers are able to apply for both unilateral, bilateral and multilateral APAs in Hong Kong. This is helpful as the demand for APAs is likely to increase with the translation of BEPS action plans and the introduction of new transfer pricing rules to Hong Kong.

5.3 Tax Administration for the BEPS Project

In introducing the statutory transfer pricing regime, the government has proposed provisions on administrative penalties, which will be in the form of additional tax

64 See State Administration of Taxation, PRC, "Hong Kong SAR of the PRC (Submitted by the People's Republic of China) - Status of List of Reservations and Notifications at the Time of Signature", above n. 15.

65 Inland Revenue (Amendment) (No. 3) Ordinance 2016.

66 IRD, "Automatic Exchange of Financial Account Information", https://www.ird.gov.hk/eng/tax/dta_aeoi.htm (accessed on 7 June 2018).

67 IRD, "Comprehensive Double Taxation Agreements concluded", above n. 39; IRD, "Tax Information Exchange Agreements concluded", https://www.ird.gov.hk/eng/tax/dta_tiea_agreement.htm.

68 Inland Revenue (Amendment) Ordinance 2018, effective on 1 January 2019. See also n. 22.

not exceeding the amount of tax undercharged for any non-compliance.[69] The penalty is set at a level lower than the current penalty on other types of tax non-compliance.[70] It is thought that such measure will demonstrate Hong Kong's commitment to combating cross-border tax avoidance and countering harmful tax practice on one hand, and attempt to alleviate compliance burdens on both taxpayers and tax administration on the other (Ernst and Young, 2018; KPMG, 2017).

Another impact brought about by the BEPS project on tax administration is the enhancement of the foreign tax credit (FTC) system. The introduction of statutory transfer pricing rules and the further expansion of the tax treaty network in Hong Kong is likely to entail more claims for double taxation relief. In view of such increase, the government has proposed to improve the existing FTC system.[71] First, the period for claiming tax credits will be extended from two years to six years,[72] which is the same as the time limit for correction of assessment due to error or omission,[73] and which will help accommodate the needs for double taxation relief arising from transfer pricing adjustments. Second, the conditions for granting tax credits will be strengthened. A taxpayer will be required to take all necessary steps to minimise the amount of foreign taxes before claiming a tax credit.[74] It is also mandatory that taxpayers notify the IRD of any adjustment to their foreign tax payments that would result in excessive credits.[75]

The revamping of the tax legislative framework to implement the BEPS package is accompanied by the updating of the department notes by the IRD. Such notes have provided practical guidelines for the implementation of the new and revised tax rules in line with international taxation requirements. One of the latest updates is related to the concessionary tax regime for aircraft leasing as a response to implementing Action 5 on combating harmful tax practices.[76] The half-tax rate treatment provided for offshore aircraft leasing activities has been extended to onshore aircraft leasing activities so as to remove the ring-fencing feature in the previous regime (Wong and Kun, 2017, pp. 46-47). To help taxpayers follow the new tax rules, the IRD issued department note DIPN No. 54 in 2017. The note elucidates a number of important issues, such as the requirement that a corporation must have its central management and control (CMC) in Hong Kong in order to be eligible for the half-tax rate concession. The note explains the factors that will be considered by the IRD in determining whether the corporation's CMC is in Hong

69 Inland Revenue (Amendment) (No. 6) Ordinance 2018, s. 80.

70 Inland Revenue Ordinance, s. 82A.

71 Inland Revenue (Amendment) (No. 6) Ordinance 2018, ss 50AAL-50AAO. See also Legislative Council, Hong Kong SAR, Legislative Council Brief - Inland Revenue (Amendment) (No. 6) Bill 2017, above n. 44, pp. 6-7. This latter publication explains the purpose of revising the FTC system.

72 Inland Revenue (Amendment) (No. 6) Ordinance 2018, s. 50AAM.

73 Inland Revenue Ordinance, s. 70A.

74 Inland Revenue (Amendment) (No. 6) Ordinance 2018, s. 50AA.

75 Inland Revenue (Amendment) (No. 6) Ordinance 2018, s. 50AA.

76 IRD, DIPN No. 54, "Taxation of Aircraft Leasing Activities", above n. 43.

Kong.[77] The approach to using department notes to assist taxpayers understanding and applying tax provisions is a good way to enhance legal clarity and certainty as well as to encourage tax compliance.

5.4 Concluding Remarks: The Future of Tax Reform in Hong Kong

Hong Kong has been widely regarded as an international financial centre, and its tax system is known as simple, efficient and predictable. Notably, the territorial source principle and the low tax policy that have been applied for over half a century make the city an attractive place for international trade and investment. The reshuffle of the international tax standards and rules by the OECD and the BEPS project has significantly impacted Hong Kong's tax system. The government has taken concrete measures to meet new international requirements and it endeavours to be a cooperative member of the international tax community, which is necessary and helpful to keep its competitiveness in the global economy. However, to further Hong Kong's competitive edge, the government will need to make more efforts, particularly in view of the effects of a new round of tax reforms in major economies and the international trend of reducing corporate tax rates. The introduction of certain tax rate reductions and additional incentives for research and development by the government most recently is a good start to keep Hong Kong competitive in the world (Siu and Yeung, 2017).

References

Chen, Albert H. Y. (2004), "The Constitutional Controversy of Spring 2004", 34(2) *Hong Kong Law Journal* 215-226.

Deloitte (2016), "BEPS Actions Implementation by Country: Hong Kong", September; version as at July 2017, https://www2.deloitte.com/content/dam/Deloitte/global/Documents/Tax/dttl-tax-beps-actions-implementation-hong-kong.pdf (accessed on 6 June 2018).

Ernst and Young (EY) (2018), "Hong Kong Introduces Tax and Transfer Pricing Legislation to Counter Base Erosion and Profit Shifting", Tax Alert, 2 January, http://www.ey.com/Publication/vwLUAssets/ey-international-tax-and-tp-tax-alert-2-jan-2018/$FILE/ey-international-tax-and-tp-tax-alert-2-jan-2018.pdf (accessed on 7 June 2018).

Financial Services and the Treasury Bureau and Inland Revenue Department, Hong Kong SAR (2017), "Consultation Report on Measures to Counter Base Erosion and Profit Shifting", July, https://www.fstb.gov.hk/tb/en/docs/BEPS-ConsultationReport-e.pdf.

Gagnon-Bélanger, Rosette (2016), "Current vs. Envisioned Parliamentary System in Hong Kong Special Administrative Region", 39(3) *Canadian Parliamentary Review* 16-21, http://www.revparl.ca/39/3/39n3e_16_GagnonBelanger.pdf.

77 IRD, DIPN No. 54, "Taxation of Aircraft Leasing Activities", above n. 43, paras 61-65.

KPMG (2017), "Hong Kong Introduces BEPS Bill Marking a Significant Step Up In Its Transfer Pricing Enforcement Regime", Hong Kong Tax Alert – Issue 24, 29 December, https://home.kpmg.com/cn/en/home/insights/2017/12/tax-alert-24-hk-hong-kong-introduces-beps-bill.html (accessed on 7 June 2018).

Ng, Tiffany (2016), "Measures to Counter Base Erosion and Profit Shifting", Hong Kong Legislative Council Secretariat, Research Office Information Note IN02/16-17, 30 November, https://www.legco.gov.hk/research-publications/english/1617in02-measures-to-counter-base-erosion-and-profit-shifting-20161130-e.pdf.

Organisation for Economic Co-operation and Development (OECD) and Council of Europe (2011), *The Multilateral Convention on Mutual Administrative Assistance in Tax Matters: Amended by the 2010 Protocol* (Paris: OECD).

Organisation for Economic Co-operation and Development (OECD) (2013), *Global Forum on Transparency and Exchange of Information for Tax Purposes Peer Reviews: Hong Kong, China 2013: Phase 2: Implementation of the Standard in Practice* (Paris: OECD).

Organisation for Economic Co-operation and Development (OECD) (2015a), *Action 5 – 2015 Final Report: Countering Harmful Tax Practices More Effectively, Taking into Account Transparency and Substance* (Paris: OECD).

Organisation for Economic Co-operation and Development (OECD) (2015b), *Action 7 – 2015 Final Report: Preventing the Artificial Avoidance of Permanent Establishment Status* (Paris: OECD).

Organisation for Economic Co-operation and Development (OECD) (2016), *Global Forum on Transparency and Exchange of Information for Tax Purposes, Tax Transparency: 2016 Report on Progress* (Paris: OECD).

Organisation for Economic Co-operation and Development (OECD) (2017a), *OECD Transfer Pricing Guidelines for Multinational Enterprises and Tax Administrations 2017*, May (Paris: OECD).

Organisation for Economic Co-operation and Development (OECD) (2017b), *Inclusive Framework on BEPS, Action 5: Harmful Tax Practices - 2017 Progress Report on Preferential Regimes*, OECD/G20 Base Erosion and Profit Shifting Project, October (Paris: OECD), http://www.oecd.org/tax/beps/harmful-tax-practices-2017-progress-report-on-preferential-regimes-9789264283954-en.htm.

Organisation for Economic Co-operation and Development (OECD) (2018), *BEPS Action 13: Guidance on the Implementation of Country-by-Country Reporting*, February (Paris: OECD), http://www.oecd.org/ctp/guidance-on-the-implementation-of-country-by-country-reporting-beps-action-13.pdf.

PricewaterhouseCoopers Hong Kong (PwC) (2018a), "Hong Kong Government Issued the Bill on BEPS Actions", News Flash – Hong Kong Tax, Issue 1, January, https://www.pwchk.com/en/tax/hongkongtax-news-jan2018-1.pdf (accessed on 7 June 2018).

PricewaterhouseCoopers Hong Kong (PwC) (2018b), "Draft Transfer Pricing Legislation Comes to Hong Kong", Tax Insights, 11 January, https://www.pwc.com/gx/en/tax/newsletters/pricing-knowledge-network/assets/pwc-tp-hk-draft-legislation.pdf (accessed on 7 June 2018).

Sawyer, Adrian (2017) "An Update on Hong Kong's Exchange of Information Developments and Engaging with BEPS", 25(2) *Asia Pacific Law Review* 170-189.

Siu, Phila and Raymond Yeung (2017), "Tax Breaks and R&D Touted to Keep Hong Kong Competitive as Carrie Lam Delivers Policy Speech", *South China Morning Post*, 12 October, http://www.scmp.com/news/hong-kong/economy/article/2114944/carrie-lam-says-tax-breaks-profits-and-rd-among-measures-keep (accessed on 7 June 2018).

Taxation Institute of Hong Kong (2016), "2016-2017 Budget Proposals", submission to Financial Secretary, Hong Kong Government, 11 January, http://www.tihk.org.hk/v2/about/budget (accessed on 6 June 2018).

Wong, Katrina and Kathy Kun (2017), "Hong Kong's Proposed Preferential Tax Regime for Offshore Aircraft Leasing Activities Extended to Cover Onshore Market", 13(5) *aplus* (Hong Kong Institute of Certified Public Accountants) 45-47, http://app1.hkicpa.org.hk/APLUS/2017/05/pdf/45_Large_Souce.pdf (accessed on 6 June 2018).

6 The Adoption of BEPS in India

Abdul Muheet Chowdhary*

Abstract

BEPS has been a concern for India long before the OECD began its initiative, specifically in the areas of transfer pricing, permanent establishments, royalty payments, thin capitalisation, treaty abuse and digital services. India accordingly played a leading role in the formulation of the BEPS Action Plan. It was involved from the outset and is strongly committed to its execution. Within a relatively short time span it has made substantial progress in implementation and has initiated both legislative and administrative steps in virtually all the BEPS Actions. The exceptions are Action 14, where it is opposed to mandatory and binding arbitration, and Actions 2, 11 and 12, where policy discussions are still underway. Some of the BEPS project is actually a validation of issues India has raised for a long time, especially in transfer pricing of intangibles. Implementation will continue at a rapid pace, given strong political commitment across the spectrum.

6.1 Introduction

A South Asian nation, India is the world's largest democracy with a population of 1.3 billion (second only to China) and is a constitutional federal republic with the President as head of state and Prime Minister as head of government. The system is replicated at the state/provincial level with the Governor as the nominal head and the Chief Minister as the head of government in practice. The third tier of government consists of urban local bodies such as municipalities and rural local bodies known as *panchayats*. India is the world's seventh largest economy with a nominal GDP of USD 2.2 trillion and is the fastest growing major economy with a growth rate of 6.75 per cent for 2017-18 and an estimated growth rate of 7-7.5 per cent for 2018-19. India is a primarily agrarian economy with around 50 per cent of its population engaged in this sector. However services are the main contributor to GDP and have a share of 55.2 per cent in Gross Value Added (GVA) with the key

* Consultant, Policy Planning and Research Division, Ministry of External Affairs, Government of India. The credit for this chapter goes overwhelmingly to Rahul Navin, Additional Director General (Vigilance), Central Board of Direct Taxes, Government of India. The views expressed in this chapter are personal views only.

services being finance, retail, communications and information technology. India is a developing country and is a net capital importer. It is a member of the G20 but not the Organisation for Economic Co-operation and Development (OECD), though it participated in the Base Erosion and Profit Shifting (BEPS) project on an equal footing.

Tax powers are distributed between the Union (centre), states and local governments. The details for the Union and states are contained in Part XII of the Constitution (articles 264-300A) while for rural and urban local governments they are contained in articles 243H and 243X respectively. Article 265 states that any tax introduced needs to be backed by an accompanying law, passed either by Parliament or the state legislature.

The Union exclusively collects income tax under the provisions of the *Income-tax Act, 1961* (Income-tax Act) and redistributes the revenue to the states based on the recommendations of a technocratic constitutional body known as the Finance Commission. In this sense India is a centre-heavy federation with a strong redistributive structure. Under the Income-tax Act, every person is required to pay income tax if their income exceeds the threshold and only real income is taxable. The taxes are collected by the Central Board of Direct Taxes (CBDT) which is responsible for policy formulation and administers the direct tax laws through the Income Tax Department. The CBDT is a statutory authority established under the *Central Board of Revenue Act, 1963*. International tax matters are handled at the policy level by the Foreign Tax and Tax Research (FT&TR) Division of the Income Tax Department. The administration of international tax and transfer pricing is done by specialised directorates. On the indirect tax front, a major reform was undertaken in the year 2016 with the introduction of a Goods and Services Tax (GST) which subsumed several existing indirect taxes.

India is unique in that around 94 per cent of the population does not pay income tax, leading the Finance Minister to wryly remark that it is a "tax non-compliant society" (Jaitley, 2017, para. 141). As of FY 2016-17 the effective taxpayer base is 82.7 million (Jaitley, 2018, para. 145). Of these, the majority are salaried professionals. Agricultural income has always been tax exempt owing to the low income levels of the average farmer and so about half the population is automatically out of the direct tax net.

6.2 India's Response to the G20/OECD BEPS Tax Reform Program

Base Erosion and Profit Shifting (BEPS) has been a concern for India long before the start of the G20-OECD BEPS project. India has consistently raised BEPS concerns arising out of outdated and problematic international tax rules, specifically on transfer pricing, permanent establishments, royalty payments, thin capitalisation, treaty abuse and digital services.

At the domestic level, the Indian government sought to address such concerns unilaterally through innovations in transfer pricing and anti-avoidance rules. To reduce litigation and bring in certainty, India introduced the concept of a "safe harbour" in transfer pricing, which is defined as circumstances in which the tax authorities shall accept the transfer price declared by the taxpayer. To curtail tax dodging, it introduced General Anti-Avoidance Rule (GAAR) provisions in 2012, which will be used where the main purpose of an arrangement is to obtain a tax benefit.

At the multilateral level, India played a leading role in international forums to address BEPS issues not just on its own account but also for other developing countries, notably through the United Nations (UN) in its Committee of Experts on International Cooperation in Tax Matters as well as its earlier avatar, the Group of Experts. The essential issue was the allocation of tax rights, and India was critical of the OECD's Model Tax Convention on Income and Capital and the OECD Transfer Pricing Guidelines, both of which were devised solely by OECD members to protect their interests and accordingly did not recognise the right of taxation of source countries in many cases.[1]

India also soundly rejected attempts by the OECD to promote its standards - which were devised by 34 countries - as "universal". It was consistently pointed out that genuinely international standards can only be prepared with the participation of all countries. To this end India had also called for the establishment of an intergovernmental tax commission at the UN, which would have balanced representation from both developed and developing countries.[2]

Thus when the G20-OECD BEPS project was initiated, it was a validation by the OECD of issues that India had raised for a very long time. India actively participated but insisted, along with other non-OECD G20 countries, that the recommendations should be developed through a global consensus and not by the OECD countries only. After detailed negotiations, the OECD modified its rules for associating non-OECD G20 countries on an equal footing and a formal letter requesting such countries to become an Associate was issued, which meant that they could participate on an equal footing with OECD countries, including participation in its Bureau in the Committee overseeing the project in the discussions and in the decision-making process (Ministry of Finance, 2017, p. 194). Indian delegates participated in the meetings of the Focus Group, Working Parties and Committee on Fiscal Affairs (CFA) Bureau Plus on an equal footing in finalising BEPS deliverables with the objectives of: (a) collaborating with other countries in development of recommendations, and (b) safeguarding the interests of developing countries in the

1 See letter from Sanjay Kumar Mishra (Joint Secretary (FT&TR-I), Central Board of Direct Taxes, Government of India) to Alexander Trepelkov (Director, Financing for Development Office, United Nations Department of Economic and Social Affairs) dated 12 March 2012, www.un.org/esa/ffd/tax/2012ICTM/LetterIndia.pdf (accessed on 12 June 2018).

2 Ibid.

formulation of new standards (Ministry of Finance, 2017). Today, the BEPS project has support across the political spectrum and there is commitment at the highest levels for its implementation.

6.3 India and the BEPS Inclusive Framework

India is a member in the Steering Group of the BEPS Inclusive Framework and is collaborating with the G20, developing countries and international organisations to ensure that there is a level playing field amongst various economies. It has started complying with all four minimum standards in different degrees.

6.3.1 Action 5: Harmful Tax Practices

The BEPS recommendation is that: i) substantial activity be required for preferential regimes, and ii) transparency be improved by compulsory spontaneous exchange of rulings. The Forum on Harmful Tax Practices (FHTP) has been reviewing royalty regimes to assess whether they are harmful. India's new patent regime was introduced through section 115BBF of the Income-tax Act to incentivise companies to carry out research and development activities in the country itself. As per this section, any income by way of royalty in respect of a patent developed and registered in India shall be taxable at the rate of 10 per cent (plus applicable surcharge and cess) on the gross amount of royalty. This was subjected to peer review in the Forum on Harmful Tax Practices (FHTP) in 2016 after which it was concluded that it was not harmful.

India has also started complying with spontaneous exchange of information on tax rulings and has put in place a system to facilitate this. India is a party to the Convention on Mutual Administrative Assistance in Tax Matters, has double tax avoidance agreements (DTAAs) and Tax Information Exchange Agreements with 94 jurisdictions and is a signatory to the South Asian Association for Regional Cooperation (SAARC) Agreement. This network of agreements covers 141 jurisdictions in total.

The Income Tax Department issues the following rulings: a) cross-border unilateral advance pricing agreements (APAs), issued by the CBDT, and b) permanent establishment (PE) rulings, issued by the Authority on Advanced Rulings (AAR). APA rulings are not published while PE rulings are published. All APAs entered into up to 31 March 2016 are defined as "past rulings". For future PE rulings, once they are issued by the Delhi office of the AAR, they are sent to the CBDT's centralised office as well as its field offices. A departmental representative of the CBDT is posted in the AAR and checks the rulings to determine if they are PE rulings. The CBDT identifies potential exchange jurisdictions from information available in the ruling, which would include the information on the residence of the head office, or of the PE. In the case of future APA rulings, they are identified by two designated offices from a centralised database which is updated whenever a unilateral APA is signed.

India issued 69 past rulings and for the period 1 April 2016 -1 February 2017 issued 126 future rulings (OECD, 2017, p. 139). For both PE rulings and APAs, information on the immediate parent and ultimate parent company was not included in the application for the ruling. It has been highlighted by India that these terms are not defined in the Action 5 report and it proposed a plan to amend the process for issuing future rulings to require this information, using definitions that are consistent with accounting or legal provisions in India's domestic laws. The OECD has given the go-ahead for using this method for both past and future rulings.

The OECD through its 2018 peer review has recommended that India improve execution efforts, specifically in submitting information to the competent authority (CBDT) and exchanging information on past rulings. Compliance is underway on these recommendations.

6.3.2 Action 6: Treaty Abuse

The BEPS recommendation is that: i) limitation of benefits (LOB) and principal purposes test (PPT) rules be inserted into the OECD Model Convention, and ii) tax treaties should clearly state that their objectives include avoiding non-taxation or reduced taxation, including through treaty shopping arrangements. Certain offshore jurisdictions are major conduits for round tripping funds into India in the form of foreign direct investment (FDI). After a change of government in 2014, India has begun renegotiating treaties with certain jurisdictions seen as tax havens to close these loopholes. It has modified its DTAAs with Mauritius, Cyprus and Singapore to provide for source taxation of capital gains and introduced stringent LOB clauses. Further, India has complied with these by ratifying the Multilateral Instrument (MLI) in June 2017 and this will automatically update its LOB and PPT clauses with other ratifying countries.

Another instrument to tackle treaty abuse is the General Anti-Avoidance Regime (GAAR). These provisions are contained in Chapter X-A of the Income-tax Act and further details on the conditions under which they will apply are in Rules 10U to 10UC of the Income-tax Rules, 1962. These are used when the main purpose of an arrangement is to obtain a tax benefit. Any of the following four tests may be used to determine this: i) arm's length test; ii) misuse or abuse test; iii) commercial substance test, and iv) *bona fide* purpose test. Tax auditors are required to report any avoidance arrangements. An Approving Panel determines whether it is an impermissible avoidance arrangement and the directions it issues are binding on the assessee as well as the income-tax authorities. If it is determined as impermissible, then the transaction may be either disregarded or re-characterised or its value re-determined.

The same income can be taxed twice in the hands of different tax payers and no relief is available for adjustments made in the hands of one taxpayer to another.The GAAR does not apply to non-resident financial institution investors (FIIs) and to such FIIs that choose not to take any benefit under an agreement under section 90 or section 90A of the Income-tax Act. It also does not apply to arrangements where the tax benefit is less than INR 30 million. The GAAR is applicable from FY 2017-18 (AY 2018-19) onwards.

6.3.3 Action 13: Country-by-Country Reporting

India signed the Multilateral Competent Authority Agreement on the Exchange of Country-by-Country Reports (CbCR) in May 2016. A solid legislative framework is in place to facilitate this. The essential elements of the CbCR regime have been included in the Income-tax Act by amending sections 92D, 271AA and 273B and inserting new sections 271GB and 286. The remaining aspects have been prescribed through rules. Section 286 provides for the furnishing of a CbCR of an international group by its constituent or parent entity which has total consolidated group revenue exceeding INR 55 billion. Section 92D provides for the keeping and maintaining of the Master File by every constituent entity of an international group which has a consolidated revenue exceeding INR 5 billion and either aggregate value of international transactions as per the books of accounts exceeding INR 500 million or aggregate value of international transactions in respect of intangible property exceeding INR 10 million. The submission details for the CbCR and Master File are contained in Form 3CEAD and Form 3CEAA, respectively. An international group having multiple Indian constituent entities can designate one constituent entity to file the Master File. The first round of CbCR will have had to be filed by 31 March 2018.

The reporting requirements for the Master File are largely in line with the OECD template, with the following additional requirements (PwC, 2017): i) list and address of all entities of the international group (instead of solely "operating entities"); ii) descriptions of the functions performed, assets employed, risks assumed by constituent entities of the international group that contribute to at least 10 per cent of revenues or assets or profits on an individual basis, and iii) list and address of all entities engaged in the development and management of intangibles.

Stakeholders have expressed concerns regarding data security, confidentiality and usage details. Discussions are ongoing to assuage these concerns.

6.3.4 Action 14: Mutual Agreement Procedure

The Mutual Agreement Procedure (MAP) is a dispute resolution mechanism contained in article 25 of the OECD Model Tax Convention which has been turned into one of the four minimum standards. Action 14 recommends that disputes be addressed through the MAP. India's DTAAs contain a MAP article which is used to resolve double taxation disputes. The MAP can also be entered into under Section 90 or 90A of the Income-tax Act. Bilateral meetings for resolving tax disputes under the MAP take place regularly with countries such as US, UK, Japan, etc. and it is seen as a useful instrument in resolving longstanding and complex issues of double taxation.

Certain developed countries such as the US, UK, Switzerland, etc. have made a unilateral commitment to provide for mandatory binding MAP arbitration in their bilateral tax treaties as a mechanism to guarantee that "treaty-related disputes will be resolved within a specified timeframe". However India does not hold this view and is firmly opposed to mandatory and binding arbitration. This is seen as impinging on the sovereign rights of developing countries and limiting their ability to apply their domestic laws for taxing non-residents and foreign countries. India also opposed the proposal to make arbitration binding even if one party disagrees, which is different from MAP as currently followed, where both sides need to agree.

6.4 India and the Other BEPS Actions

6.4.1 Action 1: Digital Economy

The Action 1 report outlines an "equalisation levy" as one of three options that countries can introduce in their domestic laws or bilateral treaties as a BEPS safeguard. India introduced an equalisation levy at a rate of 6 per cent on online advertisements and this has come into effect from June 2016. A Chapter titled "Equalisation Levy" was inserted in the *Finance Act 2016*, comprising sections 163-180. The levy was chosen as it would be a tax on payment for digital transactions, not income, and would hence not require any change in existing DTAAs. The levy is applicable only on payments made for business or profession purposes exceeding INR 100,000 made by a person resident in India or a permanent establishment of a non-resident person to a non-resident enterprise. Income arising from payments subjected to the levy will be exempted from income-tax. To encourage compliance, there is the caveat that if the levy is not paid, the income tax exemption will no longer apply.

6.4.2 Action 3: Controlled Foreign Companies

The Direct Taxes Code is a draft Indian law that seeks to modernise and replace the Income-tax Act. Controlled Foreign Corporation (CFC) provisions were envisaged under this law and may yet be a part of the final Bill when it is introduced in Parliament. However as yet there are no statutes on CFCs. Indian authorities are still studying the matter and seek to avoid drastic policy changes which would impact Indian companies and outbound investment. It must be noted that though India has Place of Effective Management (POEM) rules, these are not the same concept as CFC rules.

6.4.3 Action 4: Interest Deductions and Other Financial Payments

Action 4 recommends that countries introduce a fixed ratio rule which limits an entity's net deductions for interest and payments economically equivalent to interest to a percentage of its earnings before interest, taxes, depreciation and amortisation (EBITDA). Prior to the BEPS project, India did not have thin capitalisation rules. During litigation, the courts tended to side with the defendants and in *DIT v.*

Besix Kier Dabhol SA [2012] 210 Taxmann 151 the Bombay High Court held that "tax authorities cannot disregard the interest payments as tax deductibles".

This loophole has now been closed. A new section 94B "Limitation on interest deduction in certain cases" has been introduced in Chapter X of the Income-tax Act in 2017. It states that interest expenses claimed by an entity to its associated enterprises shall be restricted to 30 per cent of EBITDA which is deductible in computing income chargeable under the head "Profits and gains of business or profession" or interest paid or payable to an associated enterprise, whichever is less. The provision is applicable to an Indian company, or a permanent establishment of a foreign company which pays interest to a non-resident or to a permanent establishment of a non-resident and which is an "associated enterprise" of the borrower.

The debt shall be deemed to be treated as issued by an associated enterprise where it provides an implicit or explicit guarantee to the lender or deposits a corresponding and matching amount of funds with the lender. The disallowance of excess interest will be made even if the borrowing is for the purpose of business and the rate of interest is at arm's length. The provision will apply only for interest expense deductions exceeding INR 10 million, is not applicable to banks and insurance businesses and will be in force from AY 2018-19 onwards.

6.4.4 Action 7: Permanent Establishment Status

The Action 7 recommendations on changes to Article 5 of the OECD Model Convention (which is on permanent establishments) are incorporated into the MLI, which India has ratified. As a result these changes have been incorporated into India's bilateral treaties with other countries that have also ratified the MLI and accordingly India is essentially implementing this action through the MLI. Section 90(2) of India's Income-tax Act states that provisions of domestic law would prevail over corresponding provisions in the DTAAs, to the extent they are beneficial.

Accordingly, the definition of "business connection" in section 9 of the Income-tax Act has been amended such that it now includes "any business activity carried out through a person who, acting on behalf of the non-resident has and habitually exercises in India, an authority to conclude contracts on behalf of the non-resident or habitually concludes contracts or habitually plays the principal role leading to conclusion of contracts".

In the same section, the definition of "significant economic presence" has been expanded to mean:

a) transaction in respect of any goods, services or property carried out by a non-resident in India including provision of download of data or software in India, if the aggregate of payments arising from such transaction or transactions during the previous year exceeds such amount as may be prescribed; or

b) systematic and continuous soliciting of business activities or engaging in interaction with such number of users as may be prescribed, in India through digital means.

These amendments will take effect from 1 April 2019.

6.4.5 Actions 8-10: Transfer Pricing

The BEPS recommendations on transfer pricing are actually acknowledgements of issues raised by India for a long time. Indian authorities have been consistently arguing that mere legal ownership of an intangible (such as IP) is not enough to allocate the entire residual income to that entity and the tax must be levied where actual value creation takes place (Ranjan, 2015, p. 17). The BEPS reports reassert this. Accordingly, there has been no need for any major changes in Indian domestic law and it is in fact the OECD that has corrected itself and brought itself around to the Indian position. One update is that a new section 92CE has been introduced into the Income-tax Act to provide that the assessee shall be required to carry out secondary adjustment where the primary adjustment to transfer price has been made in certain situations which are detailed in the Income-tax Act (KPMG, 2017).

6.4.6 Actions 2, 11 and 12

No formal statutes have been enacted yet, but the Ministry of Finance in collaboration with other organisations in the government of India is working on these aspects of the BEPS project. Action 12 holds particular interest as that will force consultants to disclose their tax "planning" strategies.

6.4.7 Action 15: Multilateral Instrument

India was part of the Ad Hoc Group of countries that worked on finalising the text of the MLI and was part of the first set of 76 countries that signed it on 7 June 2017. India has listed all its comprehensive bilateral tax treaties as Covered Tax Agreements (CTAs). The MLI will modify India's treaties with key countries such as Canada, Cyprus, France, Japan, Luxembourg, the Netherlands, Singapore, and the UK. However certain countries such as China, Germany and Mauritius have not notified their treaties with India as CTAs, meaning that India will have to renegotiate treaties with them bilaterally, delaying BEPS implementation (Jhaveri, 2018). Further, India has taken up both the principal purpose test (PPT) and limitation of benefits (LoB) provisions and has opted for an agency PE article but many of its treaty partners have not done so, implying further tax treaty renegotiation if these have to be incorporated.

6.5 India's Unilateral Adoption of Particular BEPS Measures

India's GAAR provisions have already been discussed in section 6.3.2 above. Certain other measures are as follows.

6.5.1 Place of Effective Management (POEM) Rules

POEM has been defined in the Income-tax Act as a place where key management and commercial decisions that are necessary for the conduct of the business of an entity as a whole are, in substance, made. Most of India's tax treaties recognise POEM for determining company residence as a tie breaker rule for avoidance of double taxation. POEM is to be determined on a year to year basis and the process will be primarily based on whether or not the company is engaged in active business outside India. The details are contained in section 6(3) of the Income-tax Act.

6.5.2 Black Money Act

Parliament passed the *Black Money (Undisclosed Foreign Income and Assets) and Imposition of Tax Act* in 2015. The Act replaced the Income-tax Act for taxation of foreign income. In summary, "[i]t penalises the concealment of foreign income, and provides for criminal liability for attempting to evade tax in relation to foreign income".[3]

Separately, the income tax return form now contains a "Schedule FA" where tax payers must report their foreign assets. This was introduced in FY 2011-12.

6.5.3 Taxation Laws Act

The Taxation Laws (Second Amendment) Act was enacted in 2016 which enabled levy of tax at a higher rate on the undisclosed income under which a person could declare undisclosed cash by paying tax, surcharge and penalty totalling to 50 per cent of the undisclosed income. Further, 25 per cent of the undisclosed income must be kept for four years interest free in the "प्रधान मंत्री गरीब कल्याण" (Prime Minister's Welfare of the Poor) Deposit Scheme.

6.5.4 PMLA

In 2015, the *Prevention of Money Laundering Act, 2002* was amended so that in case of proceeds of crime being taken out of the country, property equivalent in value within the country could be confiscated.

6.5.5 Economic Offenders Bill

Parliament passed the Fugitive Economic Offenders Act, 2018. This was introduced after a spate of high profile crimes where businesspersons owing large sums of money to banks ruthlessly fled the country. The Bill seeks to prevent their escape and allows the government to confiscate their properties if they do.

6.5.6 Automatic Exchange of Information (AEOI)

India joined a group of 48 countries as early adopters to new global standards for automatically exchanging information from 2017. It is taking several steps to effec-

3 PRS Legislative Research, http://www.prsindia.org/billtrack/the-undisclosed-foreign-income-and-assets-imposition-of-tax-bill-2015-3697/ (accessed on 12 June 2018).

tively engage with problematic jurisdictions such as Switzerland, British Virgin Islands, Jersey and Liechtenstein. It is also actively participating in the development of a Common Transmission System under the aegis of the Forum on Tax Administration (FTA). This will create an architecture for secure and rapid AEOI. Similarly, India is participating in the Joint International Taskforce on Shared Intelligence and Collaboration (JITSIC) that enables coordinated action among member states to jointly tackle tax evasion and avoidance. This too is under the FTA.

Additionally, black money or undisclosed income is a major political issue in India. A Special Investigative Team on Black Money was constituted in May 2014 under the leadership of two former Judges of the Supreme Court. It has been tasked with finding ways and means of recovering Indian revenue that has been illegally hidden abroad. Its work is ongoing and it periodically submits reports to the Supreme Court.

6.6 Tax Administration in Relation to International Tax Reform in India

A Multi Agency Group has been created consisting of officers from the CBDT, Reserve Bank of India, Enforcement Directorate and Financial Intelligence Unit for coordinated and effective investigation in the "Panama Papers" and "Paradise Papers" cases. A task force on shell companies has been constituted under the joint leadership of the Revenue Secretary and Secretary, Ministry of Corporate Affairs in February 2017.

The CBDT issued a Central Action Plan in June 2016 which, read together with the Manual on Exchange of Information, explains the process and need to make exchange of information references when seeking information under tax treaties. The Plan also mandates that every Commissioner of Income Tax will organise training and sensitisation programs for making proper references under tax treaties. Training programs are also in place to ensure that information received from treaty partners is used effectively to counter tax avoidance. Efforts are in progress on strengthening the directorates of international taxation, transfer pricing and advanced pricing agreements by providing them with more staff and resources.

India also provides training to other countries. Talks with the Commonwealth Association of Tax Administrators (CATA) are at an advanced stage to conduct capacity building programs for the member countries of the region at the National Academy of Direct Taxes.

6.7 The Future of International Tax Reform for India

The next steps on the BEPS agenda for India are bringing in rules on CFCs, hybrid instruments, firming up a framework for BEPS-related data collection and making companies and tax consultants disclose their tax "planning" strategies. India will continue to give high priority to taxing the digital economy. New challenges are being thrown up by innovations such as Software as a Service (SaaS). Accordingly, the concepts of business connection and PE will need to be redefined and India is likely to press for these changes. The equalisation levy is only a temporary measure and efforts will be continuing to find a more holistic solution.

India will continue to crack down on tax havens and amend its treaties either bilaterally or through the MLI. To prevent illicit financial outflows, it will support the strengthening of the AEOI mechanism and implementation of Common Reporting Standards on a fully reciprocal global basis.

India will continue to advocate its interests and the interests of fellow developing countries at the forefront of other multilateral forums such as the G20, BRICS and CIAT. Having suffered the ravages of colonialism and imperialism, India sees itself as having a historical responsibility towards deepening North-South cooperation and framing a more just international economic order. Black money and international tax evasion are major political issues in India and there is strong commitment from the Indian polity towards addressing them both domestically and internationally through multilateral cooperation.

India will continue to support the UN in having a larger say in international tax matters, including supporting the creation of a UN intergovernmental tax commission. India is so far the only country in the world which has contributed money to the Trust Fund of the UN Committee of Experts on International Cooperation in Tax Matters.[4] That it does so despite its poverty and massive domestic challenges is a testament to its commitment to multilateralism and a more equitable international tax system. It will continue to engage with the OECD but this will be more out of necessity than choice. India has consistently maintained that the 36 countries of the OECD cannot claim monopoly over the realm of international taxation. It has accordingly played a leading role in the G77's efforts for the creation of a UN intergovernmental tax commission.

Engagement with Russia, China, Brazil and South Africa through the BRICS format will increase in the field of tax cooperation. It may even take the form of coordinated efforts to assist other developing countries, thus providing them a non-OECD alternative.

---

4 See United Nations, "India contributes US$100,000 for fund to ensure developing countries' role in international cooperation on critical tax matters" (3 July 2018), https://www.un.org/sustainabledevelopment/blog/2018/07/india-contributes-us100000-for-fund-to-ensure-developing-countries-role-in-international-cooperation-on-critical-tax-matters/.

References

Jaitley, Hon. Arun (Minister of Finance) (2017), *Budget 2017-2018: Budget Speech,* 1 February, https://www.indiabudget.gov.in/budget2017-2018/ub2017-18/bs/bs.pdf (accessed on 12 June 2018).

Jaitley, Hon. Arun (Minister of Finance) (2018), *Budget 2018-2019: Budget Speech,* 1 February, https://www.indiabudget.gov.in/ub2018-19/bs/bs.pdf (accessed on 12 June 2018).

Jhaveri, Vipul (2018), "BEPS Adoption Calls for Tax Treaty Renegotiations", *The Hindu, Business Line,* 19 April, https://www.thehindubusinessline.com/opinion/beps-adoption-calls-for-tax-treaty-renegotiations/article23606173.ece (accessed on 12 June 2018).

KPMG (2017), "CBDT notifies rules for the computation mechanism of interest income pursuant to secondary adjustments", *Tax Flash News,* 20 June, a http://www.in.kpmg.com/taxflashnews/KPMG-Flash-News-CBDT-notifies-rules-for-computation-of-interest-income-2.pdf (accessed on 11 July 2018).

Ministry of Finance, Government of India (2017), *Annual Report 2016-17,* https://dea.gov.in/sites/default/files/Annual%20Report-2016-17-E.pdf (accessed on 12 June 2018).

Organisation for Economic Co-operation and Development (OECD) (2017), *Inclusive Framework on BEPS, Action 5: Harmful Tax Practices – Peer Review Reports on the Exchange of Information on Tax Rulings* (Paris: OECD).

PricewaterhouseCoopers (PwC) (2017), "Indian Rules on Master File and Country-by-Country-Reporting Requirements", Tax Insights, 21 December, https://www.pwc.com/gx/en/tax/newsletters/pricing-knowledge-network/assets/pwc-tp-india-cbcr.pdf (accessed on 12 June 2018).

Ranjan, Akhilesh (Joint Secretary – Ministry of Finance) (2015), "In Conversation with Akhilesh Ranjan", *Ernst and Young India Tax Insights,* Issue 6, October, 12-19, http://www.ey.com/Publication/vwLUAssets/ey-india-tax-insights-sixth-edition/$FILE/ey-india-tax-insights-sixth-edition.pdf (accessed on 12 June 2018).

7 The Adoption of BEPS in Indonesia

Arifin Rosid and T. Qivi Hady Daholi*

Abstract

As the global initiatives of the G20/OECD BEPS program, comprising 15 Actions and associated recommendations, are in now place, it is essential to understand how each country, particularly at a domestic level, has responded and implemented this cohesive approach. This chapter aims to provide detailed updates with respect to the implementation of OECD recommendations, including substantive legislative changes, in the Indonesian context. It facilitates a better understanding of how the Indonesian government has adapted its domestic measures to align with international standards and what administrative international tax-related reforms are now in place, as well as the challenges and opportunities now before the Indonesian government.

7.1 Introduction

Indonesia, with its government a presidential system, is currently the world's third largest democratic country. The Indonesian presidential system takes the form of a "unitary republic" which relies on separation of powers into three parts, namely executive, legislative, and judicial stances. Two decades ago in 1998, Indonesia experienced a major political transition from an authoritarian to democratic country. This was followed in 2004 by the first peaceful direct presidential election in which Susilo Bambang Yudhoyono took office for a five-year term. In 2014, the election of President Joko Widodo as the first president outside the military and political establishment has indicated Indonesia's sustainable political stability. Since these developments, Indonesia has exhibited the dynamics of a growing democracy, a lively parliament, and a strong economic resiliency.

The primary source of Indonesian government revenues is taxation. For instance, in 2016, tax revenue contributed 83 per cent of government revenue (Ministry of Finance (MoF), 2018). The Directorate General of Taxation (DGT) is respon-

* Both authors are senior officers at the Directorate General of Taxation, Ministry of Finance of the Republic of Indonesia. This chapter should not be reported as representing the views of the Directorate General of Taxation. The views expressed are those of the authors and do not necessarily reflect the official positions or the policy of the institution where they serve.

sible for achieving this outcome. It is an institution established under the Ministry of Finance - and categorised therefore as a Single Directorate in the Ministry of Finance (SDMOF) by the Organisation for Economic Co-operation and Development (OECD, 2013) - and has three main functions: (i) collecting tax revenue; (ii) formulating tax policy, and (iii) administering tax revenue at the national level. The head office of the DGT is led by a Director General and consists of the Secretariat of the DGT, twelve Directorates, and a Data and Document Processing office. In performing its operations, the DGT is also supported by 31 regional tax offices and 331 tax offices located across the country (DGT, 2016).

In 1983 Indonesia undertook a major reform of its tax system by boldly switching from an official-assessment to a self-assessment system. The latter granted taxpayers both responsibility and trust since the new law accorded them the responsibility to determine, calculate, pay and report their tax obligations to the tax authority independently. For this reason, the 1983 tax reform represented a crucial starting point for a series of further major changes in tax laws.

Indonesia is one of the world's most populous countries, with a population of over 252 million (BPS, 2018). It is the largest archipelago country in the world, stretching across an area between Australia and the Asian continent, and between the Indian and the Pacific Oceans, encompassing more than 17,000 islands (more than 6,000 of which are inhabited).[1] In terms of economic size, Indonesia's Gross Domestic Product (GDP) ranks 15th among 195 countries, with a figure of USD 932 million in 2017, the largest in southeast Asia. Indonesia's GDP per capita was USD 3,570 in 2016 and the country is categorised by the World Bank as a lower-middle income country.[2] It is worth noting that this figure is double that of the comparable figure in 2007 when the GDP per capita in Indonesia was USD 1,765.[3] Indonesia is currently southeast Asia's only member of the G20 but it is not a member of the OECD (OECD, 2016), and it is recognised as one of the six major emerging economies that will account for more than half of all global growth (World Bank, 2011).

Indonesia is currently the 27th largest importer in the world and is also a net capital importer. Its inbound foreign direct investment (FDI) capital is roughly five times as large as its outbound capital (International Monetary Fund, 2017). Indonesia's largest export commodity is palm oil, while its largest import commodity is refined petroleum.

1 See United States-Indonesia Society, http://www.usindo.org/information-on-u-s-and-indonesia/about-indonesia/ (accessed on 5 May 2018).

2 See World Bank, "GDP per capita (current US$)", https://data.worldbank.org/indicator/ny.gdp.pcap.cd (accessed on 9 April 2018).

3 See CountryEconomy.com, "Indonesia GDP – Gross Domestic Product", https://countryeconomy.com/gdp/indonesia (accessed on 1 May 2018).

7.2 The Indonesian Government's Response to the G20/OECD BEPS Program of Tax Reform

Indonesia's initial reaction towards the BEPS project has been proactive. Indonesia, represented by the DGT, has been very active in expressing its interest in implementing many of the BEPS project measures and is now in the process of reviewing and refining some of its relevant domestic legislation. For instance, in the initial stage of the project, Indonesia agreed to facilitate a study conducted by the OECD relating to BEPS and has signed a declaration agreement to support this study (Arifin, 2014). In addition to this supportive role, Indonesia also expressed its interest in becoming an Associate Member of the BEPS project. Administratively, Indonesia's joining of the BEPS project comes with the consequence of a contribution payment of approximately EUR 51,000 annually. Initially, the Indonesian Ministry of Finance did not allocate any such membership payment for year 2013. For this reason, on behalf of the Ministry of Finance, the Fiscal Policy Office officially accepted the OECD invitation for Indonesia to become an Associate Member of the BEPS project in late 2013 by indicating Indonesia's readiness to participate in the project as well as the payment for its membership contribution starting in 2014 (Arifin, 2014). Accordingly, Indonesia is one of the Initial BEPS Associates (Ernst & Young, 2016).

Prior to the G20/OECD initiative, BEPS had long been a concern for the Indonesian government. As an early participant in the Global Forum for Tax Transparency and Exchange of Information, Indonesia took the view that BEPS activities can represent a high risk to state tax revenues, tax sovereignty, and confidence in the integrity of the tax system. It is a well-known notion that many international entities and high wealth individuals generally attempt to minimise their tax obligations by arranging their business activities to obtain tax savings and adopt tax planning schemes that exploit the differences in income treatment and tax rates among countries around the globe. While the detrimental impacts of BEPS activities are generally harmful for both developed and developing countries, the negative consequences on the latter appear to be more severe since developing countries, such as Indonesia, generally rely more heavily on tax revenue to finance their public budget.

As a result of this awareness, several robust anti-avoidance legislative measures are already in place in Indonesian tax laws. These involve five areas. First, the Indonesian Income Tax Law (IITL), as last amended by Law No. 36 of 2008, has an extensive definition of income by adopting a "substance over form" principle.[4] Broadly speaking, this provision establishes basic guidance in determining taxable income and can be used as one of the legal measures to address unacceptable tax avoidance and/or tax evasion.

4 According to Article 4 of IITL, income is defined as "any increase in economics capacity received by or accrued by a taxpayer from Indonesia as well as from offshore, which may be utilized for consumption or increasing the taxpayer's wealth, in whatever name and form, including ...".

Second, the introduction of debt-to-equity regulations has been explicitly provided for in Article 18(1) of the IITL. This principal provision has provided the Minister of Finance an authorisation to issue a regulation on the debt to equity ratio for the purposes of calculating tax payable in accordance with Indonesian tax law. Third, issues relating to controlled foreign companies (CFCs) have also been anticipated in Article 18(2) of the IITL. According to this specific legislation, the Minister of Finance is authorised to determine when a dividend is deemed to be derived by a resident taxpayer from his or her participation in an offshore company other than a public company, where: (i) the taxpayer owns at least 50 per cent of the paid in capital of the company, or (ii) the taxpayer together with one or more other resident taxpayers own at least 50 per cent of the paid in capital of the company.

Fourth, the Indonesian general transfer pricing guidelines are already in place as stipulated in Article 18(3) and (3a)-(3d) of the IITL. These regulations generally require that transactions between related parties should be carried out in a "commercially justifiable way" and on an arm's length basis. Fifth, like many other countries, Indonesia finds it challenging to examine tax liabilities linked to "related party transactions" and has taken several bold steps to join global initiatives aimed at addressing this issue. However, Indonesia appears to adopt a stricter approach in defining a special relationship for the case of "related taxpayers". According to Article 18(4) of the IITL, a so-called "special relationship" exists when: (i) there is capital participation of 25 per cent or more; (ii) there is control through management or technology; and (iii) there is control through close family relationships.[5]

7.3 The Adoption of the BEPS Inclusive Framework in Indonesia

The problem of BEPS has been a longstanding global issue and has affected the international taxation field. It takes place worldwide in a way that has a greater impact on developing countries through this profit shifting behaviour (Crivelli, De Mooij and Keen, 2015; Johannesen, Tørsløv and Wier, 2017). Base erosion and profit shifting has been defined as constituting an international tax planning strategy that exploits loopholes and mismatches in taxation regulations to minimise global tax paid.[6] Therefore, the solution to this issue cannot be merely a domestic approach or uncoordinated strategy (OECD, 2014). It requires comprehensive and collective actions that involve the international community to tackle the BEPS problem.

In responding to the BEPS phenomenon, the OECD has released an Action Plan comprising 15 Actions that can be considered the largest globally-coordinated strategy to combat profit shifting (Marian, 2016). These Actions have then been supported by G20 countries which developed the Inclusive Framework with

5 Similarly, according to the OECD (2012), management, board members, and controlling shareholders are those who can control the terms of a transaction in their favour potentially at the cost of the company.

6 OECD, "Base erosion and profit shifting", http://www.oecd.org/tax/beps/ (accessed on 28 June 2018).

the OECD. This Framework requires its members to implement four minimum standards of the BEPS Actions (Actions 5, 6, 13 and 14), and to be reviewed and monitored regarding their implementation, and also enables them to work with the OECD and G20 members in designing standards on BEPS problems (OECD, 2017a). By March 2018, 113 countries had signed up to the BEPS Inclusive Framework.

Indonesia, as a member of the G20, has shown its strong commitment to applying the OECD BEPS Actions. Indonesia has become a member of the Inclusive Framework and implemented not only the BEPS minimum standards, but also the other detailed Actions. Indonesia has also been reviewed by the OECD regarding implementation of the BEPS minimum standards, and so far, no recommendations have been made in relation to the implementation, apart from Action 14 that will be reviewed by the end of 2018. The details of Indonesia's responses on the OECD Action Plan are set out further below.

7.3.1 Action 5 – Countering Harmful Tax Practices More Effectively

The OECD began to take action to counter harmful tax practices from 1998 through its *Harmful Tax Competition: An Emerging Global Issue* report in that year (noted in OECD, 2017b). Although the report was published 20 years ago, it is still relevant as the basis for the future strategy in combating harmful tax regimes. This report constituted the foundation for the OECD in establishing the Forum on Harmful Tax Practices (FHTP) and its continuing BEPS Action 5. This Action is dedicated to transforming the effort in countering harmful tax practices by enhancing transparency and preventing non-substantial activities in preferential tax regimes.

In Action 5, the scope of the FHTP's work and the criteria of a harmful tax regime have been determined. The FHTP work comprises the activity and the tax treatment for geographically mobile activities, such as financial services, and arrangements involving the use of intangibles (OECD, 2015d). Therefore, one of the FHTP's objectives is requiring substantial activities for intangible property (IP) regimes. The effort in Action 5 introduced the nexus approach in which the existence of research and development (R&D) activities (as reflected in the proportion of R&D expenditure) are required to be associated with tax incentives (OECD, 2015d). Likewise, Action 5 proposes the criteria for the FHTP in reviewing non-IP regimes, such as headquarters regimes, and funds management regimes, in which generally the same principles are applied as for IP regimes. The policy regulated in Action 5 is designed to ensure the alignment between the taxation of profit and the associated value-creation activities (OECD, 2015d).

In response to the needs in this area, Indonesia joined the Inclusive Framework and also the FHTP. Consequently, Indonesia is committed to being reviewed regarding the tax facility regime in its jurisdiction. There are various tax incentives in Indonesia; for instance, a tax facility for industry that is classified as a pioneer industry, a reduced tax rate for publicly listed companies and small-medium taxpayers, and a tax holiday for certain industries. For Action 5 purposes, the tax facilities granted by the Indonesian government were classified into publicly-listed companies, investment allowance, special economic zone, and tax holiday regimes. These regimes were reviewed by the FHTP and the result stated that all of them were outside the scope of the FHTP's work. Therefore, the OECD (2017b) has declared that no harmful tax regimes exist in Indonesia and no recommendation has been made regarding Indonesia's tax regime in relation to BEPS Action 5.

7.3.2 Action 6 – Preventing Treaty Abuse

Combating profit shifting by preventing multinational enterprises (MNEs) from using tax treaties improperly is considered one of the primary missions of the BEPS project (Miller and Oats, 2016). With respect to that objective, the OECD released BEPS Action 6 which identifies various tax treaty abuse activities, such as treaty shopping in which an international operation is deliberately structured in order to obtain advantage from a specific tax treaty (OECD, 2015e; Miller and Oats, 2016). Action 6 was developed as a response to tax planning strategies by providing recommendations concerning tax treaty design, clarifying that tax treaties are not expected to create double non-taxation, and developing local legal frameworks to inhibit the granting of treaty benefits in improper situations (OECD, 2015e). This Action Plan introduced several minimum standards in developing tax treaties and also provides supplementary provisions for the OECD Model Tax Convention (MTC), which are:

1 a clear expression that declares that the states involved in a tax treaty arrangement intend to prevent tax avoidance or evasion activities;

2 a specific anti-avoidance rule, the limitation on benefits clause (LOB), which restricts the treaty benefit to the appropriate person or company only as stipulated in the tax treaty arrangement; and

3 a general anti-avoidance rule, the principal purpose test (PPT), which examines the intention of the person or company who expects to be granted the treaty benefit.

Through this Action Plan, it is expected that the treaty benefit will be granted appropriately and the opportunities to employ treaty shopping or other treaty abuse activities can be reduced.

In response to Action 6, Indonesia has implemented this Action by the enactment of Director General Regulation Number 10/PJ/2017 (PER-10/2017), dated 19 June 2017 regarding the implementation procedure for double tax treaties. These new provisions have adopted the minimum standard in Action 6 and announce the requirements to be fulfilled in order to receive treaty benefit. If the person or company is unable to meet the criteria enacted in PER-10/2017, the treaty benefits will be denied for their case.

This measure regulates the criteria that must be met by a non-resident taxpayer (NRT) to obtain tax treaty benefit. In order to enjoy such benefit, an NRT must submit a Certificate of Domicile (COD) using the standard form in PER-10/2017. The form as stipulated in PER-10/2017 consists of a DGT-2 form which is used by a Banking NRT, pension fund NRT, or NRT who receives or earns income from a custodian, and a DGT-1 form which is used by any NRT who does not use DGT-2. In addition, PER-10/2017 also provides the requirement that should be fulfilled by Individual NRTs and Entity NRTs to be considered as beneficial owners. The beneficial owner shall be the individual or entity that does not act as agent, nominee, or conduit and has capacity to undertake their business activity in Indonesia.

The application of PPT and LOB provisions as indicated in Action 6 of the minimum standard will be implemented in Indonesian tax treaties as Indonesia has signed the Multilateral Instrument (MLI). Likewise, such implementation can be discerned in chapters VI and VII of PER-10/2017. The provisions in those chapters constitute the implementation of Action 6 recommendations, albeit that there is no clear expression of the application of PPT or LOB therein. However, the review has nevertheless been scheduled for the implementation of these rules. Chapter VI regulates the COD form and the requirements that an NRT must meet when using those forms. The COD forms shall state that the NRT has economic motives when incorporating their business in Indonesia, and the business must have economic substance in Indonesia. Furthermore, Chapter VII, titled Treaty Abuse, has stipulated the conditions in which treaty abuse is not considered to occur, which are: (i) there is economic substance in incorporating or conducting transactions; (ii) the legal form is aligned with economic substance; (iii) there is a relevant level of autonomy in performance of business through its own management; (iv) sufficient assets are involved in conducting business activity in Indonesia; (v) there are sufficient employees in terms of number and expertise involved in the conduct of business in Indonesia, and (vi) an active business activity exists other than receiving passive income from Indonesia.

7.3.3 Action 13 – Re-examining Transfer Pricing Documentation

Action 13 introduces provisions for three-tiered standardised transfer pricing documentation, which comprises: (i) the Master File, which contains information about the multinational entity (MNE) as a group; (ii) the Local File, which includes the description of the local entity, and (iii) Country-by-Country Reporting (CbCR), which provides information regarding the financial indicators of the MNE group by tax jurisdiction and lists the MNE's entities as well as its functions in every jurisdiction where the MNE operates (OECD, 2015g). This documentation is required for MNE groups with total consolidated revenue exceeding EUR 750 million.

In this transfer pricing documentation regime, the CbC report is the only document that is included in the BEPS minimum standards. CbC reports will be exchanged among tax authorities that have signed the Multilateral Competent Authority Agreement (MCAA) on the Exchange of CbCR. This agreement specifies the situations and conditions for obtaining and using CbCR. Indonesia signed the MCAA on 26 January 2017, and to April 2018, there have been 52 jurisdictions that have already chosen Indonesia as their country partner for reciprocal exchange of CbCR.

In response to the Inclusive Framework requirement Indonesia had already enacted domestic regulations in implementing Action 13, which are:

1 Minister of Finance Regulation Number 213/PMK.03/2016 (PMK-213/2016), dated 30 December 2016 regarding transfer pricing documentation. This regulation introduces the implementation of three-tiered transfer pricing documentation in Indonesia aligned with OECD Action 13 recommendations; and

2 Director General Regulation Number 29/PJ/2017 (PER-29/2017), dated 29 December 2017 regarding the administration procedures for CbCR. This measure constitutes the detailed regulation for CbCR which defines the entities that are obliged to prepare CbC reports, the requirement for filing CbC reports, and the deadline for filing CbC reports. PER-29/2017 also introduces the obligation to submit notification stating whether such a corporate taxpayer is obliged to submit CbC reports or not. The requirement to submit notification to the DGT is imposed on any constituent entities or members of a business group that conduct an affiliated transaction.

In broad terms, both PMK-213/2016 and PER-29/2017 are aligned with Action 13 recommendations. However, there are several additional measures implemented in adopting this Action due to the specific needs of the Indonesian tax authority. The adjustments are:

1 the obligation to prepare CbC reports is imposed on every Indonesian business group which has total consolidated revenue at least IDR 11 trillion (equal to EUR 750 million), regardless of the existence of any group member abroad. Hence, if the Indonesian business group only operates in Indonesia, it is still required to prepare CbC reports if its consolidated revenue exceeds the CbCR threshold; and

2 the obligation to prepare a CbCR worksheet for an Indonesian Ultimate Parent Entity (UPE) in preparing its CbC reports. The UPE can be considered the entity that controls the other business group members where there is no other entity that will consolidate its financial statements. The CbCR worksheet is required in assisting the Indonesian UPE to prepare its CbC reports and the worksheet must be submitted together with the notification and CbCR submission. Since the worksheet is not part of OECD Action 13 CbCR, it will not be exchanged with other competent tax authorities.

The implementation of Action 13 in Indonesia, particularly for CbCR, has been reviewed by the OECD. The review has led to the acceptance of the domestic law for CbCR in place in Indonesia without any further recommendations by the OECD. Therefore, Indonesia's domestic law has complied with the Action 13 minimum standard.

7.3.4 Action 14 – Making the Dispute Resolution Mechanism More Effective

Actions taken in combating profit shifting will often result in tax disputes between taxpayers and tax authorities. The dispute can relate to double taxation, tax treaty interpretation, or transfer pricing adjustment. Generally, the procedure to resolve such a dispute has been enacted in Article 25 of the OECD Model Tax Convention through the Mutual Agreement Procedure (MAP) (OECD, 2015h). However, specific action is inevitably needed to provide recommendations for resolving tax disputes effectively, efficiently, and in a timely manner as well as to strengthen the procedure stipulated in Article 25. In this way, certainty and predictability for taxpayers when a tax dispute arises can be ensured (OECD, 2015h).

Action 14 contains the objectives, minimum standard, best practices, and monitoring process for dispute resolution. There are three main objectives for the implementation of Action 14, which are: (i) ensuring that the MAP procedure is employed in good faith and in a timely manner; (ii) ensuring an administrative process for averting treaty disputes and resolving disputes expeditiously, and (iii) ensuring rightful taxpayers are able to lodge a MAP request.

Each of these objectives has been elaborated into minimum standards. Similarly, Action 14 provides the best practices for the minimum standards which could be applied by any countries joining this project. Since Action 14 was included in the BEPS minimum standards, the project has also defined the framework for the Action 14 monitoring process.

As at mid-May 2018, Indonesia has not yet enacted any specific measures in response to Action 14. However, Indonesia has already included Article 25 in almost all its tax treaties. Of 67 tax treaties with other countries, only one treaty does not include Article 25, the treaty with Saudi Arabia (Mulyani, 2016). Furthermore, Indonesia has already put international taxation dispute mechanisms in place for resolving disputes through the MAP, and preventing disputes through Advance Pricing Agreements (APAs). These procedures were enacted separately in Minister of Finance Regulation Number 240/PMK.03/2014 (PMK-240/2014) which regulates the procedure for MAP, and Minister of Finance Number 7/PMK.03/2015 (PMK-7/2015) regarding the procedure for APAs. Even though these regulations were released before the publication of Action 14, generally the content of these measures is directed to Action 14's recommendations. Recently, the Indonesian tax authority has been developing new regulations in response to the minimum standard in Action 14.

Regulation PMK-240/2014 specifies the taxpayers who can raise MAP requests, namely Indonesian taxpayers, through the Directorate General of Taxation, and taxpayers in partner countries through the tax authority in the treaty partner country. The MAP will cover double taxation issues due to transfer pricing adjustments, dual residence issues, and disputes in tax treaty application. When the dispute arises, the taxpayer can make a request for the MAP as well as an objection and appeal request to the DGT. However, if the dispute is raised before the tax court and the court has already issued its decision, the taxpayer cannot lodge an MAP request, or in the case of an ongoing MAP request, the process will be stopped. Taxpayers can apply for the MAP in accordance with the timeline as enacted in tax treaties. In general, PMK-240/2014 provides that a dispute should be concluded within three years after the first consultation held between the DGT and the tax authority of the treaty partner country. If the MAP process cannot be completed in three years, the timeframe will be extended as agreed between the DGT and the treaty partner.

Separately, PMK-7/2015 regulates the procedure to prevent disputes through an APA which can be lodged by Indonesian taxpayers and non-resident taxpayers. They must have operated their business in Indonesia for at least three years to be eligible to apply for an APA. By raising the APA mechanisms, there will be an agreement between the DGT and taxpayers or a treaty partner's tax authority regarding the transfer price for affiliated transactions in the future. The result of an APA will cover the transaction over the next three fiscal years in the case of a unilateral APA, or four fiscal years for a bilateral APA. However, an outcome that differs from Action 14 is that PMK-7/2015 does not allow rollback for the period of years before the APA is submitted.

7.4 The Adoption of the Other BEPS Actions

7.4.1 Action 1 – Addressing the Tax Challenge of the Digital Economy

BEPS Action 1 specifically responds to the tax challenge created by the digital economy. Profit shifting and tax avoidance activity is exacerbated by the feature of the digital economy of being able to perform business activity without any significant presence (OECD, 2015a). Additionally, flexibility in relocating commercial activity to the most advantageous jurisdiction, transferring assets, and carrying out business remotely have been facilitated by the advance of technology (OECD, 2015a). Consequently, MNEs can avoid taxable presence which results in avoiding taxes in both source and intermediate countries (OECD, 2015a). Therefore, Action 1 offers several recommendations in facing these issues, which are: (i) taxing based on significant economic presence; (ii) imposing withholding tax; (iii) introducing an equalisation levy, and (iv) requiring non-resident taxpayers to register for value-added tax (VAT) purposes where they operate (OECD, 2015a).

Indonesia, as the world's fourth most populated country, constitutes a potential market for digital business. A study by Google and Temasek has found that the number of internet users in Indonesia is predicted to grow from 92 million users in 2015 to 215 million users in 2020 (Google, Inc. and Temasek Holdings (Private) Ltd, 2016). Based on this calculation, Indonesia is considered "the fastest growing internet market in the world". Accordingly, a McKinsey report in 2016 revealed that digital technology could boost the growth of labour and productivity and give added value of USD 155 million to Indonesian GDP by 2025 (Das et al., 2016).

Notwithstanding the rapid growth of the digital market in Indonesia, specific legislation has not so far been enacted in response to the recommendations on Action 1. The current regulations which contain provisions related to the taxation of e-commerce are Presidential Regulation Number 74 year 2017 (PERPRES-74/2017) regarding the roadmap for e-commerce in years 2017-2019, Circular Letter of Directorate General of Taxation (DGT) Number 62 year 2013 regarding confirmation of tax treatment for e-commerce transactions (SE-62/2013), and Circular Letter of Directorate General of Taxation (DGT) Number 04 year 2017 regarding determination of permanent establishment (PE) for non-resident taxpayers which provide application or content services through the internet (SE-04/2017).

Regulation PERPRES-74/2017 provides guidance and reference for government, both central and local, for stipulating the provisions and actions to accelerate e-commerce trade in Indonesia. This regulation also provides guidance for stakeholders in conducting a national trade system on an e-commerce basis. Regarding the taxation aspects, PERPRES-74/2017 requires simplification of tax procedures, tax incentives for e-commerce business investors, design of a registration system for e-commerce entrepreneurs, and implementation of equality of tax treatment as between foreign and local e-commerce enterprises. SE-62/2013 sets out the detail of regulation for taxing e-commerce business. This letter provides taxation details both for income tax and value added tax as they relate to e-commerce transactions. Furthermore, this regulation requires the operator or service users to withhold the associated tax depending on the transaction type and the related parties' tax obligations.

By contrast, Circular SE-04/2017 is the only measure that has regulated international taxation aspects of e-commerce in Indonesia. To some extent, SE-04/2017 could be regarded as Indonesia's response to the Action 1 recommendation regarding PE determination using a significant economic presence. This implementation corresponds to the category for PE determination for an application or content service provider. As stipulated in this Circular, a PE can be formed as a fixed place of business, including room for sales or marketing, a computer included in a server or data centre, an electronic agent, or any automatic tools owned by non-resident taxpayers, which are used for performing business in Indonesia. The application of these categories to PE determination constitutes a breakthrough in the Indonesian taxation field. While many issues still remain regarding the establishment of a PE involving a computer, server, or Internet Service Provider (ISP), Indonesia has already enacted regulation on this matter by analysing the activity of e-commerce which is carried out through a computer or the internet. Nevertheless, the determination of a PE must take into account the provisions of the tax treaty agreement with the relevant treaty partner and should not override the treaty arrangement.

7.4.2 Action 3 – Strengthening CFC Rules

Multinational companies could design their organisational structure for tax purposes, for instance through establishment of subsidiaries in tax haven jurisdictions, so that the distribution of their earnings from overseas subsidiaries will be deliberately deferred. Such an activity results in postponement of tax payments that causes capital exporting jurisdictions to suffer from deferral of tax revenue (Miller and Oats, 2016). BEPS Action 3 gives recommendations to prevent this strategy by designing effective rules in curbing tax haven abuse involving the use of controlled foreign companies (CFCs) (OECD, 2015b). Miller and Oats (2016) have found that CFC rules constitute the most effective measure in curtailing this problem.

Action 3 suggests that the design of CFC rules ought to provide for: (i) the definition and description of the type of entity constituting a CFC and the extent to which an entity will be considered a CFC; (ii) the CFC exemptions and threshold; (iii) the type of income subject to CFC rules; (iii) procedures on how to calculate the income; (iv) rules for attributing income, and (v) the mechanism on how to prevent double taxation.

As a response to the CFC recommendations, Indonesia has enacted Minister of Finance Regulation Number 107/PMK.03/2017 (PMK-107/2017) considering the determination of the timing for dividend receipt and its computation for a resident taxpayer which owns a share in a foreign company and does not sell their share on the stock exchange. In PMK-107/2017, a resident taxpayer which owns at least a 50 per cent share in a CFC is regarded as receiving income distribution in the form of a deemed dividend on its capital participation in a non-listed overseas company. This provision covers both directly and indirectly owned foreign entities. It also provides some examples on calculating the amount of capital participation and deemed dividend, the determination of timing for the deemed dividend receipt, and the computation of allowable tax credit.

Further, PMK-107/2017 defines a CFC to consist of:

1 a direct CFC, which constitutes a foreign company that is directly owned by a resident taxpayer or collectively owned with other resident taxpayers, with a minimum total participation of 50 per cent; and
2 an indirect CFC, which is a foreign company that is indirectly controlled by a resident taxpayer through a directly controlled CFC, or directly controlled CFC together with other indirectly controlled CFCs, with at least 50 per cent ownership at each level of share participation (not using proportional calculation of share).

Indonesian resident taxpayers owning such entities must recognise income distribution from the CFC in the form of a deemed dividend. To prevent deferral, the revenue attribution is recognised four months after the last day of the CFC's tax return submissions or seven months after the end of the fiscal year if the CFC is not required to submit tax returns.

Generally, the tax base for the deemed dividend calculation is net income after tax, including other income, under the accounting principle applied in the CFC's jurisdiction. However, the calculation is different depending on the CFC's type:

1 for direct CFCs, the deemed dividend is computed by multiplying the tax base by the percentage share in the direct CFC; and
2 for indirect CFCs, the deemed dividend is calculated by multiplying the tax base of the indirect CFC by the effective percentage ownership in the indirect CFC.

To prevent double taxation, the resident taxpayer can credit the actual tax paid or withheld in the CFC's jurisdiction. A simulation of the calculation has been provided in PMK-107/2017. For taxpayers who claim the tax credit, they must attach the following documents in their annual tax return: (i) financial statement; (ii) copy of CFC's tax return (if any); (iii) calculation or detailed list of profit after tax in the last five years; and (iv) evidence of tax payment or tax withheld for the dividend received.

7.4.3 Action 4 – Limiting Base Erosion Involving Interest Deductions and Other Financial Payments

The objective of Action 4 was to combat the tax planning strategies conducted by MNEs which employ intragroup lending, so that such a group can generate global interest deductions in which the amount of interest exceeds that which would be paid to an unrelated party (Miller and Oats, 2016; OECD, 2015c). In curbing this base erosion through manufactured interest deductions, Action 4 recommends the application of a fixed ratio rule which restricts the interest based on a percentage of interest payment to earnings before interest, taxes, depreciation and amortisation (EBITDA) (OECD, 2015c). However, Action 4 also recognises other approaches, such as a fixed ratio based on assets or equity (widely known as thin capitalisation rules), and a worldwide group ratio.

In relation to this issue, Indonesia has enacted a regulation to curtail excessive interest deductions by taxpayers through the application of thin capitalisation rules. The approach used is a debt-to-equity ratio (DER) pursuant to Article 18, paragraph 1 of the IITL. Even though Indonesia has not implemented the best practice approach as recommended in Action 4, it has developed its own rule for limiting base erosion from intragroup financing activities. As at 2018, Indonesia's legal framework only provides for the application of a fixed ratio using equity (DER) rather than using EBITDA. On this basis, the detailed provisions of the DER were stipulated in Minister of Finance Regulation Number 169/PMK.010/2015 (PMK-169/2015) regarding the determination of a company's debt to equity ratio for income tax purposes, and the Directorate General of Taxes Regulation Number 25/PJ/2017 (PER-25/2017) regarding the implementation of PMK-169/2015 and the procedure to report foreign private loans.

Regulations PMK-169/2015 and PER-25/2017 have stipulated a maximum DER of 4:1 for Indonesian taxpayers. Consequently, where a taxpayer's actual DER exceeds the maximum permitted DER, the excess amount of its borrowing cost will be disregarded as a deductible expense for income tax purposes. The taxpayers covered by these provisions are limited liability companies not including banks, financial institutions, insurance companies, mining enterprises, and concerns in other specific areas as stipulated in PMK-169/2015. In addition, the taxpayer must consider the arm's length principle when applying the 4:1 ratio.

Regulation PMK-169/2015 provides the criteria in relation to debt and equity used for calculating the DER. Debt includes long term debt, short term debt, and interest bearing trade payable. Likewise, equity is defined in accordance with financial accounting standards, and includes non-interest bearing loans from related parties. Furthermore, PMK-169/2015 and PER-25/2017 elaborate the borrowing costs which are allowed and disallowed for tax purposes. Generally, any borrowing cost in the form of interest, premium or discount, additional cost due to the borrowing arrangement, financial expenses associated with a capital lease, cost due to guarantee of loan repayment, or foreign exchange loss related to borrowing cost shall be allowed as deductible expense. Conversely, the excess amount of borrowing cost when the taxpayer's DER surpasses the maximum allowable DER, including intragroup borrowing cost which is not aligned with the arm's length principle, and any borrowing cost related to non-taxable income or final-taxed income, shall be regarded as a non-deductible expense. In order to give comprehensive guidance, PER-25/2017 provides several simulations for calculating DER and the allowed borrowing cost, including the appropriate adjustment for particular cases. For tax filing purposes, PER-25/2017 requires taxpayers to submit DER calculations and foreign private loan reports (if any) using the form as provided in the regulation and attach these forms in the annual tax return. If taxpayers do not comply with this requirement, the annual tax return will be considered incomplete.

7.4.4 Actions 8-10 – Updating Transfer Pricing Guidelines

The update of transfer pricing guidelines has been effected through Actions 8-10. With the tag line of aligning transfer pricing with value creation, these Actions have been designed to work on three areas, which are: (i) transfer pricing for intangible transactions (Action 8); (ii) risk allocation, the impact of risk allocation on profit, and addressing issues related to the appropriate return on funding by capital-rich companies (Action 9); and (iii) other high-risk transactions which generally do not take place between independent parties, and guidance for commodity transactions (Action 10). These Actions continue to apply the arm's length principle for every transaction conducted between independent or affiliated parties. Additionally, this measure also requires prudent delineation between the legal contract and the actual transaction so that the profit allocation is aligned with the actual business activities.

The current Indonesian transfer pricing regime is based on Article 18, paragraph 3 of the IITL, regarding the authority of the Directorate General of Taxation to redetermine the transfer price of an affiliated transaction using the arm's length principle. Subsequently, based on this article, the transfer pricing guidelines for Indonesian resident taxpayers have been enacted in Director General Regulation Number PER-43/PJ/2010 (PER-43/2010) and PER-32/PJ/2011 which regulate the application of the arm's length principle for affiliated transactions, supplemented by Directorate General Regulation Number PER-22/PJ/2011 and Circular Letter of Directorate General of Taxation Number SE-50/PJ/2013 which provide guidelines for transfer pricing audits. In general, these provisions have adopted the 2010 OECD Transfer Pricing Guidelines, so that there are several differences between Indonesia's domestic rule and BEPS Actions 8-10, including:

1 there is no explicit guidance in the Indonesian regulation regarding intangibles and remuneration for development, enhancement, maintenance, protection or exploitation of intangibles (Hutagaol, 2017);

2 no clear guidance on how to perform risk analysis is provided in the Indonesian domestic rule; and

3 the Indonesian transfer pricing measure has not to date provided specific treatment for commodity transactions.

Recently, Indonesia has been working to revise its transfer pricing regulation pursuant to which the 2017 OECD transfer pricing guidelines will be adopted as well as BEPS Actions 8-10.

7.4.5 Action 15 – Developing a Multilateral Instrument

The implementation of the BEPS Action Plan will not be effective without adjustments also being made to the OECD Model Tax Convention and associated bilateral tax treaties. Yet, adjustment on an individual basis of more than 3,000 bilateral tax treaties worldwide in order to adopt the BEPS Action Plan would be infeasible and exceedingly time consuming. Therefore, an innovative approach has been developed in the form of the Multilateral Instrument (MLI) which provides an overarching framework in tackling profit shifting in a harmonised way in accordance with the BEPS Action Plan whilst still respecting tax sovereignty (OECD, 2015i - Action 15). Through implementation of the MLI, bilateral tax treaties will be enhanced by incorporating changes pursuant to the treaty-related Actions, namely Action 2 (neutralising the effect of hybrid-mismatch arrangements), Action 6 (preventing treaty abuse), Action 7 (preventing artificial avoidance of PE), and Action 14 (making dispute resolution more effective). Therefore, the implementation of Action 15 could eliminate, or at least reduce the possibility of the incidence of base erosion and profit shifting, double taxation, or double non-taxation in an effective way and timely manner.

As at March 2018, 78 jurisdictions had already agreed to implement the MLI agreement, not including six other jurisdictions that have also expressed their willingness to join the convention. Indonesia has responded towards this Action by signing the MLI on 7 June 2017. The implementation of the MLI in Indonesia will adjust the following tax treaty articles: (i) Article 3 regarding transparent entities; (ii) Article 4 regarding dual resident entities; (iii) Article 5 regarding eliminating double taxation; (iv) Article 7 regarding the principal purpose test (PPT)/simplified PPT or limitation of benefit (LOB) clause; (v) Article 9 concerning capital gains; (vi) Article 10 concerning PEs in a third contracting state; (vii) Article 13 concerning PEs; (viii) Article 16 concerning the MAP; (ix) Article 17 regarding corresponding adjustments, and (x) Article 35 regarding entry into effect of the MLI.

7.5 The Adoption of Unilateral BEPS Measures

Indonesia has attempted to adopt some unilateral measures to tackle BEPS issues as set out further below, some of which are currently in progress.

7.5.1 Diverted Profits Tax

Certain countries have undertaken unilateral moves particularly with respect to the "digital economy". With respect to this, while there is no "diverted profits tax" approach currently in place, Indonesia is currently considering imposition of a withholding tax for e-commerce transactions.

7.5.2 Tightening of General Anti-Avoidance Rules

While no specific GAAR is currently in place, the Indonesian domestic law adopts an anti-avoidance approach through an emphasis on the "special relationship" concept under transfer pricing and thin capitalisation rules.

For instance, under Article 18(3) of the IITL, the Indonesian tax authority can make adjustments to commercial transactions, particularly with respect to income and expenses, and also recharacterise debt as equity. In doing so, the DGT is authorised to determine the taxable income from transactions between related parties in accordance with the principle of common business practices that are not carried out by those in a special relationship. The effect of this approach is somewhat similar to that in Article 9 of the OECD Model Tax Convention although the wording is slightly different. Further, according to Article 16(2) of Government Regulation 80 Year 2007, taxpayers are required to provide transfer pricing documentation. However, no specific guidelines directed at taxpayers were available prior to September 2010 although DGT Regulation PER-39/PJ/2009 implicitly indicates that the OECD Transfer Pricing Guidelines should be adopted. It is worth noting that the OECD guidelines might have no direct impact upon Indonesia since Indonesia is not a member of the OECD. Filling this gap, the DGT for the first time released guidance for taxpayers relating to transfer pricing practices and related party transactions through PER-43/2010 (see section 7.4.4 above).

While the definition of "related parties" in Indonesia seems stricter than in other typical jurisdictions, this regulation highlights several general considerations to be taken into account in determining whether the pricing of related party transactions satisfies the arm's length principle. In doing so, the regulation provides certain steps to be carried out in examining whether the pricing of related party transactions is fair and in accordance with common business practices. An amended version of this regulation - DGT Regulation Number PER-32/PJ/2011 - revoked the hierarchical approach in selecting the transfer pricing method as suggested previously in the former regulations and adopts the "most appropriate method" stance instead. In addition to this, while the transactional net margin method is no longer considered the method of last resort, this regulation requires taxpayers to justify the process of selection of their adopted method.

An attempt to tighten the anti-avoidance rules is also reflected in Regulation PMK-169/2015 which deals with thin capitalisation rules (see section 7.4.3 above). This regulation adopts a "4:1 debt-to-equity ratio" in addressing BEPS issues. This means that borrowing expenses relating to debt exceeding the ratio are not deductible. It is worth noting however that this debt-to-equity ratio does not apply to certain institutions (e.g., banks, financial institutions, insurance and reinsurance businesses, oil and gas and mining industries, infrastructure industries, and industries that are subject to final income tax).

Finally, other anti-avoidance measures can also be found under Article 18(2) of the IITL regarding the Controlled Foreign Corporations (CFC) rule (recall section 7.4.2 above). As indicated earlier, the Ministry of Finance (MoF) is authorised to determine when a dividend is deemed to be accrued by a resident taxpayer. Under this provision, an Indonesian resident shareholder is taxed on the "deemed dividend" if in the relevant year these earnings have not been distributed. That is, the qualifying Indonesian resident shareholders will be deemed to have received the dividends from the CFC at a time determined in accordance with the following criteria: (i) in the fourth month after the CFC has to file its annual income tax return; or (ii) in the seventh month after the end of the fiscal year if the CFC is not obliged to file an annual tax return or no deadline is applied for lodgement of the annual tax return.[7] The amount of the deemed dividend is calculated proportionally based on the shareholding percentage and applied to the after-tax profit of the CFC.

7.5.3 Automatic Exchange of Information

In response to the prerequisites for implementing automatic exchange of information (AEOI) by September 2018, Indonesia as an initial step issued Government Regulation in Lieu of Law Number 1 Year 2017 (PERPU 1/2017) in May 2017 as the primary legal basis for EOI.[8] This regulation - upgraded and converted to Law

7 See Regulation PMK-107/2017.

8 It is worth noting that if no primary legislation had been in place by 30 June 2017, the Indonesian government would have been categorised by the Global Forum as a country that has "failed to meet its commitment".

Number 9 Year 2017 in August 2017 (LAW 9/2017) - provides a legal basis for the Indonesian tax authority to access both local and foreign customer information data from financial sectors such as banking, capital market, insurance, and other financial institutions.

Following this primary authority, on 31 May 2017, the Ministry of Finance (MoF) issued MoF Regulation Number 70/PMK.03/2017 concerning Technical Guidance on Financial Information Access for Taxation Purposes (PMK-70/2017). With respect to its implementation, this regulation covers two areas: (i) international agreements, and (ii) domestic taxation. It also establishes two types of EOI: automatic and upon request. The former is performed periodically, systematically, and continuously at a certain time in relation to certain information based on the Common Reporting Standard (CRS). The details of information that need to be automatically reported are the identity of financial account holders, identity of financial institutions, financial account numbers, financial account balances, and income related to the reported account. With respect to the reciprocal nature of the EOI, the Indonesian Competent Authority is authorised to lodge a written request for an EOI to a corresponding partner country or jurisdiction in cases where a resident taxpayer is suspected of being non-compliant.

In general, the technical guidance addresses four issues: (i) subjects, i.e., entities that are required to submit information; (ii) the mechanism on how information reporting is carried out; (iii) confidentiality concerns, and (iv) imposition of sanctions.

7.6 Administrative International Tax-Related Reform

The Indonesian government has taken several bold steps to strengthen its revenue administration, some of which are related to international tax reform. One of the recent major administrative tax reforms undertaken by the government was a tax amnesty program, which ran for nine months between July 2016 and March 2017. Under Law Number 11 Year 2016, by offering both tax incentives and immunity from prosecution, this program aimed to make it attractive for non-compliant taxpayers to declare their offshore and/or domestic assets to the Indonesian tax authorities. With revenue collected of close to 1.08 per cent of Indonesian GDP (i.e., IDR 134.99 trillion of approximately IDR 2.5 quadrillion), some considered this program to be one of the most - if not the most - successful tax amnesty programs in the world. In terms of the value of assets declared, although less than one million Indonesian taxpayers joined the program, a figure equal to 40 per cent of Indonesian gross domestic product (GDP) was declared by the participants. These figures imply that tax non-compliance remains rampant in Indonesia.

It is believed that the introduction of the AEOI procedures as proposed by the OECD, which Indonesia is planning to implement by September 2018, was one of the factors that motivated taxpayers to participate in the program. Following the end of this program, to address the underlying flaws within the tax system, the Indonesian government issued a law to equip the tax authority with a right of access to financial information for taxation purposes on May 2017 (i.e., PERPU 1/2017, as noted in section 7.5.3 above).[9] This legislation requires financial institutions to lodge a report on financial data to the DGT.

In addition to ongoing administrative tax reform undertaken over 2017 entailing five areas (i.e., organisation, human resources, information technology and data base, business process, and regulations),[10] a major driver of current administrative tax reform has been the enactment of Presidential Regulation Number 13 Year 2018 (PERPRES 13/2018) concerning Principles of Recognizing the Beneficiaries of Corporations in Preventing and Combating Money Laundering and Criminal Acts of Terrorism. In general, this regulation requires corporations to provide details of beneficiary information, defined as any individual who may appoint or dismiss the board of directors, board of commissioners, administrators or supervisors of the corporation. In addition, individuals who have the ability to control corporations are regarded as deriving the benefits of the corporation, whether directly or indirectly, and are the true owners of the funds or shares of the corporation. So far, beneficiary practices are closely related to the phenomenon of illicit financial outflows between jurisdictions. In this sense, taxes can be the reason for the beneficial owner to disguise the origin, control, or the amount of benefits received and terminate the chain of ownership to avoid or evade the tax burden. Thus, it is hoped that this regulation will not only be capable of preventing and eradicating money laundering and terrorism financing activities, but also preventing any attempts made by taxpayers to "escape" from their tax liabilities through tax avoidance and tax evasion practices.

7.7 Future International Tax Reform

While developing countries generally rely on tax revenue for their state-building, it is a widely accepted belief that the tax base in this context has been eroded by both illegal tax evasion and legal tax avoidance by MNEs. For this reason, Indonesia has actively participated in the global forum for tackling BEPS issues, for instance by becoming a member of the G20 working group, joining the Inclusive Framework for BEPS and the FHTP, and becoming an MLI signatory along with 66 other countries. As a result, Indonesia is expected to apply the BEPS Action Plan consistently, and ensure its implementation of domestic measures aligned with international standards. However, there are some challenges and opportunities in the future of international taxation in Indonesia.

9 Converted to LAW 9/2017 on August 2017.

10 See Decree of Minister of Finance Number KMK-360/KMK.03/2017 regarding Tax Reform (KMK 360/2017). It is worth noting that with respect to regulations, Indonesia is currently considering amending its tax laws: general provisions, income tax, and VAT.

7.7.1 Challenges

Indonesia is highly reliant on tax revenue as the source of income for its national budget. In the past five years, more than 70 per cent of total government revenue has been collected from taxation. Apparently, this trend will be ongoing for the next several decades. On the one hand, Indonesia is considered to be a net capital importing country so that it should provide facilities to attract inbound investment. On the other hand, the international trend in company income tax rates is one of decline and this could affect the Indonesian tax system.

The lack of administrative resources, particularly competent staff in the area of international tax practice, and burdensome tax provisions are present in Indonesia as in many other developing countries (see, for example, Sandford, 2000; Fuest and Riedel, 2010; Ring, 2017). Moreover, inadequate transparency has resulted in asymmetric information between tax authorities and taxpayers which has undermined the effectiveness of tax collection (Fuest and Riedel, 2010; Ting, 2014). This suggests that enhancement of the tax transparency regime is inevitably needed in the future. In addition to this, Indonesia also needs to take several bold steps to improve both the internal capabilities and the effectiveness of its tax administration, some of which are already in progress.

7.7.2 Opportunities

There are still several BEPS Actions which have not been implemented in Indonesia, for instance Action 7 and Action 12. Indonesia could consider adopting these Actions through its domestic rules and tax treaties. Additionally, Indonesia could adopt the recommendations in Action 1 in its income tax and VAT law proposals to address the rapid growth of Indonesian e-commerce business arising from the digital economy.[11]

On the other hand, Indonesia also needs to consider its strategy to attract foreign investment without sacrificing its statutory tax rate. There are several ways in which incentives could be offered to investors by the Indonesian government, for instance by providing tax holiday schemes for particular industries, or establishing safe harbour policies for ensuring certainty in transactions entered into with affiliated foreign entities.

Since Indonesia is a net capital importer, it seems important to protect its tax base from any profit shifting activity. The government should consider strengthening Indonesia's tax treaties to preserve the taxing rights of Indonesia as the source taxation country. The application of simplified PPT or LOB provisions as agreed in the MLI has provided a potential advantage for Indonesia in protecting its tax base. In addition to that, Indonesia could renegotiate those treaties which it considers undermine Indonesia's taxing rights by implementing a specific model aligned with domestic law (International Monetary Fund, 2017). Alternatively, Indonesia could

11 Ibid.

follow global trends in which there has been a shift from a "worldwide income" approach (as currently applied in the Indonesian tax regime) to a territorial tax system which offers simplicity and greater disincentives for tax dodging activities (International Monetary Fund, 2017).

In response to the demands on experienced staff in the international tax practice and transfer pricing areas, Indonesia could consider steps to enhance their skills by providing training in the international taxation area, or organising a secondment to other countries or international organisations involved in the international taxation field. In addition, Indonesia should enhance its tax transparency regime to reduce the information disparity between the tax authorities and taxpayers. The first steps in building this transparency regime were actually taken with the release of the CbCR regulation in December 2016. However, Indonesia could further consider implementing the BEPS Action 12 recommendations which require taxpayers to disclose their tax planning strategies through mandatory disclosure rules. The implementation of mandatory disclosure rules could provide more relevant information for tax authorities in curbing tax avoidance whilst preventing MNEs from deliberately reducing their tax base or shifting their profits out of Indonesia. By doing so, it would be possible to deal further with the problem of BEPS in Indonesia.

References

Arifin, Nanang Zainal (2014), "*BEPS dalam Kerangka Kerja Sama G20 dan Implementasinya kepada Indonesia*" (BEPS in the G20 Framework and its Application to Indonesia), https://www.kemenkeu.go.id/sites/default/files/beps%20dalam%20kerangka%20kerja%20sama%20g20%20dan%20implementasinya%20kepada%20indonesia.pdf (accessed on 27 June 2018).

BPS (Statistics Indonesia) (2018), *Statistical Year Book of Indonesia 2017*, Jakarta.

Crivelli, Ernesto, Ruud De Mooij and Michael Keen (2015), "Base Erosion, Profit Shifting and Developing Countries", IMF Working Paper WP/15/118, International Monetary Fund Fiscal Affairs Department, May.

Das, Kaushik, Michael Gryseels, Priyanka Sudhir and Khoon Tee Tan (2016), *Unlocking Indonesia's Digital Opportunity*, McKinsey & Co., October, https://www.mckinsey.com/~/media/McKinsey/Locations/Asia/Indonesia/Our%20Insights/Unlocking%20Indonesias%20digital%20opportunity/Unlocking_Indonesias_digital_opportunity.ashx (accessed on 27 June 2018).

Directorate General of Taxation (DGT) (2016), *Annual Report 2015: The Guidance Year of Taxpayer Compliance*, Jakarta.

Ernst & Young (2016), "BEPS associates increased to 82 countries", Global Tax Alert, 30 June, https://www.ey.com/gl/en/services/tax/international-tax/alert--beps-associates-increased-to-82-countries (accessed on 28 June 2018).

Fuest, Clemens and Nadine Riedel (2010), "Tax Evasion and Tax Avoidance in Developing Countries: The Role of International Profit Shifting", Oxford University Centre for Business Taxation Working Paper WP 10/12, June.

Google Inc. and Temasek Holdings (Private) Ltd (2016), *e-conomy SEA: Unlocking the $200 billion digital opportunity in Southeast Asia*, research study, May, http://apac.thinkwithgoogle.com/research-studies/e-conomy-sea-unlocking-200b-digital-opportunity.html (accessed on 23 May 2018).

Hutagaol, John (2017) "BEPS Action Plan at the Implementation Stage – An Indonesian Perspective", in Sam Sim and Mei-June Soo (eds), *Asian Voices: BEPS and Beyond* (Amsterdam: IBFD Publications), 171-178.

International Monetary Fund (IMF) (2017), "Indonesia Selected Issues", IMF Country Report No. 17/48, Washington, DC.

Johannesen, Niels, Thomas Tørsløv and Ludvig Wier (2017), "Are Less Developed Countries More Exposed to Multinational Tax Avoidance? Method and Evidence from Micro-Data", WIDER Working Paper 2016/10, revised version May, Helsinki.

Marian, Omri (2016), "The Other Eighty Percent: Private Investment Funds, International Tax Avoidance, and Tax-Exempt Investors" 6 *Brigham Young University Law Review* 1715-1765.

Miller, Angharad and Lynne Oats (2016), *Principles of International Taxation*, 5th edn (Haywards Heath: Bloomsbury Professional).

Ministry of Finance (MoF) (2018), *Nota Keuangan beserta Rancangan APBN 2018* (Financial note along with the draft state budget 2018), https://www.kemenkeu.go.id/informasi-publik/uu-apbn-dan-nota-keuangan/.

Mulyani, Yeni (2016), *"Menyelesaikan sengketa dengan Mutual Agreement Procedure"*, Inside Tax Magazine DDTC Indonesia, Jakarta.

Organisation for Economic Co-operation and Development (OECD) (2012), *Corporate Governance: Related Party Transactions and Minority Shareholder Rights* (Paris: OECD), http://www.oecd.org/corporate/ca/corporategovernanceprinciples/relatedpartytransactionsandminorityshareholderrights.htm.

Organisation for Economic Co-operation and Development (OECD) (2013), *Tax Administration 2013: Comparative Information on OECD and Other Advanced and Emerging Economies* (Paris: OECD).

Organisation for Economic Co-operation and Development (OECD) (2014), *Two-Part Report to G20 Development Working Group on the Impact of BEPS in Low Income Countries* (Paris: OECD).

Organisation for Economic Co-operation and Development (OECD) (2015a), *Action 1 - 2015 Final Report: Addressing the Tax Challenges of the Digital Economy* (Paris: OECD).

Organisation for Economic Co-operation and Development (OECD) (2015b), *Action 3 - 2015 Final Report: Designing Effective Controlled Foreign Company Rules* (Paris: OECD).

Organisation for Economic Co-operation and Development (OECD) (2015c), *Action 4 - 2015 Final Report: Limiting Base Erosion Involving Interest Deductions and Other Financial Payments* (Paris: OECD).

Organisation for Economic Co-operation and Development (OECD) (2015d), *Action 5 - 2015 Final Report: Countering Harmful Tax Practices More Effectively, Taking into Account Transparency and Substance* (Paris: OECD).

Organisation for Economic Co-operation and Development (OECD) (2015e), *Action 6 - 2015 Final Report: Preventing the Granting of Treaty Benefits in Inappropriate Circumstances* (Paris: OECD).

Organisation for Economic Co-operation and Development (OECD) (2015f), *Actions 8-10 - 2015 Final Reports: Aligning Transfer Pricing Outcomes with Value Creation* (Paris: OECD).

Organisation for Economic Co-operation and Development (OECD) (2015g), *Action 13 - 2015 Final Report: Transfer Pricing Documentation and Country-by-Country Reporting* (Paris: OECD).

Organisation for Economic Co-operation and Development (OECD) (2015h), *Action 14 - 2015 Final Report: Making Dispute Resolution Mechanisms More Effective* (Paris: OECD).

Organisation for Economic Co-operation and Development (OECD) (2015i), *Action 15 -2015 Final Report: Developing a Multilateral Instrument to Modify Bilateral Tax Treaties* (Paris: OECD).

Organisation for Economic Co-operation and Development (OECD) (2016), *Active with Indonesia*, October (Paris: OECD), http://www.oecd.org/indonesia/Active-with-Indonesia.pdf (accessed on 28 June 2018).

Organisation for Economic Co-operation and Development (OECD) (2017a), *Inclusive Framework on BEPS: Progress Report July 2016-June 2017* (Paris: OECD).

Organisation for Economic Co-operation and Development (OECD) (2017b), *Harmful Tax Practices 2017: Progress Report on Preferential Regimes* (Paris: OECD).

Ring, Diane (2017), "Developing Countries in an Age of Transparency and Disclosure" 6 *Brigham Young University Law Review* 1767-1835.

Sandford, Cedric (2000), *Why Tax Systems Differ: A Comparative Study of the Political Economy of Taxation* (Bath: Fiscal Publications).

Ting, Antony (2014), "iTax - Apple's International Tax Structure and the Double Non-Taxation Issue" 1 *British Tax Review* 40-71.

World Bank (2011), "World Bank Report: Indonesia, Emerging Markets Redefine Global Economy", press release, 15 June, http://www.worldbank.org/en/news/press-release/2011/06/15/world-bank-report-indonesia-emerging-markets-redefine-global-economy (accessed on 28 June 2018).

8 The Adoption of BEPS in Japan

Masato Ohno*

Abstract

Japan is one of the most developed countries in the world and, as a member country of the OECD, has supported the new inclusive framework to tackle Base Erosion and Profit Shifting. The first meeting of the new inclusive framework was held on 30 June to 1 July 2016 in Kyoto, Japan. Japan has been proactive in adopting many of the OECD's BEPS initiatives.

8.1 Introduction

8.1.1 Geological and Economic Status

Japan is situated close to the eastern edge of the Eurasian continent. Surrounded by the Russian Federation (to the north), the Republic of Korea (west), the People's Republic of China (west), and Taiwan (south), Japan is composed of about 3,700 islands including four large islands (*Hokkaido, Honshū, Shikoku* and *Kyūshū*). Japan's population is 126.7 million as of 31 December 2017.[1]

Japan is one of the most developed countries in the world. Its GDP of USD 5,428 billion is exceeded only by the United States (USD 19,390 billion) and China (USD 12,014 billion), and is followed by Germany (USD 3,684 billion) and the United Kingdom (USD 2,624 billion).[2] Japan exports cars, semiconductors, electronic devices, steel, engines, etc., and imports oil, liquefied natural gas (LNG), clothes, pharmaceutical products, etc. In its 2017 balance of payments, Japan's current account was a surplus of JPY 21,951 billion and its financial account was a surplus of JPY 17,664 billion.[3]

---

* Professor, Graduate School of Business Sciences, University of Tsukuba.

1 Statistics Bureau, Ministry of Inland Affairs and Communications, http://www.stat.go.jp/jinsui/new.html.

2 International Monetary Fund World Economic Outlook databases, April 2018.

3 Ministry of Finance, www.mof.go.jp/international_policy/reference/balance_of_payments/bpnet.htm. Exchange rate of USD 1 equivalent to JPY 110 as at the end of July 2018.

8.1.2 Membership of the OECD and G20

Japan has been a member country of the OECD since 1964, and a member country of the G20 from the first meeting in 1999 as one of the G7 countries.

8.1.3 Political System

Japan is a constitutional monarchy. The Emperor of Japan is the symbol of the nation and of the unity of the people,[4] and acts under the advice and approval of the Cabinet.[5] Japan's institutional system is composed of three bodies: the legislature (the Diet that consists of the House of Representatives and the House of Councilors), the administration (the national government under the Prime Minister and the Cabinet), and the judiciary (the Supreme Court). The ruling party (parties) that nominates the Prime Minister was, in these twenty years, the Liberal Democratic Party (LDP) from January 1996 to September 2009, the Democratic Party (DP) from September 2009 to December 2012, and the LDP and *Komeito* from December 2012 to the present (August 2018)

8.1.4 Tax System

Governmental departments in charge of drafting tax laws for the Diet are, for national taxes and customs and tariffs, the Taxation Bureau and the Customs and Tariff Bureau of the Ministry of Finance (MOF) respectively and, for local taxes, the Autonomous Taxation Bureau of the Ministry of Internal Affairs and Communications (MIC). Implementation of tax laws enacted by the Diet is the role of: (i) the National Tax Agency (NTA) of the MOF for national taxes; (ii) the Customs and Tariff Bureau for customs and tariffs, and (iii) the Autonomous Taxation Bureau and local governments (prefectures, cities, towns and villages) for local taxes. The BEPS Project in Japan has mainly been carried out by the Taxation Bureau and the NTA.

Japan's tax revenue largely depends on income tax, corporation tax and consumption tax. Income tax, at 19,020 billion JPY and 32.2 per cent of the whole tax revenue in the Fiscal Year (FY)[6] 2018 national general budget, is the largest tax revenue raiser. Consumption tax at 29.7 per cent and corporate tax at 20.6 per cent, are the next biggest revenue contributors.

The progressive tax rates for income tax are 5, 10, 20, 23, 33, 40 and 45 per cent.[7] The corporation tax rate is 23.2 per cent[8] (and for some parts of income of small and

4 Art. 1, Constitution of Japan.

5 Art. 3, Constitution of Japan.

6 A Fiscal Year of the Japanese government begins on 1 April and ends on 31 March of the following year.

7 In the 2013 Tax Reform, the highest rate was increased from 40 per cent to 45 per cent. The 45 per cent tax rate is applied to taxable incomes of JPY 40 million or more.

8 The corporation tax rate is being decreased in recent tax reforms. Before the 2012 Tax Reform, the tax rate was 30.0 per cent.

medium-sized corporations, the reduced tax rate is 19 per cent). The consumption tax rate is 8 per cent.[9]

8.2 Response of the Government to the G20/OECD BEPS Program

The BEPS Project was carried out by the Committee on Fiscal Affairs of the OECD from its launch in June 2012 to its final report in September 2015. During this period, Masatsugu Asakawa, an experienced government official of the Ministry of Finance, took the chair of the committee.[10] Japan's Ministry of Finance, especially its Tax Bureau, International Bureau and the National Tax Agency (NTA) supported him and contributed to the project. The CFA conducted unprecedented intensive discussions from July 2013 (after the announcement of the BEPS Action Plan) to October 2015 (Final Reports).

Base erosion and profit shifting has been a concern of the Japanese government. Japan's Diet (the legislative body) has continually enacted anti-avoidance rules applicable to international transactions, such as CFC rules in 1978,[11] transfer pricing taxation in 1986,[12] thin capitalisation rules in 1992,[13] corporate inversion rules in 2007,[14] excessive interest rules in 2012,[15] exit tax (expatriation tax) rules in 2015,[16] and destination-based consumption taxation on digital contents provided from businesses overseas in 2015.[17] Taxpayers, however, have constantly invented new tax-avoidance schemes with the assistance of foreign and domestic advisors or with the involvement of foreign financial institutions or other entities. For the Japanese tax authority, it seems that there is no room for being uncommitted to the BEPS project.

---

9 The consumption tax was introduced in April 1989 with a 3 per cent tax rate. The rate was increased to 5 per cent in April 1997 and to 8 per cent in April 2014. The tax rate was expected to be increased to 10 per cent in October 2015, but the hike was postponed to April 2017, then postponed again to October 2019.

10 Asakawa was the chairman of the Committee from January 2011 to December 2016. In the Japanese Ministry of Finance, he was Deputy Vice Minister of Finance for International Affairs when he held the chair of the Committee, and Vice Minister of Finance for International Affairs when he left the chair.

11 Articles 40-4 (for individuals) and Article 66-6 (for corporations) of the *Special Taxation Measures Act* (STMA: Act No. 26 of 1957).

12 STMA, Art. 66-5 (presently 66-4).

13 STMA, Art. 66-5. Under this rule, if the amount of debt borrowed from related parties exceeds the amount of three times the borrower's capital, interest payments corresponding to such excess amount cannot be deducted as expenses.

14 STMA, Arts 40-7 (for individuals) and 66-9-2 (for corporations).

15 STMA, Art. 66-5-2. Under this rule, if the amount of net interest payment paid to related parties exceeds 50 per cent of a corporation's income, such excess payment cannot be deducted as expenses.

16 Articles 60-2 and 60-3 of the *Income Tax Act* (Act No. 33 of 1965).

17 Articles 2, 4 and 5 of the *Consumption Tax Act* (Act No. 108 of 1988) as revised in 2015. After the revision, a reverse charge system is applied to the foreign business to domestic business supply of some kinds of digital contents via the internet.

On the other hand, the Japanese business community has expressed some concerns over the issues of the BEPS project. They consider that it has been foreign multinationals that have been using abusive tax avoidance schemes to decrease their tax burdens, but not Japanese companies. Therefore, it seems that the businesses of Japan partially welcome the project as an opportunity to make a level playing field with foreign multinationals for business competition, while maintaining some reservations about the increase of administrative burdens.

8.3 The BEPS Inclusive Framework

As one of the member countries of the OECD, Japan supported the new inclusive framework to tackle Base Erosion and Profit Shifting. The first meeting of the new inclusive framework was held on 30 June to 1 July 2016 in Kyoto, Japan. The meeting, that more than 80 countries and jurisdictions attended, was hosted by Taro Aso, Minister of Finance, and Masatsugu Asakawa, Vice Minister of Finance for International Affairs and Chairman of the Committee on Fiscal Affairs, OECD. The inclusive framework focuses on ensuring implementation of the four minimum standards, i.e.: (i) harmful tax practices; (ii) tax treaty abuse; (iii) Country-by-Country reporting, and (iv) dispute resolution mechanisms, which will be subject to a peer review process.

8.3.1 Action 5: Harmful Tax Competition

Under the BEPS Action 5 final report, jurisdictions were required to exchange unilateral rulings with taxpayers automatically. An example of such a unilateral ruling is a unilateral Advance Pricing Arrangement in transfer pricing cases. According to the OECD's Peer Review Report (OECD, 2017, pp. 175-176), the NTA transmitted 66 past unilateral APA rulings to its counterparts by 31 December 2016, and 27 other unilateral APA rulings after that date without delay. In Japan, the number of unilateral APA cases is small compared with the number of bilateral or multilateral APA cases shown in section 8.3.4 below.

8.3.2 Action 6: Abuse of Tax Treaties

The Japanese government signed the Multilateral Instrument (MLI) on 7 June 2017 in Paris. Japan did not make any reservation on Article 7 paragraph 1 of the MLI, and therefore Article 7 paragraph 1, that provides for the "one-of-the-main-purposes test" will be applicable to most of the tax treaties Japan has concluded with other MLI jurisdictions (unless these other jurisdictions make reservations on the clause). The MLI was approved by the House of Representatives on 19 April 2018 and by the House of Councilors on 19 May 2018.[18]

Apart from the MLI, Japan already has the "main-purpose test" or "one-of-the-main-purposes test" in several of its tax treaties, such as the Japan-New Zealand

18 The Japanese government deposited the instrument of ratification to the OECD on 26 September 2018, and the MLI will be put into effect for Japan on 1 January 2019.

Treaty (Article 23), Japan-Sweden Treaty (Article 21C), Japan-Germany Treaty (Article 21), Japan-Portuguese Treaty (Article 21), Japan-Hong Kong Treaty (Article 26), etc. Therefore, these tests have already been accepted as Japan's tax treaty policy.

8.3.3 Action 13: Country-by-Country Reporting

The Japanese government revised its transfer pricing rules in 2016 and required taxpayers to submit the Country-by-Country (CbC) report[19] and the master file[20] in addition to the local file which taxpayers have been obliged to prepare since 2010.[21] These new rules are applied to taxation periods of the final parent entity that begin after 1 April 2016, if the total amount of turnover of such group is JPY 100 billion or more. If a taxpayer does not submit the Country-by-Country report or the master file, a criminal fine of up to JPY 300,000 may be imposed.[22] The OECD's peer-review report of 2018 concluded that Japan's implementation of the Action 13 minimum standards met all applicable terms of reference (OECD, 2018, p. 382).

8.3.4. Action 14: Dispute Resolution Mechanism

The competent authority in charge of mutual agreement procedure (MAP) negotiation for double taxation cases is the Office of Mutual Agreement Procedures of the NTA's head office. In Operational Year (OY) 2016,[23] the numbers of cases for transfer pricing adjustments were 25 received, 28 settled and 94 carried forward,[24] and for transfer pricing APAs, 131 received, 143 settled and 343 carried forward.[25]

The Office of Mutual Agreement Procedures had 44 staff in OY 2016, increased from 19 in OY 2007.[26] The procedure of mutual consultation is provided for by

19 New Art. 66-4-4 of the STMA.

20 New Art. 66-4-5 of the STMA.

21 Before the 2016 tax reform, taxpayers had had to submit documents which proved that their transfer pricing was at arm's length if the tax auditor so requested. Article 66-5 (6) of the STMA (1986 tax reform; presently Art. 66-4 (6) of the STMA). In the 2010 Tax Reform, the detailed list of such documents was added in Article 22-10 of the Ministerial Ordinance Implementing the STMA (Ministerial Order of the Ministry of Finance, No. 15, 1957), but it did not include the master file and the Country-by-Country report.

22 With regard to the Country-by-Country report, Art. 66-4-4 of the STMA. With regard to the master file, Art. 66-4-5 of the STMA.

23 An Operational Year (OY) of the NTA begins on 1 July and ends on 30 June of the following year.

24 National Tax Agency, "Mutual Consultation in the 2016 Operational Year", http://www.nta.go.jp/information/release/kokuzeicho/2017/sogo_kyogi/index.htm; "Attachment 1, Number of Mutual Consultation Cases", http://www.nta.go.jp/information/release/kokuzeicho/2017/sogo_kyogi/01.htm.

25 National Tax Agency, "Mutual Consultation in the 2016 Operational Year", http://www.nta.go.jp/information/release/kokuzeicho/2017/sogo_kyogi/index.htm; "Attachment 1, Number of Mutual Consultation Cases", http://www.nta.go.jp/information/release/kokuzeicho/2017/sogo_kyogi/01.htm.

26 Hata (2018, p. 25). Mr. Hata is Director of the Office of Mutual Agreement Procedures.

"the Commissioner's Directive regarding Mutual Agreement Procedures",[27] which includes procedures for APA cases.

The average period for settling cases was 26.0 months in OY 2015 and 29.1 months in OY 2016.[28] The average period for settling cases with non-OECD countries was 33.3 months in OY 2015 and 36.9 months in OY 2016.[29]

With regard to arbitration, it seems to be Japan's treaty policy to put the binding arbitration clause in its bilateral tax treaty if its counterparts do not refuse. Tax treaties Japan has recently entered into or amended, such as treaties with the Netherlands, Hong Kong, Portugal, New Zealand, Sweden, United Kingdom, Germany, and Chile, have the binding arbitration clause.[30] For the Multilateral Instrument, Japan chose to apply Part IV (Arbitration).

8.4 Other BEPS Actions

8.4.1 Action 1: Digital Economy

The issue of how to impose consumption tax on international digital transactions has been discussed for years in Japan, and in the 2015 Tax Reform the government changed its policy from the origin method to the destination method for taxation of international digital transactions.

After the consumption tax was introduced in 1988 and before the 2015 Tax Reform, in respect of international digital transactions (both B2B and B2C), the Japanese consumption tax law had treated the place of the supplier's office as the place of transaction.[31] Therefore, where a foreign corporation supplied digital contents (digital music, digital books, etc.) to companies or individuals that were residents of Japan, such a supply was an out-of-scope supply under the *Consumption Tax Act*. Under such a system, people preferred to purchase digital contents from foreign suppliers without paying consumption tax, and Japan-based businesses requested the government to revise the law. It was also reported in the media that Japan-based companies were moving out of Japan to foreign countries such as Singapore in order to obtain a level playing field with foreign business.

In the 2015 Tax Reform, the law was revised to treat the location of a purchaser of some kinds of digital content as the place of transaction,[32] and inbound digital contents transactions became taxable. For collecting consumption tax for such

27 Commissioner's Directive of 25 June 2001.

28 National Tax Agency, "Mutual Consultation in the 2016 Operational Year", above n. 24.

29 Ibid.

30 New treaties with the US, Austria and Denmark also have an arbitration clause but not put into effect as of 31 May 2018.

31 Article 4(3)(ii) of the *Consumption Tax Act* and Article 6(2)(vii) of the Cabinet Order to Implement the Consumption Tax Act (Cabinet Order No. 360, 1988), before the 2015 Tax Reform.

32 Articles 2(1)(viii-ii) and 4(3)(iii) of the *Consumption Tax Act* after the 2015 Tax Reform.

inbound digital contents transactions, the government introduced the reverse charge system for B2B transactions, under which Japanese purchasers have to pay consumption tax that can be credited against the amount of consumption tax they have collected when they supply their goods and services. For B2C inbound digital contents transactions, the new law requests foreign suppliers to register as taxable business persons and pay consumption tax to the Japanese government.

8.4.2 Action 2: Hybrid Mismatch

In the 2009 Tax Reform, Japan made dividends from foreign subsidiaries tax exempt,[33] expecting this reform to accelerate the "flow-back" of the profits of foreign subsidiaries to domestic parent companies (Morotomi, 2017; Herzfeld and Honda, 2018). In the 2015 Tax Reform, in order to counter double non-taxation schemes using hybrid entities, dividends from foreign subsidiaries that are treated as interest in the subsidiaries' residence country were excluded from the exemption. This was to implement the BEPS first report of September 2014.

Other measures to prevent tax avoidance using hybrid entities will be implemented through Part II (Hybrid Mismatches) of the MLI because as noted in section 8.3.2 above Japan is to join the MLI.

8.4.3 Action 3: CFC Rules

Japan introduced its CFC rules in the 1978 Tax Reform as an "anti-tax-haven tax system". At first the "Black List" method, under which tax haven jurisdictions were listed, was applied, but in 1992 it was changed to the "trigger tax rate" method. The "trigger tax rate" was 25 per cent in 1992, decreased to "20 per cent or less" in 2010, and again decreased to "less than 20 per cent" in 2015. Japan's CFC rules are applied to a domestic parent company or a resident that has a foreign subsidiary[34] whose tax burden ratio is that of the trigger tax rate or less, and where such foreign subsidiary does not meet all four of the following four standards: (i) type-of-business standard; (ii) fixed-facility standard; (iii) self-management-and-administration standard, and (iv)-(a) place-of-business standard or (iv)-(b) no-related-party-transaction standard. If the CFC rules are applied, the income of such subsidiaries is added to the income of the parent company or the resident. Even if the subsidiary meets all of the four standards, its passive income[35] is still added to the income of the parent company or the resident.

33 *Corporation Tax Act*, Art. 24-2.

34 The CFC rules will be applied if a domestic company or a resident has 10 per cent or more of a foreign subsidiary's share, and 50 per cent or more of such foreign subsidiary's share is directly or indirectly owned by one or more domestic companies or residents.

35 Passive income is: (i) dividends from a subsidiary less than 10 per cent of the stock of which is owned by the parent corporation; (ii) interest on bonds; (iii) capital gains from stock or bonds; (iv) royalties; (v) income from a lease of a ship or an aircraft, etc. Art. 66-6(4) of the STMA, before the 2017 Tax Reform.

In the 2017 Tax Reform, the CFC rules were revised to a significant extent. After the 2017 Tax Reform, the "less than 20 per cent" standard continues to be applied to the business income of a foreign subsidiary that does not meet all of the four conditions above ("targeted foreign related corporation"). Even if a foreign subsidiary meets all of the four standards mentioned above, but its tax burden ratio is less than 20 per cent, the passive income[36] of the subsidiary will be added to the parent's income. Furthermore, for a subsidiary that: (a) does not meet both of the fixed-facility standard and the self- management-and-administration standard ("paper company"); (b) has passive income of 30 per cent or more against its total assets ("cash-box company"); or (c) is founded in a jurisdiction which is not co-operative in Exchange of Information, the income of such subsidiary ("specified foreign related corporation") should be added to the parent's income if the tax burden ratio of the subsidiary is less than 30 per cent. On the other hand, some business transactions such as aircraft leasing or Hong Kong-based manufacturers managing factories in mainland China were excluded from CFC taxation.

The BEPS Action 5 final report evaluated that the Japanese CFC rules were a kind of hybrid of the entity approach and the transactional approach. Japan's private sector also evaluates that the Japanese CFC rules are consistent with the BEPS final report (Japan Federation of Economic Organisations (*Keidanren*), 2016).

8.4.4 Action 4: Interest

Japan enacted its thin capitalisation rules in 1992, under which interest paid by a domestic corporation to its foreign-related parties is denied a deduction as expenses if the amount of debt borrowed from such foreign-related parties exceeds three times the capital of the corporation.[37]

Japan also enacted excessive interest rules in 2012, under which the net interest paid by a domestic corporation to its foreign-related parties is denied a deduction as expenses if the net amount of interest paid to such foreign-related parties exceeds 50 per cent of the net income of the corporation.[38] This rule is a little different to the rule proposed by the BEPS Action 4 report, that recommended that interest should be denied deduction as expenses if its amount exceeded the company's EBITDA (Earnings Before Interest, Tax, Depreciation and Amortisation) multiplied by a fixed number.

The 2017 Tax Reform Package of the ruling parties (the LDP and *Komeito*), issued on 8 December 2016, stated in its Appendix, "The basic policy regarding future international taxation", that they would study the system for restricting the deductibility of interest in accordance with the BEPS Action 4 report.

36 The definition of passive income is slightly different from that before the 2017 tax reform.

37 STMA, Art. 66-5.

38 STMA, Art. 66-5-2.

8.4.5 Action 7: Permanent Establishment

In the 2018 Tax Reform of March 2018, the definition of a permanent establishment was changed in accordance with the BEPS Action 7 report, as a counter action to the avoidance of permanent establishment status. Under the new provisions regarding the definition of a PE, if the definition of a PE in a bilateral tax treaty is different from the definition in the *Income Tax Act* and the *Corporation Tax Act*, the definition of the tax treaty prevails.[39]

8.4.6 Actions 8-10: Transfer Pricing

The Appendix to the 2017 Tax Reform Package of the ruling parties mentioned above in section 8.4.4 stated that they would study how to treat intangibles in the transfer pricing taxation, including the introduction of the "commensurate with income" provision, in order to counter the transfer of intellectual property to foreign jurisdictions with low tax rate.

The Japanese government seems to be awaiting the outcome of discussions of the OECD Working Party 6 regarding the OECD Transfer Pricing Guidelines.

8.4.7 Action 12: Mandatory Disclosure Rules

After the BEPS Action 12 final report on Mandatory Disclosure Rules (MDR) was issued in October 2015, the Tax System Council (*zeisei chousakai*), an advisory board of the Prime Minister, expressed their interest in the MDR regime in its discussion report of November 2016. The Appendix to the 2017 Tax Reform Package of the ruling parties noted in section 8.4.4 above also mentioned MDR as a system to be studied.

8.4.8 Action 13: Multilateral Instrument

As mentioned in section 8.3.2 above, the Japanese government signed the Multilateral Instrument (MLI) on 7 June 2017 in Paris. The approval of the Diet has already been given. Tentatively, Japan has accepted major parts of the MLI including Article 7 (Prevention of Treaty Abuse), Part V (Improving Dispute Resolution) and Part VI (Arbitration), but Japan made a reservation to Paragraph 1 of Article 23 ("Baseball Arbitration").

Japan has tentatively made reservations to some other clauses of the MLI, such as Article 11 "Application of tax agreement to restrict a party's right to tax its own residents" and Article 14 "Splitting-up of contracts".

39 New Article 2(1)(viii-iv) of the *Income Tax Act* and new Article 2(xii-xix) of the *Corporation Tax Act*.

8.5 Unilateral BEPS Measures

8.5.1 In General

It seems that the Japanese tax authority does not prefer to legislate any original (or innovative) anti-avoidance rules but lays its policy weight on following well-accepted international rules, such as CFC rules, transfer pricing taxation, thin capitalisation, or corporate inversion rules.

In Japan, it is widely accepted (by academics, the tax administration, tax lawyers and judges) that: (i) taxes should be imposed only by statutes of the Diet, and (ii) the taxable events (*Steuertatbestand*) should be as clear as possible. Those are two of important requirements under the Principle of Statute-based Taxation.[40] In this context, in respect of preventing or nullifying abusive tax avoidance, a consensus has been reached that the Diet should enact Special Anti-Avoidance Rules (SAARs) as soon as the tax authority finds a new type of scheme. For General Anti-Avoidance Rules (GAARs), however, scholars' opinions are divided.[41] Opponents to the GAARs argue that the conditions of taxation in a GAAR clause are vague as part of the essential nature of the clause, and therefore legislating for GAARs would be against the Principle of Statute-based Taxation. On the other hand, proponents argue that GAARs are necessary to counter newly developed tax avoidance schemes because the Diet (and the tax authority) cannot predict all kinds of schemes at the time of enacting legislation. The author thinks that the former group comprises the majority of academics while the latter has persuasive voices in the context of the situation where many foreign jurisdictions have introduced GAARs in recent years.

8.5.2 General Anti-Avoidance Rules Applied for Family Companies and in Other Situations

Although Japanese tax law does not have GAARs, it has quasi-GAARs applicable to family corporations (that account for more than 96 per cent of all corporations) and in other particular situations such as corporate reorganisation, transaction by permanent establishments, or consolidated tax returns.

Article 132(1) of the *Corporation Tax Act* provides (emphasis added):[42]

> "In making correction or determination of a corporation tax on corporations prescribed in the following, if the district director realises that the

40 This principle comes from Article 84 of the Constitution of Japan (1947) that provides: "No new tax shall be imposed or existing one modified except by law or under such conditions as law may prescribe".

41 In July 1961, the Tax System Council (*zeisei chousakai*), an advisory board to the Prime Minister, submitted a report regarding the enactment of the General Act of National Taxes and made the recommendation to insert a General Anti-Avoidance Rule such as that of then West Germany. The *General Act of National Taxes* was enacted in 1962 (Act No. 66 of 1962), but the GAAR was not provided for because of the opposition of tax scholars and practitioners.

42 Translation: Sozeishiryokan, "Corporation Tax Act of Japan (2017)", http://www.sozeishiryokan.or.jp/corporation_tax/corporation_tax2017e.html.

admission of transaction or book entries of the corporations would result in *improper decrease* of the burden of the corporation tax on the corporations, the district director may compute the tax base of corporation tax, the amount of net loss, or the amount of corporation tax on the corporations according to his recognition, notwithstanding transactions or books entries by the corporations.

(i) A family corporation which is a domestic corporation.

(ii) ......"

A "family corporation" is a corporation with more than 50 per cent of the shares of which are held by less than 3 persons and related persons (such as relatives within 6-degrees of kinship or related corporations).[43] Similar provisions are contained in the *Income Tax Act* and the *Inheritance Tax Act*. For example, under Article 152(1) of the *Income Tax Act*, the district director of the district tax office may compute the amount of income, tax, loss, etc., of a resident who is a shareholder of, or has a special relationship with, a family corporation if the district director realises that the admission of transaction or book entries of the corporations would result in an *improper decrease* of the burden of the income tax on the resident, notwithstanding transactions or books entries by the family corporations.

These rules have been criticised on the basis that the term "*improper decrease*" is too vague, but in a 1978 decision[44] the Supreme Court dismissed a taxpayer's assertion that they violate Article 84 of the Constitution.[45] On the other hand, it has not been an easy task for the Diet and the tax authority to propose a tax reform to clarify the meaning of "*improper decrease*" because there is no consensus whether Japan should have GAARs or not. In this situation, the Diet reproduced articles that contain the term "*improper decrease*" when it enacted new Special Anti-Avoidance Rules applied to corporate reorganisations,[46] consolidated tax returns,[47] or permanent establishments.[48]

In its 2017 decision,[49] the Supreme Court interpreted the meaning of the term "*improper decrease*" of Article 132-2, stating (emphasis added):

"......the meaning of "improper decrease of the burden of the corporation tax" of Article 132-2 of the [Corporation Tax] Act means that a transaction or book entries of the corporation induces a decrease of the burden

---

43 Defined at Article 2(x) of the *Corporation Tax Act*.

44 Decision of the Supreme Court (2nd chamber) of 21 April 1978, Monthly Litigation Reporter (*Shomu Geppo*) Vol. 24, No. 8, p. 1694.

45 See n. 40, above.

46 Article 132-2 of the *Corporation Tax Act*, Article 157(4) of the *Income Tax Act*, etc., (introduced in the 2001 tax reform).

47 Article 132-3 of the *Corporation Tax Act* (introduced by Act No. 79 of 2002).

48 Article 147-2 of the *Corporation Tax Act* (introduced in the 2014 tax reform).

49 Decision of the Supreme Court (1st Chamber) of 29 February 2016, Supreme Court Reporter Vol. 70, No. 2, p. 242.

of corporation tax by *abusing provisions* relating corporate reorganisation *as methods of tax avoidance*, according to *the purpose and object of the provision*."

This Supreme Court decision has led to discussions as to whether the meaning of "improper decrease" of Articles 132, 132-2, 132-3 and 147-2 should be interpreted in the same way or differently.

8.5.3 Automatic Exchange of Information

Japan committed to the automatic exchange of information under the Common Reporting Standards (CRS) set by the OECD in 2014.

Before 2014, in joint statements with the United States on 21 June 2012 and 11 June 2013, Japan committed to the US Foreign Account Tax Compliance Act (FATCA) in the following way:

- the Japanese government instructs Japanese financial institutions (such as banks or insurance companies) to register at the Internal Revenue Service (IRS) of the US;
- Japanese financial institutions provide the IRS with information of their US clients who agree that their information would be provided to the IRS;
- Japanese financial institutions provide only the number of its US clients who do not agree that their information would be provided to the IRS;
- the IRS requests Japan's National Tax Agency (NTA) to provide detailed information about the clients who do not agree that their information would be provided to the IRS, under the information exchange clause of the Japan-US Tax Treaty;
- the competent authority of the NTA inquires of the financial institution about the information of such clients,[50] and
- the competent authority of the NTA provides to the IRS such information provided to it by the financial institutions.

This is the so-called "Model 2 Agreement", compared to the reciprocal "Model 1 Agreement" that the UK, Germany, France, Italy and Spain have concluded with the US. The Model 2 Agreement is not reciprocal, but the Japanese government seems not to have had time to revise its law in order to obligate financial institutions to provide information of their US clients.

In the 2015 Tax Reform, persons who have an account in a financial institution have become obliged to provide financial institutions with information on their name, birthdate, resident country, etc., and financial institutions have become obliged to provide the tax authority with their clients' information.[51] This new rule was enacted to enable the Japanese tax authority to implement information exchange under the CRS.

50 The refusal to the inquiries may be criminally penalised under Japanese tax law.

51 New Article 10-5 of the *Act Relating to Special Measures of the Income Tax Act, the Corporation Tax Act and the Local Tax Act for Implementing Tax Conventions, etc.* (Act No. 46 of 1969).

8.5.4 Overseas Money-Remittance Report

Under Act No. 119 of 1997, a person who remits money overseas or receives money overseas of more than JPY 1 million must submit a report to a financial institution that is in charge of the transfer of the money,[52] and such financial institution must submit that report to the tax authority.[53] A failure to carry out such reporting may result in a criminal fine of up to JPY 500,000 and/or imprisonment of up to one year.[54]

8.5.5 Overseas Property Report

Under the abovementioned Act No. 119 of 1997, a person who has overseas properties of more than JPY 50 million must submit a report called "Overseas Property Report" to the tax authority by 15 March each year.[55] A failure of such reporting may result in a criminal fine of up to JPY 500,000 and/or imprisonment of up to one year.[56] The rate of additional tax for understatement or non-statement will be increased (in case of income tax) or decreased (in case of income tax or inheritance tax) depending upon whether a taxpayer has submitted such documentation honestly.[57]

8.6 Tax Administration

On 25 October 2016, the National Tax Agency published "The International Strategic Total Plan" (National Tax Agency, 2016),[58] referring to the BEPS Project, CRS and other measures. On 19 December 2017, the NTA published "The International Strategic Total Plan: The present situation and the way forward" (National Tax Agency, 2017b).[59] In the December 2017 document, the NTA reported that:

- the NTA created a new position "Director of International Taxation" in 2017 as a position responsible for international taxation[60] in its Taxation Department (TD);

52 Article 3 of Act No. 119 of 1997.
53 Article 4 of Act No. 119 of 1997.
54 Article 9 of Act No. 119 of 1997.
55 Article 5 of Act No. 119 of 1997. 15 March is the due date of income tax return filing.
56 Article 10 of Act No. 119 of 1997.
57 Article 6 of Act No. 119 of 1997.
58 See press release, http://www.nta.go.jp/information/release/kokuzeicho/2016/kokusai_kazei/index.htm (accessed on 6 August 2018).
59 See http://www.nta.go.jp/taxes/shiraberu/kokusai/strategy/index.htm.
60 The NTA already has the positions of "Director, International Examination" in the Large Enterprises Examination Division of the Examination and Criminal Investigation Department (ECID), "Director of the International Operations Division", for exchange of information and international cooperation, in the Commissioner's Secretariat (CS), and "Director of the Office of Mutual Agreement Procedures", in charge of mutual consultations, in the CS. In respect of tax auditing, the ECID is responsible for the audit of large corporations the capital of which is JPY 100 million or more, and the Taxation Department for the audit of other corporations and all individual taxpayers. See National Tax Agency (2017a, p. 10).

- the NTA established the "HNWI Project Team" relating to high net wealth individuals in each of 12 Regional Taxation Bureaus (RTBs) in 2017;
- the NTA is requesting an increase of the number of international tax auditors.

The December 2017 document also stated that the NTA would utilise information resources such as: (i) the money remittance / receiving report; (ii) the overseas property report; (iii) information exchanged under tax treaties; (iv) information exchanged under the Common Reporting Standard (CRS), and (v) information exchanged under the CbC reporting system. The document further stated that the NTA would strengthen its global network relating to matters such as: (i) mutual assistance for collection; (ii) automatic exchange of information provided by foreign jurisdictions under relevant tax treaties and the CRS framework; (iii) expediting mutual agreement procedures, and (iv) participating in international discussions.

8.7 The Future of BEPS

In this author's view, the BEPS Project was a very beneficial first step for the coordination of international taxation, as well as for preventing abusive tax planning. The final reports of the BEPS Project have indicated the way forward to the unification of tax systems of jurisdictions, and such unification seems to be in the process of being realised gradually but steadily. Information exchange systems of tax authorities, such as the CRS, CbC reporting and exchanging of tax rulings have developed dramatically. The BEPS Project also gave an opportunity for jurisdictions to reach a common understanding in relation to international taxation as far as possible. It is remarkable that such an audacious project was completed in the short period of three years, belying the common understanding that the process of making new international tax rules only moves glacially.

It is not realistic, however, to expect that all jurisdictions will maintain their pace and implement their tax laws in a similarly harmonious way in the future. Even immediately before and after the BEPS final reports were issued, some jurisdictions devised their own unique anti-avoidance rules, such as the Diverted Profits Tax of the UK and Australia. Several new concepts such as Digital Service Tax, Significant Digital Presence or Digital PE are emerging. Negative evaluations should not be given for such new legislation because each jurisdiction has its own authority to invent and implement its own rules, and our tax systems would not develop if we denied such new ideas. At the same time, however, international cooperation is necessary to integrate such rules, to implement such rules efficiently and effectively, and to avoid double taxation and double non-taxation for taxpayers.

The post-BEPS world also contains some new concerns. If one jurisdiction uses information exchanged under the newly developed system by the BEPS Project with an interpretation that is different from that agreed in the project, private enterprises will be at risk of double taxation and administrative burdens. In this context, protecting taxpayers' rights in the post-BEPS world is also a concern of businesses and scholars. It is a duty of jurisdictions, tax authorities and the international tax community to supervise and review the implementation process of the BEPS Project.

References

Hata, Mikio (2018), "Recent Situation of Mutual Agreement Procedures", 38(4) *Monthly Journal of International Taxation* 14-41.

Herzfeld, Mindy and Mitsuhiro Honda (2018), "Moving to Territorial: Lessons From Japan", 89 *Tax Notes International* 119-123.

Japan Federation of Economic Organisations (*Keidanren*) (2016), "Proposals on Future International Taxation after the BEPS Project", 19 April, http://www.keidanren.or.jp/policy/2016/024_honbun.html (accessed on 6 August 2018).

Morotomi, Toru (2017), "Japan's Shift to Territoriality in 2009 and the Recent Corporate Tax Reform: A Japan-United States Comparison of Taxing Income from Multinationals", 14(2) *Pittsburgh Tax Review* 173-217.

National Tax Agency, Japan (2016), "International Strategy Total Plan – Current situation and future direction of international taxation initiatives", Tokyo, October, www.nta.go.jp/information/release/kokuzeicho/2016/kokusai_kazei/pdf/04.pdf.

National Tax Agency, Japan (2017a), *National Tax Agency Report 2017*, Tokyo, June.

National Tax Agency, Japan (2017b), "The International Strategic Total Plan: The present situation and the way forward", Tokyo, December, http://www.nta.go.jp/taxes/shiraberu/kokusai/strategy/pdf/action_policy_201712.pdf.

Organisation for Economic Co-operation and Development (OECD) (2017), *Inclusive Framework on BEPS: Action 5, Harmful Tax Practices – Peer Review Reports on the Exchange of Information on Tax Rulings* (Paris: OECD).

Organisation for Economic Co-operation and Development (OECD) (2018), *Inclusive Framework on BEPS: Action 13, Country-by-Country Reporting – Compilation of Peer Review Reports (Phase 1)* (Paris: OECD).

9 The Adoption of BEPS in Korea

Hyejung Byun[*] and Seung Jong Yang[**]

Abstract

Base erosion and profit shifting activities have been a concern in Korea for many years and critical public commentary had strengthened government resolve to tackle these abuses even prior to the OECD's BEPS initiative. Korea is expected to progressively adopt most of the BEPS actions through enactment or modifications of domestic tax laws, as well as in its tax treaties, in line with the BEPS Action plans. However, it will take some time for all the recommendations to eventually be incorporated into Korea's domestic laws and tax treaties following the necessary legal and administrative processes. It may be noted that Korea should endeavour to implement the BEPS recommendations as appropriate while also giving careful consideration to its economic situation.

9.1 Introduction

Korea, officially the Republic of Korea, is a country in East Asia, constituting the southern part of the Korean Peninsula and lying east of the Asian mainland. It comprises an estimated population of 51.4 million residents inhabiting an area of 99,392 square kilometers.

In the 1970s and 1980s, the Korean economy enjoyed substantial growth. The country was transformed into a G20 major economy and joined the Organisation for Economic Co-operation and Development (OECD) in 1996.[1] As of 2018, Korea is the world's 12th largest economy by nominal GDP and the 11th largest in purchasing power parity terms. It is a global leader in the industrial and technological sectors, being the world's 5th largest exporter and 8th largest importer. Its export-driven economy primarily focuses production on electronics, automobiles, ships, machinery, petrochemicals and robotics.

Korea has a presidential system of government with a relatively independent chief executive. Like many democratic countries, Korea's government comprises three branches: executive, judicial, and legislative. The executive and legislative branches operate primarily at the national level, although various ministries in the executive branch also carry out local functions. The judicial branch operates at

* Associate Professor, Graduate School of Science in Taxation, University of Seoul, Seoul, Korea.

** Tax Partner, Kim & Chang, Seoul, Korea.

1 By contrast, note that, according to UNCTADstat, Korea is classified as a developing country.

both the national and local levels. Currently 18 ministries exist in the government. The major administrative divisions are eight provinces, one special self-governing province, six metropolitan cities, one special city and one metropolitan autonomous city.

The National Tax Service (NTS), which is mainly in charge of the assessment and collection of internal taxes, was established as an external organisation of the Ministry of Finance on 3 March 1966, taking over the Taxation Bureau of the Ministry of Finance. Headed by the Commissioner, it is responsible for tax administration by directing, supervising, and controlling regional and district tax offices.[2] The NTS consists of 10 bureaus, namely the Planning & Coordination Bureau, the Information System Bureau, the Taxpayer Advocacy Bureau, the International Taxation Bureau, the Collection, Legal Affairs & PR Bureau, the Individual Taxation Bureau, the Corporate Taxation Bureau, the Property Taxation Bureau, the Investigation Bureau and the Earned Income Tax Bureau. There are three affiliated organisations, comprising the National Tax Officials Training Institute, the NTS Liquor License Support Center and the National Tax Consultation Center. The NTS also has six regional tax offices, in Seoul, Busan, Daegu, Daejeon, Gwangju and Suwon, and 117 district tax offices across the country.

Taxes in Korea comprise national and local taxes. National taxes are divided into internal taxes, customs duties, and three earmarked taxes. The local taxes include province taxes and city and county taxes. The national internal taxes consist of direct and indirect taxes and each consists of five internal taxes. Of these ten taxes, Income Tax, Corporation Tax, and Value Added Tax make up the bulk of Korean tax revenue. There are also three national earmarked taxes, namely the Transportation Energy and Environment Tax, Education Tax and Special Tax for Rural Development; the revenues from these sources go directly to pre-designated government programs. There are 11 local taxes, and they are divided into province and city and county taxes. At the provincial level, there are four ordinary taxes and two earmarked taxes.[3] At the city and county level, there are five ordinary taxes.[4]

---

2 The Commissioner of the National Tax Service, a vice-ministerial level official in legal terms, is customarily considered to be a ministerial level official due to the importance of the National Tax Service. Therefore, the Commissioner of the agency attends meetings of minister-level officials, and the Vice-Commissioner of the agency attends meetings where other agencies would send their Commissioners.

3 The ordinary taxes include Acquisition Tax, Registration and License Tax, Leisure Tax and Local Consumption Tax, and the earmarked taxes include Community Resource and Facility Tax and Local Education Tax.

4 These are Inhabitant Tax, Property Tax, Automobile Tax, Local Income Tax and Tobacco Consumption Tax.

9.2 Korea's Response to the G20/OECD BEPS Program of Tax Reform

Base erosion and profit shifting activities have been a concern in Korea for many years and critical public commentary had strengthened government resolve to tackle these abuses even prior to the G20/OECD initiatives. Along the way, the BEPS project began in 2013 with OECD and G20 countries, in a context of financial crisis and major controversy over tax affairs. In 2015, the Korean government announced that it was reviewing the BEPS Action recommendations and intended to incorporate the recommendations into the domestic laws.

Anti-avoidance regimes had already existed in Korea before the BEPS project commenced. The transfer pricing regulations were introduced in 1996 and extensively amended in 2010 to reflect changes made to the OECD Transfer Pricing Guidelines.[5] Both controlled foreign company (CFC) rules and thin capitalisation rules were introduced in 1997.

In recent years, reforms related to BEPS have been actively implemented in Korea as in many other countries. The tax authorities have made significant efforts to strengthen relevant regulations and bring the regulations more into line with the BEPS project outcomes.

9.3 Korea and the BEPS Inclusive Framework

Korea has signed up to the BEPS Inclusive Framework. The mandate of the Inclusive Framework is a focus on the implementation of four BEPS minimum standards, including those relating to harmful tax practices, tax treaty abuse, Country-by-Country Reporting requirements for transfer pricing and improvements in cross-border tax dispute resolution.

9.3.1 Action 5: Peer Review and Monitoring

Action 5, entitled "countering harmful tax practices more effectively, considering transparency and substance", consists of two elements: whether preferential tax regimes have harmful features, and whether a framework exists for the compulsory spontaneous exchange of information on tax rulings (the transparency framework).

9.3.1.1 *Preferential Tax Regimes*

The existing Korean tax laws do not run counter to the BEPS recommendations

5 The transfer pricing regulations are contained in the Law for the Coordination of International Tax Affairs (LCITA). Prior to the introduction of the LCITA, transfer prices imposed in relation to domestic and cross-border transactions were both regulated by the Corporate Income Tax Law (CITL). In an effort to update and conform Korean transfer pricing regulations to internationally recognised rules and principles, the LCITA was promulgated on 6 December 1995 and then supplemented by an Enforcement Decree (LCITA-ED) and an Enforcement Regulation (LCITA-ER), issued on 30 December 1995 and 30 March 1996, respectively.

regarding harmful tax practices. In accordance with the OECD's BEPS Action 5 Final Report (OECD, 2015), the intellectual property regimes in Korea, which include special taxation for transfer or acquisition of technology, were reviewed from October 2015 and as at 4 October 2017 were found not harmful (OECD, 2017, p. 17). It was also determined that the regimes of foreign investment zone, free economic zone and free trade zone are out of the scope of the preferential regimes (OECD, 2017, p. 20).

On this topic, however, on 5 December 2017, the European Union included Korea in its list of non-cooperative tax jurisdictions, noting a harmful preferential tax regime related to Korea's foreign investment tax incentives that are only granted to non-residents. On 23 January 2018, the EU removed Korea from the list after Korea's tax policy announcement in December 2017 which included revisions to its tax support system "to bring it in line with global standards" (Bang, 2018; Kim and Jang, 2018). In particular, the reform Bill as announced on 30 July 2018 ends a national corporation tax exemption for foreign companies investing in "new growth sector businesses and in specially designated areas" for new applications filed on or after 1 January 2019 (Ernst and Young, 2018b, p. 2).

9.3.1.2 *Transparency Framework*

To implement the legal basis for the transparency framework and complete the administrative work to ensure that exchange of information on rulings is implemented, Korea has legislated to exchange information received from taxpayers as part of applications for advance pricing agreements (APAs). The amended law has been effective from 13 February 2018.[6] Before the amendment, the relevant domestic regulation specifically restricted the tax administration's use of information that is submitted in an application of an APA only to the review of the APA and follow-up procedures related to the APA.

Under Korea's legal system, treaty provisions enabling administrative power such as exchange of information cannot automatically override the legal provision regarding the restrictions on use of APA information. Therefore, the amendment is regarded as improving how Korea cooperates with other countries' tax agencies on the collection of tax from multinational enterprises.

9.3.2 Action 6: Preventing Treaty Abuse

Korea's domestic laws include a rule requiring a substance-over-form approach to interpretation which also applies to deny treaty benefits arising from treaty abuse.[7] As a supplement to this rule, Korea has taken up the option under Action 6 of applying a principal purpose test under future treaties and renegotiated treaties

6 Enforcement Decree for the Coordination of International Tax Affairs (LCITA-ED), §9(5).

7 Law for the Coordination of International Tax Affairs (LCITA), § 2-2. For further details of the use of this provision by Korean authorities in treaty disputes and the domestic cases on the provision, see Park and Kim (2018).

to deny treaty benefits where one of the principal purposes of the arrangement was the gaining of those benefits. It has been noted that the emphasis in the Action 6 recommendations on the purpose of the agreement may provide an alternative focus to the concept of beneficial ownership in substance as a basis to limit treaty shopping (Nam, Lee and Sung, 2017, p. 482).

The *Convention Between the Republic of Korea and the Czech Republic for the Avoidance of Double Taxation and the Prevention of Fiscal Evasion with respect to Taxes on Income* (Korea-Czech Tax Treaty), signed on 12 January 2018 and awaiting parliamentary approval, is the first bilateral tax treaty Korea has concluded which complies with the minimum standard on Action 6, including the revised preamble and principal purpose test.

9.3.3 Action 13: Transfer Pricing Documentation

Korean rules require two categories of transfer pricing documentation, namely documents associated with the tax return and those with a tax audit (Kim, 2018, p. 367). Tax return documentation encompasses a Declaration of Transfer Pricing Method, Summary of Cross-Border Transactions, and Summary of Foreign Affiliate Income Statements, while in a tax audit a variety of other documents may be required to assist auditors in forming a view about the extent to which transfer prices meet the arm's length standard.

In accordance with the BEPS initiative, new legislation has been enacted to require qualifying taxpayers in Korea to submit the Combined Report of International Transactions (CRIT), consisting of a Master File, a Local File, and a Country-by-Country Report (CbC Report), for fiscal years commencing on or after 1 January 2016 (Kim, 2018; PwC, 2016). The CRIT requirements introduced initially in December 2015 represented a substantial change in Korean practice towards filing of information as part of annual lodgement of return rather than as part of an audit (Kim, 2018, p. 368).

Qualifying taxpayers are MNE groups operating in Korea and meeting a KRW 1 trillion consolidated revenue threshold in the prior year. This rule applies to ultimate parent entities resident in Korea as well as constituent entities resident in Korea if the group's ultimate parent is resident in a jurisdiction that does not require CbC Reports or the ultimate parent's jurisdiction does not automatically exchange CbC Reports with the Korean tax authorities.

The required content of the CbC Report is in line with BEPS Action 13 guidelines, including aggregate tax information for each jurisdiction in which the group operates and details of all constituent entities. The CbC Report is exchanged with other jurisdictions with which Korea has entered into a competent authority agreement for exchange. For exchange purposes, Korea signed the Multilateral Competent Authority Agreement on the automatic exchange of CbC reports on 30 June 2016.

Through the amendments made to the Law for the Coordination of International Tax Affairs (LCITA) as part of the tax reform bill enacted on 20 December 2016, the Ministry of Strategy and Finance (now Ministry of Economy and Finance, MOEF) allows taxpayers to submit the CRIT within 12 months after the end of the fiscal year, thereby easing the timing constraint on taxpayers to prepare and submit the required documents with respect to international intercompany transactions.[8] Thus, the first reporting was due by 31 December 2017 for calendar year taxpayers.

Furthermore, the MOEF made amendments to the Enforcement Decree of the LCITA (LCITA-ED), enacting measures to supplement the regulations on BEPS documentation requirements and revise the penalty rules on failure to submit the required information.[9] The 2018 tax reform legislation increased the penalty for failure to file a Master File, a Local File, or a CbC Report from KRW 10 million to KRW 30 million per item of documentation (Cho et al., 2018). The penalties can also apply where the foregoing documentation is filed with false information.

However, when and if the taxpayer maintains and provides data verifying the method for an arm's length price applied in filing an income tax or corporate tax return and is acknowledged as having selected and applied the method for an arm's length price based on a reasonable determination, the taxpayer is exempted from the penalty.[10]

9.3.4 Action 14: Tax Treaty Dispute Resolution

Korea's 93 tax treaties all include a provision relating to mutual agreement procedure (MAP), Korea has an established MAP program. The OECD has noted that Korea has "considerable experience with resolving MAP cases" and "a large MAP inventory with a modest number of new cases submitted each year" (OECD, 2018, p. 9; Ernst and Young, 2018a). One of the authors of this chapter has, however, recently spoken with UNSW Professor John Taylor about the comprehensive revision of the Korea-Australia (1982) DTA. This is a process which could extend to the updating of the MAP provisions separately from the MLI (see Wong and Stewart, 2017, reporting the co-presentation of Byun and Taylor at the Australia-Korea Foundation workshop, Canberra, 9-10 November 2017).

The MAP provisions in those tax treaties that Korea has concluded mostly follow paragraphs 1 through 3 of Article 25 of the OECD Model Tax Convention

8 As of 1 August 2018, the Ministry of Strategy and Finance changed its official English name to the Ministry of Economy and Finance. This is to clarify to the international community, including international organisations and institutions, "the Ministry's role of being in charge of the overall economic policies in Korea": see Ministry of Economy and Finance, "'Ministry of Strategy and Finance' Changes Its Official English Name to 'Ministry of Economy and Finance'", press release (1 August 2018), english.moef.go.kr/ec/selectTbEconomicDtl.do;jsessionid=VbmeP6IcpqNfjvgDz3Kso235.node20?boardCd=E0010&seq=4524&boardCdKey=N.

9 The OECD model legislation does not include provisions regarding penalties to be imposed if an entity fails to comply with the reporting requirements for the CbC Report.

10 LCITA, § 13.

on Income and on Capital 2014. The OECD Peer Review has found that they are "largely consistent with the requirements of the Action 14 minimum standard", apart from the existence of some treaties lacking appropriate time limits and provisions for consultation between the competent authorities (OECD, 2018, p. 9; for further details, see also Ernst and Young, 2018a). One element of the process also potentially inconsistent with Action 14, noted further below, is an overriding domestic rule preventing MAP proceedings which the taxpayers involved are seeking to use for tax avoidance purposes, which may extend to proceedings involving disputes about the rules preventing treaty abuse themselves.

Korea has signed the Multilateral Instrument (MLI), through which a number of its tax treaties are modified to fulfil the requirements under the Action 14 Minimum Standard. Korea will update via bilateral negotiations all the other tax treaties which are not modified upon entry into force of the Multilateral Instrument to be compliant with the requirements under the Action 14 Minimum Standard, but it has not yet put a plan in place for that purpose.

In terms of prevention of disputes, Korea has a bilateral advance pricing agreement (APA) program including provision for taxpayers to request application of the agreed prices to past transactions (roll-backs). Korea's MAP provisions meet the Action 14 Minimum Standards (with the possible exception of the rules for disputes involving treaty anti-abuse provisions), including availability of MAP in all appropriate cases and procedures for consultation where the competent authority intends to decline the application for MAP proceedings. Korea also has clear and comprehensive MAP guidance.

As noted above, one caveat in the review findings relates to Korea's domestic law rule allowing the competent authority not to initiate an MAP proceeding which the parties are seeking to use for tax avoidance purposes. This provision gives rise to the the risk that MAP will not be available in cases where the rules to prevent treaty abuse have been applied, contrary to the requirements of Action 14.

The inclusion of MAP arbitration is possible under Korean law but in general is not part of Korea's tax treaty policy. This is also stipulated in its MAP guidance. In addition, Korea has reserved its position in relation to Article 25(5) of the OECD Model Tax Convention relating to the arbitration provisions.

Although Korea has not incorporated an arbitration clause in its tax treaties as a final stage to the MAP, the Convention Between the Republic of Korea and Switzerland for the Avoidance of Double Taxation with Respect to Taxes on Income includes a most-favoured nation clause on arbitration. This provision stipulates that if Korea includes an arbitration provision in one of its tax treaties, it shall enter into negotiations with its treaty partner with whom the most-favoured nation clause was agreed with a view to including an arbitration provision in that treaty as well.

9.4 Korea's Response to the Other BEPS Actions

9.4.1 Action 1: Digital Economy

Korea has implemented reforms relating to the digital economy through its value added tax (VAT) law, extending the tax to the importation of electronic services into Korea. The reform implements a foreign service provider registration model imposing the VAT liability on the provider, which has been effective since 1 July 2015 (Nam, Lee and Sung, 2017).

An electronic service is widely defined for the purposes of these rules and includes games, audio or video files, electronic documents and software. The 2018 Proposal extends the definition to include cloud computing.

A registered foreign service provider must pay VAT quarterly, but is not required to issue a VAT invoice. If the electronic service is provided through an intermediary such as an open market platform or an intermediary agent for payment, the VAT obligations apply to the platform or agent, as the case may be.

More broadly, it has also recently been reported that the Korean government has been mulling income tax reforms to impose tax on multinational technology firms as a result of domestic political pressure and the work of its officials participating in the OECD digital economy taskforce (Jun, 2018, also cited by LeFebvre, 2018). The reform reportedly may include defining a local place of business to include a cache server but otherwise the specific form that such measures may take is not yet clear.

9.4.2 Action 2: Hybrid Mismatch Rules

As a commitment to implementing the hybrid mismatch rules recommended by the BEPS Action 2, the 2018 Tax Reform Legislation, which entered into force on 1 January 2018, introduces restrictions on interest deductions for cross-border hybrid mismatch arrangements.[11] The restrictions apply to transactions between a domestic corporation, including a Korean branch of a foreign corporation and its foreign related party and operate to deny deductions for payments under financial instruments not fully subject to tax (i.e., none or less than 10 per cent of the payment has been included in taxable income) in the other jurisdiction in question through to the end of the following fiscal year in that jurisdiction (Cho et al., 2018).

A claw-back provision also applies in relation to deductions made of any non-taxable portion of payment (Cho et al., 2018).

9.4.3 Action 3: Controlled Foreign Companies

Korea introduced CFC rules in 1997. To curb perceived tax avoidance through foreign retention, Korea extended application of its CFC rules to passive income as of 1 January 2015. The obligation to submit information on CFCs has been reinforced

11 LCITC, §16-3.

in the 2017 tax reform legislation, under which a new penalty of up to KRW 100 million of additional tax may be levied for failure to comply.[12]

Some discrepancies between Korea's CFC rules and the requirements of Action 3 have been identified, such as the lack of coverage of partnerships and branches under the current regime and absence of an allowance for foreign losses (Kim and Kim, 2017, pp. 473-474), so that some revision of Korea's CFC laws is possible in the future.

9.4.4 Action 4: Fixed-Ratio Interest Expense Limitation

The 2018 tax reform legislation introduced a fixed-ratio rule to limit related-party interest deductions to 30 per cent of a domestic corporation's adjusted taxable income for transactions involving domestic and foreign related parties, apart from financial and insurance companies (Cho et al., 2018). From 1 January 2019, a Korean corporation's deduction of interest payments to foreign related parties will be limited to the lower of the amount resulting from application of the fixed-ratio rule, that is 30 per cent of the domestic corporation's adjusted taxable income or the Korean thin capitalisation rules.

Korea's thin capitalisation rules have a debt-to-equity ratio of 2:1, with a 6:1 ratio for financial institutions.[13] Where a Korean company borrows from its foreign controlling shareholders, any equity interest payable on the portion exceeding the debt-to-equity ratios is characterised as dividends that are not deductible for Korean tax purposes.

The domestic corporation must use the method that results in a larger disallowance of interest expense deduction computed either under the new interest expense limitation rule or 2:1 debt-to-equity safe harbour rules.

9.4.5 Action 7: Permanent Establishments

The 2018 tax reform proposal as announced by the MOEF on 30 July 2018 includes a range of amendments to Korea's domestic law provisions on permanent establishments in keeping with the November 2017 updates to Article 5 of the OECD Model Tax Convention.

It should be noted, however, that Korea's tax law generally adopts the approach of allowing treaty provisions to prevail over domestic law in case of an inconsistency (Lee, 2018, p. 380), so the application of the proposed amendments will still need to be considered in the case of each treaty. Moreover, Korea has reserved the application of the Action 7 recommendations as part of its adoption of the MLI, pending evidence of the effectiveness of the MLI (Lee, 2018, p. 388).

Nevertheless, the proposed amendments are set out in domestic law: (i) that certain fixed places relating to purchase or storage of merchandise will only be

12 LCITA, §12.

13 Corporate Income Tax Act, Article 28(2). See Nam, Lee and Sung (2017).

excluded from the PE definition if the relevant activity is of a preparatory or auxiliary character; (ii) restrictions on the application of the preparatory or auxiliary character test to prevent abuse; (iii) further deeming provisions for when domestic persons may constitute an agency PE (see Ernst and Young, 2018b).

9.4.6 Actions 8-10: Transfer Pricing

Korea has been diligently changing transfer pricing rules and administrative practice to align with the OECD guidelines, but Actions 8, 9 and 10 are yet to be fully reflected in its domestic laws. Recent commentary has noted that Korea's transfer pricing regime is "closely modelled" on the OECD Transfer Pricing Guidelines and reference can be made to them in interpreting the rules, but that the Guidelines are not legally binding (Kim, 2018, p. 366, n. 6).

9.4.7 Action 15: Multilateral Instrument

On 7 June 2017, Korea and 67 other jurisdictions signed the Multilateral Convention to Implement Tax Treaty Related Measures to Prevent BEPS (the MLI) in Paris. Korea has identified 63 tax treaties to be considered Covered Tax Agreements (CTAs), i.e., tax treaties to be amended through the MLI. Some treaties have been excluded simply due to the fact that negotiations are currently taking place for a bilateral protocol relating to MLI positions.

Korea has elected to apply key minimum standards including the new preamble to treaties under Article 6 and the denial of treaty benefits in inappropriate circumstances under Article 7 (KPMG International, 2017, p. 20).

Korea also submitted a provisional list of reservations and notifications (MLI positions) in respect of the various provisions of the MLI (Ernst and Young, 2017). The reservations apply, in summary, to: Article 3 (transparent entities); Article 4 (dual resident entities); Article 5 (methods for elimination of double taxation); Article 8 (dividend transfer transactions); Article 9 (capital gains on shares or interests deriving their value principally from immovable property); Article 10 (anti-abuse rule relating to PEs in third countries); Article 11 (application of agreements restricting rights to tax own residents), and Articles 12-15 (avoidance of PE status). Other limited reservations and notifications have also been made in respect of other MLI provisions. In summary, however, the provisional reservations and notifications made by Korea have been described as "quite balanced and consistent with the double tax treaty negotiation policies followed by Korea during the past years" (Ernst and Young, 2017, p. 7). The definitive MLI positions will be provided upon the deposit of its instrument of ratification, acceptance or approval of the MLI.

9.5 Unilateral BEPS Measures Adopted by Korea

Korea has continued to build its network of agreements with governments providing for exchange of information, including the agreement with the United States relating to the Foreign Account Tax Compliance Act (FATCA), which took effect in

July 2014. Accordingly, domestic laws were also amended. The exchange of information rules apply both to non-resident entities and Korean residents. Failure to meet information submission requirements is subject to a penalty of up to KRW 30 million.

The 2018 Proposal announced on 30 July 2018 expands the duty of reporting overseas financial accounts held by overseas companies to individual owners of a company with 100 per cent ownership, including beneficial owners, an expansion from corporate owners of the company and requires corporations, along with individual citizens, to explain unreported offshore accounts. Penalties for not reporting overseas property transactions are increased and explanations for unreported investment overseas, including property investment, are required.

The 2018 proposal increased exit taxes: taxes of up to 25 per cent are imposed on the sales of corporate shares and a tax on the sales of property shares has been introduced. The government is also looking at ways to collect taxes from foreign companies in the wake of domestic complaints about the practice.

9.6 Tax Administration in Relation to International Tax Reform in Korea

It has been noted that the government has formed a task force comprised of NTS officers and tax professionals to assist in the effective implementation of the OECD BEPS proposals (KPMG International, 2017, p. 21). It has also set up a BEPS response centre to help Korean companies respond to BEPS developments.

9.7 Future of International Tax Reform for Korea

Korea, like many other countries, is engaged in and influenced by the profound international tax changes that are underway. Even though the OECD is aiming for coordinated implementation, countries are proceeding at somewhat different paces in implementing the BEPS recommendations. Thus, it is reasonable that each government scrutinises how the BEPS recommendations will affect its existing rules, and then embarks upon the process of changing existing rules and introducing new rules into its tax law system. Korea's move to increase its corporate income tax rate in 2018 is also a notable development which contrasts with the continued rate reduction approach still being pursued by many other countries at present.

In addition, governments should also note that localisation of BEPS recommendations to domestic circumstances is necessary. This is particularly appropriate in Korea's case considering its economic situation. In recent years, the economy has shown signs of weakness: the economic growth rate is forecast to be lower at 3 per cent; unemployment is at its highest level in 17 years; private consumption growth has slowed, held back by falling consumer confidence and rising unemployment, and fixed investment has fallen.

Taxes are a significant factor when businesses are determining where to locate their production facilities and make their investments. It is also accepted that foreign direct investment can generate new jobs, bring in new technologies and, more generally, promote growth and employment (OECD, 2008). Tax policies may also support direct investment abroad with the economic benefits that investment in that form can also provide. In this respect, as has been a matter of public debate for some time (see Jeong, 2015), the Korean government is facing a critical crossroad in both its economy and tax system. Therefore, it should endeavour to find the best way to implement the BEPS recommendations while also giving careful consideration to its economic situation.

References

Bang, Jun-ho (2018), "EU removes South Korea from tax haven blacklist", Hani.co.kr, 24 January, http://english.hani.co.kr/arti/english_edition/e_business/829213.html (accessed on 24 September 2018).

Cho, Shuck Il, Chris Finnerty, Kazuyo Parsch, Bee-Khun Yap and Min Yong Kwon (2018), "Korea Enacts 2018 Tax Reform Bill", 29(4) *Journal of International Taxation* 13-14.

Ernst and Young (2017), "Korea signs Multilateral Convention to Implement Tax Treaty Related Measures to Prevent BEPS", Global Tax Alert, 26 July, https://www.ey.com/Publication/vwLUAssets/Korea_signs_Multilateral_Convention_to_Implement_Tax_Treaty_Related_Measures_to_Prevent_BEPS/$FILE/2017G_04339-171Gbl_Korea%20signs%20MC%20to%20Implement%20Tax%20Treaty%20Related%20Measures%20to%20Prevent%20BEPS.pdf

Ernst and Young (2018a), "OECD releases Korea's peer review report on implementation of Action 14 minimum standard", Global Tax Alert, 16 May, https://www.ey.com/Publication/vwLUAssets/OECD_releases_Koreas_peer_review_report_on_implementation_of_Action_14_minimum_standard/$FILE/ 2018G_02145-181Gbl_Korea%20-%20OECD%20BEPS%20Action%2014%20peer%20review%20report.pdf.

Ernst and Young (2018b), "Korea announces 2018 tax reform proposals", *Global Tax Alert*, 15 August, https://www.ey.com/Publication/vwLUAssets/Korea_announces_2018_tax_reform_proposals/$FILE/2018G_010769-18Gbl_Korea%20announces%202018%20tax%20reform%20proposals.pdf.

Jeong, Seeun (2015), "The Korean economy and its tax system at a crossroads", paper presented at the Theory of Crisis-Proof Regulation conference, Paris, 10-12 June, https://theorie-regulation.org/colloques/colloque-rr-2015/programme-rr2015/.

Jun, Ji-hye (2018), "Korea moving to tax Google, Apple, Amazon", *Korea Times*, 2 August, https://www.koreatimes.co.kr/www/tech/2018/08/133_253245.html.

Kim, Jung-hong and Young-Ok Kim (2017), "Republic of Korea", *Cahiers de Droit Fiscal International Vol. 102A: Assessing BEPS: Origins, Standards, and Responses* 463-481.

Kim, Seung Ho and Sung Doo Jang (2018), "Recent Tax Issues in Korea: Increase in Corporate Income Tax Rate and Listing on EU Blacklist", 89 *Tax Notes International* 943-947.

Kim, Young-Joo (2018), "The Current Transfer Pricing Environment for Multinational Enterprises in Korea", 72(6) *Bulletin for International Taxation* 366-373.

KPMG International (2017), *OECD BEPS Action Plan: Moving from Talk to Action in the Asia Pacific Region*, October, https://assets.kpmg.com/content/dam/kpmg/xx/pdf/2017/10/2017-beps-aspac.pdf?.

Lee, Kyung Geun (2018), "Recent Issues Regarding Permanent Establishments in Korea", 72(6) *Bulletin for International Taxation* 380-390.

LeFebvre, Rob (2018), "South Korea wants to tax companies like Apple and Google", engadget, 2 August, https://www.engadget.com/2018/08/02/south-korea-tax-global-companies-apple-google/.

Nam, Tae-Yeon, Hoon Lee and Kenny Sung (2017), "Korea – Early Mover on BEPS, More to Come", in Sam Sim and Mei-June Soo (eds.), *Asian Voices: BEPS and Beyond* (Amsterdam: IFBD Publications), 473-496.

Organisation for Economic Co-operation and Development (OECD) (2008), "Tax Effects on Foreign Direct Investment", *Policy Brief*, Paris, February.

Organisation for Economic Co-operation and Development (OECD) (2015), *Action 5 – 2015 Final Report: Countering Harmful Tax Practices More Effectively, Taking into Account Transparency and Substance* (Paris: OECD).

Organisation for Economic Co-operation and Development (OECD) (2017), *Inclusive Framework on BEPS, Action 5: Harmful Tax Practices - 2017 Progress Report on Preferential Regimes*, OECD/G20 Base Erosion and Profit Shifting Project (Paris: OECD).

Organisation for Economic Co-operation and Development (OECD) (2018), *Inclusive Framework on BEPS, Action 14: Making Dispute Resolution More Effective – MAP Peer Review Report, Korea (Stage 1)*, 12 March (Paris: OECD).

Park, Hun and Sun Young Kim (2018), "International Tax Cases Involving Substance-over-Form Rules in Korea", 72(6) *Bulletin for International Taxation* 395-402.

PwC (2016), "Korea introduces new transfer pricing documentation requirements", *Tax Insights*, 20 January, https://www.pwc.com.au/tax/taxtalk/assets/alerts/korea-introduces-new-transfer-pricing-documentation-requirements-jan-2016.pdf.

Wong, Teck Chi and Miranda Stewart (2017), "New Approaches to Tax and Welfare in Australia and Korea", Austaxpolicy: Tax and Transfer Policy Blog, 13 December, http://www.austaxpolicy.com/new-approaches-tax-welfare-australia-korea/.

10 The Adoption of BEPS in Malaysia

Jeyapalan Kasipillai* **and Veerinderjeet Singh****

Abstract

The OECD's BEPS initiatives constitute the most significant international tax reform in the twenty-first century. Malaysia has signed the Multilateral Convention Initiatives (MLI) to implement tax treaty-related measures to prevent or minimise BEPS practices. Hence, it is crucial for accounting managers and tax specialists to fully understand the impact of the anti-BEPS measures and the MLI on their groups' operations.

10.1 Introduction

Malaysia is a relatively small developing country with an area of 329,847 km^2 (127,355 square miles) and a population of around 34 million. Malaysia is not a member of the Organisation for Economic Co-operation and Development (OECD) nor is it a member of the G20.

In Malaysia, the Federal Government imposes taxes in both of the broad categories of direct and indirect taxation. The *Income Tax Act 1967* (ITA 1967) is the principal income tax legislation imposing income tax. It came into effect on 1 January 1968 replacing the then Income Tax Ordinance 1947. Other direct taxes are the petroleum income tax, real property gains tax and stamp duty. Indirect taxes are import duty, export duty, excise duty and the goods and services tax (GST) (which is replaced by a sales tax and service tax (SST) as had been imposed prior to commencement of the GST in 2015, in line with the pledge made by the new Government that was elected on 9 May 2018).

Malaysia sits at 59 of 94 countries on the Financial Complexity Index Ranking. Its main industries are integrated circuits, manufactured goods, petroleum and palm oil related industries.

10.1.1 Federal Tax Revenue

Tax revenue (including specified non-tax revenue) continues to be the main source of income for the Government of Malaysia. In 2017, 51.6 per cent of the federal government revenue was from direct taxes and the remainder was from

* Professor, Monash University, Malaysia.

** Group Chairman, Axcelasia Group, Kuala Lumpur, Malaysia and Adjunct Professor, Monash University Malaysia.

indirect taxes (28.1 per cent) and relevant non-tax revenues (20.3 per cent). Non-tax revenues include investment income, licenses, permits, registration fees, road tax, fines, petroleum royalties and service fees. Direct taxes, in nominal values, collected in 2017 amounted to MYR 119.67 billion, compared to MYR 125.57 billion in 2016, a decrease of 4.7 per cent. In 2018, the collection of direct taxes is expected to increase by 6.8 per cent to MYR 127.7 billion compared to previous years.

From the year of assessment (YA) 2016, the income tax rate for non-resident individuals was increased by 3 percentage points from 25 per cent to 28 per cent. The highest tax rate for resident individuals stood at 28 per cent from YA 2016. From YA 2018, 260,000 individuals will benefit from not paying income tax following a two percentage point reduction in the individual tax rate for those earning between MYR 20,000 and 70,000 (as announced in the 2018 Budget presented in October 2017). The corporate income tax rate in 2017 for Malaysia is 24 per cent. In 2017, income tax (including petroleum income tax) accounted for 93 per cent of total direct taxes while GST accounted for 69 per cent of total indirect taxes.

Malaysia introduced its GST in April 2015 to generate a sustainable revenue stream in the hope that its implementation would reduce the country's budget deficit given the then fall in oil prices. In 2017, revenue collection expanded by 3 per cent to MYR 119.7 billion and the fiscal deficit was 3 per cent of Gross Domestic Product compared with 3.1 per cent in 2016.[1]

The new Malaysian Government (known as the Coalition of Hope or *Pakatan Harapan*) that was formed effective from 10 May 2018 announced on 16 May 2018 that the GST would be set at zero per cent effective for a 3-month period from 1 June 2018 to 31 August 2018.[2]

10.1.2 Malaysian Tax Administration

The responsibility for the administration of direct taxes is with the Director General of Inland Revenue (DGIR) who is the Chief Executive Officer of the Inland Revenue Board (IRB). The operations of the IRB are highly decentralised. Currently, the IRB has over 70 branches throughout Malaysia.

1 Kraal, Thiagarajah and Kasipillai (2017) highlight that low oil prices have impacted Malaysian Government petroleum-related revenue, resulting in Budget revisions in 2015 and 2016. Malaysia's GST has, however, partly offset lower petroleum revenues. From the petroleum industry perspective, low oil prices are having a structural impact, although reactions differ depending on whether an entity is extractive, service or refining orientated.

2 See report of the statement in *The Star* online, 16 May 2018, https://www.thestar.com.my/news/nation/2018/05/16/gst-zero-rated-from-june-1/ (accessed on 13 June 2018). The statement from the Ministry of Finance indicated that the reduction of the rate from the current 6 per cent to 0 per cent will be implemented nationwide until a further announcement is made on the new Sales Tax and Service Tax. See also Royal Malaysian Customs Department, "Frequently Asked Questions (FAQ) Transitional 6% - 0% (Without prejudice)", 30 May 2018, http://www.customs.gov.my/en/Documents/FAQ%20TRANSITIONAL%20GST/FAQ%20(BI)%20-%20UPDATED%2030.5.18%202PM.pdf (accessed on 13 June 2018).

The Royal Malaysian Customs Department (RMCD) is responsible for the enforcement of legislation relating to indirect taxation. The types of indirect taxes include customs duties, excise duty and GST.

10.2 Malaysia's Response to the G20/OECD BEPS Tax Reform Program

Malaysia is committed to adhering to the internationally agreed exchange of information standards for tax purposes to ensure that the tax system is competitive, while maintaining its own taxing rights. In tabling the 2018 Budget in Parliament on 27 October 2017, the Finance Minister reiterated Malaysia's cooperation with the international community on the changing landscape in international taxation (Razak, 2017, para. 52):

> "Malaysia is committed to economic information sharing introduced by the OECD. These include the implementation of Base Erosion and Profit Shifting Plan of Action and as well as the Automatic Exchange of Information commencing September 2018."

The Minister also outlined the initiatives undertaken by Malaysia thus far, which will be covered below.

The anti-BEPS measures introduced by the OECD constitute the most important international tax reform during the last decade. On 28 January 2018, Malaysia signed the Multilateral Instrument (MLI) to implement tax treaty-related measures to prevent BEPS. In this regard, Malaysia is committed to meeting the internationally-agreed tax standards.

By signing the MLI, Malaysia, together with other countries including Australia, China, India, Indonesia, Japan and Singapore, has taken measures to introduce the practices under international standards, including the implementation of Base Erosion and Profit Shifting (BEPS) action plans.

10.3 The Inclusive Framework and Four Minimum Standards

The OECD formally announced on 6 March 2017 that Malaysia had become part of the Inclusive Framework on BEPS. Malaysia became the 94th country to become so. The inclusive framework allows participating countries to work with the OECD on:

a) developing a monitoring process with regard to the four minimum standards of BEPS-related issues, and
b) reviewing and implementing the whole BEPS package.

The four minimum standards are:

i countering harmful practices effectively (BEPS Action Point 5);
ii preventing tax treaty abuse (BEPS Action Point 6);
iii implementing country-by-country (CbC) reporting for transfer pricing (BEPS Action Point 13); and
iv making cross-border tax disputes more effective (BEPS Action Point 14).

Malaysia's commitment to the OECD initiatives and the BEPS inclusive framework is indicated by their commitment to be an Associate under the inclusive framework. They are a member of the Forum on Harmful Tax Practices, the Global Forum on Transparency and Exchange of Information for Tax Purposes, a party to the Convention on Mutual Administrative Assistance on Tax Matters, party to the Multilateral Competent Authorities Agreement on Country-by-Country Reporting, party to the Multilateral Competent Authorities Agreement on the Common Reporting Standards, ad-hoc member of the Multilateral Instrument Framework, commitment to the implementation of the Automatic Exchange of Information and the streamlining of tax incentives to be in line with FHTP criteria.

10.3.1 BEPS Action 5: Countering Harmful Tax Practices More Effectively, Taking into Account Transparency and Substance

Following several issues raised in OECD forums on Malaysia's special incentives, offshore insurance and leasing and special economic regions, Malaysia is committed to reviewing tax incentives for principal hubs, the biotechnology industry, multimedia superior corridor (MSC) Malaysia, pioneer status, Labuan leasing, Labuan financial services, inward reinsurance and offshore insurance regime and special economic regions, to be in line with Action 5 and it will be streamlining the relevant tax incentives to the Forum on Harmful Tax Practices (FHTP) criteria. The relevant amendments are expected to be gazetted before 1 January 2019.[3]

Malaysia has its own preferential regime on the island of Labuan which was established in 1991 with the main legislation being the *Labuan Business Activity Tax Act 1990* (LBTA) and the *Labuan Companies Act 1990*. Preferential tax regimes selected by the OECD's Forum on Harmful Tax Practices are those that apply to mobile business income, such as income from financial and related services, and income from intellectual property, which can be shifted by multinationals with relative ease.

Following discussions and presentations at the FHTP, the revised guidelines on leasing activity in Labuan were accepted. The new guidelines issued on 29 December 2017 impose substance requirements on spending and resources to be employed in Labuan. Companies are required to establish substantial activities and perform strategic functions in Labuan. Companies are required to establish a physical presence, carry out key leasing activities in Labuan, incur adequate business spending and staffing and have sufficient working capital.

In respect of other financial services, Malaysia is required to curtail dealings with residents and dealings in local currency (Malaysian Ringgit, MYR). For example,

3 See Ministry of Finance, Malaysia, "Malaysia's Commitment to International Tax Standard: Malaysia's Participation in Forum on Harmful Tax Practices (FHTP) OECD Taxation Initiatives" (17 August 2018), http://www.treasury.gov.my/index.php/en/tax/malaysia-s-commitment-in-international-tax-standard.html.

under the *Labuan Business Activity Tax Act 1990*, generally dealing with residents and in MYR is not permitted except if approved by the Minister of Finance. It is expected that legislative amendments in this regard will be introduced in the near future.

Upon Malaysia's amendment to its Labuan leasing regime to remove harmful features and its commitment to amending four of its intellectual property (IP) regimes by the end of 2018, the European Union Code of Conduct Group recommended updates to the December 2017 Economic and Financial Affairs Council's conclusions on the so-called EU blacklist of non-cooperative jurisdictions (see OECD 17 May 2018 press release).[4] Labuan is now in the grey list.

10.3.2 BEPS Action 13: Income Tax (Country-by-Country Reporting) Rules 2016

Malaysia has signed the Multilateral Competent Authority agreement for the automatic exchange of CbC reports. Malaysia issued the Income Tax (Country-by-Country Reporting) Rules (CbCR Rules) and these came into effect on 1 January 2017. The CbCR Rules are in line with the OECD's recommendations for Action 13. New or modified existing local documentation now includes elements of OECD Action 13 Local File content (but local documentation is not replaced by the Action 13 Local File). No rules on master file reporting requirements have been released, but adoption is applicable for years beginning on or after 1 January 2018.

The Rules were gazetted on 23 December 2016 and came into operation on 1 January 2017. The Rules apply to a multinational corporate group which meets the conditions specified in Rule 2 of the Rules including having total consolidated group revenue of at least MYR 3 billion in the financial year preceding the reporting financial year (reporting financial year means that financial year of which the financial and operational results are reflected in the CbC Report). The ultimate holding company of a multinational group that is resident in Malaysia is responsible for preparing and filing the CbC Report to the Malaysian Inland Revenue Board (IRB) within one year from the end of the reporting financial year.

10.3.3 BEPS Action 14: Mutual Agreement Procedure

Malaysia will fully adopt the Mutual Agreement Procedure (MAP) article in its double tax agreements (DTAs). When a Malaysian resident taxpayer encounters taxation, which is not in accordance with the intended application of the DTA provisions, they can seek assistance from the Malaysian Inland Revenue Board (IRB) to contact the treaty partner to resolve the dispute. Malaysia has elected not to adopt the mandatory arbitration provisions.

4 See OECD, "OECD releases decisions on 11 preferential regimes of BEPS Inclusive Framework Members" (17 May 2018), http://www.oecd.org/tax/oecd-releases-decisions-on-11-preferential-regimes-of-beps-inclusive-framework-members.htm.

The IRB issued an updated set of MAP guidelines on 19 December 2017 replacing the 4 December 2014 Guidelines.[5] The IRB announced the update to the MAP guidelines in a release, which stated that the amendments were intended to fulfil Malaysia's obligations as a member of the OECD base erosion and profit shifting project's Inclusive Framework. The MAP guidelines now align with BEPS Action 14 minimum standards.

The guidelines stipulate that the Malaysian competent authority will accept requests for access to MAP within the applicable time limit if the issue relates to a Malaysian treaty partner, it is evident that the actions of one or more countries have resulted in double taxation inconsistent with the treaty, and neither country has decided to consider the issues raised as a matter of policy. Competent authority assistance requests generally relate to transfer pricing, tax residency or the existence of a permanent establishment, withholding taxes, or the characterisation of income.

The guidelines require that taxpayers request and attend a pre-filing meeting before submitting a formal request. Pre-filing meeting requests must be submitted in writing and be accompanied by adequate documentation to allow a preliminary assessment of the issues. Regarding timing of an application, the guidelines state that the three-year limit contained in article 25(1) of the OECD Model Tax Convention applies in the absence of an explicit time limit in the applicable treaty.

The updated procedures also apply to bilateral and multilateral advance pricing agreement (APA) procedures and should be read together with Malaysia's guidelines on APAs. To be eligible for a bilateral or multilateral APA, a Malaysian taxpayer must have more than MYR 100 million (USD 25.1 million) in annual revenue and the covered transactions must exceed 50 per cent of revenue for sales, 50 per cent of expenses for purchases, or MYR 25 million (USD 6.3 million) for all other transactions.

The guidelines urge taxpayers to cooperate fully with the Malaysian competent authority throughout the process and provide all requested information in a timely manner. Submitting incorrect information or failing to provide information requested may be grounds for terminating MAP negotiations. The onus is on the taxpayer to keep the Malaysian competent authority informed of all material changes in the information or documentation previously submitted as part of, or in connection with, the request, as well as new information or documentation that becomes known or is created after the request is filed and which is relevant to the issues under consideration. The guidelines also instruct taxpayers to provide both competent authorities with the same information at the same time. It is to the taxpayer's benefit to be fully cooperative and transparent to ensure an efficient MAP process. The timely provision of requested information is essential to enable the

5 See IRB, "Mutual Agreement Procedure Guidelines" (19 December 2017), http://lampiran1.hasil.gov.my/pdf/pdfam/MAP_Guidelines_2017.pdf.

competent authorities to reach an equitable and expeditious conclusion. Applying for access to the MAP does not affect taxpayers' appeal rights under domestic law and all information submitted is covered by Malaysia's confidentiality protection.

10.4 Malaysia's Response to Other BEPS Actions

As mentioned in section 10.2, on 28 January 2018, Malaysia signed the Multilateral Convention to implement tax treaty related measures to prevent Base Erosion and Profit Shifting (MLI). In essence, the MLI facilitates the implementation of tax treaty related measures to counter BEPS. With the signing of the MLI, Malaysia's DTAs now must be read together with the MLI provisions. Malaysia has submitted a list of agreements with 73 jurisdictions (see Appendix for a list of the 73 jurisdictions) that it would designate as Covered Tax Agreements (CTAs), that is, double tax treaties (DTAs) to be amended through the MLI. The 73 DTAs represent 71 existing comprehensive tax treaties (currently in force) and two tax treaties, with Senegal and Poland, that have been gazetted but have yet to come into force. With respect to a specific tax treaty, the changes to the DTA will enter into effect after both parties to the treaty have deposited instruments of acceptance, ratification or approval of the MLI and a specified time has passed.

Malaysia's positions on the treaty-based BEPS measures are summarised below.

Malaysia will adopt the Principal Purpose Test (PPT), under which treaty benefits will be denied if it is "reasonable to conclude" from the facts that "the principal purpose or one of the principal purposes" of entering into a transaction or an arrangement was to obtain such tax benefits (unless the transaction is in accordance with the object and purpose of the treaty); a statement of intent will also be included in DTAs that a DTA is to eliminate double taxation without creating opportunities for non-taxation or reduced taxation through tax evasion or avoidance.

Action 6 aims at providing an additional level of protection against treaty shopping where a further test must be met before a treaty benefit is granted. For example, when applying the reduced withholding tax rate for interest under Article 11 of a treaty, apart from meeting the treaty conditions (e.g., tax residency, beneficial ownership and the arm's length test), the PPT needs to be fulfilled. Multinational corporations would need to revisit their existing holding and financing structures to ensure that they are BEPS compliant.

10.4.1 Action 7: Preventing the Artificial Avoidance of Permanent Establishment (PE)

Malaysia will adopt the following positions:

i creation of an agency PE when the agent habitually plays a principal role leading to the conclusion of contracts with routine approval of the principal;

ii an agent will not be considered to be an independent agent if he/she acts exclusively or almost exclusively on behalf of a closely related enterprise (specific activity exemption);

iii proposed wording in Action 7 (i.e., PE exemption should only be available if the specific activity listed is of a preparatory or auxiliary character); and

iv with the adoption of Action 7, the operating models of multinational corporations need to be analysed with a view to assessing the implications (as Malaysia has not opted out of the anti-fragmentation provision).

A non-PE position taken previously may no longer be valid. An operating model involving a marketing company in another country (or in Malaysia) may now create a PE due to the lowering of the threshold for a PE. The reliance on the PE exclusion in the past may no longer be tenable given that each activity must now be "preparatory or auxiliary" in character. In addition, with the anti-fragmentation provision, it is also crucial to analyse the operations of the company or its related companies in another jurisdiction holistically to the anti-fragmentation clause which will apply to the "splitting-up of contracts".

Malaysia will fully adopt the Mutual Agreement Procedure Article in its DTAs (see section 10.3.3 above). When a Malaysian resident taxpayer encounters taxation, which is not in accordance with the intended application of the DTA provisions, the taxpayer can seek assistance from the Malaysian IRB to contact the treaty partner to resolve the dispute.

10.4.2 Action 15: Multilateral Convention

Malaysia intends that the MLI will apply to all of its 71 existing comprehensive DTAs (except that with Poland) and two tax treaties that have been gazetted but have not yet entered into force (i.e. Senegal and Poland). Once both treaties are in force, they will be CTAs.

With respect to a specific tax treaty, the changes to the DTA will enter into effect after both parties to the treaty have deposited instruments of ratification, acceptance or approval of the MLI and a specified time has passed. As a next step, Malaysia will work towards the ratification of the MLI.

As is evident from what is being initiated by the Government, the MLI is a major step in the BEPS implementation process. The signing of the MLI signifies Malaysia's commitment to implementing BEPS action plans and reflects its serious intent to adopt international standards and combat international tax avoidance. With the signing of the MLI, introduction of CbCR and review of the robustness of its tax incentives, Malaysia has demonstrated its commitment to implementing the four minimum standards under the BEPS project in the areas of harmful tax practices, tax treaty abuse, country-by-country reporting requirements for transfer pricing, and improvements in cross-border tax dispute resolution.

10.5 Malaysia's Unilateral Adoption of BEPS Measures

10.5.1 Action 1: Digital Economy

The Malaysian government has demonstrated a keen interest in the taxation issues affecting the digital economy. The MIRB has been tasked with monitoring the development of the digital economy and the taxation of digital businesses.

10.5.2 Action 2: Hybrid Mismatch Arrangements

Malaysia has reserved its right not to include treaty-based measures relating to Action 2 (Neutralising the Effects of Hybrid Mismatch Arrangements) except for the provision relating to transparent entities.

10.5.3 Action 4: Interest Deductions and other Financial Payments

Apart from the four minimum standards discussed above, Malaysia is also adopting another non-minimum standard by way of the proposed Earnings Stripping Rules (in line with Action 4 on limiting interest deduction).

Further to the 2018 Budget announcement in October 2017, the IRB has issued draft guidelines to the professional bodies for comments on the Earnings Stripping Rules. This initiative is expected to come to effect for financial years starting on or after 1 January 2019. A *de minimis* rule threshold of MYR 500,000 is proposed with a fixed ratio of 20 per cent of tax EBITDA on interest expense on all forms of debt.

10.5.4 Actions 8-10: Transfer Pricing

Malaysia's tax system is not complex and anti-avoidance measures have followed international trends. As such, there are no unilateral measures taken to counter shifting of profits in cross-border transactions, with transfer pricing provisions introduced not too long ago being the main changes in line with the OECD guidelines.[6] The general anti-avoidance provisions enacted from the introduction of the ITA 1967 remain in force to date. Malaysia does not have any diverted profits tax, controlled foreign company (CFC) rules, etc.

10.5.5 Action 13: Country-by-Country Reporting

In keeping with international trends, the automatic exchange of information (AEOI) and Common Reporting Standard (CRS) regime was implemented in Malaysia in late December 2016, which included the Income Tax (Automatic Exchange of Financial Account Information) Rules 2016 (AEOI Rules). Recently, there have been some developments in the AEOI and CRS sphere in Malaysia as follows:

6 See IRB, "Transfer Pricing", listing Income Tax (Transfer Pricing) Rules 2012, Transfer Pricing Guidelines 2012 and subsequent updates to the Guidelines "to reinforce the existing standard", at: http://www.hasil.gov.my/bt_goindex.php?bt_kump=5&bt_skum=20&bt_posi=1&bt_unit=1&bt_sequ=3&bt_lgv=2 (accessed on 14 June 2018).

i effective 23 December 2017, the AEOI Rules were amended pursuant to the Income Tax (Automatic Exchange of Financial Account Information) (Amendment) Rules 2017 (2017 Amendment Rules);

ii in January 2018, the IRB published the List of Reportable Jurisdictions and the List of Participating Jurisdictions;

iii on 5 February 2018, the IRB issued the Common Reporting Standard Guidance Notes in respect of the compliance requirements for the AEOI Rules (Guidance Notes);

iv on 5 February 2018, the Labuan Business Activity Tax (Automatic Exchange of Financial Account Information) Regulations 2018 (Labuan AEOI Regulations) were gazetted and are deemed operational from 1 July 2017.

Apart from the above measures, no unilateral measures have been adopted by Malaysia in respect of anti-BEPS initiatives.

10.6 Malaysia's Tax Administration and International Tax Reform

The IRB has established a BEPS Action Committee to look into how the action plan could be translated and implemented in Malaysia. It acts as the coordinating forum to discuss results from various BEPS meetings, suggestions or follow up on certain issues, and implications for domestic law, as well as recommendations to the Government, where applicable.

Due to the IRB's involvement in some of the Working Party meetings at the OECD, the IRB is more familiar with certain Actions, such as 8, 9, 10, and 13 than the proposals overall.

The BEPS Project's impact on tax administration and policy-making in Malaysia is reflected in amendments to the transfer pricing rules and guidelines in 2016 to incorporate the outcomes of Actions 8, 9, 10, and 13. The rules on CbC reporting were issued at the end of 2016. Malaysia generally takes a similar approach to that of India and China on issues such as marketing intangibles, location premium, etc., but there will be challenges with regard to implementation. While the IRB aims to learn from others, any actions/changes identified will take time to be incorporated.

The IRB has also set up a special audit unit known as the Aggressive Tax Planning unit to focus on local and cross-border tax planning measures adopted by corporations operating in Malaysia.

Administratively, there will not be any drastic changes within the IRB. However, there will be human resources and capacity building issues, especially in dealing with the outcomes of Action 13, for instance the need to increase the number of trained officers dealing with the anticipated increase in data and information from the AEOI arrangement and CbC reporting, and the number of officers who are sufficiently skilled to carry out audits on multinational enterprises and to handle the increase in dispute resolution cases that are expected to arise post-BEPS. Transfer pricing is a very specialised area and the IRB will need to look into ways of training and retaining skilled resources. There is also the issue of increased investments/ costs in IT systems if CbC reporting is fully adopted to cater for the exchange mechanism through AEOI.

Malaysia's experience in resolving transfer pricing disputes through the Mutual Agreement Procedure (MAP) under existing regulations has been favourable, although there have been few transfer pricing cases. Hence at this point in time, there is no necessity or urgency to consider a mandatory binding MAP arbitration in the tax treaties.

While discussions and work are being carried out in relation to certain Action items as mentioned above, some areas such as the digital economy and mandatory disclosure rules do require further study and data to support the implementation of future plans.

The IRB participates in consultations and meetings with international organisations such as the OECD and the United Nations. The United Nations is the most inclusive, and Malaysia was represented through the Committee of Experts in International Co-operation in Tax Matters, and more specifically in the Subcommittee on Article 9 which also deals with the transfer pricing related aspects of BEPS. The IRB intends to continue to participate in post-BEPS discussions such as the toolkits development and other capacity-building initiatives.

Without technical assistance, increased capacity and more involved participation in the BEPS process, we are likely to see individual country actions rather than a coordinated approach in the Asia-Pacific region.

10.7 The Future of International Tax Reform in Malaysia

Malaysia, being a net capital importing country, will closely follow international trends and adopt a more reactive than proactive approach as can be seen in recent and past trends. Given that Malaysia fundamentally has a territorial income tax system, Malaysia does not need to adopt many of the measures that other countries have introduced to counter tax evasion and avoidance. So, Malaysia will continue to observe and adopt what is relevant and in line with its economic objectives.

Of course, with Malaysia being an active party in OECD initiatives, certain of its tax incentives have come under scrutiny and these will need some modifications to meet acceptance by the OECD. In this context, Malaysia will have to take notice of international tax developments and study these proactively instead of ignoring them. In that sense, Malaysia is very much involved and has engaged in international tax developments unlike in the past.

Appendix

Malaysia: Double Tax Agreements[7]

1. Albania 2. Australia 3. Austria 4. Bahrain 5. Bangladesh 6. Belgium 7. Bosnia Herzegovina 8. Brunei Darussalam 9. Canada 10.Chile 11.China 12.Croatia 13.Crech Republic 14.Demark 15.Egypt 16.Fiji 17.Finland 18.France 19.Germany 20.Hong Kong 21.Hungary 22.India 23.Indonesia 24.Iran 25.Ireland 26. Italy 27. Japan 28. Jordan 29. Kazakhstan 30. Korea 31. Kuwait 32. Kyrgyz Republic 33. Laos 34. Lebanon 35. Luxembourg 36. Malta 37. Mauritius 38. Mongolia 39. Morocco 40. Myanmar 41. Namibia 42. Netherlands 43. New Zealand 44. Norway 45. Pakistan 46. Papua New Guinea 47. Philippines 48. Poland (new DTA) 49. Qatar 50. Romania 51. Russia 52. San Marino 53. Saudi Arabia 54. Senegal 55. Seychelles 56. Singapore 57. Slovak Republic 58. South Africa 59. Spain 60. Sri Lanka 61. Sudan 62. Sweden 63. Switzerland 64. Syria 65. Thailand 66. Turkey 67. Turkmenistan 68. United Arab Emirates 69. United Kingdom 70. Uzbekistan 71. Venezuela 72. Vietnam 73. Zimbabwe.

References

Kraal, Diane, Lydia Thiagarajah and Jeyapalan Kasipillai (2017), "Low Oil Price Shock in Malaysia: Government Fiscal Impact and Petroleum Industry Reactions", 32(4) *Australian Tax Forum* 681-708.

Razak, Hon. Najib (Prime Minister and Minister of Finance) (2017), *Budget 2018: Budget Speech*, 27 October, http://www.treasury.gov.my/pdf/budget/speech/bs18.pdf (accessed on 14 June 2018).

7 As mentioned in section 10.3.2, the 73 Double Tax Agreements (DTAs) represent the 71 existing comprehensive tax treaties (currently in force) excluding that with Poland and the two tax treaties with Senegal and Poland that have been gazetted but have yet to come into force.

11 The Adoption of BEPS in the Netherlands

Irma Johanna Mosquera Valderrama*

Abstract

The approach of the Netherlands to tackling tax evasion and tax avoidance has changed over the course of the years 2015 to 2018. These changes are to a great extent the result of the priority of the Dutch government to ensure that "the Netherlands' image as a country that makes it easy for multinationals to avoid taxation" is overturned by appropriate measures. As a member of the OECD, the Netherlands has participated in the design of the content of the BEPS Actions and in the BEPS Inclusive Framework. In general, the Netherlands has adopted all BEPS Actions and it has committed to the BEPS Multilateral Instrument for almost all its tax treaty network and with very few reservations. More recently, in February 2018, the State Secretary of Finance published two Policy Letters, one to introduce the Tax Policy Agenda and the other to introduce measures to tackle tax avoidance and tax evasion. The Dutch government has proposed in the Tax Policy Agenda several measures to counteract tax avoidance including the adoption of the EU Anti-Avoidance Tax Directives (ATAD 1 and ATAD 2) with some stricter requirements. If the measure relating to ATAD 1 is approved by the Dutch Parliament, the result will be a stricter rule than the minimum standard of ATAD 1. In order to address the needs of investors, the Netherlands is also proposing favourable rules such as the elimination of the Dutch dividend withholding tax and reduction of the corporate income tax rate. As of July 2018, these measures are still under discussion.

11.1 Introduction

The Netherlands is a sovereign state and constitutional monarchy with a population of approximately 17 million people. The Netherlands is a developed country and member of the Organisation for Economic Co-operation and Development

* Associate Professor of Tax Law, Faculty of Law University of Leiden, the Netherlands. The author can be contacted at i.j.mosquera.valderrama@law.leidenuniv.nl. The writing and research for this chapter is in part the result of ERC research currently being carried out in the framework of the GLOBTAXGOV Project (2018-2023). The GLOBTAXGOV Project investigates international tax law making including the adoption of OECD and EU standards by 12 countries. The GLOBTAXGOV Project has received funding from the European Research Council (ERC) under the European Union's Seven Framework Programme (FP/2007-2013) (ERC Grant agreement n. 758671).

(OECD) and of the European Union, but not of the G20.[1] It is also a capital export country with an open economy and the ninth largest export economy in the world, ranked 55 of 94 in the Financial Complexity Index ranking[2] and 32 of 190 in the World Bank Ease of Doing Business ranking (World Bank, 2018).

The tax system in the Netherlands has specific features that have contributed to its attractiveness to investors. Among these features[3] are advance rulings to provide certainty, an extensive tax treaty network,[4] no statutory withholding tax on outgoing interest and royalty payments,[5] and participation exemption. Due to these features, the Netherlands has also been regarded as an attractive jurisdiction in which to locate holding companies and to structure international transactions worldwide.

These features have resulted in several civil society reports[6] and parliamentary discussions[7] where the role of the Netherlands in tax avoidance has been addressed. As a consequence, the Dutch government has introduced some changes to its domestic and international tax policy. One of these changes was the decision in 2013 of the Dutch Government to introduce treaty abuse provisions in tax

1 The European Union is a member of the G20, and therefore the Netherlands in principle participates in the G20 but not as member on its own. By contrast, Germany and France are members of both the European Union and the G20.

2 TMF Group, *The Financial Complexity Index 2017*, June 2017, http://www.tmud.org.tr/Files/Arsiv/FinansalRaporlama.pdf (accessed on 9 July 2018).

3 One such feature that will not be discussed here is the Fiscal Unity Regime providing tax consolidation for Dutch activities within a corporate group. This Regime is currently under review following two recent judgments of the Court of Justice of the European Union (CJEU) since some of the features of the Regime have been regarded by the CJEU as contrary to the EU freedom of establishment. See Judgment of 22 February 2018, Joined Cases *X BV* (C-398/16) and *X NV* (C-399/16) *v Staatssecretaris van Financiën*.

4 The Netherlands has 92 treaties which apply to 94 jurisdictions since "the Netherlands still continues to apply the 1986 treaty with the former USSR to Tajikistan and the 1982 treaty with former Yugoslavia to Bosnia and Herzegovina, Montenegro and Serbia". Only two tax treaties are not yet in force, i.e., tax treaties with Kenya and Malawi. See OECD (2017b, p. 14, nn 1 & 2).

5 See section 11.7 below.

6 See for instance the Centre for Research on Multinational Corporations (SOMO) (2006, 2013).

7 Documents of the Second Chamber of Parliament, 2017-2018, no. 794. In these documents, the State Secretary of Finance replied to some questions from a member of the Second Chamber regarding news articles (in the Guardian UK, and the NOS Dutch news) on the role of the Netherlands in treaty shopping. See Boffey (2017) and De Rooy and Brands (2017). More recently, in a Letter of 9 May 2018 of the State Secretary of Finance to the Dutch Parliament (2018-0000069166), the State Secretary of Finance answered 211 questions regarding the Dutch Tax Policy (*Fiscale beleidsagenda).* Some of the questions also addressed tax avoidance including also the BEPS Actions and the EU Directives (ATAD 1 and ATAD 2): see Dutch Government, "Answers to parliamentary questions about fiscal policy agenda", 9 May 2018, https://www.rijksoverheid.nl/ministeries/ministerie-van-financien/documenten/kamerstukken/2018/05/09/beantwoording-kamervragen-over-fiscale-beleidsagenda (accessed on 9 July 2018).

treaties with at least 23[8] countries including some African and Eastern European countries.[9]

More recently, in February 2018, the State Secretary of Finance published two Policy Letters, one to introduce the Tax Policy Agenda and the other to introduce measures to tackle tax avoidance and tax evasion.[10] The Dutch government has proposed in the Tax Policy Agenda several measures to counteract tax avoidance including the adoption of the EU Anti-Avoidance Tax Directives, and the further enhancement of transparency including exchange of information. The Dutch government states that the priority of the government is to tackle tax evasion and tax avoidance and to ensure that "the Netherlands' image as a country that makes it easy for multinationals to avoid taxation"[11] is overturned by appropriate measures. However, to keep the Netherlands attractive for companies, the Dutch government has proposed to the Second Chamber of the Legislature several measures that will benefit companies in general. The first is the elimination of the Dutch dividend withholding tax and the second is the reduction of corporate income tax rate (currently 20-25 per cent[12]). As of July 2018, these measures are still under discussion.

Another discussion that has been initiated by civil society reports is the use of "letterbox" companies located in the Netherlands.[13] These letterbox companies benefit from the ruling practice in the Netherlands and are also used for treaty shopping. Following the discussions in the Second Chamber,[14] the Dutch government has stated in the Tax Policy Agenda that substance requirements to apply for a ruling will be introduced for letterbox companies. The Dutch government has also decided to introduce a withholding tax for dividends, interest and royalties paid to low tax jurisdictions (see further section 11.7 below).

8 Some of these treaties have been signed but are not yet in force while other treaties are still in the process of negotiation. These 23 countries have been also joined the BEPS Multilateral Instrument (MLI). See section 11.2 below.

9 Letter from the Minister for Foreign Trade and Development Cooperation and the State Secretary of Finance of 30 August 2013 to the Second Chamber. Documents of the Second Chamber 2012-2013 25087 nr. 60.

10 Policy Letter of the State Secretary of Finance on Tackling Tax Avoidance and Tax Evasion, 23 February 2018, https://www.government.nl/topics/tax-avoidance/documents/policy-notes/2018/02/27/policy-letter-on-tackling-tax-avoidance-and-tax-evasion (accessed on 9 July 2018).

11 Ibid, p. 2. See also Documents of the Second Chamber of Parliament, 2017-2018, 32140, no. 33, p. 5.

12 As of 2019 to be gradually reduced until 2021 where it will be 16-21 per cent. *Herziening Belastingstelsel. Brief van de Staassecretaris vna Financien naar de Twede Kamer*. Documents of the Second Chamber of Parliament, 2017-2018, no. 32140, p. 11.

13 "Letterbox companies" are companies without any substance. See, for example, Centre for Research on Multinational Corporations (2015).

14 For instance, in the parliamentary discussion of the Paradise papers and the ruling practice: Documents of the Second Chamber of Parliament, 2017-2018, 25087, no. 180.

11.2 The Response of the Netherlands to the G20/OECD BEPS Program

The Netherlands has been committed to the BEPS Project since its origins. In addition, as a member of the BEPS 44 group,[15] the Netherlands has participated actively in the drafting of the BEPS Actions. The Netherlands has also committed to the G20/OECD BEPS Project including the BEPS Inclusive Framework and to the BEPS Multilateral Instrument (MLI).

Notwithstanding the commitment of the Netherlands as a country to BEPS, it is important to keep in mind that the position of the Dutch government is to seek the adoption of the BEPS measures by means of binding instruments mainly at the EU level through EU Directives and of the MLI at the national level. For instance, at the EU level, the Netherlands has advocated for the implementation of the BEPS Project measures in the EU Directives.[16] For the Dutch government, EU Directives are hard law measures that can safeguard the principles of equality and certainty for the taxpayer.[17] Two of the Directives that have implemented some of the BEPS measures (Actions 2, 3 and 4) are the Anti-Tax Avoidance Directives (ATAD 1 and ATAD 2 – see further section 11.4.2 below).[18]

Another binding instrument that has been used by the Netherlands is the MLI. The Dutch government is in favour of including the provisions of the MLI in almost all of its tax treaties,[19] except for the treaties which are currently under (re-)negotiation (9 treaties).[20] In relation to the treaties with 23 developing countries which are currently being renegotiated to include a treaty anti-abuse clause, the Netherlands has also decided to include the MLI provisions in these treaties.[21]

15 The BEPS 44 group comprises the members of the OECD, G20 and the OECD accession countries during the adoption of the BEPS Project.

16 Even more importantly, during the time that the Netherlands held the EU Presidency (which ended in June 2016), the Netherlands stated that the adoption of ATAD 1 was one of the main goals of the Dutch Presidency. Documents of the Second Chamber of Parliament, 2014-2015, 25087, no. 102 and 2017-2018, 25087, no. 182.

17 Documents of the Second Chamber of Parliament, 2017-2018, no. 794.

18 ATAD 1 should be transposed into domestic law by 1 January 2019 and ATAD 2 by 1 January 2020.

19 The MLI applies to the Netherlands and to countries within the Kingdom of the Netherlands that have chosen to apply the MLI. Of Curaçao, Sint Maarten and Aruba, only Curaçao has made use of this option and therefore the MLI will apply to almost all tax treaties concluded by the Netherlands (82 tax treaties) and to all tax treaties concluded by Curaçao (two tax treaties at present: one with Malta and the other (concluded by the (then) Netherlands Antilles) with Norway).

20 In Letter of 21 March 2017 to the Dutch Parliament, the State Secretary of Finance stated that the countries that are currently under (re-)negotiation are Belgium, Germany, France, Denmark, Poland, Spain, Ireland, Bulgaria and Brazil. For these countries, the provisions of the MLI will be taken into account during the negotiation. Documents of the Second Chamber 2016-2017 25087 nr. 148, p. 16. See also Section 11.2.2.2 below. Documents of the Second Chamber 2016-2017, 25087 nr. 135, p. 4.

21 In Letter of 21 March 2017 to the Dutch Parliament, the State Secretary of Finance stated that

11.3 The Netherlands and the BEPS Inclusive Framework

The Netherlands has committed to the implementation of the four BEPS Minimum Standards. In addition, the position of the Dutch government is that all countries could benefit from participating in the BEPS Project. Therefore, the Netherlands has since 2015 actively supported the participation of developing countries in the discussions regarding the adoption of the BEPS Actions.[22]

In addition to supporting the participation of developing countries, the Netherlands is in favour of capacity building, for instance through the Platform for Collaboration on Tax,[23] and it is currently participating in a pilot (twinning) project with Georgia for the implementation of BEPS.[24]

Regarding the adoption of the minimum standards, the Dutch government is currently working on the adoption of these standards into domestic law. In the case of two of the four minimum standards, i.e., BEPS Action 13 (Country-by-Country Reporting) and Action 5 (spontaneous exchange of rulings and preferential regimes (Innovation Box)), the Netherlands has already adopted legislative measures. These measures include the drafting of templates that make possible the exchange

---

the main reason is that in case the re-negotiations to introduce a treaty anti-abuse rule (main purpose test) are not successful, then the MLI can be an alternative way to include the treaty ant-abuse rule (principal purpose test). For the Netherlands, both rules are similar. From the 23 , the countries which are still in the re-negotiation process are: Bangladesh, Kirgizia, Morocco, Moldavia, Uganda, Sri-Lanka, and Vietnam. Documents of the Second Chamber 2016-2017 25087 nr. 148, p. 17. See also Letter of 4 July 2018 to the Dutch Parliament (2018-0000112064) and Annex 1 Note in response to the questions from the Dutch Parliament on the MLI Legislative Proposal Reference 34 853 (R2096), p. 7, https://www.rijksoverheid.nl/documenten/kamerstukken/2018/07/04/aanbiedingsbrief-nota-multilateraal-verdrag (accessed on 9 July 2018).

22 For instance, the Netherlands was one of the initiators in the OECD to invite 14 developing countries and some representatives of regional tax organisations in Africa and Latin America to participate in several BEPS discussion groups. See Letter from the State Secretary of Finance to the Second Chamber dated 5 October 2015, p. 2. Reference IZV/2015/657 M.

23 In order to assist developing countries, and to coordinate the cooperation regarding international tax issues for low-income countries, in April 2016, the International Monetary Fund, World Bank, United Nations and OECD launched the Platform for Collaboration on Tax. One of the Platform's main tasks is to develop toolkits to assist developing countries in implementing efficiently BEPS Action items. These toolkits contain reports, guidance, model legislation, train-the-trainers materials and other tools which are designed to support capacity building. See http://www.worldbank.org/en/programs/platform-for-tax-collaboration (accessed on 9 July 2018).

24 As explained by the Ministry of Finance of Georgia, "[o]n June 20, 2017, the Ministry of Finance of Georgia and the Ministry of Finance of the Netherlands signed a bilateral twinning program within the Inclusive Framework on BEPS. The twinning program seeks to strengthen the capacity of new members of the Inclusive Framework on BEPS to participate effectively in its work. The following topics were outlined as working are as within this project: - Transfer Pricing and Country-by-Country Reporting; Application of Double Tax Conventions; BEPS policy issues; Inclusive Framework on BEPS reviews". P2017 Presentation by the Ministry of Finance of Georgia, "International Taxation: Report on Progress 2017", p. 15, https://mof.ge/images/File/angarishebi/Progress-report-2017_MoF-final.pdf (accessed on 9 July 2018).

of Country-by-Country reports, the exchange of rulings with several countries and the amendment of its Innovation Box in accordance with OECD guidelines (new Innovation Box). The other two minimum standards, i.e., Action 6 (prevention of treaty abuse) and Action 14 (more effective dispute resolution mechanisms) have been also adopted by the Netherlands mainly through its commitment to the MLI.

11.3.1 BEPS Action 5

11.3.1.1 Spontaneous Exchange of Rulings

The Netherlands is one of the countries that has been reviewed regarding the standard on exchange of information of certain rulings (BEPS Action 5).[25] The peer review contains the input of 10 countries[26] and it refers to the ruling practice of the Netherlands up to 31 December 2016 (this included review of the exchange of approximately 2,180 rulings).[27] Following the peer review, the Dutch government expressed its commitment to follow all recommendations and to exchange all past and current rulings[28] by 31 December 2017.[29]

The peer review states that in general, exchange of information by the Netherlands takes place with the correct format and the information provided is complete; however, seven countries mentioned delays in respect of exchange of rulings (mainly past rulings). Therefore, the review recommended that the Netherlands: (i) complete its information gathering process on past rulings as soon as possible; (ii) continue to ensure that all information on past rulings is exchanged as soon as possible, and fulfil its commitment to complete the exchange of information on past rulings by no later than 31 December 2017 (delays), and (iii) ensure that all information on past rulings, including rulings on new entrants to the intellectual property (IP) regime, is exchanged as soon as possible (OECD, 2017a, pp. 13 and 203).

The Netherlands has not only exchanged rulings with the OECD and G20 countries, but it has also decided to exchange rulings with members (as at 2016) of the BEPS Inclusive Framework and also with countries that are not members of the

25 The first batch of countries reviewed are the countries that participated in the BEPS 44 group. See OECD (2017a).

26 The peer review does not mention which 10 countries.

27 In total, 10,000 rulings should be exchanged by member countries of the BEPS 44 group. From these 10,000, the Netherlands has approximately 2,180 rulings to be exchanged. The number of rulings to be exchanged was one of the reasons why the Netherlands could not comply with the timely exchange of information. Other reasons were also the need for manual search of rulings given by local tax inspectors. Letter from the State Secretary of Finance to the Chairman of the Second Chamber, dated 4 December 2017. Reference: 2017-0000227792, p. 3.

28 Past rulings are rulings given in the period between 1 January 2010 and 1 April 2016 and new rulings after 1 April 2016.

29 Letter from the State Secretary of Finance to the Chairman of the Second Chamber, dated 4 December 2017. Reference: 2017-0000227792. The Policy Letter of the State Secretary of Finance on Tackling Tax Avoidance and Tax Evasion, 23 February 2018, n. 10 above, p. 16, stated that "as at 31 December 2017, the Netherlands had shared information on 4,462 'past' rulings".

Inclusive Framework but with which the Netherlands has a treaty that makes possible spontaneous exchange of information.[30] In total, the Netherlands' network of agreements makes possible the spontaneous exchange of rulings with 142 jurisdictions.

Since 2016, the Dutch government has been in the process of introducing several changes to its ruling practice, including the automation and centralisation of the rulings collection point in one office, i.e., the Central Liaison Office,[31] the review of the ruling practice and the recruitment of additional staff dedicated to the exchange of information on rulings (from five in 2016 to 15 to 20 full-time employees in 2017).[32]

The goal of the Dutch government is to have the revised tax ruling practice in place by 1 January 2019, considering "the forthcoming legislative changes and social, economic and practical considerations".[33] Therefore, two reviews and wider consultations have been scheduled. The two reviews have already taken place, being: (i) the review by a commission consisting of members of the tax administration and Ministry of Finance on the quality of the ruling practice (report submitted in 2017), and (ii) the review by a commission of independent experts from academia and the tax administration and Ministry of Finance[34] on the conformity of the ruling practice with the law, regulations, and case law, which would provide recommendations in relation to the ruling practice (report submitted on 10 April 2018).

The first Commission concluded that in general the administrative procedures for exchange of rulings have been followed, except for few rulings.[35] The second Commission concluded that the rulings (a representative number of the rulings

30 In addition to the treaty network it also includes the countries signatories of the OECD-Council of Europe Convention on Mutual Administrative Assistance in Tax Matters: (OECD, 2017a, p. 206).

31 Previously only some rulings were kept at the Central Liaison Office, and other rulings were kept at the office of the local tax inspector. This resulted in several delays since the rulings needed to be searched manually by each local inspector office. In any case where the information in the ruling was not sufficient to fill in the template for the exchange, the template needed to be sent to "the taxpayer or the tax adviser to ask them to complete any missing information including on the relevant related parties". This also generated delays in the exchange of past rulings. OECD (2017a, para. 7) and Documents of the second chamber 2017-2018 25087 nr. 180, p. 1.

32 OECD (2017a, para. 18).

33 Policy Letter of the State Secretary of Finance on Tackling Tax Avoidance and Tax Evasion, 23 February 2018, above n. 10, p. 16.

34 Six members were appointed, two from academia, and four from the Tax Administration and/or Ministry of Finance. In order to guarantee independence, these four members are not members of the Advance Pricing Agreement-Advance Tax Ruling Team and have not been involved in the rulings analysed by the Commission. Annex to the 21st Midyear report dated 18 April 2018-Tax Administrations, identified "blg-839374" Annex to the Documents of the Second Chamber 2017-2018 34651;31066 nr. E, At 30, p. 1.

35 See report Documents of the Second Chamber 2016-2017, 25087, nr. 153 and 2017-2018, 25087, nr. 187.

were analysed[36]) are in accordance with the law, regulations and case law.[37] Regarding the recommendations, the Commission stated that the publication of all rulings is not desirable. However, transparency is necessary and therefore the Commission recommended a periodical reporting of the number of rulings given and also of the policy regarding the granting of the rulings (addressing questions such as who and under which conditions a specific taxpayer can be granted a ruling). Furthermore, the Commission considered that more openness is necessary in relation to the way the specific (tax) concepts or terms are being interpreted in the ruling practice.[38] These two reviews will be followed by wider public consultations and discussions in the Parliament in the following months.

11.3.1.2 *Preferential Tax Regimes*

Regarding the preferential tax regimes including IP regimes covered by BEPS Action 5, the Netherlands has introduced several changes to the innovation box to comply with BEPS and EU requirements. In 2016, the innovation box was changed regarding the introduction of the double requirement to apply for the preferential regime[39] and the introduction of the "modified nexus approach"[40] that limits the application of such a regime.[41] These changes were introduced taking into account EU developments[42] and following a public internet consultation by the government

36 Thirty-one of 488 rulings given in 2017. Annex to the 21st mid-year report dated 18 April 2018-Tax Administrations, identified "blg-839374" Annex to the Documents of the Second Chamber 2017-2018 34651;31066 nr. E At 30, p. 2.

37 Documents of the Second Chamber 2017-2018 25087 nr. 180, p. 2. The report of the Commission is available in the Annex to 21st Mid-year report.

38 Annex to the 21st mid-year report dated 18 April 2018-Tax Administrations, identified "blg-839374" Annex to the Documents of the Second Chamber 2017-2018 34651;31066 nr. E At 30, p. 9.

39 Accordingly, several rules were introduced that also make a distinction between large and small taxpayers (with less than EUR 37.5 million in gross revenue over a five-year period from all IP assets). As rightly described by Hemels (2017), "as of 2017, the innovation box can only be applied to software, a patent or a plant variety right granted to the taxpayer or for which the taxpayer has applied, a license to distribute medication and IP assets for which a utility model or a supplementary protection certificate has been granted or an exclusive license for the limited use of these assets. Furthermore, having a R&D-statement is obligatory for all of these assets. This is called the double entrance-requirement. Small taxpayer may apply the innovation box to any IP asset for which they have obtained an R&D statement: a single entrance requirement".

40 On the nexus approach and the subsequently modified nexus approach, see OECD (2015).

41 The nexus approach limits the benefits of the regime in case R&D activities are outsourced to related parties.

42 These EU developments mainly related to the EU political agreement regarding the "modified nexus approach" for beneficial tax regimes for IP rights, i.e., IP regimes on 20 November 2014. According to the EU's political agreement "the modified nexus approach should be implemented by 30 June 2016, with the possibility of applying transitional rules until 30 June 2021": Lukkien and Roelofsen (2017, p. 559). The Code of Conduct Group agreed in November 2014 that all existing patent box regimes should be assessed according to the modified nexus approach which ensures that they present sufficient economic substance with the Member State concerned. In this context, the Code of Conduct Group concluded that all existing patent box regimes were not compatible with the modified nexus approach and should be put in line

in 2016 for all stakeholders,[43] and several discussions between the government and the Dutch Parliament.[44] The legislation to comply with BEPS Action 5 entered in force on 1 January 2017 (with a grandfathering period until 2022 for certain intangible assets). Later in 2017, an increase in the effective rate from 5 per cent to 7 per cent was proposed by the government. This new rate entered into force on 1 January 2018.

The peer review report on exchange of rulings above (section 11.3.1.1) also stated that the Netherlands "offers an intellectual property regime that is subject to the transparency requirements under the Action 5 Report" (OECD, 2017a, p. 208). Nevertheless, some outstanding issues regarding the exchange of these rulings were addressed by the peer review report, mainly relating to delays in the completion of the exchange of past rulings regarding all new entrants (benefiting from the grandfathering IP regime) from 6 February 2015 to 31 March 2016.

11.3.2 BEPS Action 6

Regarding Action 6, the Netherlands has committed through the BEPS Inclusive Framework mainly to the application of articles 6 and 7 of the MLI to its tax treaties. Article 6(1) of the MLI provides as a minimum standard that the countries shall introduce modifications to the preamble of their tax treaties to include reference to the prevention of double non-taxation.[45] In addition, in article 6(3), an option is given to countries also to state in the preamble that the countries "desire to further develop their economic relationship and to enhance their co-operation in tax matters". The Netherlands has adopted the text of the preamble in its tax treaties and has also chosen to introduce the additional text of article 6(3). This new preamble will also influence the interpretation and application of tax treaties.[46]

---

with the latter (doc. 16553/1/14 REV 1). As of 2018, almost all (but France) have made changes to comply with EU requirements. See Council of the European Union (2016, pp. 1-4) and (2017, pp. 5-7).

43 Policy Letter of the State Secretary of Finance on Tackling Tax Avoidance and Tax Evasion, 23 February 2018, above n. 10, p. 22.

44 The policy documents regarding the changes to the innovation box have been made available in 2017 at the government website to comply with the request of a taxpayer in accordance to the Dutch Transparency Law WOB (*Wet Openbaarheid van bestuur*). Therefore, 47 documents (in Dutch, approx. 500 pages) are available at: https://www.rijksoverheid.nl/documenten/wob-verzoeken/2017/08/25/besluit-op-wob-verzoek-innovatiebox (accessed on 9 July 2018).

45 Art. 6 states that the text to be introduced in the preamble should be: "Intending to eliminate double taxation with respect to the taxes covered by this agreement without creating opportunities for non-taxation or reduced taxation through tax evasion or avoidance (including through treaty-shopping arrangements aimed at obtaining reliefs provided in this agreement for the indirect benefit of residents of third jurisdictions)".

46 The Netherlands has expressed its intention to use the text of art. 6(1) for the interpretation and application of tax treaties taking also into account the Vienna Convention on the Law of the Treaties, mainly art. 31(1), containing the principle of good faith and art. 31(2) stating that the preamble belongs to the context of the treaty. Documents of the Second Chamber 2017-2018 25087 nr. 184, p. 17.

Article 7(1) of the MLI provides the minimum standard of principal purpose test (PPT) to prevent treaty abuse.[47] On 20 December 2017, a legislative proposal to the Second Chamber to approve the MLI was presented. In the explanatory letter to the proposal, the State Secretary stated the PPT will be offered to all treaty partners including those that have signed the MLI and those who have not yet signed. In this way, the Netherlands goes further than the commitments in the BEPS Inclusive Framework.[48] The Netherlands has chosen to apply the PPT with the discretionary relief provided in article 7(4).[49]

Furthermore, for the Dutch government, the PPT is consistent with the provisions of the main purpose test which has been introduced in some tax treaties, since the way that the test is applied is the same in both provisions. Therefore, the Netherlands does not make reservations to the tax treaties that include the main purpose test. However, the Dutch government also mentions one difference between the two provisions. In the main purpose test, the intentions of the taxpayer are relevant for the application of the provision[50] whereas the PPT states that "one of

47 Art. 7(1) states: "Notwithstanding any provisions of a Covered Tax Agreement, a benefit under the Covered Tax Agreement shall not be granted in respect of an item of income or capital if it is reasonable to conclude, having regard to all relevant facts and circumstances, that obtaining that benefit was one of the principal purposes of any arrangement or transaction that resulted directly or indirectly in that benefit, unless it is established that granting that benefit in these circumstances would be in accordance with the object and purpose of the relevant provisions of the Covered Tax Agreement".

48 The Netherlands has committed to the following anti-abuse measures of the MLI and offered them to all treaty partners: limit treaty benefits in case of hybrid mismatches (with some specific reservations); one year minimum holding period to counteract dividend stripping; one year lock-back period for interests in immovable property entities; no treaty benefits for passive income in low tax permanent establishments; anti-abuse measures regarding permanent establishment (mainly regarding commissionaire arrangements, limit scope of exception for preparatory or auxiliary activities, measure against fragmentation to avoid permanent establishment status, measures against splitting up contracts) (with some specific reservations). Policy Letter of the State Secretary of Finance on Tackling Tax Avoidance and Tax Evasion, 23 February 2018, above n 10, p. 11.

49 See the Netherlands BEPS MLI position, "Status of List of Reservations and Notifications at the Time of Signature", http://www.oecd.org/tax/treaties/beps-mli-position-netherlands.pdf. See also documents to the second chamber 2017-2018 25087 nr. 184, pp. 19 and 65.

50 The main purpose test has been applied to tax treaties mainly in respect of dividends, interest and royalties (arts 10, 11 and 12) and also taking into account the discussion by civil society organisations regarding the Netherlands and developing countries. One example is the tax treaty between the Netherlands and Malawi (amended in 2015), arts 10, 11 and 12. Art. 11(9) introduces the following wording: "No relief shall be available under this Article if it was the main purpose or one of the main purposes of any person concerned with the creation or assignment of the debt-claim in respect of which the interest is paid to take advantage of this Article by means of that creation or assignment. The competent authority of the Contracting State which has to grant the benefits shall consult with the competent authority of the other Contracting State before denying the benefits under this paragraph". See also the United Kingdom-Netherlands tax treaty that introduces the main purpose in arts 10, 11 and 12. For instance art. 11(5) states: "No relief shall be available under this Article if it was the main purpose or one of the main purposes of any person concerned with the assignment of the

the principal purposes" is to obtain the tax treaty benefit. This means that even if the tax purpose is not decisive, the principal purpose test will still apply.[51] According to the Dutch government, the reason for the reference to "one of the principal purposes" in the principal purpose test is to prevent an outcome where the test does not work when there is a rank order of different purposes of the taxpayer (e.g., commercial, business, and tax purposes).[52]

11.3.3 BEPS Action 13

In 2016, the Netherlands introduced legislation in the Corporate Income Tax Act[53] for Country-by-Country Reporting (CbCR) to comply with the minimum standard in OECD BEPS Action 13 including the CbCR rules, and the transfer pricing documentation of the master file and local file. The tax administration has developed specific tools for the filing of Country-by-Country reports,[54] and it has also engaged in dissemination of the rules mainly through presentations to companies and tax advisors. In addition, the tax administration has also engaged in discussions with companies and tax advisors regarding the implementation of CbCR.[55] In 2017, the Netherlands introduced some changes to comply with EU reporting rules including the Automatic Exchange of Information.[56]

The Netherlands has also advocated in favour of making public Country-by-Country reporting of multinationals enterprises.[57] In addition, the Dutch

interest, or with the creation or assignment of the debt-claim in respect of which the interest is paid, or with the establishment, acquisition or maintenance of the company that is the beneficial owner of the interest and the conduct of its operations, to take advantage of this Article. In any case where a Contracting State intends to apply this paragraph, its competent authority shall in advance consult with the competent authority of the other Contracting State".

51 For an analysis of the application of the principal purpose test, see De Broe and Luts (2015, p. 132); Lang (2014); Weber (2017).

52 Letter of the State Secretary of Finance 21 March 2017. Documents of the Second chamber 2016-2017, 25087 nr. 148, p. 23.

53 Arts 29b-29h Corporate Income Tax (*Vpb*) 1969.

54 These tools are available at the website of the tax administration. For instance: *2016 Handleiding - Gegevensaanlevering van landenrapporten* ("Country by-Country Reporting"), https://www.belastingdienst.nl/wps/wcm/connect/bldcontentnl/belastingdienst/zakelijk/internationaal/vermogen/country_by_country_reporting/ (accessed on 9 July 2018).

55 Twentieth Mid-year report Dutch Tax Administration, identifier "blg-826046". Annex to the Documents of the Second Chamber 2017-2018 31066 nr. 389, p. 12.

56 Mainly the extension of the Directive on Administrative Cooperation to Country-by-Country Reporting. Council Directive (EU) 2016/881) of 25 May 2016 amending Directive 2011/16/EU as regards mandatory automatic exchange of information in the field of taxation. See also: https://ec.europa.eu/taxation_customs/business/tax-cooperation-control/administrative-cooperation/enhanced-administrative-cooperation-field-direct-taxation_en#by_country (accessed on 9 July 2018).

57 The Policy Letter on Tackling Tax Evasion and Tax Avoidance also addresses the EU proposal stating that the said proposal "would require multinationals with global annual turnover of more than EUR 750 million to publish information on the nature of their activities, number of employees, net turnover, profit or loss before tax, corporation tax obligations, corporation tax

government, mainly following the recommendations of the Legislator (Second Chamber), has advocated for complete transparency of countries' information, thus not aggregated data but itemised by country.[58] However, the adoption of this initiative has encountered some problems at EU level, "since a small group of member states think the matter should be treated as a tax proposal (where voting must be unanimous) and not as an accounting proposal (where voting is by qualified majority)".[59]

In general, as rightly stated by Lukkien and Roelofsen (2017, p. 569), "the Netherlands rules on CbCR and on master and local files are very close to the text included in the OECD Report on Action 13". However, it is important to keep in mind that the features of the Dutch tax system also influence the way that CbCR will work in the Netherlands. For instance, one feature is the application of the general anti-avoidance doctrine of *fraus legis* and the defensible position of the taxpayer, addressed by this author elsewhere (Kok and Mosquera Valderrama, 2018). In a case where there is a *fraus legis* and the position of the taxpayer is regarded as a defensible position, then the penalty will not be imposed. This may also have consequences for CbCR since the taxpayer can argue in the explanation of the CbCR, master file and local filing, that the choices made by the taxpayer were based on a defensible position and that, therefore, there should be no penalty. So far as this author is aware, this tax law feature does not exist in other countries. For the position to be defensible, it is required that the taxpayer use the legislation available

paid and accumulated profit. This information would be broken down by EU Member State and by third country on the list of non-cooperative tax jurisdictions and aggregated in respect of other countries". Policy Letter of the State Secretary of Finance on Tackling Tax Avoidance and Tax Evasion, 23 February 2018, above n. 10, p. 19.

58 The Policy Letter on Tackling Tax Evasion and Tax Avoidance also addresses that the Netherlands is taking into account the Dutch Chamber (mainly motion by Parliament member Merkies) recommendations "suggested during the negotiations that information from third countries should also be specified by country rather than aggregated". Policy Letter of the State Secretary of Finance on Tackling Tax Avoidance and Tax Evasion, 23 February 2018, above n. 10, p. 19. See also Documents of the Second Chamber, 2015-2016 21501-07 nr. 136 and nr. 1385.

59 Policy Letter of the State Secretary of Finance on Tackling Tax Avoidance and Tax Evasion, 23 February 2018, above n. 10, p. 19. See also European Commission, "Introducing public country-by-country reporting for multinational enterprises – Questions and Answers", press release (12 April 2016), http://europa.eu/rapid/press-release_MEMO-16-1351_en.htm (accessed on 9 July 2018). The European Commission states in item 5 that the legal basis is the Accounting Directive, and that the measure refers to the financial reporting obligation. According to the EU Commission, "This Directive does not propose the harmonisation of taxes, but instead refers to financial reporting obligations as regards income tax information. This is why Article 50 of the Treaty on the Functioning of the Union, which concerns the right of establishment and is the regular legal basis for initiatives in the area of company law, accounting and corporate financial reporting has been determined to be the appropriate legal basis. Today's legal proposal amends the Accounting Directive (2013/34/EU) and is therefore based on the same legal basis. This means that this proposal is subject to qualified majority voting, not unanimity as is the case for legislation dealing with the harmonisation of tax rules".

at that moment for the transaction or for the tax structure, and that there are not precedents in case law that could have resulted in *fraus legis*.

Finally, some estimations regarding the Country-by-Country reports for the 2016 tax year have been already provided by the tax administration. In the 2017 mid-year report by the Dutch tax administration to the Legislature (Second Chamber), the tax administration stated that it was expected to receive approximately 3,150 country reports for the 2016 tax year (i.e., 150 from parent companies located in the Netherlands, and 3,000 via exchange of information with other countries).[60]

11.3.4 BEPS Action 14

The Netherlands was also one of the first "batch" of countries to be peer reviewed regarding Stage 1[61] of Action 14 (September 2017). The peer review contains the input of 21 countries[62] and it refers to the mutual agreement procedure (MAP) cases from 1 January 2014.[63] In general, the peer countries emphasised the good working relationship of the Netherlands with regard to the MAP. Furthermore, the peer review report concluded that, overall, the Netherlands' tax treaties meet most of the elements of the Action 14 minimum standard,[64] but there are some areas for improvement for some of the treaties.

The main recommendations were: (i) to amend the remaining treaties to include a provision requiring implementation of mutual agreements reached notwithstanding any time limits imposed by domestic law; (ii) to include in the remaining treaties[65] the full equivalent of article 25(1) as amended by BEPS Action 14 in order to

60 Twentieth mid-year report Dutch Tax Administration, identifier "blg-826046". Annex to the Documents of the Second Chamber 2017-2018 31066 nr. 389, p. 11.

61 According to OECD (2016, p. 5), "[t]he Assessment Methodology establishes detailed procedures and guidelines for a two-stage approach to the peer review and monitoring process. Stage 1 involves the review of a Member's implementation of the minimum standard based on its legal framework for MAP and the application of this framework in practice. Stage 2 involves the review of the measures taken by the Member to address any shortcomings identified in its Stage 1 Peer Review".

62 The 21 countries are: Australia, Austria, Belgium, Canada, Denmark, France, Germany, Greece, India, Ireland, Italy, Japan, Korea, Norway, People's Republic of China, Portugal, Spain, Sweden, Switzerland, the United Kingdom and the United States. For the peer review, "these peers represent approximately 80% of post-2015 MAP cases in the Netherlands, inventory on 31 December 2016". Furthermore, the peer review also asked input from taxpayers, but taxpayers did not provide any input. OECD (2017b, p. 12).

63 The peer review report stated that "while the review of the minimum standard commitment only starts from 1 January 2016, the Netherlands opted to provide information on a period starting from 1 January 2014 ('the look back period') and also requested peer input relating to the look back period". OECD (2017b, p. 12).

64 According to the peer review report, all 92 treaties concluded by the Netherlands "provide for a mutual agreement procedure for resolving disputes on the interpretation and application of the provisions of the tax treaty. In addition, 42 of these treaties provide for an arbitration procedure as a final stage to the mutual agreement procedure": OECD (2017b, p. 11).

65 According to the Netherlands peer review report (OECD, 2017b, p. 22), from the 92 treaties, 71 treaties contain the wording of art. 25(1) and therefore only 21 treaties do not contain the

make it possible for taxpayers to present their MAP cases "either to the competent authorities of both contracting states or to the competent authority of which they are resident or national in case of application of the no-discrimination provision",[66] and (iii) to ensure that the competent authority functions independently from the tax administration personnel directly involved in the adjustment at issue.[67]

The Netherlands also committed to: (i) introduce in its 92 treaties "a bilateral notification and/or consultation procedure for cases in which its competent authority considered the objection raised in a MAP request not to be justified",[68] and (ii) include in the practical information on MAP further detail on the relationship between MAP and audit settlements in order to clarify that audit settlements do not preclude access to MAP.[69]

One important element of the MLI that has also received attention in the Netherlands is the introduction of mandatory arbitration in tax treaties. For the Dutch government, the use of arbitration can contribute to disputes being resolved in a reasonable time, since countries will be encouraged to reach an agreement. The position of the Dutch government is that two years should be a sufficient period of time (which is also the starting position from the MLI).[70] However, pursuant to the MLI countries can also replace the two-year term with a three-year term.[71]

11.4 The Netherlands and the Other BEPS Actions

The Netherlands has followed the developments at the EU level mainly regarding BEPS Actions 1, 2, 3, 4 and 12. In respect of Actions 8-10, the Netherlands is following the OECD developments and in respect of Actions 7 and 15 the Netherlands has adopted most of the anti-abuse provisions of the MLI including the ones dealing with permanent establishment (except for the splitting-up contracts provision). The following paragraphs will briefly describe some of these developments as of April 2018. In subsequent months, more work is to be done mainly regarding Actions 2, 3 and 4 due to the transposition of the Anti-Tax Avoidance Directives into domestic legislation.

---

provision of art. 25(1), but 9 of the 19 treaties are considered to be in line mainly due to the interaction of art. 25(1) with the application of the non-discrimination provision. Therefore, only 10 should be amended. The final two treaties require either double taxation not in accordance with the convention (to the contrary art. 25(1) requires taxation not in accordance with the convention) and the other treaty does not allow the filing of a MAP request irrespective of domestic remedies.

66 OECD (2017b, pp. 9 and 22).

67 OECD (2017b, p. 10).

68 OECD (2017b, pp. 9 and 26).

69 Although in practice, as stated in the peer review report, "the Netherlands has granted access to the MAP in eligible cases, even if there was an audit settlement between the tax authority and a taxpayer". OECD (2017b, pp. 10 and 30).

70 Documents of the Second chamber 2016-2017 25087 nr. 148.

71 Art. 19(1)b provides for a term of two years, but art. 19(11) gives the party the right to replace the two-year term with a three-year term.

11.4.1 BEPS Action 1

As of April 2018, BEPS Action 1 is still a work in progress mainly due to the OECD and EU work that has not been finished. Following the work by the OECD on BEPS Action 1, the OECD has published on 16 March 2018, an interim report addressing the tax challenges of the digital economy (OECD, 2018). As stated by the OECD, this report sets out the Inclusive Framework's agreed direction of work on digitalisation and the international tax rules through to 2020. According to the OECD press release, the country members of the Inclusive Framework have agreed to work on the implications of digitalisation for taxation.[72] However, while countries agree that there should be a long-term solution, there are still some differences regarding the adoption of interim measures.[73] Therefore, the next several months will be relevant for the discussion of the OECD initiatives, also taking into account the impact of the EU proposals for the Directives below.

On 21 March 2018, the EU Commission proposed new rules (i.e. Directives) to ensure the fair taxation of the digital economy. The first proposal is for a common reform of the EU tax rules for digital activities including the introduction of the concept of a virtual permanent establishment. The second proposal is for the introduction of an interim tax on certain revenue from digital activities.[74] These two proposals will be submitted to the EU Council for adoption after prior consultation with the European Parliament, and therefore, it is expected that these proposals will be further discussed by the EU Member States in the coming months.

The State Secretary of Finance in the Tax Policy Letter stated that most of the EU states agree that the digital economy should be addressed through the OECD/G20 initiatives since the digital economy is a worldwide phenomenon that it is not limited to EU countries only. The Dutch government has also stated that it will engage in a dialogue with scientists, civil society organisations and representatives of technology companies and digital platforms to obtain a better picture of the business as well as to see in what way the value creation in modern technologies differs from that in the traditional business models, and which short and long-term

72 OECD, "Tax Challenges Arising from Digitalisation: More than 110 countries agree to work towards a consensus-based solution", press release (16 March 2018), http://www.oecd.org/tax/beps/tax-challenges-arising-from-digitalisation-more-than-110-countries-agree-to-work-towards-a-consensus-basedsolution.htm. (accessed on 9 July 2018).

73 The press release states that "[w]hile agreeing to work towards a long-term solution by 2020, some countries believe that there is a strong imperative to act quickly and are in favour of the introduction of interim measures, while other countries are opposed to them and consider that such measures will give rise to risks and adverse consequences. Those countries in favour have identified a number of considerations that they believe need to be taken into account to limit the possible adverse side-effects": ibid.

74 See for the content of the proposals and official documents, the information available at the website of the EU Commission, "Fair Taxation of the Digital Economy", https://ec.europa.eu/taxation_customs/business/company-tax/fair-taxation-digital-economy_en (accessed on 9 July 2018).

solutions are desirable.[75]

11.4.2 BEPS Actions 2, 3 and 4

BEPS Actions 2, 3 and 4 are being implemented in the Netherlands by transposing the Anti-Tax Avoidance Directives (ATAD 1 and ATAD 2). In general, ATAD 1 implements the OECD developments of Actions 2, 3 and 4 dealing with interest limitation, hybrid mismatches, and CFC rules.[76] However, ATAD 1 also goes beyond the BEPS recommendations by introducing two further provisions, i.e. exit taxation and a general anti-avoidance rule (GAAR).[77] These two provisions will also be implemented by the Netherlands. ATAD 2 addresses hybrid mismatches with third countries.[78]

The Netherlands is currently in the process of transposing ATAD 1 and ATAD 2 into its domestic legislation. The legislative proposals are expected to be submitted to the Second Chamber before the summer of 2018 (ATAD 1) and by 2019 (ATAD 2).[79] The process of implementation has also included a public internet consultation regarding the measures of ATAD 1 and the impact on businesses.[80] The implementation of ATAD 2 will also include an internet consultation which will take place as soon as possible in 2018 (most likely after the summer),[81] and thereafter the legislative proposal will be submitted to the Second Chamber (most likely at the beginning of 2019).

In general, the Netherlands follows the provisions of ATAD 1, but in respect of the general interest deduction rule (Action 4),[82] the Dutch government has decided:

---

75 Tax Policy Agenda letter of 23 February 2018, Documents of the Second Chamber 2017-2018, 32140 nr. 33, p. 19.

76 BEPS Actions 2, 3 and 4 respectively.

77 Council Directive (EU) 2016/1164 of 12 July 2016 laying down rules against tax avoidance practices that directly affect the functioning of the internal market. Paras 10 and 11 and arts 5 and 6 of the Directive, http://eur-lex.europa.eu/legal-content/EN/TXT/PDF/?uri=CELEX:32016L1164&from=EN (accessed on 9 July 2018).

78 BEPS Action 2. Council Directive (EU) 2017/952 of 29 May 2017 amending Directive (EU) 2016/1164 as regards hybrid mismatches with third countries, eur-lex.europa.eu/legal-content/EN/TXT/?uri=uriserv:OJ.L_.2017.144.01.0001.01.ENG&toc=OJ:L:2017:144:TOC (accessed on 9 July 2018).

79 As of April 2018, the Netherlands is in the process of preparing the legislative proposal to implement ATAD 1 which is expected to be submitted before the summer 2018 to the Dutch Second Chamber.

80 Results of the consultation available (in Dutch) at: https://www.internetconsultatie.nl/consultatiedocumentatad1/reacties (accessed on 9 July 2018).

81 One of the reasons given by the Dutch government is the complexity of the issue of hybrid mismatches mainly due to the different types of mismatches and the interface between different legal systems. See Policy Letter of the State Secretary of Finance on Tackling Tax Avoidance and Tax Evasion, 23 February 2018, above n. 10, p. 8.

82 This rule is also called an earning stripping rule, and as stated in the Policy Letter of 28 February, "it will limit the deduction of net interest owed by a taxpayer on bank and intra-group loans. The deduction of the net interest owed is limited to a maximum of 30% of the

(i) not to include a group exemption; (ii) to lower the threshold from EUR 3 million to EUR 1 million up to which net interest may always be deducted, and (iii) not to apply the grandfathering rules to existing loans. These changes (if approved by the Dutch Parliament[83]) result in a stricter rule than the minimum standard of ATAD 1.

In respect of the controlled foreign company (CFC) rules provided in ATAD 1, the Dutch government has chosen to adopt "Model A", since the position of the Dutch government is that Model A is stricter than "Model B". In Model A it is necessary to assess whether the CFC carries on a substantive economic activity.[84] For the Dutch government, the use of Model A and the criterion of substantive economic activity will also apply "to tackle tax avoidance through entities or permanent establishments in a country with a low statutory rate or a country on the EU list of non-cooperative countries".[85] The CFC needs to satisfy the substantive economic activity requirements, which includes a payroll of EUR 100,000 and office space that is available for at least 24 months.[86]

In general, it could be argued that the interest deduction rule in ATAD 1 will be the rule that will impact business more significantly, since the other measures already exist in the Netherlands (substance requirements, exit taxation, and GAAR) or are already receiving consideration by tax advisors as to alternative ways to

gross operating result". See Policy Letter of the State Secretary of Finance on Tackling Tax Avoidance and Tax Evasion, 23 February 2018, above n. 10, p. 4.

83 At the time of writing (July 2018), the Legislative Proposal has been addressed in several documents of the Second Chamber and it is expected that the Legislative Proposal will be discussed in the Parliament around or after summer 2018. For instance in a Letter of 9 May 2018 (2018-0000069704) the State Secretary of Finance provided answers to some questions of the Parliament mainly regarding the group exemption and the exemption of the earning stripping rule regarding infrastructure projects. Letter of the State Secretary of Finance answering questions on the Letter of 23 February 2018 Tackling Tax Avoidance and Tax Evasion Reference, pp. 4-6, https://www.rijksoverheid.nl/onderwerpen/belastingontwijking/documenten/kamerstukken/2018/05/09/antwoorden-vragen-n.a.v.-de-brief-aanpak-belastingontwijking-en-belastingontduiking (accessed on 9 July 2018).

84 "Under the Model A, the amount of income is determined on the basis of several specific categories of income (dividends, interest, financial leasing, royalties, etc). Under Model B the income is determined on the basis of the arm's length principle. This means that non-arm's length transactions within a group are adjusted as if they were transactions between independent parties". Policy Letter of the State Secretary of Finance on Tackling Tax Avoidance and Tax Evasion, 23 February 2018, above n. 10, p. 6.

85 Policy Letter of the State Secretary of Finance on Tackling Tax Avoidance and Tax Evasion, 23 February 2018, above n. 10, p. 6. This list has been published by the EU since 2017, and the most recent change has taken place. See European Commission, "Common EU list of third country jurisdictions for tax purposes", https://ec.europa.eu/taxation_customs/tax-common-eu-list_en (accessed on 9 July 2018).

86 The Dutch government has also stated that these substance requirements have been also introduced for the purposes of the dividend tax withholding exemption. In addition, the Letter states that "the government will consult the business community in order to establish a clearer picture of the administrative burden imposed by the government's decision and if, possible, further reduce it". Policy Letter of the State Secretary of Finance on Tackling Tax Avoidance and Tax Evasion, 23 February 2018, above n. 10, p. 7.

proceed for tax structuring (mainly regarding ATAD 2 that will no longer make possible the use of hybrid mismatches in the CV/BV structures involving particular limited partnership and operating company arrangements).

11.4.3 BEPS Actions 8-10

The Netherlands has adopted the new OECD transfer pricing guidelines that introduce the measures in BEPS Actions 8 to 10. The new rules of transfer pricing aim to "prevent the shifting of profits to countries where the value is not created".[87] For the Dutch government, the profits should be allocated to and taxed in the countries where "the important functions have been or are being performed".[88] Therefore, the State Secretary of Finance has expressed his intention to amend the Transfer Pricing Decree in 2018 in line with the new OECD guidelines.[89]

11.4.4 BEPS Action 12

At the EU level, the Netherlands has committed to the proposed Directive for automatic exchange of information regarding reportable cross-border arrangements[90] (implementing BEPS Action 12). The proposal would require financial intermediaries, e.g., tax advisors, lawyers, civil-law notaries and TCPSs (service providers such as trust offices) to notify the tax authorities of potentially aggressive cross-border tax planning schemes.[91]

11.4.5 BEPS Actions 7 and 15

In general, the Netherlands has committed to the MLI including also the introduction of almost all of the MLI anti-avoidance measures[92] with only four partial or full reservations.[93] For the Netherlands, the MLI anti-abuse provisions are an effective instrument to tackle tax avoidance also for developing countries.[94] These MLI anti-abuse provisions deal mainly with hybrid entities, permanent establishments and treaty abuse (i.e., the minimum standards of the principal purpose test).

87 Ibid, p. 12.

88 Ibid, p. 13.

89 Ibid.

90 See COM (2017) 335 final.

91 See COM/2016/0198 final.

92 Letter of the State Secretary of Finance of 28 October 2016. Documents of the Second Chamber 2016-2017, 25087 nr. 135, p. 3 and Letter of the State Secretary of Finance of 28 October 2016, Documents of the Second Chamber 2016-2017, 25087 nr. 148, p. 18.

93 The reservations are: (i) limited reservation to some tax treaties with detailed rules regarding hybrid entities, art. 3 of the MLI; (ii) full reservation to the saving clause, art. 11(3)(a) of the MLI; (iii) limited reservation to some tax treaties regarding the splitting-up of contracts provision, art. 14 of the MLI, and (iv) limited reservation to some tax treaties that already contain a binding arbitration clause (arts 18 to 26 of the MLI). See Documents of the Second Chamber 2017-2018 34853 (R2096) Nr. 3, p. 8.

94 Legislative Proposal to approve the MLI. Documents of the Second Chamber of Parliament, 2017-2018, 25087, no. 184.

According to the Dutch Government, the anti-abuse provisions of the MLI will prevent the extensive treaty network of the Netherlands being used for undesired tax structures (for instance the use of empty shell companies without real economic reality). In addition, the anti-abuse provisions make it possible for countries to tax the activities taking place in their own territory.[95] However, the Dutch Government has noted that not all countries are willing to adopt these anti-abuse provisions, but rather only the ones that are regarded as the four BEPS Minimum Standards. This means then that, from the MLI, mainly the preamble to the treaties and the anti-abuse provision of the principal purpose test (Articles 6 and 7 of the MLI, in accordance with Action 6) will be in place since they are minimum standards, but other provisions will only be included depending on the approach of the various countries in question. This may create an inconsistent application of the MLI and the mismatching of choices made by countries may result in multiple mini-treaty negotiations.[96]

Regarding permanent establishments, one reservation made by the Netherlands to the MLI deals with the splitting-up of contracts in the exploration for or exploitation of natural resources.[97] The main reason for this reservation is that the Netherlands has tax treaties that include periods of less than 30 days giving rise to the existence of a permanent establishment for these activities.[98] However, the provisions of article14 of the MLI do not take into account periods that are less than 30 days. The explanatory statement to the MLI states that the provisions regarding permanent establishments are not considered a minimum standard and that since the provisions regarding natural resources have been carefully negotiated by countries, a reservation in relation to the splitting-up of contracts may be justified.[99]

95 Tax Policy Letter to the Dutch Parliament, p. 1, Number: 2017-0000237466.

96 For a discussion of the MLI, the mismatches and the reservations, see García Antón (2017); Bravo (2016).

97 As stated in the position of the Netherlands to art. 14. Pursuant to Article 14(3)(b) of the Convention, the Netherlands reserves the right for the entirety of Article 14 not to apply with respect to provisions of its Covered Tax Agreements relating to the exploration for or exploitation of natural resources. See the Netherlands BEPS MLI position, "Status of List of Reservations and Notifications at the Time of Signature", at: http://www.oecd.org/tax/treaties/beps-mli-position-netherlands.pdf (accessed on 9 July 2018).

98 Documents of the Second chamber 25087 nr. 184, p. 27.

99 "... recognizing that a Covered Tax Agreement could contain anti-contract splitting rules that are specifically addressed to the exploration for or exploitation of natural resources, and that these provisions are frequently carefully negotiated, paragraph 3(b) allows a Party to reserve on the application of Article 14(1) only with respect to the existence of a permanent establishment relating to the exploration for or exploitation of natural resources". Explanatory Statement to the Multilateral Convention to Implement Tax Treaty Related Measures to Prevent Base Erosion and Profit Shifting, art. 14(3), p. 46, https://www.oecd.org/tax/treaties/explanatory-statement-multilateral-convention-to-implement-tax-treaty-related-measures-to-prevent-BEPS.pdf (accessed on 9 July 2018).

11.5 Unilateral BEPS Measures by the Netherlands

For the Dutch Government, the BEPS Project is a multilateral solution, and it is the best solution to tackle tax avoidance. The Netherlands is against unilateral solutions, and therefore, the approach of the Dutch government is to implement the BEPS Actions in the domestic law and to transpose the EU Directives (e.g. ATAD 1 and ATAD 2).[100]

Notwithstanding the above, the Netherlands continues applying its domestic anti-abuse measures including the application of the general anti-avoidance rule (GAAR) of *fraus legis*,[101] that aims to tackle tax-avoidance situations that contravene the object and purpose of the law,[102] and of specific anti-avoidance rules (SAARs) such as limitation of interest deductions among others.[103]

11.6 Tax Administration in Relation to International Tax Reform in the Netherlands

The Netherlands is currently working on the implementation of the BEPS Actions including those in the EU Directives (e.g., ATAD 1 and ATAD 2). Some of the BEPS Minimum Standards such as amendments to the Innovation Box (Action 5) and Country-by-Country Reporting (Action 13) have already been introduced in domestic legislation and are now in force (see sections 11.3.1 and 11.3.3 above).

The Dutch government has stated that in general the BEPS Project and MLI do not require additional staff and have not created an extra administrative burden. The only concern has been in relation to the exchange of rulings which has required amendments to the Dutch tax rules and drafting of specific guidelines for the tax administration in charge of issuing the rulings. Therefore, specific budget changes have been estimated for the enforcement and supervision of the ruling practice,

100 As rightly stated by Lukkien and Roelsofsen (2017, p. 549), the Dutch government "has acknowledged the role that Dutch companies play in international structures and at the same time emphasized that the vast majority of BEPS concerns cannot be resolved by taking unilateral measures, which runs the risk of unnecessarily harming the investment climate".

101 On the application of *fraus legis* to BEPS, mainly to Action 13 (CbCR), see section 11.3.3 above.

102 See for a recent analysis of *fraus legis* in the Netherlands including also the EU and BEPS developments Kok and Mosquera Valderrama (2018).

103 These have been addressed by De Wilde and Wisman (2017, pp. 458-459) and include (among others), in addition to the limitation on interest provision:

- provisions addressing non-resident corporate shareholder taxation for both equity income and debt-receivable income;
- provisions addressing dividend tax-avoidance arrangements and dividend-stripping strategies;
- provisions to prevent undue tax deferral in cases of shareholding transfers;
- mechanisms countering undue tax avoidance in the area of certain shareholding and asset transfers involving the tax consolation regime; and
- mechanisms countering undue tax avoidance and tax deferral relating to business restructurings.

as well as for the hiring of additional staff on this matter.[104] Some of the problems identified in the ruling practice have been explained in section 11.3.1.1 above.

11.7 The Future of International Tax Reform for the Netherlands

The approach of the Netherlands towards BEPS and on the need to introduce additional measures to tackle tax evasion and tax avoidance has changed over the course of the years 2015 to 2018. In 2015, when the BEPS Project was introduced, the Dutch government committed to the BEPS Project but also stated that it had to be implemented in a way that was consistent with the tax policy approach of the Netherlands at the time, mainly with regard to the strong points of the Dutch tax system[105] including the approach of equal treatment of Dutch and international companies (resulting in the 0 per cent withholding tax rates in royalty and interest flows, and the participation exemption).[106]

In addition, the Dutch government stated that the introduction of BEPS measures should be proportional, and therefore, for instance, in the case of exchange of rulings (Action 5), the Dutch government stated that "steps must be taken to ensure that the implementation costs remain proportionate to the expected benefits".[107]

Since 2015, however, there have been several discussions in the Dutch Parliament including in relation to the implementation of ATAD 1 and ATAD 2, the publication of the leaked tax materials involving the "Panama Papers" and "Paradise Papers", and the civil society and political discussions regarding the image of the Netherlands as a country perceived as facilitating tax avoidance (see section 11.1 above). Some of these discussions have resulted in the Netherlands introducing stricter requirements to deal with BEPS and changes to two of its main features that have until now being regarded as important for the investment climate (i.e., ruling practices and the treatment of interest and royalty payments).

By 2018, in the Policy Letter of the State Secretary of Finance to the Parliament regarding the implementation of measures to tackle tax evasion and tax avoidance

104 The costs for enforcement are estimated at EUR 300,000 (incidentally) and EUR 250,000 (structurally) and for additional staff, full-time equivalent 3.0 incidentally, and full-time equivalent 2.5 structurally. Dutch Second Chamber documents 2017-2018 34853 no. 3, p. 40.

105 The State Secretary of Finance stated in Letter of October 2015 that: "The government considers the main strong points of our tax system to be our extensive treaty network, the participation exemption, absence of withholding tax on interest and royalties, our efficient Tax Administration and our efficient dispute resolution procedures. These elements help to create a transparent, clear and attractive tax climate for international businesses".

106 See Letters 2 June 2015 and Letter 5 October 2015 (number 25087 nr. 102. *Brief regering: Internationale belastingen en belastingontwijking – Internationaal fiscal (verdrags) beleid*, p. 1).

107 This statement was made in relation to the automatic exchange of rulings (BEPS Action 5) but also in relation to treaty abuse measures (Action 6). The government stated that: "disproportionate countermeasures could have major consequences for the Dutch tax climate for businesses". Letter of 5 October 2015 from the State Secretary for Finance to the Second Chamber presenting an assessment of the outcome of the BEPS and the outlook for the Dutch tax climate for businesses, reference IZV/2015/657 M.

(February 2018[108]), the Dutch government announced that to tackle tax avoidance, the Netherlands will go beyond the BEPS standards regarding the interest deduction and treaty abuse measures of Actions 4 and 6 (see sections 11.4.2 and 11.3.2 respectively).

The Dutch government is also considering to introduce a withholding tax on dividends, interest and royalty flows to low-tax jurisdictions. The introduction of this withholding tax may result in a different treatment of companies in the Netherlands mainly for the outgoing dividends, interest and royalties and changes to the long-term tax treaty policy of the Netherlands.[109] However, the government justifies this measure in order "to prevent the Netherlands from being used primarily to erode the tax base of other countries".[110]

In the same Policy Letter and in respect of the ruling practice, the Dutch government stated that "businesses will have to meet stricter requirements regarding their presence in the Netherlands before they can obtain certainty in advance".[111] In addition, it also expressed its commitment to the exchange of rulings to create transparency for foreign tax authorities. However, and unlike the approach of 2015, no appeal by the Dutch government has been made to proportional consideration of the implementation costs of a new ruling practice *vis-à-vis* the expected benefits. So far as the author is aware, no impact assessment of the changes to the ruling practice has been made. The developments in the exchange of rulings and the ruling practice have been elaborated in section 11.3.1 above.

11.8 Final Remarks

In light of the description of the Netherlands' policies and adoption of BEPS measures in this chapter, it can be concluded that the Netherlands has committed to BEPS, but it has also decided to go further by introducing stricter requirements regarding interest deduction and treaty abuse (BEPS Actions 4 and 6). One interesting best practice in the adoption of these changes is that the Dutch government includes the participation of relevant stakeholders (business, business associa-

108 Policy Letter of the State Secretary of Finance on Tackling Tax Avoidance and Tax Evasion, 23 February 2018, above n. 10, p. 2.

109 The memorandum on Dutch tax treaty policy of 2011 published by the Ministry of Finance stated the position of the Netherlands in respect of withholding tax on interest and royalties. Accordingly, "The Netherlands seeks to agree on exclusive resident state taxation for interest and royalties. On request of the treaty partner, the Netherlands is willing to consider reasonable anti-abuse provisions".

110 Policy Letter of the State Secretary of Finance on Tackling Tax Avoidance and Tax Evasion, 23 February 2018, above n. 10, p. 2.

111 In the Policy Letter of 23 February 2018, the State Secretary of Finance announced that the substance requirements "are the same as the substance requirements introduced in the *Holding Cooperative Withholding Obligation and Withholding Exemption Extension Act*, that is to say a payroll of EUR 100,000 and office space that is available for at least 24 months". Policy Letter the State Secretary of Finance on Tackling Tax Avoidance and Tax Evasion, 23 February 2018, above n. 10, p. 17.

tions, civil society and scholars) in these discussions and, therefore, the changes to the tax system receive input from all relevant parties.

Finally, the Dutch government has decided to make changes to its long-term tax treaty policy (treatment of outgoing interest and royalties) and to introduce stricter substance requirements for companies operating in the Netherlands. The objective is to prevent the Netherlands being used to erode the tax base of other countries. Neither the withholding tax nor the substance requirements for companies were part of the BEPS Project. Nevertheless, it can be safely argued that these measures will not represent an obstacle to the BEPS Project and, on the contrary, will reinforce the measures to tackle BEPS and the objective of the Netherlands to overturn its image as a tax haven or a country used for treaty shopping.

References

Boffey, Daniel (2017), "Netherlands and UK are biggest channels for corporate tax avoidance", *The Guardian*, 26 July, https://www.theguardian.com/world/2017/jul/25/netherlands-and-uk-are-biggest-channels-for-corporate-tax-avoidance (accessed on 9 July 2018).

Bravo, Nathalie (2016), "The Multilateral Tax Instrument and Its Relationship with Tax Treaties", 8(3) *World Tax Journal* 279-304.

Centre for Research on Multinational Corporations (SOMO) (2006), *The Netherlands: A tax haven?* (Amsterdam: SOMO), https://www.somo.nl/nl/the-netherlands-a-tax-haven/ (accessed on 9 July 2018).

Centre for Research on Multinational Corporations (SOMO) (2013), *Should the Netherlands sign tax treaties with developing countries?* (Amsterdam: SOMO), https://www.somo.nl/wp-content/uploads/2013/06/Should-the-Netherlands-sign-tax-treaties-with-developing-countries.pdf (accessed on 9 July 2018).

Centre for Research on Multinational Corporations (SOMO) (2015), *Fool's Gold: How Canadian firm Eldorado Gold destroys the Greek environment and dodges tax through Dutch mailbox companies* (Amsterdam: SOMO), https://www.somo.nl/wp-content/uploads/2015/03/Fools-Gold-Eldorado-Gold.pdf (accessed on 9 July 2018).

Council of the European Union, General Secretariat (2016), "I/A Item Note: Report by the Code of Conduct Group (Business Taxation) to ECOFIN – Patent boxes: the state of play and the way forward", 13924/16, 3 November, http://data.consilium.europa.eu/doc/document/ST-13924-2016-INIT/en/pdf (accessed on 9 July 2018).

Council of the European Union (2017), "Report: Code of Conduct Group (Business Taxation)", 14784/17, 24 November, http://data.consilium.europa.eu/doc/document/ST-14784-2017-INIT/en/pdf.

De Broe, Luc and Joris Luts (2015), "BEPS Action 6: Tax Treaty Abuse", 43(2) *Intertax* 122-146.

De Rooy, Marleen and Aida Brands (2017), "Nederland ligt nog altijd dwars bij EU-aanpak belastingontwijking", *Nederlandse Omroep Stichtung*, 5 December, https://nos.nl/artikel/2206095-nederland-ligt-nog-altijd-dwars-bij-eu-aanpak-belastingontwijking.html (accessed on 9 July 2018).

De Wilde, Maarten and Ciska Wisman (2017), "Netherlands", in Ana Paula Dourado (ed.), *Tax Avoidance Revisited in the EU BEPS Context: EATLP Annual Congress Munich, 2-4 June 2016* (Amsterdam: IBFD Publications), 455-536.

García Antón, Ricardo (2017), "Untangling the Role of Reservations in the OECD Multilateral Instrument: The OECD Legal Hybrids", 71(10) *Bulletin for International Taxation* 544-552.

Hemels, Sigrid (2017), "The Netherlands", Country Report presented at the *Implementing Key BEPS Actions: Where Do We Stand?* conference, 29 June to 1 July, Rust, Austria. Conference volume forthcoming, IBFD Publications.

Kok, Reinout and Irma Johanna Mosquera Valderrama (2018), "The Netherlands", *Cahiers de Droit Fiscal International Vol. 103A: Anti-Avoidance Measures of General Nature and Scope – GAAR and Other Rules* 5-22.

Lang, Michael (2014), "BEPS Action 6: Introducing an Antiabuse Rule in Tax Treaties", 74 *Tax Notes International* 655-664.

Lukkien, Margriet and Aart Roelofsen (2017), "Netherlands", *Cahiers de Droit Fiscal International Vol. 102A: Assessing BEPS: Origins, Standards, and Responses* 549-570.

Organisation for Economic Co-operation and Development (OECD) (2015), *OECD/G20 Base Erosion and Profit Shifting Project: Action 5 – Agreement on Modified Nexus Approach for IP Regimes* (Paris: OECD), http://www.oecd.org/ctp/beps-action-5-agreement-on-modified-nexus-approach-for-ip-regimes.pdf (accessed on 9 July 2018).

Organisation for Economic Co-operation and Development (OECD) (2016), *BEPS Action 14 on More Effective Dispute Resolution Mechanisms: Peer Review Documents* (Paris: OECD), http://www.oecd.org/tax/beps/beps-action-14-on-more-effective-dispute-resolution-peer-review-documents.pdf.

Organisation for Economic Co-operation and Development (OECD) (2017a), *Inclusive Framework on BEPS, Action 5: Harmful Tax Practices – Peer Review Reports on the Exchange of Information on Tax Rulings* (Paris: OECD).

Organisation for Economic Co-operation and Development (OECD) (2017b), *Inclusive Framework on BEPS, Action 14: Making Dispute Resolution More Effective – MAP Peer Review Report, The Netherlands (Stage 1)* (Paris: OECD).

Organisation for Economic Co-operation and Development (OECD) (2018), *Inclusive Framework on BEPS: Tax Challenges Arising from Digitalisation – Interim Report 2018* (Paris: OECD).

Weber, Dennis (2017), "The Reasonableness Test of the Principal Purpose Test Rule in OECD BEPS Action 6 (Tax Treaty Abuse) versus the EU Principle of Legal Certainty and the EU Abuse of Law Case Law", 10(1) *Erasmus Law Review* 48-59.

World Bank (2018), *Doing Business 2018: Reforming to Create Jobs* (Washington, DC: World Bank), http://www.doingbusiness.org/~/media/WBG/DoingBusiness/Documents/Annual-Reports/English/DB2018-Full-Report.pdf (accessed on 9 July 2018).

12 The Adoption of BEPS in New Zealand

Adrian Sawyer* **and Richard McGill****

Abstract

New Zealand is a firm supporter of the G20/OECD's BEPS project, having been involved from the early discussions through to endorsing the BEPS Action Plan and undertaking domestic legislative reform. Major developments include New Zealand being in the first 10 jurisdictions to deposit their instrument of ratification of the Multilateral Convention to Implement Tax Treaty Related Measures to Prevent BEPS (MLI) with the OECD, and to be actively involved in exchanging information. As from 1 July 2018, New Zealand enacted legislation to give effect to the majority of necessary changes to ensure it is "BEPS compliant", although aspects of the permanent establishment (PE) and transfer pricing (TP) amendments go beyond the BEPS requirements. New Zealand has not ruled out further unilateral action, including a possible diverted profits tax similar to that in Australia. Importantly, all policy and legislative proposals are developed through New Zealand's unique Generic Tax Policy Process (GTPP). Future reform includes expected introduction of legislation to lower the threshold of goods and services tax on imported goods.

12.1 Introduction

New Zealand has a unicameral Westminster-style Parliament, which since 1996 has operated through a Mixed Member Proportional (MMP)-style election process. This means that the makeup of Parliament is principally determined by the party vote. The last General Election was held in September 2017, with a new left-of-centre coalition government formed (Labour-NZ First and Labour-Greens). This new government appears to be largely following the same path as its predecessor in terms of international tax reform, especially with respect to implementing the G20/OECD's BEPS initiative.

Inland Revenue is the New Zealand tax authority. It operates in a transparent and consultative manner, with policy proposals and draft legislation open

* Professor, University of Canterbury, Christchurch, New Zealand.

** Partner, PwC New Zealand, Christchurch, New Zealand.

This chapter states the position in New Zealand as at 30 September 2018.

for submissions as part of New Zealand's Generic Tax Policy Process (GTPP) (see Sawyer, 2013; Inland Revenue, 2017e). The GTPP is a transparent framework that clearly shows the process by which tax policy is developed and where consultation is undertaken with the wider public. Currently Inland Revenue is undergoing its largest transformation as part of the NZD 1.6 billion Business Transformation project, which will not only see a new digital revenue administration platform, but major changes in tax administration in New Zealand.[1]

The New Zealand tax system is based on a broad-base low-rate (BBLR) approach. This commenced in the late 1980s when the then Labour Government radically reformed the New Zealand tax system through introducing BBLR as the core revenue tax model. The idea was to broaden the tax base to allow for a much lower and consistently applied top tax rate to be imposed (for example, the top personal rate was reduced from 60 per cent to 33 per cent). This was achieved by removing tax exemptions, introducing a broad-based goods and services tax (GST), the introduction of dividend imputation, and other initiatives. Currently the main tax bases are: income tax for individuals, corporate income tax, and GST. The major "gaps" include the absence of a comprehensive capital gains tax and other forms of wealth taxes. The New Zealand government and Inland Revenue have always maintained that New Zealand has a robust international tax system and is not impacted by aggressive tax planning to anywhere near the same extent as other jurisdictions.

New Zealand's specific international tax regimes are similar to many international norms, especially with respect to a number of regimes, including its regimes for controlled foreign companies (CFCs), thin capitalisation, transfer pricing (although less formalistic than many jurisdictions) and foreign investment funds (FIFs), and its comprehensive network of around 40 double tax agreements (DTAs), largely based on the Organisation for Economic Co-operation and Development (OECD) Model Tax Convention. One area of difference is that of its foreign trusts, which is discussed in the next section below.

New Zealand is a member of the OECD, joining in 1973. It is an active member within the OECD, operating to a greater extent than may be expected of a small nation of less than 5 million people. It is not a member of the G20, being much too small in size (GDP and population) to warrant inclusion. New Zealand is an established developed country with GDP per capita of USD 39,800 (NZD 57,700) as at the end of 2017. In the Financial Complexity Index Ranking, New Zealand sits at 68 from 94.

New Zealand is in the Australasian (or Oceania) region, being the second largest economy in this region (after Australia). It is the 44th largest export country in the world. It is a net capital importer, principally an importer of capital goods while being an exporter of consumption goods. Its main exports are concentrated milk

---

1 See James and Sawyer (2018); see also Inland Revenue's website: http://www.ird.govt.nz/transformation/bt-programme/bt-programme-section-contents.html.

and other agricultural products, and tourism. New Zealand's major imports are cars and electronics.

12.2 New Zealand's Response to G20/OECD BEPS Program

New Zealand has actively engaged with the G20/OECD BEPS program. This has included Inland Revenue policy and investigations staff working on specific actions at the OECD's head office in Paris. New Zealand's approach to BEPS generally is to work with the OECD (unsurprising given it is a member) to ensure that its international tax rules provide a robust way of taxing multinational enterprises (MNEs). This needs to be balanced against ensuring that New Zealand remains a good place to base an exporting business, as well as to encourage inward investment given that New Zealand is a net capital importer.

New Zealand has previously implemented various measures to address some specific BEPS-type concerns. For instance, legislation has been previously enacted to strengthen the non-resident withholding tax (NRWT) rules (see Inland Revenue, 2017c), limit the use of look-through companies (LTCs) as conduit vehicles (Inland Revenue, 2017b), impose GST on online services consumed in New Zealand (Inland Revenue, 2016), confirm that New Zealand's general anti-avoidance rule (GAAR) overrides tax treaties,[2] and implement automatic exchange of information with other tax authorities.[3] Other earlier changes have included a strengthening of New Zealand's thin capitalisation rules (Inland Revenue, 2014), as well as a number of anti-arbitrage measures for when mismatches occur with cross-border transactions.

While New Zealand is not an early adopter of BEPS measures, it has certainly not been slow to review its tax system and identify areas in need of change. New Zealand has also worked to ensure that the reforms needed to the domestic tax system to incorporate the BEPS program are progressed through the domestic ratification process. As noted earlier, it would be fair to say that the New Zealand government and Inland Revenue were not initially overly concerned about the BEPS initiatives proposed by the G20/OECD, as they maintained that New Zealand has a robust international tax system and is not impacted by significant aggressive tax planning to anywhere near the same extent as other jurisdictions. The fallout from the Panama Papers, however, led to a major change in the reporting obligations of foreign trusts (Littlewood, 2017; Inland Revenue, 2017a). While not part of the Shewan report (Inquiry into Foreign Trust Disclosure Rules, 2016), the changing

2 See Inland Revenue (Policy and Strategy), "Relationship between double tax agreements and anti-avoidance rules", regulatory impact statement on the Taxation (Annual Rates for 2016-17, Closely Held Companies, and Remedial Matters) Bill (February 2016), http://taxpolicy.ird.govt.nz/publications/2016-ris-archcrm-bill/relationship-between-dtas-and-anti-avoidance-rules.

3 For further details on New Zealand's implementation of AEOI, see Inland Revenue, "Implementing automatic exchange of information (AEOI)" (as at 4 April 2017), http://taxpolicy.ird.govt.nz/topical-issues/implementing-aeoi.

environment led to a review of New Zealand's preparedness for BEPS. Driving this change in approach were various misleading news reports that MNEs operating in New Zealand were not paying their fair share of tax.[4] As result, politicians "got on the band wagon" and demanded that urgent action be taken. This was largely a perceived but not a real risk. The then National-led government needed to be seen to be doing something about the perceived risk prior to the election. The New Zealand government feared that if it did not enact changes quickly enough it could potentially have issues with other countries beating it to a response through unilateral actions. Consequently, legislative reform was considered to be necessary, in addition to embracing the BEPS inclusive framework.

New Zealand already has a robust GAAR in section BG 1 of the *Income Tax Act 2007* (ITA 2007), which has been in place for over one hundred years with respect to income tax. There is also a similar GAAR in section 76 of the *Goods and Services Tax Act 1985*, along with a number of specific anti-avoidance rules (SAARs). With the sections framed in very broad terms, it has been left to the New Zealand courts to interpret and apply the provisions, with the Supreme Court establishing the parliamentary contemplation test in 2008.[5]

As noted above, New Zealand also applies transfer pricing rules largely following OECD guidelines, has both a comprehensive CFC regime and thin capitalisation regime, and a network of 40 DTAs with its major trading partners. However, a review undertaken by officials on behalf of the New Zealand Government will see significant modifications to New Zealand's approach to BEPS. These issues have recently been addressed through legislation passed in June 2018 by the New Zealand Parliament in the form of the *Taxation (Neutralising Base Erosion and Profit Shifting) Act 2018* (the June 2018 Act). The Finance and Expenditure Select Committee (FEC) reported back on 15 May 2018 to the Parliament on the 2017 Bill for this enactment. While the FEC recommended some technical and drafting changes to the Bill, the proposals have remained essentially the same as in the initial version of this Bill (and as subsequently enacted).

Broadly, the June 2018 Act seeks to protect New Zealand's tax base from erosion through abuse of the tax system.[6] It is designed to counter strategies used by some MNEs to pay little or no tax in New Zealand. The June 2018 Act changes New Zealand domestic law to meet G20/OECD recommendations for best practice to address BEPS. The measures contained in the June 2018 Act prevent MNEs from using:

---

4 For example, the *New Zealand Herald* published an article in 2016 (Nippert, 2016) that examined the effective tax rates (ETRs) of the top 20 large businesses in NZ, and found these to be low. It concluded, without undertaking wider in-depth analysis that this must be because of BEPS type abuses. See further Elliffe (2016).

5 The key decision of the Supreme Court delivered in 2008 is *Ben Nevis Forestry Ventures Limited v Commissioner of Inland Revenue* [2008] NZSC 115. The leading decision in the NZ courts on cross-border anti-avoidance issues is: *Alesco NZ v Commissioner of Inland Revenue* [2013] NZCA 40.

6 For an extensive discussion on the June 2018 Bill, see Nario and Looi (2018).

- artificially high interest rates on loans from related parties to shift profits out of New Zealand (interest limitation rules);[7]
- artificial arrangements to avoid having a taxable presence (permanent establishment) in New Zealand;
- related party transactions (transfer pricing payments) to shift profits into their offshore group members in a manner that does not reflect the actual economic activities undertaken in New Zealand and offshore;
- hybrid and branch mismatches that exploit differences between countries' tax rules to achieve an advantageous tax position; and
- certain tactics to hinder an Inland Revenue investigation, such as withholding relevant information that is held by an offshore group member.

12.3 The BEPS Inclusive Framework

12.3.1 Action 5

New Zealand has no harmful tax practices as identified by the G20/OECD. This was confirmed by the OECD in a review in 2012.[8] New Zealand has an active unilateral and bilateral advance pricing agreement (APA) process[9] and a comprehensive binding rulings regime.[10] New Zealand is already exchanging redacted Inland Revenue taxpayer binding ruling information with foreign tax administrators, where these binding rulings fall within one of the six categories highlighted as part of Action 5.[11] This exchange of binding rulings applies to past rulings issued on or after 1 January 2010 and which are still in effect on or after 1 January 2014. It also applies to rulings issued on or after 1 April 2016.

12.3.2 Action 6

With respect to Action 6, New Zealand already has an anti-treaty shopping/limitation-on-benefits provision in its model tax treaty that it uses in negotiations.[12]

7 It is interesting to observe that the reportable tax position (RTP) that was introduced here is very much a unilateral response and out of step with any OECD BEPS recommendation.

8 This is in a Confidential OECD report supplied to the New Zealand Government (report number withheld).

9 See further Inland Revenue's website: http://www.ird.govt.nz/transfer-pricing/practice/transfer-pricing-practice-apas.html.

10 See Part 5A of the TAA 1994.

11 These six categories are:
- rulings relating to preferential regimes;
- unilateral APAs or other cross-border unilateral rulings in respect of transfer pricing;
- cross-border rulings providing for a downward adjustment of taxable profits;
- PE rulings;
- related-party conduit rulings; and
- any other type of ruling agreed by the Forum on Harmful Tax Practices that, in the absence of spontaneous information exchange, gives rise to BEPS concerns.

12 New Zealand's model from which it bases its treaty negotiations is similar to the OECD's Model Tax Convention on Income and on Capital (2017).

As such, a clause has already been included in recent tax treaties.[13] New Zealand signed the OECD's Multilateral Convention to Implement Tax Treaty Related Measures to Prevent BEPS (MLI) in June 2017 and will adopt the minimum standards via the MLI.[14] The legislation to give effect to this by way of enabling ratification is supported by the FEC as evidenced by its report in February 2018. In this report, the FEC states:[15]

> This treaty is a core part of New Zealand's policy response to base erosion and profit shifting, and the OECD's recommendations. We consider it important that New Zealand take all steps it can to ensure compliance with tax legislation, and therefore support the treaty.

Also in this report the FEC provides the National Interest Analysis.[16] On 14 May 2018, New Zealand ratified the MLI, by way of the Double Tax Agreements (Multilateral Convention to Implement Tax Treaty Related Measures to Prevent Base Erosion and Profit Shifting) Order 2018 (the Order).[17] New Zealand submitted its MLI position at the time of signature, listing its Reservations and Notifications and included 36 DTAs that it wishes to be covered by the MLI. The MLI will enter into force for New Zealand:

- if New Zealand is one of the first five jurisdictions to ratify the MLI, on the first day of the month following the expiration of three months after the fifth instrument of ratification has been deposited with the Secretary-General of the OECD; or
- otherwise, on the first day of the month following the expiration of three months after New Zealand has deposited its instrument of ratification with the Secretary-General of the OECD (see Article 34 of the MLI).

While not in the first five jurisdictions to deposit their ratification with the OECD, New Zealand was in the first 10 to do so, depositing its instrument on 27 June 2018.[18] Consequently the MLI will come into force for New Zealand with effect from 1 October 2018, three months after deposition of the ratification instrument. After that, the provisions will take effect in relation to each of New Zealand's DTAs that are covered by the MLI on a staggered basis depending on the provision and when New Zealand's DTA partners ratify the MLI (see Article 35 of the MLI). Once

13 For recent DTAs signed by New Zealand, see: http://taxpolicy.ird.govt.nz/tax-treaties#dta.

14 The ratification process is now complete – see the Finance and Expenditure Committee website: www.parliament.nz/resource/en-NZ/SCR_76418/9d567aacef47a07b911ab74af532e165a2b5a 2b9

15 Finance and Expenditure Committee, "International treaty examination of the Multilateral Convention to Implement Tax Treaty Related Measures to Prevent Base Erosion and Profit Shifting: Report of the Finance and Expenditure Committee" (February 2018), https://www.parliament.nz/en/pb/sc/reports/document/SCR_76418/international-treaty-examination-of-the-multilateral-convention.

16 Ibid, Appendix.

17 This was published in New Zealand's Official Gazette of 17 May 2018.

18 New Zealand has since advised that it will also add its DTA with Fiji to the list of covered agreements, bringing the total to 37.

the MLI takes effect in relation to a particular DTA, that agreement will have effect as modified by the MLI.[19]

12.3.3 Action 13

In terms of Action 13, New Zealand signed the Multilateral Competent Authority Agreement on the Exchange of Country-by-Country Reports (CbCR) in 2016, and is collecting CbCR information from New Zealand headquartered groups under its general information gathering powers, including section 17 of the *Tax Administration Act 1994* (TAA 1994). Originally Inland Revenue was of the view that these general powers would be sufficient. In the June 2018 Act, there is a further legislative change that provides Inland Revenue with additional powers, namely through new section 78G of the TAA 1994. This new section provides:

> 78G Country-by-country report from large multinational group
>
> 1 A large multinational group with an ultimate owner that is a New Zealand resident must provide to the Commissioner a report, for each period set by the Commissioner, that includes—
>
> a) the information described in the OECD transfer pricing guidelines, Chapter V, Annex III; and
>
> b) other information that is required by the Commissioner.
>
> 2 The report for a period must be provided to the Commissioner by the date that is 12 months after the end of the period.

This enhancement to existing powers comes with a new penalty of up to NZD 100,000 should the information not be provided as requested (see new section 139AB of TAA 1994).

In New Zealand, CbCR applies to MNEs headquartered in New Zealand with annual consolidated group revenue equal to or exceeding EUR 750 million in the previous year, with effect for fiscal years beginning on or after 1 January 2016. The report must be filed within 12 months after the reporting year-end. It needs to be submitted in English, with New Zealand adopting the OECD's XML Schema standardised electronic format. There is no Local notification requirement in New

19 The dates on which the MLI comes into force and when it takes effect in relation to each DTA, and the extent of the modification to each DTA, will be publicised by Inland Revenue at: http://taxpolicy.ird.govt.nz/tax-treaties. See also: Double Tax Agreements (Multilateral Convention to Implement Tax Treaty Related Measures to Prevent Base Erosion and Profit Shifting) Order 2018, http://www.legislation.govt.nz/regulation/public/2018/0072/latest/whole.html. Overall the MLI entered into force generally on 1 July 2018 following depositing of the ratification instrument of the first five jurisdictions: Austria, Isle of Man, Jersey, Poland and Slovenia; see further OECD, "Landmark tax agreement to strengthen tax treaties enters into force with additional countries joining" (27 June 2018), http://www.oecd.org/tax/beps/landmark-tax-agreement-to-strengthen-tax-treaties-enters-into-force-with-additional-countries-joining.htm.

Zealand for foreign-owned MNEs with a New Zealand presence that will be lodging CbCR in another jurisdiction, unless requested by Inland Revenue. Inland Revenue expects taxpayers to maintain Master file and local file documentation format. While the format of documentation is not explicitly stated in New Zealand tax legislation, taxpayers are required to demonstrate their compliance with the OECD's Transfer Pricing Guidelines[20] with appropriate documentation.[21] It has also been observed that compliant transfer pricing documentation is now essential in order for a taxpayer to discharge its onus proof that its transfer prices have been set in accordance with the arm's length principle.[22]

More generally in relation to AEOI, from 1 July 2017, financial institutions need to meet obligations under the OECD Common Reporting Standard (CRS) for AEOI with respect to financial account information. The *Taxation (Business Tax, Exchange of Information, and Remedial Matters) Act 2017*, which received Royal Assent on 21 February 2017, sets out the requirements. New Zealand's approach is essentially to incorporate the CRS directly into New Zealand law by reference, and to require the application of the CRS to be consistent with the Commentary on the OECD Model Tax Convention.[23]

Furthermore, in relation to transfer pricing, with the enactment of the June 2018 Act, while no additional transfer pricing requirements have been introduced, a report will need to be filed that sets out the information required by the OECD's Transfer Pricing Guidelines[24] and other information the Commissioner of Inland Revenue requires. This should occur in the second half of 2018.

12.3.4 Action 14

In terms of Action 14, New Zealand is committed to binding arbitration. Specifically, New Zealand's approach is to adopt what is referred to as "final offer" or "last best offer" arbitration (in Article 23(1)), but will accept "independent opinion" arbitration if the other party to the Covered Tax Agreement (CTA) chooses this (by entering a reservation under Article 23(2)). In the case of "independent opinion" arbitration, New Zealand will adopt Article 24(2) and (3) which means that the arbitrators' decision will not be binding on the competent authorities (CAs) if they come to an alternative resolution of all unresolved issues within three calendar months of the delivery of the arbitrators' decision.

---

20 See OECD, *Transfer Pricing Guidelines for Multinational Enterprises and Tax Administrations* (2017).

21 The current report format (IR 1032) is available on Inland Revenue's website: www.ird.govt.nz/resources/9/f/9f96d3a8-1c8b-49e4-852f-3ec3bcbc8a31/ir1032.PDF.

22 It is worth noting that the June 2018 Act has shifted the onus from Inland Revenue to the taxpayer regardless of whether documentation has been prepared. This is an important signal that taxpayers must prepare documentation in order to support arm's length pricing.

23 OECD, Commentaries on the Articles of the Model Tax Convention.

24 See OECD, *Transfer Pricing Guidelines for Multinational Enterprises and Tax Administrations* (2017), Chapter V, Annex III.

New Zealand also proposes to require undertakings of confidentiality by all parties involved in arbitration (Article 23(5)) and reserves the right not to include arbitration provisions in Covered Tax Agreements with jurisdictions that do not require the same (Article 23(6) and (7)). New Zealand intends to enter a free form reservation in respect to arbitration to carve out cases that involve the application of New Zealand's general anti-avoidance rule contained in section BG 1 of the ITA 2007.[25]

12.4 Response to Other BEPS Actions

12.4.1 Action 1

In response to Action 1, legislation extending the New Zealand GST to certain cross-border services has been enacted (pursuant to the *Taxation (Residential Land Withholding Tax, GST on Online Services, and Student Loans) Act 2016*). The Government has released a discussion paper setting out its proposed approach to imposing GST on cross-border low value goods that will take effect from 1 October 2019, assuming the proposals are eventually enacted.[26] The proposed scope of the rules is as follows:[27]

- offshore suppliers would be required to register, collect and return GST on supplies of goods to New Zealand consumers if the value of the goods is NZD 400 or less. Tariffs and cost recovery charges would no longer be collected on goods valued at or below this value;[28]
- goods supplied to GST-registered businesses would be excluded unless the offshore supplier decided to zero-rate the supply (this would allow offshore suppliers to claim costs associated with business-to-business supplies);
- offshore suppliers would be required to charge GST unless the recipient identified themselves as a GST-registered business or provided their GST registration number or NZ Business Number; and

---

25 See further the Appendix to New Zealand's implementation of the Multilateral Convention to Implement Tax Treaty Related Measures to Prevent BEPS, at: http://taxpolicy.ird.govt.nz/publications/2017-ip-beps-mli-nz/appendix.

26 New Zealand Government (2018). Submissions closed on 29 June 2018.

27 It is worthwhile noting that the Tax Working Group (TWG) established by the Government in December 2017 was consulted on several possible approaches. These are:
- at the point of sale: offshore suppliers would be required to register for, collect and return GST ("offshore supplier registration");
- between the point of sale and delivery: courier companies and New Zealand Post would collect GST, tariffs and cost recovery charges ("extended status quo");
- after delivery of the goods: recipients would pay GST directly to the government after the goods have been delivered ("pay after delivery").

The TWG recommended that the New Zealand Government implement an offshore supplier registration model for collecting GST on low-value imported goods. The other options were not considered feasible in the short term.

28 It is worth noting that low value imports below NZD 400 are not subject to GST, and that the registration threshold will be NZD 60,000. This change will only impact the larger foreign online retailers.

- a reverse charge (that is, when the recipient of the goods accounts for the GST) would apply to GST-registered recipients that use goods for non-taxable purposes (such as private purposes).

In terms of the registration requirements and return filing:

- offshore suppliers would be required to register if their total supplies of goods and services to New Zealand exceed NZD 60,000 a year (the registration threshold);
- offshore marketplaces and re-deliverers would be required to register and return GST if they meet the registration threshold;
- a simplified "pay only" registration system is proposed to minimise compliance costs for offshore suppliers; and
- quarterly GST filing is proposed for offshore suppliers of low-value goods.

12.4.2 Action 2

In terms of Action 2, the New Zealand Government's response is set out in the June 2018 Act.[29] The earlier Bill, when reported back to Parliament by the FEC, left the vast majority of the proposals concerning hybrid and branch mismatches unchanged.[30] These provisions, along with most others in the Bill, have been enacted and will apply for income years commencing on or after 1 July 2018.

New Zealand already has a comprehensive CFC regime, and has determined as a result that no further reform is expected in light of the G20/OECD recommendations with respect to Action 3. Should this not prove to be the case, then New Zealand is expected to prepare policy changes and implement new legislation to redress the deficiencies.

12.4.3 Action 4

For Action 4, the Government's response is set out in the June 2018 Act. The earlier Bill contained rules limiting interest deductions for loans from related parties. In its report on the Bill, the FEC largely endorsed the proposals, although they recommended some changes which should reduce compliance costs in relation to undertaking a credit rating analysis for related-party borrowing. As noted in section 12.2, the RTP is different to the usual international approach. It is causing a significant number of problems, including that it:

- captures more MNEs due to the extended definition of an associated person;
- often works to limit the interest deduction given a parent company's credit rating will generally be lower than that of a subsidiary (for some inbound investments, such as forestry, this makes the New Zealand venture no longer profitable);

29 The Bill (and subsequent June 2018 Act) is available on Inland Revenue's Tax Policy website, along with the regulatory impact statements: see http://taxpolicy.ird.govt.nz/bills/52-3.

30 For further discussion on the hybrid mismatch approach taken by the New Zealand government, see Patterson and North (2017).

- only applies to inbound debt – Inland Revenue still expects outbound debt to be priced under OECD principles, which is inconsistent (effectively Inland Revenue is "eating and having its cake"!);
- Inland Revenue expects NRWT to be calculated on interest calculated under the old approach; and
- will result in double taxation.

Some drafting errors were also corrected as recommended by officials. There are expected to continue to be cross-border interest rate mismatches. As such, the vast majority of the changes in the Bill (which have been enacted) commence for taxpayers for income years starting on or after 1 July 2018.

12.4.4 Action 7

With respect to Action 7, New Zealand has not reserved on the MLI articles relating to the amended definition of permanent establishment and therefore will not adopt those articles. Currently consultation is underway on unilateral options to consider the avoidance of PE status; the measures would apply where a related entity (e.g., a wholly-owned subsidiary) carries out sales activities for a non-resident in New Zealand under an arrangement that is contrary to the purpose of the PE provisions. In the FEC's report on the Bill, officials recommended a significant extension to the original proposals to include employees of MNEs (with turnover exceeding EUR 750 million) that fly in and out of New Zealand. With respect to other changes to the permanent establishment (PE) rules, the FEC recommended proceeding with them subject to some clarification. These amendments have updated the source rules, thereby expanding the PE concept, such that:

- the PE rules specifically target situations such as direct sales facilitated locally (this is the same as the Australian Multinational Anti-Avoidance Law (MAAL));
- overrides DTAs (a protective measure if the counterparty has not signed up to the MLI); and
- it only applies to large MNEs.

There remains some concern over the statutory language used. These changes have largely been included in the June 2018 Act.

12.4.5 Actions 8-10

For Actions 8-10, New Zealand endorses the OECD's latest Transfer Pricing Guidelines with Inland Revenue stating that it will apply these strengthened guidelines. The June 2018 Act amends the transfer pricing rules so that:

- legal form is disregarded if it does not align with the economic substance of a transaction;
- Inland Revenue is allowed to reconstruct transfer pricing arrangements which are not commercially rational because they involve terms that third

parties would not be willing to agree to;

- specific reference is made to arm's length conditions and the OECD guidelines;
- they codify the need to comply with the OECD's country-by-country reporting requirements;
- the time bar is increased from four years to seven years in circumstances where an audit has been commenced;
- the burden of proof for demonstrating that a taxpayer's transfer pricing position aligns with arm's length conditions is shifted from Inland Revenue to the taxpayer (which makes it essential for taxpayers to have sufficient documentation);
- the rules also apply when non-resident investors are "acting in concert" to effectively control a New Zealand entity, such as through a private equity manager (an expansion of the PE rules).

Concern has been expressed by tax practitioners and others that these proposals (particularly the extension of the time bar to seven years and change in the burden of proof) go further than is required by the BEPS Actions 8-10, especially with regard to the RTP. The response from officials was to note the concerns but to largely accept the proposed reforms as set out in the Bill.[31] Some clarity in drafting has been recommended and carried through into the June 2018 Act.

Furthermore, with respect to thin capitalisation, some changes have been recommended by the FEC to the original proposals. The exclusion criteria for deferred tax liabilities have been extended to cover non-depreciable assets (and assets with a zero rate for depreciation). Grandparenting of the existing 110 per cent safe harbour of worldwide debt for five years is a positive change. However, officials recommended that the FEC decline the vast majority of submissions.

12.4.6 Action 11

As Action 11 is an OECD measure, New Zealand is not taking any specific steps of its own in relation to this action. It is expected that New Zealand will provide some input into the OCED's work on this action. However, since 2015, Inland Revenue has conducted an annual International Questionnaire that collects key data to assess BEPS risks.[32] The most recent survey covered almost 600 foreign-owned corporations. Additional data collection from significant enterprises is being considered as part of the Business Transformation program of work.[33]

31 See further: http://taxpolicy.ird.govt.nz/publications/2018-or-nbeps-bill/transfer-pricing-and-c-c-reporting.

32 See Inland Revenue's website: http://www.ird.govt.nz/international/business/questionnaire/.

33 See n. 1 above.

12.4.7 Action 12

With Action 12, no major reforms have been signalled in this area from a New Zealand perspective. Nevertheless, as noted above, Inland Revenue issues an annual International Questionnaire to MNEs.[34] This questionnaire is concise, being only two pages in length, and therefore aims to keep compliance costs down. Furthermore, this questionnaire is in two main parts, with one page requiring key metrics and another page containing mostly "Yes"/"No" type questions. Contextual comments can be added where necessary, with guidance notes provided. Should this approach prove to be insufficient, Inland Revenue can be expected to increase the information requirements, and/or seek legislative amendment (similar to the proposed new section 78G of the TAA 1994 in relation to CbCR, discussed earlier in section 12.3).

12.4.8 Action 15

For Action 15, 28 of New Zealand's 40 DTAs are expected to be covered by the MLI after it has been signed by both parties.[35] New Zealand's strategy has been to be comprehensive and adopt as many MLI provisions as possible. Unfortunately a number of key Asia-Pacific countries that have a DTA with New Zealand have not signed the MLI and their intentions with respect to the MLI are not yet clear.[36] The New Zealand Government will not issue consolidated versions of its existing tax treaties that are modified by the MLI. This is consistent with their existing treatment of amending protocols to tax treaties that are negotiated from time to time.

12.5 Unilateral BEPS Measures

New Zealand has adopted, and is considering further, unilateral measures to address avoidance as a response to BEPS. One area where legislation has been enacted, as noted in section 12.2 above, is a broadening of the application of NRWT. This occurred in March 2017. Furthermore, as noted earlier (section 12.4), consultation has now been completed on proposed unilateral actions to counter excessive interest deductions, avoidance of PE status and transfer pricing,[37] through enactment of the June 2018 Act. The FEC reported back on the earlier Bill, largely recommending the proposed changes be implemented. Many of these go beyond the minimum that is required to be BEPS-compliant, but have been included in the 2018 Act.

Before the September 2017 General Election, the then Minister of Revenue stated that if New Zealand's measures to address BEPS did not work sufficiently

34 The two-page international questionnaire is http://www.ird.govt.nz/resources/3/3/33a41e51-5bdf-427e-b22a-aff6eb64ee19/international-questionnaire-2017.pdf.

35 These DTAs are referred to in Appendix C to Inland Revenue (2017d).

36 These nations include: Fiji, Philippines, Papua New Guinea, Samoa, Taiwan, Thailand and Vietnam.

37 Other than the RTP there are no other transfer pricing rule changes that would be described as being unilateral.

well, the Government would contemplate enacting a form of diverted profits tax similar to that in Australia. The current Labour-led Government has not publicly commented on its stance with respect to whether it will consider a diverted profits tax. Officials are expected to advise ministers as to whether a diverted profits tax should be developed for future implementation in New Zealand. It is a matter of "watch this space".

Currently there are no proposals to tighten the income tax GAAR (as set out in section BG 1 of the ITA 2007) or exchange of information rules or introduce voluntary transparency measures beyond either those required by BEPS or that New Zealand already has in place.

12.6 Tax Administration and Tax Reform in New Zealand

As noted in section 12.1, New Zealand has its unique Generic Tax Policy Process.[38] The GTPP has three main objectives. They are to:

- encourage early consideration of key policy elements and trade-offs of proposals, such as their revenue impact, compliance and administrative costs, and economic and social objectives;
- provide opportunities for substantial external contribution to policy formulation; and
- clarify the responsibilities and accountabilities of participants in the process, particularly those of the Policy Advice Division of Inland Revenue and the New Zealand Treasury.

There are five phases in the GTPP: Strategic; Tactical; Operational; Legislative; and Implementation and Review. Inland Revenue is primarily responsible for the detailed design, implementation and review of tax policy, namely the operational, legislative, and implementation and review phases of the process. Inland Revenue also take part in the strategic and tactical phases of the process, along with the New Zealand Treasury.

All of the BEPS-related measures have gone through, or are working through, the GTPP, ensuring that as far as possible, the process is transparent and consultative. Nevertheless, this does not mean that the requests made in submissions will be accepted. It is relatively rare for those making submissions to successfully convince officials and Parliament (through the FEC) of the need for major change to underlying policy relating to draft legislation. The BEPS bill, which led to the recently enacted June 2018 Act, is a prime example of the difficulty faced by such parties in having the recommendations in their submissions accepted. Drafting issues that need clarification are more likely to be accepted. Some success may be achieved on the earlier policy proposals if the proposed policy raises potential unintended consequences.

38 See Sawyer (2013) and Inland Revenue, "How we develop tax policy", http://taxpolicy.ird.govt.nz/how-we-develop-tax-policy.

In terms of Inland Revenue's new powers to investigate MNEs, submissions on the earlier Bill (that led to the June 2018 Act) to reduce these extended powers were largely rejected. However, the FEC did accept some parts of the submissions. For example:

- the proposed criminal penalty that could be imposed on New Zealand members of MNE groups for not providing information requested about an offshore group member was recommended to be removed; and
- changes were made so that New Zealand members within a wholly-owned group will only be treated as agents for the unpaid tax liabilities of non-resident group members if the New Zealand member is a New Zealand resident company or has a PE in New Zealand. Furthermore, New Zealand members that are assessed as agents will be able to dispute those assessments.

Currently the most significant tax administration reform in New Zealand is the Business Transformation project, which is a core part of the digitalisation of tax in New Zealand.[39] In Inland Revenue's 2017 Annual Report (Inland Revenue, 2017f, p. 96), it was stated:

> "Business Transformation* is a multiyear, multistage change programme that involves our people, processes, policy and technology. The activities within this appropriation will enable a modern, digital revenue system by:
>
> - simplifying policy and legislative settings
> - making more intelligent use of information to proactively ensure customers get it right from the start
> - fitting revenue processes seamlessly into people's lives
> - transforming our organisational capabilities
> - implementing a modern technology platform (START) that is digitally based and highly automated.
>
> More information is also available on the IRD Business Transformation website, http://www.ird.govt.nz/transformation*."

Specifically Business Transformation has as one of its goals to save money for both Inland Revenue, its "customers" (that is, taxpayers), and New Zealand as a whole. Business Transformation is also intended to make the tax system more certain, at least with respect to administration functions. Another goal of Business Transformation is to have all of the administration of tax and social policy products moved to the new software and all relevant legislative changes completed by 2020 or 2021. From an international tax perspective, MNEs will need to utilise the new systems and platforms just like other business taxpayers.

Inland Revenue takes a proactive approach to working with MNEs, especially in relation to CbCR. Sadiq and Sawyer (2018, pp. 29-30) comment, following an

39 See n. 1 above.

interview with a senior Inland Revenue official, that Inland Revenue determined that it would approach directly the 19 New Zealand-headquartered MNEs that need to report under CbCR rather than through their agents. In effect Inland Revenue has cut the agents out of the process. Communications on CbCR should go to *both* the agent and the taxpayer so that agents are kept in the loop regarding tax reporting and can assist their clients if need be. Consequently, Inland Revenue has largely left it to the taxpayer to contact their agent. This is somewhat of a trend in New Zealand when it comes to international cross-border activity involving MNEs, such as with the annual international tax questionnaire principally provided directly to the MNEs' agents (with a copy to the MNE) to complete regarding the MNE's cross-border activities.

Going forward, Sadiq and Sawyer (2018) observe that there is no intention from Inland Revenue to introduce new voluntary disclosure requirements (or mandatory disclosure) in addition to the current statutory voluntary disclosure regime available to all taxpayers, for either CbCR or AEOI. The most important document in relation to CbCR for Inland Revenue will be the IR1032 spreadsheet, buttressed by the new section 78G of the TAA 1994 requiring information to be provided (with the backup of a significant new penalty for a failure to comply). Sadiq and Sawyer (2018) conclude that Inland Revenue appears to be taking a pragmatic approach, with MNE taxpayers encouraged to be upfront.

12.7 Future of International Tax Reform in New Zealand

New Zealand is seen internationally as an innovative country when it comes to tax policy development, and one that has a major focus on balancing the needs of the government with the imposition of costs on taxpayers. Its broad-base low-rate framework underpins a philosophy that seeks to avoid unnecessary complexity and, where feasible, implement pragmatic solutions. The generic tax policy process emphasises transparency and consultation as fundamental concepts.

With respect to working with the OECD, New Zealand plays a significant role for a small jurisdiction. While it will not become a member of the G20 (should the G20 expand), New Zealand is expected to play a significant role in further OECD reforms. That said, New Zealand does not see itself as an earlier adopter or leader in ratifying and implementing OECD reforms. It takes what can be seen as a "mid field" approach, ensuring that it is not seen as a late adopter or possibly a reluctant adopter. Going forward with respect to BEPS, while New Zealand has chosen to pursue very few unilateral actions, there remains the possibility that it will seriously contemplate a diverted profits tax. The new Government has yet to give a clear signal although BEPS issues remain on the Tax Policy Work Program for 2018-19.[40]

40 See: http://taxpolicy.ird.govt.nz/work-programme.

The BEPS Bill was enacted on 27 June 2018 largely in the form that it was reported back to the Parliament by the FEC, incorporating the recommendations of officials for some drafting changes and a number of technical amendments. Enactment on 27 June 2018 was crucial as a number of the reforms come into effect for income years commencing on or after 1 July 2018.

In terms of the proposals relating to the importation of low value goods, should the proposed approach in the current discussion document be adopted, then draft legislation will need to be prepared and introduced to Parliament (and go out for consultation through the FEC). These changes, if implemented, are not due to take effect until 1 October 2019.

The Tax Working Group (TWG),[41] established in December 2017 by the new Labour-led Government, is also considering aspects of New Zealand's international tax regime, although its terms of reference do not permit it to revisit the key policy behind New Zealand's response to BEPS. The TWG has released a background paper on NZ's international tax developments.[42] This document was principally prepared by officials as background information for the TWG. A number of policy issues are raised, including a diverted profits tax (for which advice is to be provided to ministers), along with some form of equalisation tax.[43] The TWG released its interim report in September 2018 (Tax Working Group, 2018).

Thus it would be fair to say that further reform in the international tax area can be expected in New Zealand, including both fully implementing BEPS measures, along with possibly further unilateral BEPS measures (such as a diverted profits tax), and non-BEPS reforms to the international tax regime more generally. One further point is that, should Australia decide to reduce its standard corporate tax rate below 30 per cent to a rate lower than New Zealand's 28 per cent (25 per cent has been mooted), then we can expect New Zealand to promptly review its rate with the prospect of a reduction to ensure New Zealand remains competitive to international business.

References

Elliffe, Craig (2016), "Others' tax tactics worth a look for NZ", *New Zealand Herald* (30 March), https://www.nzherald.co.nz/business/news/article.cfm?c_id=3&objectid=11613551.

Inland Revenue (2014), "Thin Capitalisation Rules", 26(7) *Tax Information Bulletin* 50-57, http://www.ird.govt.nz/resources/d/3/d32110af-dd35-44c7-95ef-

41 See further: https://taxworkinggroup.govt.nz/.

42 See Officials Position Paper for Session 5 of the Tax Working Group, "International Issues in Taxing International Business Income" (March 2018), https://taxworkinggroup.govt.nz/resources/position-paper-taxing-international-business-income. In addition to providing the TWG with an overview to New Zealand's engagement with BEPS, this document focuses on the area of the digital economy with policy issues for the TWG's consideration.

43 Ibid.

470b4800294e/tib-vol26-no7.pdf.

Inland Revenue (2016), "GST on cross-border supplies of remote services", special report, May, http://taxpolicy.ird.govt.nz/sites/default/files/2016-sr-gst-cross-border-supplies.pdf.

Inland Revenue (2017a), "Foreign trust disclosure rules", special report, March, http://taxpolicy.ird.govt.nz/sites/default/files/2017-sr-foreign-trust.pdf.

Inland Revenue (2017b), "Closely held companies", special report, April, http://taxpolicy.ird.govt.nz/sites/default/files/2017-sr-chcs.pdf.

Inland Revenue (2017c), "NRWT: Related party and branch lending", special report, April, http://taxpolicy.ird.govt.nz/sites/default/files/2017-sr-nrwt.pdf.

Inland Revenue (2017d), "Policy Report: New Zealand's Adoption of the OECD's Multilateral Instrument", 18 April, http://taxpolicy.ird.govt.nz/publications/2017-other-beps/04-report-ir2017-260-mli.

Inland Revenue (2017e), "Regulatory Stewardship Strategy", August, http://taxpolicy.ird.govt.nz/sites/default/files/2017-other-regulatory-stewardship.pdf.

Inland Revenue (2017f), *Annual Report*, Wellington, October.

Inquiry into Foreign Trust Disclosure Rules (John Shewan, chair) (2016), *Government Inquiry into Foreign Trust Disclosure Rules – Report*, Wellington, 27 June (Shewan Report).

James, Simon and Adrian Sawyer (2018), "Digitalization of Tax: Comparing New Zealand and United Kingdom Approaches", Paper presented at the Thirteenth International Tax Administration Conference, Sydney, 5-6 April 2018.

Littlewood, Michael (2017), "Foreign Trusts, the Panama Papers and the Shewan Report" [2017] 1 *New Zealand Law Review* 59-90.

New Zealand Government (2018), *GST on low-value imported goods: An offshore supplier registration system: A government discussion document*, Wellington, May, http://taxpolicy.ird.govt.nz/sites/default/files/2018-dd-gst-low-value-goods.pdf.

Nario, Jai and Kian Looi (2018), "New Zealand's Proposed Response to the BEPS Action Plans: The Proposals, the Impact, and Potential Concerns", 89 *Tax Notes International* 1287-1295.

Nippert, Matt (2016), "Internet giants shifting millions overseas", *New Zealand Herald* (26 March 2016).

Patterson, David and Peter North (2017), "A Tailored Approach for New Zealand to the OECD's Proposals to Neutralise 'Hybrid Mismatch Arrangements'", [2017] 2 *New Zealand Law Review* 323-364.

Sadiq, Kerrie and Adrian Sawyer (2018), "Enhanced Tax Reporting Requirements under the BEPS Project: Preparing the Profession", *Company and Securities Law Journal*, forthcoming.

Sawyer, Adrian (2013), "Reviewing Tax Policy Development in New Zealand: Lessons from a Delicate Balancing of 'Law and Politics'", 28(2) *Australian Tax Forum* 401-425.

Tax Working Group (2018). *Future of Tax: Interim Report* (September); available at: https://taxworkinggroup.govt.nz/resources/future-tax-interim-report.

13 The Adoption of BEPS in Nigeria

Mustapha Ndajiwo* **and**
Ifeanyichukwu Azuka Aniyie**

Abstract

This chapter discusses the efforts made by Nigeria in the implementation of the BEPS recommendations. With that as a premise, the chapter concludes that there is a lot to look forward to in Nigeria regarding international tax reforms. Specifically, it highlights the fact that in the post-BEPS era, Nigeria would have to focus attention on the digitalised economy because of its size and growth trajectory.

13.1 Introduction

Nigeria accounts for an estimated 70 percent of exports from the Economic Community of West African States (ECOWAS) group (International Monetary Fund (IMF), 2018) and it is the largest country in Africa in terms of population and size of economy. It emerged as a net exporter in 2017 with a trade balance of NGN 4,035.5 billion compared to a negative trade balance of NGN 290.1 billion in 2016 (National Bureau of Statistics, 2017). The economy is, however, characterised by high inflation, a high fiscal deficit as well as fragile subnational balance sheet, the existence of multiple foreign exchange rates, a persistently high Consumer Price Index, etc. (IMF, 2018). Nigeria has a human development index (HDI) of 0.527 which puts it in the low development category of the Human Development Index (United Nations Development Programme, 2016). Its tax revenue to GDP ratio of 5 per cent is currently one of the lowest on the continent (African Tax Administration Forum (ATAF), 2017).

Since independence in 1960, Nigeria has experienced military and civilian rule for almost equivalent periods of time.[1] Nigeria is currently a federation; a structure originating from the Richards Constitution of 1945 (Omiunu and Aniyie, 2018).

* PhD candidate, University of South Africa.

** Associate Research Fellow, Institute of Oil, Gas, Energy, Environment and Sustainable Development (OGEES), Afe Babalola University, Nigeria and LLD candidate, University of Pretoria. The authors share accruing credits and liability for errors equally. The information in this chapter is the product of the authors' knowledge and understanding of developments in the Nigerian tax system as at 25 September 2018.

1 1960-1966 (first civilian republic), 1977-1979 (military interregnum), 1979-1983 (second civilian republic), 1983-1999 (military interregnum), 1999 to date (fourth civilian republic).

This constitutional federal structure is currently enshrined in the Constitution of the Federal Republic of Nigeria 1999 (CFRN). The CFRN also delineates the legislative powers of government into the exclusive legislative list (ELL)[2] (which is the sole preserve of the federal government) and the concurrent legislative list (CLL) (to which both the federal and state governments have legislative capacity).[3] Furthermore, items 9 and 10 of the CLL empower the government of a state to legislate for the collection, by its local government councils, of any tax not reserved for the federal government.

Presently, Nigeria consists of three tiers of government: the federal government at the top, the 36 subnational governments and the Federal Capital Territory (FCT) administration at the centre as well as 774 local government councils (inclusive of the six Area Councils of the FCT) at the bottom. The distinct consequence of the above configuration is the demarcation of Nigeria into three tiers of tax systems (i.e., the federal, state and local government tax systems) and a total of 812 tax jurisdictions (i.e., one for each of the distinct governments responsible for each jurisdiction that constitutes the federation that is Nigeria). The administrative jurisdiction of each tier of government is spelt out by the CFRN and other legislation.[4]

13.2 Nigeria's Response to BEPS

It is surmised that Nigeria's response to the G20/OECD BEPS Framework has been largely reactive. This conclusion is premised on the fact that but for its pre-2015 tax treaty network and the revoked Income Tax (Transfer Pricing) Regulations (No.1) 2012 (old TPR),[5] none of the recommended measures were in place before 2015. Nigeria did not have thin capitalisation or controlled foreign corporation (CFC) rules in place. However, the administrative classification of a taxpayer as a CFC or identification as having foreign ownership was (and is still) an audit trigger. This is because it is one of the indices taken into consideration by the revenue authority when determining if an entity qualifies for audit in Nigeria (Federal Inland Revenue Service, 2012, p. 7). It however has general anti-avoidance rules (GAARs) pursuant to which the appropriate tax authority can disregard a transaction or disposition where it is of the opinion that the transaction/disposition is not

2 This contains 67 items amongst which are customs and excise duties, stamp duties and the taxation of incomes, profits and capital gains. See CFRN, Second Schedule, Part I, Items 16, 58 and 59.

3 Noteworthy is the fact the legislative capacity of the state governments is subject to the application of the doctrine of covering the field. The doctrine applies to give supremacy to the law of the federal government where states and the federal government have concurrent law-making powers on a subject; and where both validly make legislation on the subject that of a state is regarded as inconsistent and void. The doctrine is a constitutional principle by virtue of CFRN, s. 4(5).

4 See Aniyie (2018, pp. 620-621) for a synopsis of the Nigerian tax system and the jurisdiction of the respective tiers of government.

5 This was revoked by the Income Tax (Transfer Pricing) Regulations 2018 (TPR).

in fact given effect to or that the transaction/disposition reduces or would reduce the amount of tax payable; or direct that such adjustments be made to counteract the reduction of tax liability effected by the transaction/disposition before the party thereto is assessed accordingly.[6] These GAAR provisions were further strengthened by the old TPR which *inter alia* sought to ensure that Nigeria was able to tax on an appropriate basis corresponding to the economic activities embarked upon by taxable persons within its territory and reduce the risk of double taxation.[7]

13.3 BEPS Inclusive Framework and its Consequences for Nigeria

Nigeria is committed to the BEPS minimum standards. Its membership of the Inclusive Framework on BEPS and the Steering Group of the Inclusive Framework on BEPS is testament to this (OECD, 2017a). Furthermore, as is required, it has commenced complying with the minimum standards. This section presents evidence of the level of compliance with the minimum standards.

13.3.1 Action 5: Peer Review and Monitoring

Nigeria's obligation under the respective tax treaties and the *Convention on Mutual Administrative Assistance in Tax Matters* (the Multilateral Convention),[8] the *Federal Inland Revenue Service Establishment Act 2007* (FIRSEA), a pre-BEPS legislative enactment,[9] provides the necessary legal framework for spontaneous exchange of information on rulings covered by the transparency framework subsumed in Action 5. Section 50(5) of the FIRSEA states that:

> Where any agreement or arrangement with any other country with respect to relief from double taxation of income or profits includes provisions for the exchange of information with that country for the purpose of implementing that relief or preventing avoidance of tax, the obligation as

6 See section 17 of the *Personal Income Tax Act* Cap P8 Laws of the Federation of Nigeria 2004 (PITA); section 22 of the *Companies Income Tax Act* (CITA) Cap. C21 Laws of the Federation of Nigeria 2004; and section 15 of the *Petroleum Profits Tax Act* (PPTA) Cap. P13 Laws of the Federation of Nigeria 2004. However, Onyejekwe (2018) concludes that Nigerian tax officers are reluctant to apply section 22 CITA to transactions because of its vague and ambiguous language; and that this causes uncertainty in the law as well as hampers the effective implantation of legislation and policies. Take note that the TPR extended the purpose of Nigeria's TP regime. In addition to providing a framework for the making of adjustment of profit due under the CITA, PITA and PPTA from related party transactions, the TPR provides a basis for the consideration of the impact of the adjustment made to the profits of taxpayers on any consequential capital gains tax and value added tax due/paid pursuant to the relevant legislation. This was provided for under the old Regulations regime. See regulation 1, TPR. *Cf.* regulation 1, old TPR.

7 See regulations 1-3, TPR.

8 Nigeria signed on 29 May 2013 without any reservation and it entered into force on 1 September 2015.

9 The commencement date of the FIRSEA is 16 April 2007.

to secrecy imposed by this section shall not prevent the disclosure of such information to the authorized officers of the Government of such country.

With regard to the key elements of the transparency framework, work is currently in progress for the design of the mechanism to collect all of the rulings within the scope of the framework from the functional units concerned.[10] The exchange of information element is settled within FIRS, this function is being performed by the Tax Policy, Legislation and Advisory Department using a documented exchange of information (EoI) manual which contains well-defined processes. The EoI manual and the FIRSEA[11] form the basis of the guarantee of the confidentiality of the information received.

13.3.2 Action 6: Preventing Treaty Abuse

In compliance with Action 6, Nigeria became a signatory to the Multilateral Convention to Implement Tax Treaty Related Measures to Prevent Base Erosion and Profit Shifting (MLI) on the 17 August 2017. With the adoption of this approach, it avoided the cost associated with bilateral renegotiation of its existing tax treaties.

13.3.3 Action 13: Country-by-Country Reporting

A BEPS outcome is the signing of the Multilateral Competent Authority Agreement on the Exchange of Country-By-Country Reports (CbC MCAA) on 27 January 2016. The CbC MCAA was ratified on 3 August 2016 by the Federal Executive Council. Furthermore, to give effect to the CbC MCAA, the Federal Government approved the *Income Tax (Country by Country Reporting) Regulations 2018* (CbCR) in January 2018.[12] These regulations also usher in a mandatory regime that would provide FIRS with information about the magnitude of income derived from Nigeria (relative to global income) by multinational enterprises (MNEs) and strengthen the country's transfer pricing architecture. For the MNEs, the three-tiered reporting template that is required under Action 13 could serve as a risk management tool.

13.3.4 Action 14: Tax Treaty Dispute Resolution

Being a signatory to the MLI provides Nigeria with a cost-effective means to meeting the tax treaty-related elements of this minimum standard. This is because through this route it has improved the mutual agreement procedures (MAP) of all its tax treaties. However, with regard to mandatory binding arbitration of tax disputes to complement the MAP, Nigeria has chosen the path of non-compliance.

10 These are the Tax Policy, Legislation and Advisory; and the International Tax Departments of FIRS.

11 See FIRSEA, ss 39 and 50(1).

12 The CbCR gives effect to the CbC MCAA; ss 8(1)(i) and (t), 8(2), 26 and 27(1) of the FIRSEA; ss 58 and 60 of CITA; ss 31 and 32 of PPTA and Regulation 6 of TRP. It became effective beginning 1 January 2018. See regulations 1 and 17 of the CbCR.

It is surmised that the aforementioned stance is a consequence of the current range of the municipal jurisprudence relating to tax dispute resolution. Section 251(1)(b) of the CFRN, amongst other things, provides that the Federal High Court (FHC) has exclusive jurisdiction over matters relating to the taxation of companies. The Court of Appeal interpreted this provision in *Esso Petroleum and Production Nigeria Limited & SNEPCO v. NNPC*[13] and *Shell Nigeria Exploration and Production & 3 others v. FIRS and Another*[14] to mean that an arbitral panel lacks jurisdiction to hear a tax-related matter; hence holding that tax matters are not arbitrable.

13.4 Adoption/Response to the Other BEPS Actions

13.4.1 Action 1: Digital Economy

Nigeria is yet to implement the BEPS Action 1 recommendations and there is currently no specific tax legislation that addresses the digitalisation of the economy (Ndajiwo, 2016). This is despite Nigeria having an active internet population of over 100 million (Nigerian Communications Commission, 2018) which has made it a strategic market for digital giants. Nonetheless, a framework is being put together that would remedy the situation (International Bureau for Fiscal Documentation, 2018). It is left to be seen which of the emerging rules currently being implemented around the world Nigeria would adopt for the implementation of Action 1.[15]

13.4.2 Actions 2 and 3: Hybrid Mismatch Arrangements and Controlled Foreign Companies

There is no evidence to indicate that Nigeria has adopted or is implementing Actions 2 and 3. It lacks rules in the context of BEPS recommendations targeted at hybrid mismatch arrangements and CFCs. However, as noted in section 13.2, the classification of a taxpayer as a CFC or the establishment of it having foreign ownership is an audit trigger (Federal Inland Revenue Service, 2012, p. 7).

13.4.3 Action 4: Interest Deductions and Other Financial Payments

There is currently no interest deduction limitation rule in Nigeria as recommended by Action 4. Again, a framework is being designed to remedy the situation (International Bureau for Fiscal Documentation, 2018). Thus, it is expected that there will be regulation to address this issue.

13.4.4 Action 7: Permanent Establishment Status

The signing on to the MLI by Nigeria is considered an indication of its desire to amend the definition of permanent establishment in its DTAs that are below the

13 (Appeal No. CA/A/507/2012; unreported, delivered on 22 July 2016).

14 (Appeal No. CA/A/208/2012; unreported, delivered 31 August 2016).

15 The OECD Task Force on the Digital Economy lists (1) alternative applications of the permanent establishment threshold; (2) use of withholding taxes; (3) use of turnover taxes; and (4) specific turnover taxes as the measures being adopted unilaterally across the globe. See generally, OECD (2018, pp. 133-159).

Action 7 standard. Also, Nigeria plans to include a new PE definition in its treaty-negotiating template for the future (International Bureau for Fiscal Documentation, 2018).

13.4.5 Actions 8-10: Transfer Pricing

As stated earlier, the TPR encompasses the GAAR subsumed in Nigeria's tax legislation[16] and provides guidance as well as the framework for the enforcement of the TPR (Abdulrazaq, 2016). Pursuant to the TPR, FIRS can adjust transactions considered artificial or fictitious. Noteworthy is the fact that, although the TPR is consistent with the UN Practical Manual on Transfer Pricing (UN TP Manual) and the OECD Transfer Pricing Guidelines for Multinational Enterprises and Tax Administrations 2017 (OECD TPG), regulation 19(1) of the TPR provides that where there are inconsistencies between the provisions of any applicable municipal laws, rules, regulations, the UN TP Manual and the OECD TPG, the provisions of the relevant law shall prevail.

Regulation 5 of the TPR gives guidance on the selection of the appropriate TP method. However, it does not provide any specific guidelines on the application of each method, nor does it provide guidance for the functional analysis (International Bureau for Fiscal Documentation, 2018). It also provides that taxpayers can choose any other method if the five specified methods are not appropriate. However, this is not unassailable as sub-regulation (3) provides that:

> When examining whether or not the taxable profit resulting from a taxpayer's controlled transaction or transactions is consistent with the arm's length principle, the Service shall base its review on the transfer pricing method used by taxable person, where such method is appropriate to the transaction, or on a transfer pricing method the Service consider most appropriate.

As was hitherto stated, Nigeria enacted a new transfer pricing regulation in 2018.[17] Compared to the old Regulations, the TPR introduced significant changes and they are as follows:

1. *Intragroup services pricing*

Regulation 6 stipulates *inter alia* modalities for the determination of whether or not the service charge for a transaction between taxpayer and connected person is at arm's length. Before the enactment of the TPR, recourse was to general provisions within the appropriate legislation for guidance in determination of whether the intergroup services pricing was at arm's length (OECD, 2017b). Currently, the regime for the intragroup services pricing is underpinned by a benefit and shareholder's activity tests. Pursuant to the former, FIRS's focus is the determination of whether (a) there was actually provision/rendering of the priced service; (b) the service provided the taxpayer with economic or commercial value; (c) third

16 See n. 6, above.
17 See n. 5, above.

party in comparable circumstances would at the price paid by the taxpayer, procure same service from an independent party or would choose to perform same in-house for itself; and (d) the amount is similar to what would have been agreed to by independent persons for comparable service in comparable circumstances.[18] Note that none of the foregoing is mutually exclusive and where FIRS is not convinced as to the existence of any, the associated cost of the intragroup service would be disallowed. On its part, the shareholder's activity test as entrenched in the TPR holds all cost associated with activities that have been performed by an entity in its capacity as a shareholder in a connected person inconsistent with the arm's length principle.[19] Regulation 6(2) of the TPR further provides that such inconsistent cost includes any associated with activities relating to (a) the juridical structure of the parent company; (b) the reporting and compliance obligation of the parent company; or (c) investors' cost except where the shareholding was directly or indirectly acquired by the shareholder and/or it benefits or is expected to benefit the shareholder.

2. *Intangibles*

Generally, regulation 7 of the TPR introduced a performance cum risk-oriented approach to the determination of whether the pricing of an intangible is at arm's length. This provision makes the determination of the arm's length price a functional analysis which takes into cognisance the role performed and specific risks assumed in connection with the development, enhancement, maintenance, protection and exploitation of the intangible property in question by the licensor (OECD, 2017b). This brings it into line with the OECD TPG.

A peculiarity of the provision is sub-regulation (5) which caps tax deduction in favour of a licensee at 5 percent of earnings before interest, tax, depreciation and amortisation (EBITDA) where the transaction was a transfer between related parties of rights in an intangible asset instead of an alienation. It is surmised that the ATAF is the origin of this provision as it recommends that:

> Where a person engages in a transaction with a connected person that involves the transfer of rights in an intangible, other than the alienation of an intangible, the deduction allowable for tax purposes in that transaction shall not exceed X% of the [tax EBITDA + plus royalties payable] derived from the commercial activity conducted by the person in which the rights transferred are exploited (ATAF, n.d., p. 4).

3. *Capital-rich, low-function companies*

Regulation 8 entrenches the orientation put forward by BEPS Action 8-10 on the allocation of value within a group. Pursuant to it, capital-rich, low-function companies[20] in a group for tax purposes will not be allocated profits (or losses) associ-

18 See regulation 6(1), TPR.
19 See regulation 6(2), TPR.
20 See regulation 27, TPR for definition of Capital-rich, low-function companies.

ated with the control of the financial risk associated with their funding. It further provides that in such circumstances the profit (or loss) associated with the risk assumption would be reallocated to the entity or entities in the group that manage those risks and have the capacity to bear them; while leaving the capital-rich, low-function entity with a minimum risk-free return for its activity.

4. Removal of Advance Pricing Agreement (APA) threshold

Regulation 9(2) of the TPR removed the transaction threshold to the negotiation of an APA that existed by virtue of regulation 7(2)(d) of the old TPR. Hitherto, the condition was that the taxpayer must have a NGN250 million cumulative transaction threshold in every year of assessment for it to qualify for negotiation of an APA with FIRS.

5. Documentation

Regulation 17(3) provides that connected persons whose total value of controlled transactions is less than NGN300 million are exempt from maintaining the contemporaneous documentation made compulsory by regulation 16 of the TPR. Regulation 17(6) further provides that where an entity makes a procurement from a third party on behalf of a connected person, the latter (i.e. the connected person) shall as part of the contemporaneous documentation made compulsory by regulation 16, keep contracts, invoices, bills, etc. issued by the third party from whom the procurement was made.

6. Safe harbour

Regulation 22 of the TPR has changed safe harbour provisions with Nigeria's transfer pricing regimes. The current position is that a taxpayer would be exempted from requirements of regulation 16 (i.e. the preparation of transfer pricing documentation) where its controlled or related party transactions are priced in accordance with specific guidelines that may be published by FIRS from time to time. Under the old regime (regulation 15 of the old TPR), safe harbour exemptions were granted only when the pricing was in accordance with a Nigerian statutory provision or has been approved by a regulatory agency established by law in Nigeria subject to the satisfaction of FIRS.

7. Dispute resolution

Regulation 21 introduced the following variation to the internal dispute resolution processes of the transfer pricing regime at FIRS:

a) It increased the membership of the Decision Review Panel (DRP) from 3 to 5 persons;

b) It gave the legal department of FIRS a permanent seat on the panel; and

c) Made the right to refer a case to the DRP that of the Head of the transfer pricing function in FIRS instead of the situation under the old TPR where the right to refer an assessment from the FIRS to the DRP was that of the taxpayer.

Furthermore, it is contended that under the TPR the DRP cannot issue a formal assessment or an adjustment. This power is not provided for by regulation 21 of the TPR as was the case under the regulation 14(5) of the old TPR. Also, it is not apparent from regulation 21 of the TPR if taxpayers would be allowed physical representation at the DRP.

8. Penalties for default

Below are the defaults in the TPR and associated penalties.

a) Failure to make or submit declaration under regulation 13(1) and (2) of the TPR within the specified time attracts a penalty of NGN 10 million in addition to NGN 10, 000 for every day failure continues pursuant to regulation 13(8) of the TPR.

b) Failure to file updated transfer pricing declaration in terms of regulation 13(5)[21] of the TPR to notify the happening of any of the event listed in regulation (13) 4[22] and 6[23] of the TPR attracts a fine of NGN 25,000 for every day in which the default continues.

c) Failure to declare controlled transactions within six months of the end of the accounting year in which the transaction took place or 18 months after the date of incorporation attracts a penalty of the higher of NGN 10 million or 1 percent of the total value of all controlled transactions plus NGN 10,000 for every day in which failure continues.[24]

d) Failure to submit documentation referred to in regulation 16(1) of the TPR within 21 days of receipt of its demand by FIRS attracts a penalty of the higher of NGN 10 million or 1 percent of the value of controlled transaction and NGN 10,000 for every day in which the failure continues pursuant to regulation 16(5) of the TPR.

e) Failure to furnish FIRS with any information or document required within the time specified in the demand notice attracts a penalty of one percent of each controlled transaction for which the information or document was required plus NGN 10,000 for each day of default pursuant to regulation 17(5) of the TPR.

---

21 The update transfer pricing declaration must be submitted to FIRS within 6 months of the ending of the accounting year in which the requisite event occurred.

22 These events are the merger of a parent company with other outside the group; acquisition of up to 20 percent of a parent company by another outside the group; merger or acquisition of the entity by another outside the group; sale or acquisition of a subsidiary by an entity; any change in the structure, arrangement, circumstances of the party not mentioned above with capacity to influence, whether connected to another person or not.

23 This relates to the appointment or retirement of a director of the connected person.

24 Regulation 14 (1)-(4), TPR.

13.4.6 Action 11: BEPS Data

Not applicable to Nigeria as this an OECD measure.

13.4.7 Action 12: Disclosure of Aggressive Tax Planning Practices

Nigeria is yet to respond to or implement the recommendations of Action 12. Thus, there is no mandatory disclosure regime (MDR) pursuant to which tax intermediaries or taxpayers are obligated to report aggressive or abusive transactions, arrangements or structures to FIRS. However, there is no legal or professional restriction amidst the tax jurisprudence preventing the entrenchment of one. Actually, pursuant to section 61 of the FIRSEA, FIRS can issue MDR rules or regulations.

13.4.8 Action 15: Multilateral Instrument

Nigeria has signed the MLI. The countries whose tax treaties with Nigeria are covered by the MLI are Belgium, Canada, China, Czech Republic, Slovak Republic, France, Korea, Mauritius, Netherlands, Pakistan, Philippines, Qatar, Romania, Singapore, South Africa, Spain, Sweden, United Arab Emirates and the United Kingdom (hereafter referred to as 19 treaties). At the time of signing, Nigeria entered several reservations and notifications. The notifications entered with regard the applicability of the Articles of the MLI are summarised below:

1 Article 4(2) not applicable to the 19 treaties as they all contain similar provisions;

2 Article 6(2) is not applicable as the 19 treaties contain preamble similar to that described in Article 6(1) MLI, while Article 6(3) was chosen to apply to the 19 treaties;

3 Article 7 not applicable to tax treaties with Belgium, Canada, China, France, Korea, Mauritius, Romania, South Africa, Spain, Sweden, United Kingdom as they contain similar provisions;

4 Article 9(1) is not applicable to tax treaties with Korea, Singapore, Spain, United Arab Emirate as they contain similar provision, while Article 9(4) was chosen to apply;

5 Article 12(3)(a) and (b) are not applicable as the 19 treaties contain similar provisions;

6 Option A under Article 13(1) was chosen to apply, while Article 13(5)(a) is not applicable as the 19 treaties contain similar provisions;

7 Article 16(4)(a)(i) is not applicable as the 19 treaties contain similar provisions. Also:

   a) The scenario presented in Article 16(1) is not applicable to tax treaties with Canada and Philippines as they contain provisions that specify a period shorter than three years;

   b) The scenario presented in Article 16(1) is not applicable to tax treaties with Belgium, China, France, Korea, Mauritius, Netherlands, Qatar, Romania, Singapore, South Africa, Spain, Sweden, United Arab Emirates as they contain provisions that specify a period that is at least three years;

c) That the tax treaties with Belgium, Canada, Czech Republic, Slovak Republic, Netherlands, Pakistan, Philippines, Qatar, Romania, and the United Kingdom do not contain a provision as described in Article 16(4)(b)(ii); and

d) That the tax treaties with Belgium, France, Netherlands, Pakistan, Philippines, Romania and the United Kingdom do not contain a provision as described in Article 16(4)(c)(ii).

8 Chose to replace the reference in Article 35(1)(b) and Article 35(5)(b) to "taxable periods beginning on or after the expiration of a period" with a reference to "taxable periods beginning on or after the first day of the next calendar year beginning on or after the expiration of a period".

The reservations entered are with regard to:

1 Article 8 (Dividend Transfer Transactions): that the entirety of the Article is not to apply to the 19 treaties;

2 Article 11 (Application of Tax Agreements to Restrict a Party's Right to Tax its Own Residents): that the entirety of the Article is not to apply to the 19 treaties; and

3 Article 17 (Corresponding Adjustments): that the entirety of the Article is not to apply to the 19 treaties as they already contain similar provisions.[25]

13.5 Adoption of Unilateral BEPS Measures

There is currently no evidence that points to any unilateral actions taken by Nigeria in relation to BEPS, either with regard to tax policy or tax administration.

13.6 Relationship between Tax Administration and International Tax Reform

Information exchange is central to the BEPS actions. Nigeria as a country has taken steps to use information exchange to improve tax compliance. The Federal Inland Revenue Service as the delegated competent authority for exchange of information in Nigeria has set up an Exchange of Information Unit within its Tax Policy, Legislation and Advisory Department (Aniyie, 2018, p. 608). The EoI unit has received support from multilateral agencies such as the Global Forum on Transparency and Exchange of Information for Tax Purposes (Global Forum) through their African Project – which is aimed at equipping African tax administrators with information exchange tools to carry out their jobs more efficiently (Adu, 2017). This support is a consequence of Nigeria's membership of the Global Forum since April 2011, its

25 Note regulation 10 of the TPR which provides for corresponding adjustments.

status of being "overall largely compliant with the international standard of transparency and exchange of information for tax purposes" and the "pass mark" it received after the first and second peer review by the Global Forum (OECD, 2013; OECD 2016).

Furthermore, in a bid to protect the tax base of the country and ensure that non-resident companies are tax compliant, the FIRS set up an International Tax office in Lagos, the commercial hub of the country. This development led to an increase in tax audits of non-resident companies (EY, 2017).

13.7 Future of International Tax Reform

From the foregoing, except for Action 12, it seems Nigeria has to some extent implemented all the actions which the G20 Development Working Group on Domestic Resource Mobilisation for Developing Countries earmarked as having the greatest effect for developing countries (Oguttu, 2016). However, there is much to look forward to with regard to international tax reform in Nigeria especially from the viewpoint of the BEPS implementation. As a resource rich country, it is likely that there will be increased focus on the extractive industry, particularly the petroleum and mining sectors. There is currently no bespoke legislation for the taxation of the mining sector which is currently taxed under CITA which does not take into cognisance the peculiarity of the sector. The current petroleum profits tax regime is also fraught with challenges which range from inefficient sales practices which have been the source of revenue leaks and abuse of power to underlying structural problems associated with the machinery for the regulation of the petroleum sector (Sayne, Gillies and Katsouris, 2015).

Digitalisation in Nigeria is growing, and it is our belief that very quickly the country will try to come up with measures that will address the tax challenges that come with this new development. There are indications that the number of tax treaties in force will increase in the coming years as the implementation process of a few is currently under way. Furthermore, an expansion of the treaty network is expected, as there are a number of negotiations ongoing.

In the future, it is surmised that Nigeria will face a few legal (or related) challenges with regard to international tax reforms. The obvious involves the legislative bottlenecks with respect to the enactment of domestic legislation that is needed to support the country in the international tax arena. Law-making is an expensive and time-consuming process in Nigeria. A case in point is the Petroleum Industry Bill that has been "in the making" for 17 years. Another is the issue of mandatory binding arbitration (MBA) of tax treaty disputes. This is an issue because the extant legal jurisprudence is that the arbitration of tax disputes is unconstitutional and Nigeria is a treaty partner to countries who have either committed to adopt and implement MBA to tax treaty disputes or have such clauses in treaties with other states.

References

Abdulrazaq, Abdulateef Olatunji (2016), "Nigeria: Effect of the OECD BEPS Initiative on Nigerian Transfer Pricing Regulations", 23(6) *International Transfer Pricing Journal* 535-543.

Adu, Seun (2017), "Tax information exchange – what will change and how taxpayers should respond", PwC's Transfer Pricing Series, 29 August, https://www.pwc.com/ng/en/services/tax/publications.html (accessed on 6 July 2018).

African Tax Administration Forum (ATAF) (n.d.), "Technical Assistance", https://www.ataftax.org/newpage5 (accessed 21 September 2018).

African Tax Administration Forum (ATAF) (2017), *African Tax Outlook*, 2nd edn (Pretoria: African Tax Administration Forum).

Aniyie, Ifeanyichukwu Azuka and Emmanuel Igwe Eze (2018), "Nigeria", in Chris Evans, Michael Lang, Alexander Rust, Josef Schuch, Claus Staringer and Pasquale Pistone (eds.), *Tax Treaty Arbitration* (Amsterdam: IBFD Publications) forthcoming.

Aniyie, Ifeanyichukwu Azuka (2018), "Nigeria", in Michael Lang, Alexander Rust, Josef Schuch, Claus Staringer and Pasquale Pistone (eds.), *Improving Tax Compliance in a Globalized World* (Amsterdam: IBFD Publications), 599-623.

EY (2017), "Nigeria's Federal Inland Revenue Service creates International Tax Unit to review nonresident company transactions for permanent establishment issues", *Global Tax Alert*, 23 August.

Federal Inland Revenue Service (2012), *Tax Audit Guide*, Abuja.

International Bureau for Fiscal Documentation (2018), Nigeria – BEPS Country Monitor, Quick Reference Tables, IBFD Online, Amsterdam.

International Monetary Fund (IMF) (2018), "Nigeria, Country Report No. 18/63", Washington, DC.

National Bureau of Statistics (2017), *Foreign Trade in Goods Statistics*, Abuja.

Ndajiwo, Mustapha (2016), "E-Commerce Taxation: A Framework to Broaden the Tax Base in Nigeria", African Tax Research Network Working Paper No. 16, May.

Nigerian Communications Commission (2018), "Industry Statistics", https://www.ncc.gov.ng/stakeholder/statistics-reports/industry-overview#view-graphs-tables-5 (accessed on 28 May 2018).

Oguttu, Annet Wanyana (2016), "OECD's Action Plan on Tax Base Erosion and Profit Shifting: Part 2 – A Critique of Some Priority OECD Actions from an African Perspective – Addressing Excessive Interest Deductions, Treaty Abuse and the Avoidance of the Status of a Permanent Establishment", 70(6) *Bulletin for International Taxation* 329-354.

Omiunu, Ohiocheya and Ifeanyichukwu Azuka Aniyie (2018), "Evolution of Subnational Foreign Economic Relations in Nigeria" *South African Journal of International Affairs* (Article ID: SAIJA 1526111) advance online.

Onyejekwe, Chisa (2018), "Corporate Tax as a Utility for Economic Growth: Challenges of Compliance and Enforcement in Nigeria", 29(7) *International Company and Commercial Law Review* 449-463.

Organisation for Economic Co-operation and Development (OECD) (2013), *Global Forum on Transparency and Exchange of Information for Tax Purposes Peer Reviews: Nigeria 2013, Phase 1: Legal and Regulatory Framework* (Paris: OECD).

Organisation for Economic Co-operation and Development (OECD) (2016), *Global Forum on Transparency and Exchange of Information for Tax Purposes Peer Reviews: Nigeria 2016, Phase 2: Implementation of the Standard in Practice* (Paris: OECD).

Organisation for Economic Co-operation and Development (OECD) (2017a), *Background Brief: Inclusive Framework on BEPS* (Paris: OECD).

Organisation for Economic Co-operation and Development (OECD) (2017b), "Nigeria: Transfer Pricing Country Profile", October, https://www.oecd.org/tax/transfer-pricing/transfer-pricing-country-profile-nigeria.pdf (accessed on 25 May 2018).

Organisation for Economic Co-operation and Development (OECD) (2018), *Tax Challenges Arising from Digitalisation - Interim Report 2018: Inclusive Framework on BEPS* (Paris: OECD).

Sayne, Aaron, Alexandra Gillies and Christina Katsouris (2015), *Inside NNPC Oil Sales: A Case for Reform in Nigeria,* Natural Resource Governance Institute, August.

United Nations Development Programme (2016), *Human Development Report* (New York: United Nations Development Programme).

14 The Adoption of BEPS in Singapore

Stephen Phua[*] and Joshua Lai[**]

Abstract

This chapter analyses the extent of Singapore's commitment to the Inclusive Framework on BEPS and tracks the progress of Singapore's implementation of the four minimum standards in Actions 5, 6, 13 and 14, as well as of other Actions of the BEPS Project. The authors also raise potential concerns related to uneven implementation of BEPS standards across all jurisdictions and highlight the need to prioritise the forging of international consensus for consistent enforcement of BEPS measures.

14.1 Introduction

This chapter provides an overview of Singapore's response to the G20/Organisation for Economic Co-operation and Development (OECD) Base Erosion and Profit Shifting Project, detailing also the actions that have been taken so far to implement the standards recommended by the BEPS Project (OECD, 2013c).

Despite not being a member of the OECD or G20, Singapore remains fully committed to key international initiatives on international tax cooperation.[1] It participates actively in the BEPS Project, endorsing the BEPS objective of creating an international tax system in which "... profits should be taxed where substantive economic activities generating the profits are performed and where value is created" (Ministry of Finance (MOF), 2015). To the extent that existing tax rules and practices permit profits to be artificially shifted, Singapore actively subscribes to systematic reforms implemented globally to minimise such opportunities. It agrees that tax competition is desirable only if there is an international consensus to create

---

* Associate Professor, Director (Tax), EW Barker Centre for Law and Business, Faculty of Law, National University of Singapore.

** Senior Legal Counsel, Legal Directorate, Ministry of Finance, Singapore. The opinions expressed in this chapter are the independent and personal views of the authors. The contents do not represent, directly or indirectly, the positions of the organisations with which the authors are affiliated. We are grateful to Krystle Gan and Tneu Jia Jin for their research assistance.

1 For example, Singapore signed the Agreement between the Government of the Republic of Singapore and the Government of the United States of America to Improve International Tax Compliance and to Implement FATCA on 9 December 2014 (FATCA IGA). The FATCA IGA entered into force on 18 March 2015.

and enforce an attainable level playing field amongst all countries.

14.2 Overview of Singapore

Singapore is an island country located in the Asia-Pacific region, with a size of approximately 720 square kilometres and a population of 5.61 million as of 2017 (Singapore Department of Statistics (Singstat), 2018). Founded as a British trading colony in 1819, Singapore became fully independent in 1965 as a republic. It has a Westminster system of unicameral parliamentary government, and an elected presidency where the President holds a dual role as head of state and custodian of the nation's financial reserves.

Since independence, Singapore has prospered from stable rates of economic growth for many decades. From SGD 2.98 billion in 1965, Singapore's GDP rose to reach SGD 447 billion in 2017 (Singstat, 2018). This translates to a GDP per capita of SGD 79,697, one of the highest in the world. Singapore is an open economy that is highly dependent on international investment and trade. As at the end of 2016, Singapore has attracted SGD 1,359 billion in foreign direct investment and made SGD 784 billion in direct investments abroad.

Singapore has a pro-business environment and highly competitive economy, ranking second in the Ease of Doing Business index and third in the Economic Competitiveness index, maintained by the World Bank and International Institute for Management Development (IMD) respectively, for the year 2017. In addition, Singapore possesses a relatively modern and transparent system of financial rules and laws.[2] The socio-political environment is stable with a low crime rate. Singapore is ranked second on the Economist Intelligence Unit's Safe Cities Index 2017 (Economist, 2017), and sixth least corrupt in the Corruption Perceptions Index (Transparency International, 2017). In 2018, Singapore was named the most liveable city in Asia by Mercer in its 20th annual Quality of Living survey.[3]

The Inland Revenue Authority of Singapore (IRAS) is the principal administrative agency responsible for tax collection. In Financial Year 2017, IRAS collected about 68.2 per cent of government operating revenue, the most significant sources being corporate income tax, personal income tax and goods and services tax (GST).[4] Income tax is generally charged on a territorial basis, but does extend to

2 Singapore was ranked 85 out of 94 in the TMF Group's Financial Complexity Index 2018, which makes it one of the least financially complex jurisdiction, indicating a significant ease and certainty of doing business. See TMF Group, *Financial Complexity Index 2018*, https://www.tmf-group.com/en/news-insights/publications/2018/financial-complexity-index/ (accessed on 31 May 2018).

3 See Mercer, *2018 Quality of Living Rankings*, https://www.mercer.com/newsroom/2018-quality-of-living-survey.html (accessed on 31 May 2018).

4 See IRAS (2017c). The other taxes collected by IRAS include property tax, betting taxes and stamp duty.

foreign-sourced income remitted into Singapore.[5] Personal income tax is charged at progressive rates up to a maximum of 22 per cent -- the highest marginal rate applicable to chargeable incomes in excess of SGD 320,000, while corporate entities are taxed at a flat rate of 17 per cent. As Singapore adopts a single-tier taxation system for corporate income, dividends paid by a company resident in Singapore are tax exempt. GST is charged on the supply of goods and services made in Singapore at a single standard rate of 7 per cent.[6] Singapore also has a wide network of Double Taxation Agreements.[7]

Two other bodies are responsible for the collection of the remaining major types of taxes and levies. The Singapore Customs collects tax, customs duty and excise duty on four types of dutiable goods - petroleum, alcohol, tobacco and motor vehicles. The Land Transport Authority of Singapore is charged with the responsibility of administering the levies and taxes on the ownership and usage of motor vehicles.

Corporate income tax provides 19.1% of the Singapore Government operating revenue, while personal income tax contributes 14.2% and the goods and services tax contributes 14.3% (MOF, 2018b, p.9).

14.3 Singapore's Response to the OECD BEPS Project

Singapore has participated actively in the Global Forum on Transparency and Exchange of Information for Tax Purposes since its inception. After the United Nations' endorsement of the 2005 OECD Standard on the Exchange of Information on Request (EOIR) regime in 2008, Singapore took immediate steps to adopt the international standard that had emerged. Existing DTAs were updated, and its domestic laws were amended to remove the then existing "domestic tax interest" requirement.[8] The amendments to the Income Tax Act (Cap 134, Rev. Ed. 2014) (ITA) also removed the statutory prohibition against an exchange of bank and trust information with its treaty partners. With these changes, Singapore was able to exchange such information with any treaty partner where the applicable DTAs contain the equivalent of Articles 26(4) and (5) of the OECD Model Tax Convention on Income and Capital.[9]

5 Income Tax Act (Cap. 134, Rev. Ed. 2014), s. 10(1), which provides that income tax shall be payable upon the income of any person "accruing in or derived from Singapore or received in Singapore from outside Singapore".

6 It was recently announced that the single GST rate will be increased to 9 per cent sometime between 2021 and 2025 (MOF, 2018c).

7 It has concluded 88 comprehensive double tax treaties (84 are in force), eight limited double tax treaties and one tax information agreement.

8 The *Income Tax (Amendment) (Exchange of Information) Act 2009* that effected this change came into force on 30 October 2009. See Phua and Fun (2017, p. 1338).

9 By February 2010, Singapore had put in place exchange relationships with more than half of its treaty partners. Clauses 4 and 5 were inserted into Article 26 of the OECD Model Convention in 2005. They mandate a Contracting State to exchange information for tax purposes, upon

In 2013, OECD released a Peer Review Report on Singapore's EOIR regime. Singapore was found to have "in place appropriate organisational processes and resources to ensure effective exchange of information" and was assessed to be "largely compliant" with the OECD measures (OECD, 2013a, p. 9). As of 31 May 2018, Singapore has activated more than 60 bilateral automatic exchange relationships for information under the Common Reporting Standard (CRS). IRAS has also implemented measures to guide taxpayers on the reporting of financial accounts under the CRS (IRAS, 2017a).

Since 2013, Singapore has been an active contributor to the work of the OECD's Committee on Fiscal Affairs, including providing valuable inputs to the BEPS project (MOF, 2016b). In June 2016, Singapore committed to the Inclusive Framework on BEPS. Since then, Singapore has taken steps to implement the four minimum standards under the BEPS Project:

a) Action 5: Counter Harmful Tax Practices More Effectively, Taking into Account Transparency and Substance;
b) Action 6: Prevent Treaty Abuse;
c) Action 13: Re-examine Transfer Pricing Documentation; and
d) Action 14: Make Dispute Resolution Mechanisms More Effective.

The relevant legal developments are as follows:

- Multilateral Convention on Mutual Administrative Assistance in Tax Matters (as amended by the 2010 Protocol) (MAATM): Signed on 29 May 2013. Ratified on 20 January 2016. Entered into force on 1 May 2016. Domestic laws were amended.[10]
- Multilateral Convention to Implement Tax Treaty Related Measures to Prevent Base Erosion and Profit Shifting (MLI): Signed on 7 June 2017. Not yet ratified as at 31 May 2018. Domestic laws were amended.[11]
- Multilateral Competent Authority Agreement on Automatic Exchange of Financial Account Information under the Common Reporting Standard: Signed on 21 June 2017. Domestic laws were amended.[12] Singapore has 67

the request of the other Contracting State, even if the first-mentioned Contracting State lacks "domestic tax interest" to collect the information. Further, the first-mentioned Contracting State may not decline to supply such information on the ground that it is held by a bank or other financial institution which may have a fiduciary relationship with the taxpayer to whom the information relates.

10 Section 105BA of the ITA and Income Tax (Exchange of Information Arrangement) Order 2016 (Cap. 134, S 34/2016) (with effect from 25 January 2016).

11 With effect from 26 October 2017, section 49(7) of the ITA gives the Minister power to enter into any arrangements to give effect to the MLI.

12 See ITA, ss 105K and 105P. See also Income Tax (International Tax Compliance Agreements) (Common Reporting Standard) Regulations 2016 (Cap. 134, S 621/2016) and Income Tax (International Tax Compliance Agreements) (Multilateral Competent Authority Agreement on Automatic Exchange of Financial Account Information) Order 2018 (Cap. 134, S 29/2018).

Automatic Exchange of Information (AEOI) relationships with other countries as at 31 May 2018 (MOF, 2018a; OECD, 2018c)

- Multilateral Competent Authority Agreement on the Exchange of Country-by-Country Reports (CbCR): Signed on 21 June 2017. Domestic laws were amended.[13] Singapore has 50 CbCR exchange relationships with other countries as at 31 May 2018 (OECD, 2018c).

In addition, there were numerous public consultations to engage stakeholders on the impact of the BEPS Project (MOF, 2016a). IRAS has published guides and other explanatory materials to guide taxpayers on their compliance obligations.[14]

14.4 Progress of Implementation: The Four Minimum Standards (BEPS Actions 5, 6, 13 and 14)

This section surveys the progress of Singapore's implementation of the four minimum standards, *viz.*, Action 5 (Counter Harmful Tax Practices More Effectively, Taking into Account Transparency and Substance), Action 6 (Prevent Treaty Abuse), Action 13 (Re-examine Transfer Pricing Documentation) and Action 14 (Make Dispute Resolution Mechanisms More Effective).

14.4.1 Action 5: Counter Harmful Tax Practices More Effectively, Taking into Account Transparency and Substance

Action 5 targets harmful tax practices that exploit preferential tax regimes to facilitate base erosion and artificial profit shifting. It requires tax jurisdictions to: (1) identify tax regimes with harmful features; (2) evaluate the adequacy of existing criteria in upholding the requirement of substantial activities that generate income qualifying for any preferential treatment under a regime, and (3) improve transparency by committing to a framework of compulsory spontaneous exchange of information of related rulings with other tax jurisdictions.

In Singapore, tax incentives and preferences are strictly prescribed by statute.[15] Under the statutory framework, tax incentives are generally granted for defined periods of time on specifically defined categories of income derived from qualifying activities. As a matter of general law, grants of tax incentive awards are contingent upon an undertaking by the awardee to anchor substantive operations in Singapore and contribute meaningfully to the growth of the overall economy. In October 2016, the tax incentives in Singapore reviewed by the Forum on Harmful

13 See ITA, ss 105K and 105P. See also Income Tax (International Tax Compliance Agreements) (Country-By-Country Reporting) Regulations 2018 (Cap. 134, S 75/2018) and Income Tax (International Tax Compliance Agreements) (Multilateral Competent Authority Agreement on the Exchange of Country-By-Country Reports) Order 2018 (Cap. 134, S 72/2018).

14 See IRAS E-Tax, *e-Tax Guides*, https://www.iras.gov.sg/irashome/e-Tax-Guides/ (accessed on 31 May 2018).

15 These incentives are found in the ITA or the *Economic Expansion Incentives (Relief from Income Tax) Act* (Cap. 86, Rev. Ed. 2005).

Tax Practices were certified to be fully compliant with the prevailing international standards (OECD, 2017, pp. 17-22).

With regard to preferential regimes for intellectual property (IP), Singapore is implementing an IP Development Incentive that incorporates the "modified nexus" approach.[16] This new IP regime is designed to ensure that income from the exploitation of IP subject to preferential treatment is derived from research and development activities undertaken in Singapore. In furtherance of this objective, the Economic Development Board of Singapore has indicated that IP income will no longer be eligible for preferential tax treatment under the Pioneer Service Companies Incentive and the Development and Expansion Incentive, in conformity with the agreed grandfathering timelines under Action 5 (Economic Development Board of Singapore (EDB), 2018). On 9 May 2018, the OECD released its updated review of preferential regimes in which the IP Development Incentive was assessed to be "not harmful" (OECD, 2018d, p. 1).

With respect to transparency, Singapore has committed to the OECD BEPS framework for the compulsory spontaneous exchange of information on the following categories of rulings (OECD, 2015b):

a) rulings relating to preferential regimes;
b) unilateral Advance Pricing Arrangements (APAs) or other cross-border unilateral rulings in respect of transfer pricing;
c) cross-border rulings providing for a downward adjustment of taxable profits;
d) Permanent Establishment (PE) rulings; and
e) related party conduit rulings.

14.4.2 Action 6: Prevent Treaty Abuse

Action 6 aims to prevent "treaty shopping", an arrangement through which a nonresident of either Contracting State to a DTA inappropriately attempts to obtain the benefits of that DTA. The minimum standard in Action 6 requires the inclusion of rules in DTAs to curb treaty shopping more effectively. It recommends the inclusion of a clear statement in the title or preamble that the purpose of a tax treaty is not to facilitate tax evasion or double non-taxation of income. In addition, signatories are expected to incorporate a combination of a "limitation-on-benefits" (LOB) rule and a "principal purpose test" (PPT) rule to address all potential forms of treaty abuse.[17]

In particular, Singapore is obliged, as a signatory to the MLI, to give effect to the following mandatory obligations to prevent treaty abuse:

16 Parliament of Singapore, *Singapore Parliamentary Debates, Official Report (20 February 2017) vol. 94, Annex 5.*

17 Examples of Singapore DTAs that contain a "limitation on benefits" clause include those concluded with Estonia, Latvia and Russia.

a) Article 6 (Purpose of a Covered Tax Arrangement): a statement of intent will need to be included in the preamble of a covered tax agreement that the principal purpose of a DTA is to eliminate double taxation without creating opportunities for non-taxation or reduced taxation through tax evasion or avoidance;
b) Article 7 (Prevention of Treaty Abuse): to include general anti-abuse rules, also known as the Principal Purpose Test, in all covered tax agreements; and
c) Article 16 (Mutual Agreement Procedure): to include a mechanism to allow a Singapore resident taxpayer to seek assistance from IRAS when a taxpayer encounters taxation in a DTA jurisdiction that is not in accordance with the intended application of the DTA.

IRAS has also published an updated guidance on the application process for a Certificate of Residency (COR), which serves to establish the residence status required to claim treaty benefits under Singapore's DTAs.[18] The guidance also sets out specific circumstances in which a company may not be eligible to apply for a COR, e.g., nominee companies that are not beneficial owners of income derived from the other treaty State.

14.4.3 Action 13: Re-examine Transfer Pricing Documentation

As a general principle, Singapore adheres to the arm's length principle.[19] IRAS issues and regularly updates its Transfer Pricing Guidelines. These guidelines spell out the arm's length principle for transactions with related parties. Generally, this requires parties to prepare and maintain documents as evidence of compliance with the arm's length principle. Taxpayers are to submit the documents to IRAS within 30 days upon request, and if they are unable to submit the documents, they may be subject to penalties under Section 94(2) of the ITA.

Action 13 calls for a better coordination of transfer pricing (TP) documentation that must be shared amongst national tax administrations. Structured as a three-tiered approach, the ultimate parent entity of a multinational enterprise (MNE) is required to comply with the following obligations: (1) provide tax administrations with high-level global information regarding its global business operations and TP policies in a "master file"; (2) provide TP documentation in a "local file" specific to each country, specifying material related-party transactions and the consideration provided, as well as the methodology of the TP analysis employed; and (3) file with each tax jurisdiction in which the MNE operates an annual Country-by-Country (CbC) report containing information such as its revenue, profit before income tax, income tax paid, number of employees as well as all other relevant economic indicators.

18 See IRAS, Applying for COR/Tax Reclaim Form, www.iras.gov.sg/irashome/Businesses/Companies/Working-out-Corporate-Income-Taxes/Companies-Receiving-Foreign-Income/Applying-for-COR/-Tax-Reclaim-Form/ (accessed on 31 May 2018).

19 ITA, s. 34D. The arm's length principle requires the transaction with a related party to be made under comparable conditions and circumstances as a transaction with an independent party.

Singapore has enacted legislation to impose CbC reporting obligations.[20] Any MNE with its ultimate parent entity in Singapore, and whose group annual turnover exceeds SGD 1,125 million is required to file a CbC report with IRAS within 12 months from the last day of the financial year.[21] A failure to file a CbC report by the due date for applicable MNEs is an offence punishable by a fine not exceeding SGD 1,000 (in default 6 months' imprisonment), and a further fine of SGD 50 per day in the case of a continuing offence.[22] IRAS has also issued a guide which provides detailed information on the purpose of CbC reporting, an MNE's obligations to file a CbC report, and administrative procedures for the submission of a CbC report. The administrative measures include the OECD CbC report XML Schema (IRAS, 2017b).

IRAS will exchange CbC reports with any jurisdiction that has entered into a bilateral agreement with Singapore for the automatic exchange of CbC reports when the following conditions are met:

a) the jurisdiction has a strong rule of law system and can ensure the confidentiality of the information exchanged and prevent its unauthorised use; and
b) there is reciprocity of information being exchanged.

To date, Singapore has activated 50 CbC reporting relationships.[23]

14.4.4 Action 14: Make Dispute Resolution Mechanisms More Effective

Action 14 requires all signatories to establish effective monitoring mechanisms to ensure timely resolution of treaty-related disputes through the Mutual Agreement Procedure (MAP). Singapore has recently been certified under the OECD's Peer Review Report to be largely compliant with Action 14, having met the requirements regarding the availability and access to MAP (OECD, 2018a, p. 9). The MAP provision in the 88 tax treaties concluded by Singapore is modelled on the text of Article 25 of the OECD Model Convention.

Singapore was also found to have provided comprehensive guidance on the availability of MAP. IRAS has updated its published guides on Singapore's international tax policy and the impact of modifications to the contents of Singapore's DTAs including the MAP process. This entails a four-step process:

20 Income Tax (International Tax Compliance Agreements) (Country-by-Country Reporting) Regulations 2018 (Cap. 134, S 75/2018) and Income Tax (International Tax Compliance Agreements) (Multilateral Competent Authority Agreement on the Exchange of Country-by-Country Reports) Order 2018 (Cap. 134, S 72/2018).

21 For accounting periods beginning on or after 1 January 2017. Singapore headquartered MNEs may file a CbC report for financial years beginning on 1 January 2016 on a voluntary basis.

22 ITA, s. 105M.

23 Income Tax (International Tax Compliance Agreements) (Multilateral Competent Authority Agreement on the Exchange of Country-By-Country Reports) Order 2018 (Cap. 134, S 72/2018). The initial lists contain 42 countries when it came into effect on 1 February 2018. Currently, there are 50 activated relationships (OECD, 2018c).

1 Taxpayer submits MAP application to IRAS within the time limit specified in the MAP article of the applicable DTA;

2 IRAS evaluates the MAP application. If the application is in order, an acceptance letter will be issued within one month from the date of receipt of all necessary information;

3 IRAS informs taxpayer of the MAP outcome within one month of reaching an agreement with the competent authority of the treaty partner;

4 Implementation of the MAP outcome.

While the OECD Peer Review Report concluded that Singapore's treaty network was largely consistent with the requirements of Action 14, it highlighted two deficiencies that needed to be addressed: (i) almost one-quarter of its treaties do not contain a provision that mandates MAP to be implemented notwithstanding any time limits in domestic law; and (ii) almost 10 per cent of its treaties do not provide for the equivalent of Article 25(3) of the OECD Model Convention.

Nevertheless, the Report acknowledges Singapore's continuing efforts to update its tax treaties. Besides engaging in bilateral negotiations to amend its treaties, the Report pointed out that Singapore's signing on to the MLI ensures its tax treaty network will eventually be in full compliance with Action 14 requirements. It is also helpful that Singapore has opted for Part VI of the MLI, which should pave the way for the introduction of a mandatory and binding arbitration provision to complement and strengthen the existing MAP process in the resolution of treaty disputes.

14.5 Progress of Implementation for Non-Minimum Standard BEPS Actions

This section surveys the status and progress in the implementation of the remaining BEPS Actions.

14.5.1 Action 1: Address the Tax Challenges of the Digital Economy

Action 1 highlights the nature and pervasiveness of the emerging digital economy in almost every sector of the economy ranging from retail and financial services to education and media. As the adoption of digital technologies has become an integral aspect of most modern economies, it is difficult, if not impossible, to isolate the digital economy for the purpose of addressing the specific tax challenges posed by the rapid transformation of business models in the larger economy. At a technical level, the digital economy does not create distinct BEPS issues. Rather, the unique and novel features of some business structures may exacerbate the incongruities in the application of existing tax rules, especially in its application to income derived by a growing number of businesses with virtual operations at an unprecedented scale across many jurisdictions.

Singapore is a member of the OECD Task Force on the Digital Economy. The Task Force is charged with developing international tax rules on the digital economy. Singapore advocates the adherence to three high-level principles in dealing with these challenges (Rajah, 2017):

a) tax certainty for businesses;
b) tax neutrality between traditional and digital business models; and
c) international consensus.

As recommended in the OECD's *International VAT/GST Guidelines*, Singapore endorses the application of the destination principle in the imposition of Value Added Tax (VAT) or GST on the supply of goods and services (OECD, 2018b, p. 120). In this respect, it was announced in Budget 2018 that Singapore will impose GST on imported services with effect from 1 January 2020. A reverse charge mechanism for business-to-business (B2B) services, and an overseas vendor registration system for business-to-customer (B2C) services will be coming into effect. Imported services would include music and video streaming applications, listing fees on electronic marketplaces, and software and online subscription fees.

At the same time, IRAS has also provided more clarity on the GST treatment of exported services and the use of cryptocurrencies. Exported services are zero-rated if they fall within the ambit of international services as prescribed by section 21(3) of the GST Act.[24] With regard to cryptocurrencies, IRAS has restated in published guidance that virtual digital currencies (e.g., Bitcoin) are not legal tender in Singapore and therefore do not qualify as "money" or "currency". Instead, for GST purposes, the supply of a cryptocurrency is treated as a taxable supply of a service; accordingly, all businesses registered under the GST Act are obliged to collect and account for GST on such supplies at the standard rate of 7 per cent.

14.5.2 Action 2: Neutralise the Effects of Hybrid Mismatch Arrangements

Action 2 aims to neutralise tax advantages obtainable from hybrid mismatch arrangements that exploit incompatible characterisations of entities, financial instruments and asset transfers under the domestic laws of jurisdictions to secure "double non-taxation" or long-term deferral of taxation. A common example is a financial instrument that is treated as a debt in one country and equity in another. In such cases, a distribution from the instrument qualifies for an interest deduction in the country of the payor but is classified as a tax-exempt dividend in the country where the payee resides.

Singapore recognises the negative effects associated with the use of hybrid mismatch arrangements. Prior to Singapore becoming a BEPS associate, IRAS had issued an *e-Tax Guide* to clarify the income tax treatment of hybrid instruments. The guide provides that the true substance of a hybrid instrument is a matter of construction of the instrument as a whole. The legal form adopted may not be

24 *Goods and Services Tax Act* (Cap. 117A, Rev. Ed. 2005) (GST Act).

conclusive and the facts and circumstances surrounding an instrument (e.g., the characterisation of the instrument in the country of the issuer) may sometimes be relevant in the determination of its characterisation.

14.5.3 Action 3: Strengthen CFC Rules

As Singapore does not have a Controlled Foreign Company (CFC) regime, the BEPS recommendations in relation to the strengthening of CFC rules are not relevant. It is noteworthy, however, that the OECD recognises the tension that exists when income taxed under a CFC regime is also subject to transfer pricing rules and DTAs. In its 2015 Report, it conceded that CFC rules may target the same income as transfer pricing rules and pose a real risk of double taxation (OECD, 2015a). It cautioned that States should "carefully review the relevant provisions of their tax treaties when designing their CFC regimes in order to make sure that they are not inadvertently required to apply the exemption method to income that they wish to tax under these regimes" (OECD, 2015a, p. 69).

14.5.4 Action 4: Limit Base Erosion via Interest Deductions and Other Financial Payments

This Action seeks to tackle the BEPS implications arising from intragroup financing. To minimise the payoffs from the excessive use of intragroup debt for tax reasons, Action 4 recommends the adoption of a "fixed ratio rule" to cap the amount of interest expense an entity may deduct for tax purposes. A benchmark ratio such as net interest/EBITDA may be applied to an entity or the group.

Singapore has not disclosed any plans on Action 4 recommendations.

14.5.5 Action 7: Prevent the Artificial Avoidance of PE status

This Action focuses on the artificial avoidance of PE status. It recommends that changes be made to the prevailing core definition of PE to deal with such arrangements. As bilateral changes are impractical, the OECD decided to give effect to such a change via Part IV of the MLI (Avoidance of Permanent Establishment Status). Part IV contains four Articles to address this issue:

a) Article 12: Artificial Avoidance of Permanent Establishment Status through Commissionnaire Arrangements and Similar Strategies;

b) Article 13: Artificial Avoidance of Permanent Establishment Status through the Specific Activity Exemptions;

c) Article 14: Splitting-up of Contracts; and

d) Article 15: Definition of a Person Closely Related to an Enterprise.

As a signatory to the MLI, Singapore has entered reservations against Articles 12, 13(4), 14 and 15 to exclude them from applying to covered tax agreements.

14.5.6 Actions 8-10: Assure that Transfer Pricing Outcomes are in Line with Value Creation

Collectively, Actions 8, 9 and 10 seek to align transfer pricing outcomes with value creation. Individually, they address different transactions involving intangibles (Action 8), contractual allocation of risks (Action 9) and other high-risk transactions (Action 10).

In Singapore, all such dealings must comply with the arm's length principle. IRAS has clarified that the interpretation and application of the arm's length principle in this regard should be consistent with the OECD guidance under Actions 8, 9 and 10. This requires the attribution of profits to be aligned with value creation and taxation to take place where real economic activities are located. In its latest Guidelines, IRAS reiterated its position that it takes specific reference from Actions 8, 9 and 10 in addition to the general guidance from the OECD Transfer Pricing Guidelines for Multinational Enterprises and Tax Administration.

14.5.7 Action 11: Measuring and Monitoring BEPS

Action 11 prioritises the need to establish methodologies to collect and perform statistical analysis of data on the BEPS phenomenon and the remedies implemented pursuant to the adoption of these Actions. The data collected from Actions 5, 12, 13 would be invaluable in assessing the impact of BEPS countermeasures. Although there is consensus on the existence of BEPS, the extent to which legitimate commercial interests and government tax policies may have influenced the behaviour of some taxpayers remains uncertain. As such, it is imperative to continue to collect data and monitor the need to refine prevailing countermeasures or introduce new interventions in the future.

Like many other signatories, Singapore remains committed to the goal of "... ensuring the consistent implementation of the BEPS standards across all jurisdictions" (MOF, 2016b). As a nation that is actively adopting the BEPS Project, it is in the interest of Singapore to continue its support by assisting in the collection of data on BEPS and the implementation of the actions to address it. Having said that, it is vital that the statistical analysis of data collected leads us to a better understanding of the underlying mischief of BEPS and thereby enables the relevant authorities to calibrate remedies to more effectively address them.

14.5.8 Action 12: Require Taxpayers to Disclose their Aggressive Tax Planning Arrangements

Action 12 proposes a mandatory disclosure regime that requires taxpayers to inform the tax administrations of the use of any arrangement that carries typical hallmarks of an aggressive tax planning scheme. At this moment, Singapore does not appear to have any plans to introduce any mandatory disclosure regime of this nature.

14.5.9 Action 15: Develop a Multilateral Instrument

The MLI is a product of Action 15. Singapore was a member of an OECD ad hoc group comprising more than 100 countries that developed the MLI to implement tax treaty-related changes of the OECD BEPS Project.

14.6 Singapore's Tax Administration and International Reforms

While IRAS is the principal tax administration agency in Singapore, its parent ministry, the Ministry of Finance (MOF), is the key driver of tax policies in the country. Through the MOF and IRAS, Singapore has kept itself fully engaged in international fora relating to international tax reform developments. The MOF has a directorate charged with the responsibility of formulating tax policies and overseeing "Singapore's international tax policies such as tax treaties and the exchange of information".[25] IRAS has two divisions dedicated to international tax work, *viz.*: (i) the Tax Policy and International Tax Division, and (ii) the International Tax Affairs and Relations Division (IRAS, 2017c, p. 14). IRAS regularly participates in international conferences such as the OECD Forum on Tax Administration, the Forum on Harmful Tax Practices, and Meetings of the Steering Group to the Inclusive Framework on BEPS, amongst others (IRAS 2017c, p. 20).

Singapore's sustained participation in the international fora and the positive outcomes in the Peer Review Reports are undoubtedly attributable to the industry of its specialised teams of skilled professionals in the MOF and IRAS. Their efforts and contributions cannot be overlooked. As at 31 March 2017, IRAS reported a staff strength of 1,940 (IRAS 2017c, p. 42). This demonstrates Singapore's willingness to invest human capital and resources to build and strengthen its capabilities, systems and structures, ensuring that they continue to remain relevant and robust.

Singapore does not engage in policy-making in the abstract. To effectively communicate and implement the policies emanating from the international tax reforms that Singapore has committed to, IRAS provides the necessary support by publishing "clear and comprehensive guidance"[26] on how taxpayers should fulfil their obligations. Some of the guides that are pertinent to the BEPS Project include:

a) IRAS *e-Tax Guide* on Country-by-Country Reporting (Second Edition);
b) IRAS *e-Tax Guide* (Draft) on Common Reporting Standard;
c) IRAS *e-Tax Guide* on Transfer Pricing Guidelines (Fifth Edition);
d) IRAS *e-Tax Guide* on GST: Guide for E-Commerce (Fourth Edition);
e) IRAS *e-Tax Guide* on Avoidance of Double Taxation Agreements (Second Edition);

25 See MOF, "Directorates", https://www.mof.gov.sg/About-Us/Organisational-Structure/Directorates (accessed on 31 May 2018).

26 This phrase was used by the OECD in a Peer Review Report to describe IRAS' guidance on the MAP process. See OECD (2018a, p. 10).

f) IRAS *e-Tax Guide* on Income Tax Treatment Arising from Adoption of Financial Reporting Standard 115 (FRS 115) – Revenue from Contracts with Customers; and

g) IRAS *e-Tax Guide* on Income Tax: The General Anti-avoidance Provision and its Application (First Edition).

Taken together, this reflects Singapore's seriousness in building capabilities of its tax administrators to better appreciate the impact of and opportunities presented by international tax reform. At the same time, it has strived to remain nimble in the international fora, while still effectively communicating the rapid developments in policies to both local and global taxpayers. This demonstrates Singapore's innovative and enterprising spirit, as well as a willingness to constantly re-invent itself to keep pace with international tax reforms.

14.7 Future of International Tax Reform

A consistent advocate of the rule of law in the international community, Singapore continues to embrace international tax standards and policies that would promote a level playing field across jurisdictions. As with all early adopters of BEPS initiatives, Singapore may be concerned with the prospect of uneven implementation across jurisdictions. If opportunities for regulatory arbitrage were to arise from poor execution or weak enforcement, the remedy may prove to be worse than the disease.

In this respect, international bodies such as the OECD and G20 may wish to consider possible enforcement measures that could guard against any perverse incentive that may arise from the competitive advantage secured by non-participation or deliberate delays. At some point, there may be a need to entertain the prospect of instituting sanctions against countries that resist or demonstrate a lack of good faith in the implementation of the BEPS Actions.

As early as 2013, the OECD recognised, in a report recommending global actions against BEPS, that unilateral measures taken by countries are undesirable (OECD 2013b). The report, urging quick action for a global consensus on initiatives to combat BEPS, noted that "[i]naction in this area would likely result in some governments losing corporate tax revenue, the emergence of competing sets of international standards, and the replacement of the current consensus-based framework by *unilateral measures*, which could lead to global tax chaos marked by the massive re-emergence of double taxation" (OECD 2013b, p. 10). Indeed, an indifference to the adoption of unilateral measures that are incompatible with the Actions would undermine the global consensus and consistent implementation of BEPS standards across *all* jurisdictions.

We may highlight a few examples. The objective and scope of the US Foreign Account Tax Compliance Act (FATCA) clearly overlaps with the AEOI regime. The FATCA regime creates uncertainty for individual taxpayers and imposes additional compliance costs on reporting entities. Similarly, the UK Diverted Profits Tax (25 per cent) and the Australian Multinational Anti-Avoidance Law together with the Diverted Profits Tax (40 per cent) are generally regarded as being out of line with the BEPS recommendations. The tax rates appear to be intended as a punitive measure for the avoidance of PE status.

The authors are of the view that all countries ought to acknowledge the fundamental principle that parallel "self-help" regimes should not be allowed to undermine the significant consensus that has been forged over the BEPS Project. In addition, these parallel regimes increase the risks of unrelieved double taxation as they are likely to fall outside the scope of DTAs.

Although some of the BEPS Actions may take a longer time to be implemented, unilateral measures are highly undesirable and should be frowned upon. If no country is permitted to opt out of BEPS, in whole or in part, then it is imperative that none should be entitled to deviate from the agreed BEPS Framework. Even if such measures are designed to be temporary, they may not be easy to terminate. Therefore, the immediate threats to a successful implementation of the BEPS Project should be identified and assessed. In our view, the most imminent threats are undue delays in implementation, uneven implementation and the temptation to enact unilateral measures.

Separately, the influence of MNEs and their lobby groups should not be underestimated. There may be merit in introducing appropriate sanctions against MNEs that repeatedly flout the rules generated by the BEPS Actions. With a more transparent framework for sharing data under Action 11, monitoring of the behaviour of MNEs will be made easier. Domestically, legislation can be enacted to penalise aggressive tax avoidance schemes, or BEPS behaviour. Going forward, the biggest challenge for the OECD/G20 is to articulate and secure an international consensus on the adoption of an acceptable set of effective sanctions. The BEPS Project appears to be the beginning of a global tax reform initiative the implementation of the majority of the recommendations of which is probably going to take several years. Having begun with a "bang" that defied the most cynical, only history will judge the wisdom of the BEPS Project.

References

Economic Development Board of Singapore (EDB) (2018), "Update on the Intellectual Property Development Incentive and Changes to the Pioneer Service Companies Incentive and Development and Expansion Incentive", 22 March, https://www.edb.gov.sg/content/dam/edbsite/how-we-help/incentives-&-schemes/Update PC and DEI (EDB Circular).pdf (accessed on 31 May 2018).

Economist (Economist Intelligence Unit) (2017), *Safe Cities Index 2017: Security in a rapidly urbanising world* (London: Economist Intelligence Unit Limited).

Inland Revenue Authority of Singapore (IRAS) (2017a), *IRAS e-Tax Guide (Draft): Common Reporting Standard*, https://www.iras.gov.sg/irashome/uploadedFiles/IRASHome/Quick_Links/International_Tax/IRAS%20e-Tax%20Guide_Common%20Reporting%20Standard%20(draft).pdf (accessed on 31 May 2018).

Inland Revenue Authority of Singapore (IRAS) (2017b), *IRAS User Guide: Common Reporting Standard ("CRS"): IRAS XML Schema User Guide for CRS Return*, https://www.iras.gov.sg/irashome/uploadedFiles/IRASHome/Quick_Links/International_Tax/CRS XML User Guide (First Edition)_13Oct2017.pdf (accessed on 31 May 2018).

Inland Revenue Authority of Singapore (IRAS) (2017c), *IRAS Annual Report 2016/17*, https://www.iras.gov.sg/irashome/uploadedFiles/IRASHome/Annual_Reports/IRAS%20Annual%20Report%202016-17_final.pdf (accessed 31 May 2018).

Ministry of Finance (MOF) (2015), "Singapore Welcomes the OECD's Recommendations to Counter Base Erosion and Profit Shifting", Press Release, 6 October, https://www.mof.gov.sg/Newsroom/Press-Releases/Singapore-Welcomes-the-OECD-s-Recommendations-to-Counter-Base-Erosion-and-Profit-Shifting-(-BEPS-) (accessed on 31 May 2018).

Ministry of Finance (MOF) (2016a), *Publication on Draft Income Tax (Amendment No. 3) Bill 2016*, https://www.mof.gov.sg/Public-Consultation/Public-Consultation-Closed/2016/Public-Consultation-on-Draft-Income-Tax-Amendment-No-3-Bill-2016_(accessed on 31 May 2018).

Ministry of Finance (MOF) (2016b), "Singapore Joins Inclusive Framework for Implementing Measures Against Base Erosion and Profit Shifting", Press Release, 16 June, https://www.mof.gov.sg/Newsroom/Press-Releases/Singapore-Joins-Inclusive-Framework-for-Implementing-Measures-against-Base-Erosion-and-Profit-Shifting-(BEPS) (accessed on 31 May 2018).

Ministry of Finance (MOF) (2018a), "Singapore Activated 61 Relationships for Automatic Exchange of Financial Account Information in 2018", Press Release, 15 January, https://www.mof.gov.sg/newsroom/press-releases/singapore-activated-61-relationships-for-automatic-exchange-of-financial-account-information-in-2018 (accessed on 31 May 2018).

Ministry of Finance (MOF) (2018b), *Analysis of Revenue and Expenditure, Financial Year 2018*, Singapore.

Ministry of Finance (MOF) (2018c), *Budget, 2018: Together, A Better Future*, https://www.singaporebudget.gov.sg/data/budget_2018/download/FY2018_Budget_Statement.pdf (accessed on 31 May 2018).

Organisation for Economic Co-operation and Development (OECD) (2013a), *Global Forum on Transparency and Exchange of Information for Tax Purposes Peer Review: Singapore 2013: Phase 2: Implementation of the Standard in Practice* (Paris: OECD).

Organisation for Economic Co-operation and Development (OECD) (2013b), *Addressing Base Erosion and Profit Shifting* (Paris: OECD).

Organisation for Economic Co-operation and Development (OECD) (2013c), *Action Plan on Base Erosion and Profit Shifting* (Paris: OECD).

Organisation for Economic Co-operation and Development (OECD) (2015a), *Action 3 - Final Report: Designing Effective Controlled Foreign Company Rules*, OECD/G20 Base Erosion and Profit Shifting Project (Paris: OECD).

Organisation for Economic Co-operation and Development (OECD) (2015b), *Action 5 - 2015 Final Report: Countering Harmful Tax Practices More Effectively, Taking into Account Transparency and Substance*, OECD/G20 Base Erosion and Profit Shifting Project (Paris: OECD).

Organisation for Economic Co-operation and Development (OECD) (2017), *Inclusive Framework on BEPS, Action 5: Harmful Tax Practices - 2017 Progress Report on Preferential Regimes* (Paris: OECD).

Organisation for Economic Co-operation and Development (OECD) (2018a), *Inclusive Framework on BEPS, Action 14: Making Dispute Resolution More Effective -- MAP Peer Review Report, Singapore (Stage 1)*, March (Paris: OECD).

Organisation for Economic Co-operation and Development (OECD) (2018b), *Inclusive Framework on BEPS: Tax Challenges Arising from Digitalisation -- Interim Report 2018*, March (Paris: OECD).

Organisation for Economic Co-operation and Development (OECD) (2018c), "Country-by-Country Exchange Relationships", April, http://www.oecd.org/tax/beps/country-by-country-exchange-relationships.htm (accessed on 25 June 2018).

Organisation for Economic Co-operation and Development (OECD) (2018d), *Inclusive Framework on BEPS, Action 5: Harmful Tax Practices - 2017 Progress Report on Preferential Regimes, Update as of 9 May 2018* (Paris: OECD), http://www.oecd.org/tax/beps/update-harmful-tax-practices-2017-progress-report-on-preferential-regimes.pdf.

Phua, Stephen and Chai Sui Fun (2017) "Tax Treaty Disputes in Singapore", in Eduardo Baistrocchi (ed.), *A Global Analysis of Tax Treaty Disputes, Vol. 2* (New York: Cambridge University Press), 1304-1348.

Rajah, Hon. Ms Indranee (Senior Minister of State for Law and Finance) (2017), "Future of Taxes in Disruptive Times", speech at the SMU-TA Centre for Excellence in Taxation Conference, York Hotel, Singapore, 17 August, https://www.mof.gov.sg/Newsroom/Speeches/Speech-by-Ms-Indranee-Rajah-Senior-Minister-of-State-for-Law-and-Finance-at-SMU-TA-Centre-for-Excellence-in-Taxation-Conference-at-York-Hotel-Singapor (accessed on 9 July 2018).

Singapore Department of Statistics (Singstat) (2018), *Statistics Singapore - Latest Data*, https://www.singstat.gov.sg/whats-new/latest-data (accessed on 31 May 2018).

Transparency International (2017), *Corruption Perceptions Index 2017*, https://www.transparency.org/news/feature/corruption_perceptions_index_2017 (accessed on 31 May 2018).

15 The Adoption of BEPS in South Africa

Pieter Van Der Zwan* **and Erika de Villiers****

Abstract

While South Africa is a member of the G20, it is not a member of the OECD. However, it contributes to the OECD's work in a sustained and comprehensive manner as a key partner through enhanced engagement programs. South Africa has played an active role as an associate in the BEPS Project and is an active member of the Inclusive Framework for BEPS Implementation Steering Group. This involvement has entailed providing active feedback and inputs into the BEPS process. In addition, South Africa, through the African Tax Administration Forum (ATAF), supported the process to obtain inputs from developing countries on the rest of the African continent.

15.1 Introduction

15.1.1 The Country

South Africa is situated at the southern tip of the African continent. It is bounded by the Atlantic and Indian Oceans. The country's immediate neighbouring countries are Namibia, Botswana, Zimbabwe and Mozambique. The country's population is estimated at 56.2 million (Statistics South Africa, 2017a).

15.1.2 Political Perspective

South Africa has been a democracy since 1994. The African National Congress is the ruling political party. The party is a national liberation movement that led the struggle against apartheid. The party's leadership and certain members of parliament have however in recent years been the subject of allegations of corruption and mismanagement. A recent change in leadership has generally been viewed as a positive development by business and may improve confidence in South Africa.[1] This has been evident in strengthening of the local currency, the South African Rand (ZAR).

---

* Professor, North-West University, Potchefstroom, South Africa.

** Head of Tax Policy, South African Institute of Tax Professionals (SAIT), Johannesburg, South Africa.

1 Independent Online, "South Africa's business confidence rises 11 points", 14 March 2018, https://www.iol.co.za/business-report/economy/south-africas-business-confidence-rises-11-points-13809233 (accessed on 4 July 2018).

15.1.3 The Economy

South Africa is a developing economy.[2] Despite having well-developed infrastructure, the country faces substantial challenges relating to poverty. The unemployment rate in South Africa is a significant concern and is estimated at 27 per cent (Statistics South Africa, 2018b). The country's gini coefficient of 0.65 (Statistics South Africa, 2017b), based on per capita income, is indicative of the high levels of inequality.

The country's economy has been under pressure and reflected low economic growth for a number of years. These economic pressures are evident from the country's credit ratings having been downgraded by major credit rating agencies.[3]

The country's GDP is estimated at ZAR 4.7 trillion trillion (approximately AUD 456 billion). The major contributing sectors to the GDP are:[4]

- finance (approx. 21 per cent);
- government (approx. 17 per cent);
- trade (approx. 15 per cent);
- manufacturing (approx. 13.2 per cent);
- transport (approx. 11 per cent); and
- mining (approx. 8 per cent).

Sectors that contribute to GDP to a lesser extent are personal services, agriculture, electricity and construction.

South Africa is a net importing company (South African Institute of Race Relations, 2017, p. 156). Imported commodities include oil and petroleum products as well as equipment and vehicles. The most significant export products from South Africa are products from the mining industry (gold, coal, platinum, iron products) and vehicles (South African Institute of Race Relations, 2017, p. 166).

15.1.4 The Tax System

The South African tax system consists of a number of taxes, including income tax (including capital gains tax and various withholding taxes), value added tax (VAT), taxes on properties (including donations tax, estate duty, securities transfer tax and transfer duty on property), taxes on international trade and transactions as well as levies on certain goods (National Treasury and South African Revenue Service (SARS), 2017). Income tax and VAT contribute approximately 80 per cent of the total revenue collected (National Treasury and SARS, 2017, p. 18).

South Africa changed to a residence-based income tax system in 2000. Residents are subject to income tax on income earned from both domestic and foreign sources.

---

2 United Nations Country Classification, http://unctadstat.unctad.org/EN/Classifications.html.

3 "South Africa Credit Rating", https://countryeconomy.com/ratings/south-africa (accessed on 4 July 2018).

4 See Statistics South Africa (2018a) and South African Institute of Race Relations (2017, p. 101).

Persons who are not residents of South Africa for tax purposes are only subject to income tax on income sourced in South Africa. South Africa has an extensive network of tax treaties with its trading partners.[5] Corporate income tax is imposed at a rate of 28 per cent. Dividends distributed by companies are subject to dividends tax at a rate of 20 per cent.

VAT is imposed on the supply of goods or services by registered VAT vendors.[6] The VAT rate was increased to 15 per cent with effect from 1 April 2018.

During 2013 the Davis Tax Committee (DTC) was established with a mandate to enquire into the role of the tax system in the promotion of inclusive economic growth, employment creation, development and fiscal sustainability.[7] The DTC concluded its review during March 2018. The process has culminated in a number of reports with recommendations to be considered regarding changes to the South African tax system.[8] Amongst other issues, the DTC considered BEPS and South Africa's response to it. Some future amendments to the South African tax system may be made based on the recommendations of the DTC.

15.1.5 Tax Authority

The South African Revenue Service (SARS) is responsible for the collection of taxes and exercise of control over the import, export, manufacture, movement, storage or use of certain goods.[9] The revenue authority's operating model and organisational structure have been reviewed and changed over the past number of years (SARS, 2017a, p. 11). The organisation uses modernised tax systems and has been highly rated as efficient in collecting taxes.

It does however currently face pressure relating to revenue collection as a result of economic uncertainties and challenges, such as electricity supply constraints, labour disputes and service delivery protests that impact the economic environment (SARS, 2017a, p. 11). In addition, concerns about unfavourable public perception of poor state delivery and corruption have added to the risk to tax compliance and ultimately tax collection that may stem from a low tax morale (SARS, 2017a, p. 12). The Commissioner was suspended by the President during March 2018.[10] As a result, SARS is currently headed by an Acting Commissioner. A commission of enquiry into the tax administration and governance of the SARS was instituted by the President on 24 May 2018.

5 See SARS, "Summary of All Agreements for the Avoidance of Double Taxation", http://www.sars.gov.za/AllDocs/LegalDoclib/Agreements/LAPD-IntA-DTA-2013-01%20-%20Status%20Overview%20of%20All%20DTAs%20and%20Protocols.pdf (accessed on 4 July 2018).

6 *Value-Added Tax Act, 1991* (SA), s. 7(1).

7 See Davis Tax Committee, "About Us – Our Terms of Reference", http://www.taxcom.org.za/termsofreference.html.

8 These reports are http://www.taxcom.org.za/library.html.

9 *South African Revenue Service Act, 1997*, s. 3.

10 See SARS, "Appointment of Mark Kingon as Acting Commissioner", Media Release (20 March 2018), http://www.sars.gov.za/Media/MediaReleases/Pages/20-March-2018---Appointment-of-Mark-Kingon-as-Acting-Commissioner.aspx.

15.1.6 OECD and G20 Membership

South Africa is a member of the G20.[11] It is not a member of the OECD. South Africa contributes to the OECD's work in a sustained and comprehensive manner as a key partner through enhanced engagement programs.[12]

15.2 The Response of South Africa to the G20/OECD BEPS Program of Tax Reform

Even before the commencement of the G20/OECD BEPS program in 2013, South Africa's *Income Tax Act 1962* (as amended) (*Income Tax Act*) contained a number of measures aimed at addressing risks posed by BEPS (Oguttu, 2017). These measures included:

- reclassification rules in respect of hybrid equity and debt instruments (introduced in 1989 and 2004 respectively);[13]
- transfer pricing rules, including thin capitalisation provisions (introduced in 1995);[14]
- controlled foreign company regime (replaced the controlled foreign entity rules in 2002);[15]
- prohibition of deduction of royalties paid in respect of intellectual property to benefit from intellectual property arbitrage opportunities (introduced in 2007);[16]
- withholding taxes on certain payments made to foreign persons. This included withholding taxes on royalties,[17] fees to entertainers and sportspersons[18] and proceeds from the disposal of immovable property in South Africa;[19] and
- limited restrictions on the deductibility of interest incurred in respect of certain reorganisation transactions that posed a risk to the tax base.[20]

In addition to these measures contained in the *Income Tax Act*, South Africa is party to a number of tax treaties that contain measures, such as those suggested by the OECD in its Model Tax Convention, aimed at avoiding erosion of the tax base.

Despite the existing anti-avoidance rules contained in the tax laws, as outlined above, the South African National Treasury identified its continued exposure to

11 See "G20 Participants", https://g20.org/en/g20/g20-participants.
12 OECD, "South Africa and the OECD", http://www.oecd.org/southafrica/south-africa-and-oecd.htm.
13 *Income Tax Act*, ss 8E and 8F.
14 *Income Tax Act*, s. 31.
15 *Income Tax Act*, s. 9D.
16 *Income Tax Act*, s. 23I.
17 Currently contained in *Income Tax Act*, Ch. II, Part IVA.
18 *Income Tax Act*, Ch. II, Part IIIA.
19 *Income Tax Act*, s. 35A.
20 Contained in *Income Tax Act*, s. 23K.

the risk of base erosion prior to the release of the first progress report on the BEPS Project by the OECD. In particular, it was indicated in the 2013 Budget Review that the risk of erosion of the tax base posed by artificial and excessive debt had been on its agenda for more than two years at that time (National Treasury, 2013, p. 55). Amendments aimed at addressing this risk were announced and enacted as part of the 2013 tax law amendments cycle. The above amendments prior to the conclusion of the BEPS initiative provide an indication that South Africa has reacted proactively to the risks posed by BEPS.

South Africa played an active role as an associate in the BEPS Project and is an active member of the Inclusive Framework for BEPS Implementation Steering Group.[21] This involvement has entailed providing active feedback and inputs into the BEPS process. In addition, South Africa, through the African Tax Administration Forum (ATAF), supported the process to obtain inputs from developing countries on the rest of the African continent.

15.3 South Africa and the BEPS Inclusive Framework

South Africa is a member of the Inclusive Framework on BEPS.[22] The following section provides an overview of the impact of the four minimum standards on South Africa.

15.3.1 Action 5: Peer Review and Monitoring

15.3.1.1 Preferential Tax Regimes

South Africa introduced a headquarter company regime during 2011.[23] The headquarter company regime was aimed at making South Africa attractive as a gateway to invest into the rest of the African continent.[24] In brief, a resident company may elect to be treated as a headquarter company if:[25]

- each shareholder holds a substantial interest (at least 10 per cent of the equity shares of the company);
- 80 per cent or more of the cost of the company's assets are attributable to shares in foreign companies, debt advanced to such companies or intellectual property licensed to such companies; and
- the company derives 50 per cent or more of its income from rental, dividends, interest or royalties from the abovementioned foreign companies or gains from the disposal of the interests in the companies or the intellectual property made available to them.

21 OECD, "South Africa and the OECD", http://www.oecd.org/southafrica/south-africa-and-oecd.htm.

22 OECD, "Members of the Inclusive Framework on BEPS", May 2018, http://www.oecd.org/tax/beps/inclusive-framework-on-beps-composition.pdf.

23 *Income Tax Act*, s. 9I.

24 Explanatory Memorandum on the Taxation Laws Amendment Bill 2010, sec. 5.4.

25 *Income Tax Act*, s. 9I(2).

It is submitted that the headquarter company regime is actually closer to a holding company regime, as contemplated in paragraphs 86 to 88 of the final Action 5 report (OECD, 2015), than a headquarter regime, as described in paragraphs 74 to 75 of that report (see also Davis Tax Committee, 2016, Annexure 5, sec. 4.1).

The benefits of electing to be taxed as a headquarter company include exemption from withholding tax on dividends, interest and royalties paid by this company, relief from certain transfer pricing rules in respect of royalties and interest that pass through this company as well as an exclusion from the CFC regime.

The regime has not been successful in attracting interest from investors. The regime was one of the 43 preferential regimes reviewed by the Forum on Harmful Tax Practices (FHTP). The FHTP concluded that this headquarter company regime was potentially harmful but not actually harmful. The South African National Treasury indicated in the 2017 Budget Review that it had recently completed its self-review of preferential regimes, bringing it in line with OECD member countries (National Treasury, 2017, p. 137). It appears from this statement as if the regime will remain in place for the foreseeable future as it currently stands.

15.3.1.2 Transparency in Relation to Rulings

Taxpayers can request advance tax rulings from SARS.[26] All binding rulings are published.[27] Binding rulings issued on the application of preferential tax regimes, such as the headquarter company regime or any other tax incentive, are treated similarly to any other rulings. SARS does not currently issue rulings on pricing arrangements.[28] In addition, similarly to rulings on pricing of goods or services, it may reject ruling requests as to whether a permanent establishment is created.[29]

Based on the BEPS recommendations, the *Tax Administration Act, 2011* (as amended) *(Tax Administration Act)* has been amended to establish a framework for spontaneous exchange of information with other tax authorities.[30]

15.3.2 Action 6: Misuse of Treaty Benefits

South Africa became a signatory to the Multilateral Convention to Implement Tax Treaty Related Measures to Prevent BEPS (MLI) during July 2017.[31] As a result a number of the country's tax treaties will be amended in terms of Article 7 of the MLI to address concerns regarding treaty misuse when the MLI is ratified. South Africa has taken the provisional position to reserve its right to not apply Articles 7(1) and 7(4) to its treaties that already contain provisions that deny treaty benefits

26 *Tax Administration Act, 2011* (SA), Ch. 7.

27 *Tax Administration Act, 2011*, s. 87(2).

28 *Tax Administration Act, 2011*, s. 80(1)(a)(iii).

29 Public Notice 748 (2016), para. 2.1.5.(c).

30 Definition of "international tax standard" in *Tax Administration Act, 2011*, s. 1.

31 OECD, "Signatories and Parties to the Multilateral Convention to Implement Tax Treaty Related Measures to Prevent Base Erosion and Profit Shifting", 29 June 2018, http://www.oecd.org/tax/treaties/beps-mli-signatories-and-parties.pdf.

where the principal purpose of an arrangement is to obtain such benefits.[32] It has not provided any indication of an intent to adopt a detailed or simplified limitation on benefits test.

15.3.3 Action 13: Transfer Pricing Documentation and Country-by-Country Reporting

South Africa is a signatory to the Multilateral Competent Authority Agreement on the exchange of country-by-country reports (CbC MCAA).[33]

South Africa has issued Country-by-Country (CbC) regulations[34] that are closely modelled on the CbC reporting requirements in Action 13. Certain entities that form part of a group that includes enterprises that are resident in different jurisdictions and that has consolidated turnover exceeding ZAR 10 billion (referred to as an MNE Group) are required to submit reports to SARS.[35] The regulation requires an ultimate parent entity of an MNE Group that is a South African tax resident to file a CbC Report with SARS.[36] In addition, a constituent entity of an MNE Group that is a South African tax resident may be required to file a CbC Report with SARS if its ultimate parent is not required to file a CbC Report in its jurisdiction of tax residence, its ultimate parent is tax resident in a jurisdiction with which South Africa does not have a competent authority agreement or where there has been a systemic failure in such jurisdiction.[37] The CbC Report to be filed must contain the information set out in Action 13.[38]

During October 2017, SARS issued a further public notice that requires reporting entities that are South African tax residents to file CbC Reports and financial information, a master file as well as a local file.[39] Similarly, constituent entities that are required to file CbC Reports are also required to submit a master file and local file to SARS.[40] In addition, where a resident taxpayer's potentially affected transactions (being transactions subject to transfer pricing rules without consider-

32 Election in terms of Article 7(15)(b) of the MLI. See South Africa, "Status of List of Reservations and Notifications at the Time of Signature", http://www.oecd.org/tax/treaties/beps-mli-position-south-africa.pdf.

33 OECD, "Signatories of the Multilateral Competent Authority Agreement on Exchange of Country-by-Country Report (CbC MCAA) and Signing Dates", 15 June 2018, http://www.oecd.org/tax/beps/CbC-MCAA-Signatories.pdf.

34 Regulations for purposes of paragraph (b) of the definition of "international tax standard" in section 1 of the *Tax Administration Act, 2011* (Government notice no R1598), Government Gazette, 40516, 23 December 2016 (Regulation 1598).

35 Definition of MNE Group and Excluded MNE Group in Articles 1(2) and 1(3) of Regulation 1598.

36 Article 2(1) of Regulation 1598.

37 Article 2(2) of Regulation 1598.

38 Article 4 of Regulation 1598.

39 Public notice published in terms of section 25, requiring the submission of Country-by-Country Report, Master file and Local file returns by persons as specified in the notice (Notice no 1117), Government Gazette, 41186, 20 October 2017 (Public Notice 1117), para. 2(1).

40 Public Notice 1117, para. 2(2).

ing whether the terms and conditions reflect arm's length terms and conditions) exceed ZAR 100 million this person is required to submit a return with certain information relating to a master file and local file.[41]

The outcomes of the first annual peer review for the Action 13 minimum standard indicate that South Africa meets the terms of reference relating to the domestic legal and administrative framework, exchange of information framework and appropriate use in relation to the implementation of Action 13 (OECD, 2018, p. 673).

15.3.4 Action 14: Treaty-Related Dispute Resolution

As a signatory of the MLI, the South African National Treasury has indicated that the South African treaty model will be updated to incorporate the minimum standards. South Africa reserved the right to not apply the first sentence of Article 16(1) of the MLI.[42] It has not committed to mandatory binding mutual agreement procedure arbitration (National Treasury, 2017, p. 137).

15.4 South Africa's Responses to the Other BEPS Actions

15.4.1 Action 1: Digital Economy

South Africa introduced a requirement for foreign providers of electronic services to register as South African VAT vendors from 1 April 2014 onwards. Foreign suppliers of electronic services who make supplies exceeding ZAR 50,000 during any 12 month period are required to register as a VAT vendor.[43] A regulation that prescribes electronic services in respect of which this regime applies lists the following categories of services covered:[44]

- educational services;
- games and games of chance;
- internet-based auction services;
- miscellaneous services, including e-books, audio visual content, still images and music; and
- subscription services.

These regulations are in the process of being reviewed. It has been proposed that the definition of electronic services be broadened to any service provided for consideration by means of an electronic agent, electronic communication or the

41 Public Notice 1117, para. 2(3).

42 South Africa, "Status of List of Reservations and Notifications at the Time of Signature", above n. 32.

43 *Value-Added Tax Act, 1991*, para. (vi) of the definition of "enterprise" in s. 1 read with s. 23(1A).

44 Regulations prescribing services for the purpose of the definition of "electronic services" in section 1 of the *Value-Added Tax Act, 1991* (Government notice no. R221), Government Gazette, 37489, 28 March 2014.

internet, excluding telecommunication and certain education services.[45]

To date no specific nexus rules, withholding taxes on digital transactions or equalisation levies, as referred to in Action 1, have been implemented by South Africa. South Africa is a member of the new Task Force for the Digital Economy, which is looking at direct taxes (National Treasury, 2017, p. 137).

15.4.2 Action 2: Hybrid Mismatch Arrangements

The *Income Tax Act* contains a number of provisions specifically aimed at preventing hybrid mismatches from arising. This includes a denial of exemption of foreign dividends that were deductible in another jurisdiction[46] and classification of foreign entities as fiscally transparent that mirrors its treatment in the jurisdiction of tax residence.[47] No specific further amendments addressed at avoiding hybrid mismatches were introduced in consequence of the conclusion of the BEPS recommendations. The South African National Treasury has indicated that further refinements may be considered in the future (National Treasury, 2017, p. 137).

As a signatory to the MLI, a number of the treaties entered into by South Africa will be amended by Article 3 of the MLI.

15.4.3 Action 3: Controlled Foreign Companies

South Africa introduced its current CFC rules in 2002. With the exception of the definition of a CFC, as discussed below, no amendments were made to this regime in response to the BEPS recommendations.

The definition of a CFC was broadened in 2017 to include any foreign company where the results of that company are reflected in the consolidated financial statements prepared in terms of IFRS 10.[48] This amendment is based on one of the suggested approaches to defining whether an entity is a CFC in terms of Action 3.

15.4.4 Action 4: Interest Deductions and Other Financial Payments

A statutory interest deduction limitation was introduced in 2015.[49] This limitation affects the deductibility of interest incurred in respect of debts between persons who are in a controlled relationship where such interest is not subject to tax in South Africa in the hands of recipient.[50] The limitation employs a variable percentage of an amount that reflects the payer's earnings before interest, tax, depreciation and amortisation (EBITDA) as the basis for the limitation.[51] The South African

45 Draft Amendments to Regulations: Electronic Services for the purpose of the definition of "Electronic Services" in section 1 of the *Value-Added Tax Act* published on 21 February 2018.

46 *Income Tax Act*, proviso to s. 10B(2).

47 Definition of foreign partnership in *Income Tax Act*, s. 1(1).

48 Para. (b) of the definition of "controlled foreign company" in *Income Tax Act*, s. 9D(1).

49 *Income Tax Act*, s. 23M.

50 *Income Tax Act*, s. 23M(2).

51 *Income Tax Act*, s. 23M(3).

National Treasury has indicated that the current rules will be reviewed in light of the BEPS recommendations (National Treasury, 2017, p. 137).

15.4.5 Action 7: Permanent Establishment Status

South Africa imposes income tax on a foreign person in respect of its South African sourced income. The *Income Tax Act* contains a number of statutory source rules. This includes a source rule for amounts received from the disposal of movable goods that is linked to the definition of a permanent establishment in the OECD's Model Tax Convention (MLI).[52] It is submitted that any changes made to this definition in the MTC in response to the BEPS recommendations should automatically impact the definition in the South African *Income Tax Act*. The source of income from services is determined with reference to case law.

Where a treaty exists between South Africa and the country in which the foreign person is a tax resident, the relevant treaty will generally allocate the right to tax business profits of such person that are attributable to a permanent establishment situated in South Africa. As a signatory of the MLI, its provisions relating to permanent establishments will affect a number of treaties entered into by South Africa. South Africa has made the following elections and reservations of its rights to apply provisions of the MLI:

- it reserved the right for Article 10(1) of the MLI not to apply to its Covered Tax Agreements;
- it reserved the right for Article 11 of the MLI not to apply to its Covered Tax Agreements;
- it reserved the right for Article 12 of the MLI not to apply to its Covered Tax Agreements;
- in relation to artificial avoidance of permanent establishments through the specific activity exemptions, South Africa elected to apply Option A of Article 13 of the MLI.[53]

15.4.6 Actions 8-10: Transfer Pricing

During 2012 South Africa amended its transfer pricing rules to be more closely aligned with the OECD guidelines on transfer pricing.[54] To date SARS has not issued any final interpretation notes in relation to the revised transfer pricing provisions. The South African National Treasury has indicated that SARS is in the process of updating the transfer pricing practice note, which was issued in respect of the legislation prior to the 2012 amendment, to include new guidance on the arm's length principle and an agreed approach to determine pricing on intangibles that

---

52 *Income Tax Act*, s. 9(2)(k) and definition of "permanent establishment" in s. 1(1).

53 South Africa, "Status of List of Reservations and Notifications at the Time of Signature", above n. 32.

54 Amendment of *Income Tax Act*, s. 31 of the Income Tax Act, and Explanatory Memorandum on the Taxation Laws Amendment Bill 2010.

are hard to value (National Treasury, 2017, p. 137).

In the absence of an interpretation note, the OECD guidelines on transfer pricing remain one of the key authorities in applying transfer pricing in South Africa.[55] In light of this, the 2017 update of these guidelines to reflect the recommendations made in Actions 8 to 10 directly impacts transfer pricing in South Africa.

15.4.7 Action 11: BEPS Data

The South African National Treasury has indicated that it shares the view that effective measuring and monitoring through improved statistics and evaluation is important for curbing base erosion and profit shifting. It indicated that it will continue to work with other countries in this regard (National Treasury, 2017, p. 137).

15.4.8 Action 12: Disclosure of Aggressive Tax Planning Practices

South Africa introduced a disclosure requirement on taxpayers in 2005.[56] This system of reportable arrangements has subsequently been incorporated into the *Tax Administration Act*.[57] The disclosure obligation is on any participant in an arrangement that is reportable.[58] The South African National Treasury indicated that these reportable arrangement rules were used as a benchmark for the final BEPS Action 12 recommendations (National Treasury, 2017, p. 137).

15.4.9 Action 15: Multilateral Instrument

South Africa became a signatory to the MLI during July 2017.[59] At the time of writing, South Africa has not yet ratified the MLI domestically. The country's elections and instances where its rights to apply a provision of the MLI have been reserved are mentioned under the relevant BEPS actions affected by the particular article of the MLI, as discussed in this chapter.

15.5 South Africa and Unilateral BEPS Measures

The DTC's final BEPS report contain a specific warning that unilateral action by South Africa may adversely impact the country's global competitiveness (Davis Tax Committee, 2016, p. 36; Johnston, 2017). To date, South Africa has not implemented any unilateral BEPS measures.

In recent years, a number of specific anti-avoidance provisions have been introduced into the legislation. Some of these anti-avoidance measures are specifically aimed at cross-border transactions, for example, the introduction of section 8G that

55 Explanatory Memorandum on the Taxation Laws Amendment Bill 2010.

56 SARS, Reportable Arrangement Guide (2005).

57 *Tax Administration Act, 2011*, Ch. 4, Part B.

58 *Tax Administration Act, 2011*, s. 37(1).

59 OECD, "Signatories and Parties to the Multilateral Convention to Implement Tax Treaty Related Measures to Prevent Base Erosion and Profit Shifting", 29 June 2018, above n. 31.

counters structures used to convert taxable dividends into returns of capital or amendments to claw back certain participation exemption benefits where a person ceases to be a tax resident in South Africa. These amendments were however not necessarily aimed at the BEPS issue itself, as identified in the BEPS Project and recommendations, but rather addressed shortcomings in existing legislation.

South Africa has adopted the international standards for automatic exchange of information (AEOI).[60] The South African government signed the FATCA agreement with the United States in 2014. South African financial institutions have been required to comply with its requirements and obligations from 1 July 2014.[61] South Africa is furthermore a signatory of the Multilateral Competent Authority Agreement for the Common Reporting Standard (CRS MCAA). The country was one of the early adopters of CRS during 2016 (SARS, 2016b, p. 21). The definition of an international tax standard, which refers amongst others to the OECD Standard for Automatic Exchange of Financial Account Information in Tax Matters, was specifically inserted into the *Tax Administration Act* to establish a framework to implement and comply with the common reporting standard (CRS).[62] Regulations that set out the specific reporting requirements on reporting financial institutions were published in 2016.[63] Non-compliant taxpayers were afforded a last opportunity prior to the receipt of information from foreign tax authorities and financial institutions to declare offshore assets and income to SARS in terms of a special voluntary disclosure program (SVDP) that was available in 2017.[64]

South Africa does not have any mandatory tax transparency measures, other than disclosures required in terms of accounting standards (IAS 12 Income Taxes). The Johannesburg Stock Exchange (JSE) listing requirements do not require mandatory tax transparency reporting, even though this represents good practice that firms can adopt voluntarily (Stiglingh et al., 2017). Companies that provide additional tax-related disclosures in their annual financial statements do so at their own discretion.

---

60 OECD, "Signatories of the Multilateral Competent Authority Agreement on Automatic Exchange of Financial Account Information and Intended First Information Exchange Date", 26 June 2018, http://www.oecd.org/tax/automatic-exchange/international-framework-for-the-crs/MCAA-Signatories.pdf.

61 *Agreement between the Government of the Republic of South Africa and the Government of the United States of America to Improve International Tax Compliance and to Implement FATCA*, signed 9 June 2014, TIAS 14-1028 (entered into force 28 October 2014). Available at: http://www.sars.gov.za/AllDocs/LegalDoclib/Agreements/LAPD-IntA-EIA-2014-04%20-%20FATCA%20IGA.pdf.

62 Para. (a) of the definition of "international tax standard" in s. 1 of the *Tax Administration Act, 2011*.

63 Regulations for purposes of paragraph (a) of the definition of "international tax standard" in section 1 of the *Tax Administration Act, 2011* (Government notice no R210), Government Gazette, 39767, 2 March 2016.

64 *Rates and Monetary Amounts and Amendment of Revenue Laws Act, 2016*, Part II.

15.6 South Africa's Tax Administration in Relation to International Tax Reform

As mentioned in the specific actions, a number of amendments have been made to the *Tax Administration Act* to provide a framework for the implementation of BEPS recommendations. The next step required in this regard is to monitor and enforce compliance with these requirements as the recommendations are implemented and become effective.

One of the first BEPS-driven administrative changes to occur was that the corporate income tax return (ITR14) has been changed to incorporate information relating to BEPS. It now includes, for example, questions relating to CbC reporting. In addition, SARS has also indicated that it planned to update its risk engine rules to have a specific BEPS focus (SARS, 2016a, p. 24).

The expansion and strengthening of the SARS BEPS team's capacity and capabilities to deal with large business taxpayers is a one of the revenue authority's key initiatives (SARS, 2017a, p. 12; SARS, 2016b, p. 42). In particular, it has identified the development of the skills pipeline for auditors in the transfer pricing unit to proactively deal with BEPS and transfer pricing as a critical measure to manage risks arising from complex cross-border avoidance schemes (SARS, 2017a, p. 12). In its 2016/2017 Annual Report, SARS indicated that it has increased the number of BEPS staff resources in its large business unit (SARS, 2017b, p. 47).

The DTC noted a number of further areas in relation to tax administration that would require consideration upon the implementation of BEPS recommendations. One such area is the development and maintenance of information technology systems (Davis Tax Committee, 2017, ch. 2, sec. 27). SARS has been developing systems and published business requirement specifications (BRS) for information to be submitted in terms of BEPS initiatives implemented.[65] It is expected that these systems will be refined and expanded as further BEPS recommendations are implemented.

It is submitted that a critical element of implementation of BEPS is taxpayer certainty as the process unfolds. SARS has been, and currently still is, in the process of drafting and updating interpretation notes on the application of the transfer pricing provisions found in the *Income Tax Act*. As BEPS has a substantial transfer pricing element, the timely publication of this guidance that incorporates the BEPS recommendations will be essential. A number of interpretation notes or implementation guidance documents by SARS will arguably be required for other aspects of BEPS-related changes, for example, the implementation of the MLI.

15.7 The Future of International Tax Reform for South Africa

The South African National Treasury has acknowledged the fact that the current corporate tax rate of 28 per cent is relatively high compared to advanced and mid-

65 See, as an example, SARS (2017c) issued during September 2017.

dle-income countries, especially in a global environment where the trend has been to reduce corporate income tax rates (National Treasury, 2018, p. 43). The risk has been identified that this position may provide an incentive for companies to shift profits to jurisdictions with lower tax rates. In light of this, the need to introduce effective anti-avoidance legislation and have adequate enforcement capacity has been highlighted.

The DTC report focusing on the implementation of the BEPS recommendations may form a significant component of such anti-avoidance rules (Davis Tax Committee, 2016). The DTC identified the fact that the South African economy is one which attracts foreign direct investment but also is one from which investments flow outwards as one of the challenges that the country faces in defining an international tax policy within which to implement the BEPS recommendations. Developing a clear approach to BEPS implementation would require a balance between encouraging home-grown groups to remain competitive while still protecting the tax base from erosion (Davis Tax Committee, 2016, p. 5). The importance of not undermining investment and competitiveness in implementing measures to protect the tax base was also recognised by the National Treasury in the 2018 Budget Review (National Treasury, 2018, p. 43). The DTC BEPS report contains an analysis of South Africa's current legislation for each of the BEPS actions, factors identified as requiring specific consideration when implementing the recommendations proposed in each action, suggested further steps required and recommendations in a South African context. This may well prove to be the basis for international tax reform in South Africa in the foreseeable future.

It is submitted that South Africa faces the tough challenge of making choices on implementing BEPS recommendations and other anti-avoidance rules aimed at preventing base erosion while at the same time restoring its economy and attractiveness for foreign investment.

References

Davis Tax Committee (Judge Dennis Davis, chair) (2016), *Base Erosion and Profit Shifting (BEPS) – Second and Final Report*, Pretoria, September, http://www.taxcom.org.za/library.html.

Davis Tax Committee (Judge Dennis Davis, chair) (2017), *Report on Tax Administration*, Pretoria, September, http://www.taxcom.org.za/library.html.

Johnston, Stephanie Soong (2017), "Tax Committee Warns Against Unilateral Action on BEPS", 88 *Tax Notes International* 752-753.

National Treasury (2013), *Budget Review 2013*, 27 February, Pretoria.

National Treasury (2017), *Budget Review 2017*, 22 February, Pretoria.

National Treasury (2018), *Budget Review 2018*, 21 February, Pretoria.

National Treasury and South African Revenue Service (SARS) (2017), *Tax Statistics 2017*, 12 December, Pretoria, http://www.sars.gov.za/About/SATaxSystem/Pages/Tax-Statistics.aspx.

Oguttu, Annet Wanyana (2017), "South Africa", *Cahiers de Droit Fiscal International Vol. 102A: Assessing BEPS: Origins, Standards, and Responses* 623-720.

Organisation for Economic Co-operation and Development (OECD) (2015), *Action 5 - 2015 Final Report: Countering Harmful Tax Practices More Effectively, Taking into Account Transparency and Substance* (Paris: OECD).

Organisation for Economic Co-operation and Development (OECD) (2018), *Inclusive Framework on BEPS, Action 13: Country-by-Country Reporting – Compilation of Peer Review Reports (Phase 1)* (Paris: OECD).

South African Institute of Race Relations (2017), *South Africa Survey 2017* (Johannesburg: South African Institute of Race Relations).

South African Revenue Service (SARS) (2016a), *Annual Performance Plan 2016-2017*, Pretoria.

South African Revenue Service (SARS) (2016b), *SARS Strategic Plan 2016/17 – 2020/21*, Pretoria.

South African Revenue Service (SARS) (2017a), *Annual Performance Plan 2017-2018*, Pretoria.

South African Revenue Service (SARS) (2017b), *Annual Report 2016-2017*, Pretoria.

South African Revenue Service (SARS) (2017c), *External Business Requirements Specification: Country-by-Country and Financial Data Reporting*, September, Pretoria.

Statistics South Africa (2017a), *Mid-Year Population Estimates 2017*, July, Pretoria.

Statistics South Africa (2017b), *Poverty Trends in South Africa: An examination of absolute poverty between 2006 and 2015*, Pretoria.

Statistics South Africa (2018a), *Gross Domestic Product, Fourth Quarter 2017*, Pretoria.

Statistics South Africa (2018b), *Quarterly Labour Force Survey, Fourth Quarter 2017*, Pretoria.

Stiglingh, Madeleine, Elmar Venter, Ilinza Penning, Anna-Retha Smit, Anculien Schoeman and Theuns Steyn (2017), "Tax Transparency Reporting by the Top 50 JSE-Listed Firms", 31(2) *South African Journal of Accounting Research* 151-168.

16 The Adoption of BEPS in Thailand

Patricia Mongkhonvanit,[*] Yarika Ruangsiri[**] and Saowakon Meesang[***]

Abstract

The OECD/G20 BEPS Program has been designed as a collective international effort to ensure that base erosion and profit shifting will be efficiently tackled creating a fairer and more effective international tax system. Since BEPS is a global issue, it requires global solutions. Therefore, developed and developing economies, as well as Thailand, have joined hands to collaborate on the implementation of the OECD/G20 BEPS Program under the Inclusive Framework on BEPS. This chapter describes what has been done in Thailand to tackle BEPS and to implement the four minimum standards as well as the authors' views on what Thailand should do in order to comply with the rules and the issues that are important to ensure effective tax administration.

The chapter starts with an overview of the Thai economy and Thailand's response to the OECD/G20 BEPS Program. Then the authors' views are set out on the tax law and organisational structure reforms that should be carried out to ensure that Thailand is well-equipped to tackle BEPS. In this context the scope of the chapter not only covers the implementation of the four minimum standards under the Inclusive Framework on BEPS but also implementation of other BEPS rules that are relevant to Thailand, such as those relating to the digital economy, hybrid mismatch arrangements, interest deductions, and avoidance of permanent establishment status. In addition, the authors also discuss other measures which could be introduced to make improvements to tax administration. The BEPS measures should be designed appropriately so that the rules are effectively implemented while the economy's competitiveness and a framework for effective investment decisions are maintained.

* Inspector General, Ministry of Finance, Bangkok, Thailand.

** Deputy Director (International), Tax Policy and Planning Division, Revenue Department, Bangkok, Thailand.

*** Deputy Director (Policy), Tax Policy and Planning Division, Revenue Department, Bangkok, Thailand.

The views expressed in this article are those of authors and do not represent those of the Revenue Department of Thailand.

16.1 Introduction

Thailand's economy in terms of GDP is ranked 26th in the world in nominal terms and 20th in purchasing power parity (PPP) terms.[1] Thailand is considered to be an upper-middle income country by the World Bank.[2] The country is highly dependent on international trade, with the combined value of exports and imports equalling 123 per cent of GDP and exports (including services) accounting for nearly two-thirds of GDP. The largest share in dollar value of Thailand's exports includes machinery and computers, electrical machinery and equipment, auto parts and accessories, rubber and rubber articles, plastic and plastic articles, and gems and precious metal. In terms of imports, the largest share in dollar value is electrical machinery and equipment, mineral fuel and lubricants, machinery, and computers, gems and precious metals. The shares of industry (35 per cent) and service sectors (55 per cent) produce about 90 per cent of GDP. The agricultural sector, comprised mostly of small-scale farmings, contributes only 10 per cent of GDP but employs about one-third of the labour force.

Thailand is one of the ten members of the Association of Southeast Asian Nations (ASEAN)[3] which is a trade and social alliance intended to foster economic and social cooperation among member countries and to establish a joint market for attracting foreign trade and investment. ASEAN has developed a closer economic integration by forming an ASEAN Economic Community (AEC), which aims to create a single market and achieve the free movement of goods, services, investment, capital and skilled labour. Thailand is a member of the World Trade Organization (WTO) but not yet a member of the Organisation for Economic Co-operation and Development (OECD).

Regarding the size of the government of Thailand in 2017, government revenue is 18 per cent of GDP whereas the spending side accounts for approximately 19 per cent of GDP. The overall tax burden is about 16 per cent of GDP. The main source of government revenue comes from taxation with the share of 88 per cent of government revenue. Non-tax revenue accounts for about 12 per cent of government revenue.

Tax authorities in Thailand are governmental units under the Ministry of Finance. There are three main tax authorities, namely the Customs department (responsible for import and export duties), Excise department (responsible for specific sales tax) and Revenue department (responsible for income tax, value added tax, specific business tax, stamp duty and petroleum income tax). They operate within the central administration. The main share of tax revenue comes from the

1 International Monetary Fund, World Economic Outlook, April 2018 Database, http://www.imf.org/external/pubs/ft/weo/2018/01/weodata/index.aspx.

2 World Bank, "The World Bank in Thailand: Overview" (March 2018), http://www.worldbank.org/en/country/thailand/overview.

3 The ASEAN member states are Brunei Darussalam, Cambodia, Indonesia, Lao PDR, Malaysia, Myanmar, Philippines, Singapore, Thailand and Vietnam.

Revenue department. Corporate income tax accounts for about 25 per cent of tax revenue, 4.06 per cent of GDP, value added tax gross collection is about 30 per cent, 4.8 per cent of GDP and net collection after refunds is about 21.8 per cent of tax revenue, 3.46 per cent of GDP.

In general, the Thai tax system is based on self-assessment. The top personal income tax rate is 35 per cent. The standard rate of the corporate income tax is 20 per cent, cut from 30 per cent and 23 per cent in 2011 and 2013 respectively, in order to boost competitiveness and is considered to be in the lower end of the international range (Bogiatzis et al., 2018). Corporate income tax is imposed on companies, including other forms of legal entities, that are registered under Thai law, or that are incorporated under foreign law and carry on business in Thailand. The main corporate income tax base is net profit calculated on worldwide income but a participation exemption is granted on foreign sourced dividends if criteria are met (Sheehan and Blaine, 2017). Thailand has a wide network of treaties for the avoidance of double taxation. Currently, there are 61 tax treaties in force. Regarding anti-avoidance legislation, Thailand does not have general anti-avoidance provisions nor specific anti-avoidance provisions except for transfer pricing regulations. Thailand's transfer pricing regulations follow the OECD's Transfer Pricing Guidelines (i.e., uses the arm's length basis).

Value added tax (VAT) in Thailand is a well-designed and simple system with exemptions on some goods and services (Swire, 2017). It employs the credit-invoice method. VAT registrants charge VAT on sales (output tax) and credit VAT paid on purchases (input tax). The difference is the VAT remittance to the Revenue department. The statutory rate is 10 per cent but has been reduced, since 1999, to 7 per cent, which ranked Thailand to be amongst the lowest VAT rate countries in the world (Bogiatzis et al., 2018). The government has announced that the VAT rate will continue to remain 7 per cent at least until September 2019.[4] A reverse charge is applied on imports of services but in practice is only applicable to corporate entities which import services.

16.2 Response to the G20/OECD BEPS Program of Tax Reform

The BEPS program has been an action to create a fairer and more effective international tax system for OECD and G20 countries (OECD, 2017a). This work can be done through cooperation among countries to implement the BEPS package consistently on a global basis and to develop standards to address these issues. For decades, Thailand has been experiencing loss of tax revenue from cross-border transactions through, for example, transfer mispricing, business restructuring, and ineffective tax collection on income generated from cross-border trades of digital goods and services. It is not only developing countries but also developed countries

4 Bangkok Post, "Cabinet standing pat on 7% VAT until next year" (4 July 2018), http://www.bangkokpost.com/business/news/1496982/cabinet-standing-pat-on-7-vat-until-next-year (accessed on 2 August 2018).

which are suffering from this base erosion and profit shifting. The BEPS package clearly expresses the concerns from developed countries. In this regard, it seems that Thailand initially has taken a reactive approach to the BEPS package based on the lack of legislation and rules enacted to tackle BEPS issues as mentioned above. However we see opportunities for Thailand to be more proactive to prevent BEPS issues if the correct policy reform, especially international tax policy, is introduced.

For over half a century, Thailand has undergone major industrial and social transformation and has shifted its economy from agriculture to export-oriented manufacturing, while integrating key production, particularly automobiles and electronics, into regional value chains. Such a transformation leads to concerns regarding transfer pricing. Even before the G20/OECD BEPS initiative, the Revenue department had introduced transfer pricing concepts into the determination of appropriate market prices for tax administration purposes, namely Departmental Instruction No. Paw 113/2545 which was launched on 16 May 2002.[5] This guideline empowers revenue officers to adjust a company's revenue and expenses when calculating corporate income tax if a company receives no compensation or an amount less than the market price without justifiable reasons or pays expenses at an amount greater than the market price without justifiable reasons. The definition of market price provided by the guideline[6] is consistent with the arm's length principle under the OECD's *Transfer Pricing Guidelines*. Moreover, rulings in the form of an Advance Pricing Arrangement (APA) have also been available for taxpayers since the launch of this guideline. The Revenue department has also focused on capacity building programs to increase the number of skilled revenue officers dealing with transfer pricing issues in all relevant areas such as legal, policy, and audit divisions.

Nonetheless, the Departmental Instruction on transfer pricing is only a guideline and transfer pricing issues are becoming increasingly complex, so in order to tackle transfer pricing issues more effectively, it is crucial for Thailand to have robust legislation on transfer pricing in place which is in line with the arm's length principle and can govern taxpayers' obligations in relation to transfer pricing documentation.

Apart from the abovementioned transfer pricing practices, Thailand has limited anti-avoidance legislation. There is no specific rule applicable to hybrid instruments, and generally the tax treatment follows the contractual arrangement and accounting treatment. As for thin capitalisation rules, there is no specific tax legislation on the issue. However, there is a condition on the debt to equity ratio applicable to companies that is applied for investment promotion schemes. In this regard, Thailand is particularly vulnerable to corporate tax planning exercises by multinational enterprises (MNEs) to artificially shift profit to low or no tax countries. The BEPS program should raise the level of awareness of the Thai government of the

5 See http://www.rd.go.th/publish/6008.0.html.

6 http://www.rd.go.th/publish/fileadmin/download/GUIDANCE-ON-APA-PROCESS-EN.pdf.

need to consider the necessity to protect its tax base in these areas.

16.3 The BEPS Inclusive Framework

16.3.1 Practical Issues in Implementation of Reforms

As in the case of many countries and jurisdictions around the world, Thailand has become a member of the Inclusive Framework on BEPS in order to establish its position as an equal partner in this important forum to tackle tax avoidance, improve the coherence of international tax rules, and ensure a more transparent tax environment. Having joined the Inclusive Framework, Thailand is required to commit to the comprehensive BEPS package and its consistent implementation. Such commitment at the national level needs political support and commitment so before joining the Inclusive Framework on BEPS, the Ministry of Finance sought approval from the Cabinet.

Thailand's response to the BEPS program and decision to join the Inclusive Framework on BEPS reflects the fact that Thailand's initial reaction to BEPS has been reactive. However there are advantages as a result of being part of the Inclusive Framework and also further opportunities to improve domestic legislation to be more proactive. Nonetheless, due to a lack of capacity and resource constraints, the involvement of non-G20/OECD countries and jurisdictions in the BEPS program on an equal footing with member countries may be difficult in practice. Most of the rules are set at working group meetings and relevant forums where developing countries may not be able to raise their voices. As a result, these rules may be too rigid for them to implement within the required time periods (ActionAid, 2014).

Despite the above concerns and with support from the government, Thailand is now in the process of amending its legislation to meet the four minimum standards under the Inclusive Framework. The Revenue department has been working with the Secretariats of the Inclusive Framework, Forum on Harmful Tax Practices (FHTP) and Forum on Tax Administration (FTA) mutual agreement procedures group, and has also been welcoming assistance from international organisations so as to be able to implement the minimum requirements in due time.

16.3.2 Harmful Tax Practices

Based on the harmful tax practices framework under the 1998 Report (OECD, 1998), the regimes which fall within the scope of work of the FHTP are regimes applying to income from geographically mobile activities, such as financial and other service activities, including the provision of intangibles. Therefore, there are a number of Thai tax incentives which fall within the scope of the FHTP, namely the International Headquarters regime (IHQ), Treasury Centre regime (TC), International Trading Center regime (ITC), Regional Operating Headquarters regimes (ROHs) and International Banking Facilities regime (IBF).

These regimes were introduced not only to retain Thai multinational companies within the country but also to attract foreign companies which foresee that Thailand would be a strategic location to establish their regional and international headquarters. These regimes are mainly directed to providing incentives for the services activities within branches or affiliated enterprises, such as general management, procurement of raw materials and parts, technical support, marketing or sales promotion, research and development, human resource management or training, and financial advisory services, by providing special tax rates for income derived from such services and further rate reductions for such income from abroad. The laws require that in order to qualify for benefits under these regimes, companies must have business presences and substantial activities in Thailand.

In 2016, the FHTP reviewed the abovementioned regimes and identified that they have ringfencing features. According to the 2017 Progress Report on Preferential Tax Regimes (OECD, 2017b), the FHTP updated the status of the International Headquarters regime (IHQ), Regional Operating Headquarters regimes (ROHs), and Treasury Centre regime (TC) as "in the process of being amended" and the status of the International Trading Center regime (ITC) and International Banking Facilities regime (IBF) as "in the process of being eliminated/amended". Thailand has thus committed to amending or abolishing the regimes within the timeframe set by the FHTP. Although Thailand is committed to cooperating with the international community on the BEPS project, there are some challenges in doing so. First of all, Thailand has only just joined the Inclusive Framework and has to learn quickly all of the requirements of the FHTP. Secondly, there is a time constraint within which the legislation on abolishing regimes must be enacted which requires some time due to the legislative process. Last but not least, the business sector in Thailand maintains the need for such regimes to remain competitive within the region.

Since the 2017 Progress Report published in October 2017, Thailand has progressed the abolition and amendment of the regimes. The elimination of the International Banking Facilities (IBF) regime was approved by the Cabinet of Thailand on 5 June 2018.[7] In the case of the intellectual property (IP) provisions under the International Headquarters regime, reforms were approved by the Cabinet on 19 June 2018[8] such that as of 1 July 2018 only research and development conducted in Thailand will be eligible for tax benefits. As for the remaining regimes, the Revenue department has been in the process of conducting consultation with the business sector.

7 Deloitte, "Tax Incentives for BIBF Abolished", Tax & Legal Services Newsletter (July 2018), https://www2.deloitte.com/content/dam/Deloitte/th/Documents/tax/th-tax-newsletter-en-240718.pdf (accessed on 19 September 2018).

8 Government of Thailand, "The Cabinet meeting on Tuesday, June 19, 2018", http://www.thaigov.go.th/news/contents/details/13220 (accessed on 12 July 2018).

16.3.3 Tax Treaties: Anti-Abuse Provisions and Dispute Resolution

All of Thailand's 61 tax treaties contain Mutual Agreement Procedure (MAP) provisions but none of them have anti-abuse provisions that are in line with Action 6 (Prevent treaty abuse). Only the tax treaty between Thailand and the United States has a limitation on benefit (LOB) provision; however this treaty still needs to be amended to be fully compliant with the minimum requirements of Action 6. Moreover a number of Thailand's tax treaties contain MAP provisions which need to be amended to meet the minimum requirements of Action 14 (Make dispute resolution mechanisms more effective). Given Thailand's commitment, Thailand has complied with the requirements of Actions 6 and 14 by providing answers to questionnaires and providing the Country's MAP profile and MAP statistics.

There are two available approaches for Thailand to meet the minimum standards of Actions 6 and 14. One is to negotiate bilaterally with the treaty partners to amend the MAP provisions and to add the requirements of Action 6. Another approach is to modify the tax treaties using the Multilateral Instrument (MLI). Even though the MLI could be viewed as an instrument to expedite and streamline the implementation of the measures developed to address BEPS, the implementation of MLI itself is complicated. Therefore in some cases, treaty partners may prefer a bilateral approach.

Under bilateral negotiations, treaty partners have more flexibility to adopt the OECD's recommendations by including a "principal purpose test" (PPT), or a limitation on benefits rule supplemented by a mechanism that deals with conduit arrangements, or a combination of LOB and PPT rules. The optimal choice will be made based on legal environments and policy preferences. Application of the treaty anti-abuse provisions is not easy in practice and thus clear guidelines should be provided to taxpayers and revenue officers with respect to the provisions' interpretation and application.

With respect to the requirements of Action 14, treaty partners may prefer a taxpayer to present his or her case to the competent authority of the country where the taxpayer is a resident. In Thailand, the only guidance that has been published on the Revenue department's website relates to the APA process. However such guidance does not include details on how to access the MAP in other cases. Therefore Thailand needs to develop a MAP guideline explaining taxpayers' rights and obligations, as well as the MAP process.

16.3.4 Country-by-Country Reporting

At present, Thailand does not have legislation providing for Country-by-Country (CbC) Reporting and has not signed any competent authority agreement for automatic exchange of CbC reports. As previously mentioned, Thailand needs to implement specific transfer pricing legislation which allows the government to require transfer pricing documentation. In particular, to comply with the Inclusive Framework minimum standards, Thailand also needs legislation that will oblige

Thai MNEs to submit Country-by-Country (CbC) reports and legislation to allow such information to be exchanged automatically with her treaty partners.

16.4 The Other BEPS Actions

In addition to the four minimum standards, the BEPS Actions that Thailand should consider to be priority BEPS issues are taxation of the digital economy, limiting base erosion via interest deductions and preventing the artificial avoidance of permanent establishment status, as well as assuring that transfer pricing outcomes are in line with value creation and developing rules regarding transfer pricing documentation to enhance transparency for the tax administration. These priorities are also recognised as being the Action items in the OECD/G20 BEPS Action Plan of most relevance to developing countries (OECD, 2014).

16.4.1 Digital Economy

In this new era of globalisation, the forms of trade and types of goods and services traded have been transformed. A large volume of trade in both physical goods and virtual goods is conducted through digital platforms. In Thailand, the digital economy also plays a significant role in driving the economy. This is also reflected in the national policy to transform Thailand into a much more significant digital economy under the "Digital Thailand" Plan. The statistical survey conducted by the Electronic Transactions Development Agency (ETDA) shows that the total value of e-commerce in Thailand has increased significantly every year in the recent past. The annual growth rate in 2017 was expected to be 9.86 per cent (Leesa-nguansuk, 2017). Comparing revenue generated in e-commerce in Southeast Asian countries, Thailand is currently the third largest e-commerce market and is expected to be the second largest in 2020. Thailand's e-commerce market reported revenue in the amount of USD 3,648 million in 2018,[9] with an expectation that it will reach USD 5,850 million in 2022 (Leesa-nguansuk, 2017). As a country where a large volume of trade is conducted through the digital economy, Thailand faces challenges in how to find the right balance between collecting a fair share of tax and maintaining an environment conducive to business. To mitigate the negative impact of taxation of the digital economy, Thailand should consider implementing both income-based and non-income-based tax measures. Nonetheless, while the OECD is still in the process of developing international rules to address the tax challenges of the digital economy, Thailand should re-examine its VAT-related rules to ensure effective collection of VAT with respect to the cross-border supply of digital goods and services.

In terms of these rules for VAT collection on cross-border services, the current system in Thailand involves a reverse charge mechanism the application of which is limited to corporate entities. In order to fairly and effectively tax cross border

9 Statista, "eCommerce – Highlights, Thailand", https://www.statista.com/outlook/243/126/ecommerce/thailand# (accessed on 12 July 2018).

services, the Revenue department has decided to follow the OECD's International VAT/GST Guidelines, so that foreign service suppliers whose value of services supplied to Thailand reaches the VAT registration threshold shall collect VAT from final consumers in Thailand and pay the collected VAT to the Revenue department. Having conducted a process of public consultation, the Ministry of Finance proposed a draft bill to the Cabinet and this was approved on 19 July 2018. The proposed bill has a 180-day grace period after it comes into force in order to provide enough time for foreign service suppliers to comply with the law.

16.4.2 Hybrid Mismatch Transactions and Interest Deductions

Currently, there are no specific rules applicable to hybrid entities, and generally, the tax treatment follows the legal classification under the Thai Revenue Code and the accounting treatment of the legal entities involved. Thailand should therefore study the OECD report on neutralising the effects of hybrid mismatch arrangements as well as considering the need to apply such concepts to Thailand and their implications.

The Revenue Code, Thai domestic tax law, does not limit the amount of interest that can be deducted as a business expense. Therefore, attention should be given to the OECD report on base erosion involving interest deductions and other financial payments. As Thailand becomes increasingly open for trade and investment, some volume of foreign direct investment will be in the form of debt. Introducing a limitation on interest deductions could be effective in minimising base erosion and profit shifting. However, there are some concerns over the impact of such a move on sentiment of parties considering foreign inward investment to Thailand.

16.4.3 Permanent Establishment Status

In addition to the above issues, Thailand has seen the fast-growing number of foreign companies that conduct their businesses in Thailand through digital means seek to arrange or limit their business activities in order to avoid having a permanent establishment in Thailand. Therefore it is important for Thailand to make reforms under BEPS Action 7 (preventing the artificial avoidance of permanent establishment) one of its priorities. The existing provision under the Revenue Code is quite broad in determining whether or not a foreign company is carrying on a business in Thailand so as to be subject to income taxation on net profit. However, given the complexity of business and the nature of the modern commercial environment, it is nevertheless often found that, under tax treaties, foreign enterprises have arranged themselves so as not to be taxed in Thailand.

In dealing with the possibility of avoiding PE status, Thailand should consider incorporating new PE provisions in the country's tax treaties with a revised PE definition to cover commissionaire arrangements and to prevent avoidance of PE status through fragmentation of activities between related parties or splitting up of contracts. Moreover new PE exemption provisions should also be adopted to ensure that there will be no interpretation problem and only an enterprise that solely conducts an activity which has a preparatory or auxiliary character is deemed not to give rise to a PE.

Nevertheless, even where new PE concepts are covered under tax treaties' provisions and efforts have been made to prove that a foreign company has a PE in Thailand, another concern is how to allocate profit to such a PE. Given the existing international practice, it may often be the case that there will be no or a low amount of profit attributed to a PE in a developing country. In this regard, the ongoing work of the OECD that the profit should also be attributed to a PE based on the economic substance doctrine will be beneficial to developing countries, as well as to Thailand.

16.4.4 Tax Transparency

Apart from implementation of BEPS Actions, Thailand has also joined the Global Forum on Transparency and Exchange of Information for Tax Purposes to improve transparency and provide for exchange of information according to international standards, since information plays a crucial role not only in determining the correct amount of tax payable, but also in preventing tax avoidance and increasing voluntary tax compliance. Therefore Thailand's commitment to improve its exchange of information processes and to adopt the international standard of exchange of information will support international cooperation to prevent BEPS.

16.5 Unilateral BEPS Measures

Thailand has introduced certain measures not only to raise revenue but also to encourage formalisation of the economy and correct tax reporting, namely the factual financial reporting program and the incentive to encourage individual entrepreneurs to conduct business as a company. The Ministry of Finance aims to bring businesses into the country's formal tax system. From 1 January 2019 local financial institutions will be required to provide credit on the basis of the revenues shown in financial reports submitted to the authorities (Bogiatzis et al., 2018). Moreover, the Ministry of Finance is in the process of proposing legislation allowing the Revenue department to obtain access to bulk third party information from financial institutions. Based on these developments, it can be seen that Thailand has put significant effort into broadening of the tax base and increasing taxpayer compliance.

Regarding MNEs doing business in Thailand, the Revenue department has tightened the transfer pricing rules, is proposing VAT legislation on cross-border services, and is considering applying the OECD recommendation regarding interest deductibility. Moreover, the Revenue department closely follows developments in the EU relating to a special tax addressing taxation of digital multinational companies.

16.6 Tax Administration in Relation to International Tax Reform in Thailand

In complying with international standards to increase transparency and prevent BEPS, Thailand needs to carry out structural reform that involves organisational reform in addition to policy and legislative reform. The needs of policy and legislative reform in relation to the BEPS minimum standards and exchange of information (EOI) have already been discussed previously in this chapter. Nevertheless, effective implementation of those standards is crucial and thus Thailand needs a tax administration structure that will facilitate compliance with the relevant laws and international commitments.

Given the obligations under the Inclusive Framework on BEPS and the Global Forum, Thailand is required to follow the roadmaps set by both the OECD and the Revenue department to implement the international standards under the two forums. It is then essential for Thailand to implement those standards in a timely and efficient manner. To be well-prepared for peer reviews by the Global Forum and under the Inclusive Framework, especially with respect to BEPS Action 14, a tax authority should have a MAP unit and an EOI unit. Thailand is scheduled to be reviewed by the FTA MAP Forum in December 2019 and by the Global Forum with respect to the exchange of information on request in 2020.

In addition, implementation of the Inclusive Framework minimum standards and improving tax transparency through the new exchange of information standard will involve automatic exchanges of reports under the Country-by-Country and Common Reporting Standard regimes. The automatic exchange of information (AEOI) mechanism will lead to an influx of information such as high level information for transfer pricing risk assessment and financial account information. Protecting taxpayers' information is extremely important; therefore, Thailand will need structural reform to comply with the data safeguards and confidentiality provisions under the AEOI mechanism, as well as those for making appropriate use of the information. Information exchanged under tax treaties will need to be treated in a manner described under the relevant Exchange of Information Article.

Regarding the utilisation of the exchanged information, Thailand needs IT infrastructure that is capable of carrying out large-scale data analysis. Information can be used in risk assessment processes to improve efficiency in tax collection. For example, information received under the CRS relating to financial accounts can be mapped to individual taxpayers' information to locate high net worth individuals (HNWI). Moreover CbC reports will give information in relation to MNEs doing business in Thailand and such information can be added to automated risk assessment tools to detect the possibility of questionable transfer pricing. However the utilization of the information will have to be conducted in an appropriate manner and be governed by laws and regulations.

To effectively achieve all that has been described here, Thailand needs a well-structured capacity-building program. Such a capacity-building program should incorporate lessons from shared experiences and best practices through international cooperation. Moreover the program should include both policy and practical aspects and also provide for short-term and long-term planning strategies and resourcing, including use of training periods, target groups, experts, etc.

16.7 The Future of International Tax Reform for Thailand

Thailand is in a transition period in its compliance with international standards. The requirements for an increase in transparency and prevention of tax base erosion is likely to lead to an increase in the number of tax audits, EOI requests, and MAP cases. Therefore effective tax administration is very important. The international tax reform process must ensure fair taxation, create stability, sustain growth and promote investment.

The Revenue department should establish EOI and MAP units which will play important roles in improving tax administration. Information received through information exchanges under tax treaties and other relevant legislation including, for example, third party information, will lead to an increase in taxpayer compliance. The EOI unit can help field officers/auditors identify issues that need further investigation or make information requests under tax treaties to ensure that all actions and procedures are in accordance with international standards. Moreover an effective MAP unit is important to increase tax certainty and increase taxpayers' confidence in the tax dispute resolution process.

In addition to measures Thailand has already introduced to comply with the Inclusive Framework minimum standards, other measures, such as safe harbour rules especially in the area of transfer pricing, could be considered as tools to increase tax certainty in terms of both tax administration and tax law implementation. The scope of these rules will need to be carefully designed in order to be in line with international standards and meet the several objectives of increasing taxpayers' confidence in doing business in Thailand and promoting certainty, and at the same time protecting the nation's fair share of taxation.

References

ActionAid (2014), "The BEPS Process: Failing to Deliver for Developing Countries", September, https://www.francophonie.org/IMG/pdf/beps_16th_sept_2014_actionaid.pdf (accessed on 12 July 2018).

Bogiatzis, Adam, Hidekatsu Asada and Mohamed Rizwan Habeeb Rahuman (2018), "Sustainable Finance for Inclusive Growth in Thailand", OECD Economics Department Working Paper No. 1471, Paris, May.

Leesa-nguansuk, Suchit (2017), "E-commerce value gauged at B2.8tn", *Bangkok Post*, 28 September, https://www.bangkokpost.com/tech/local-news/1332643/e-commerce-value-gauged-at-b2-8tn (accessed on 2 August 2018).

Organisation for Economic Co-operation and Development (OECD) (1998), *Harmful Tax Competition: An Emerging Global Issue* (Paris: OECD).

Organisation for Economic Co-operation and Development (OECD) (2014), *Two-Part Report to G20 Development Working Group on the Impact of BEPS in Low Income Countries* (Paris: OECD).

Organisation for Economic Co-operation and Development (OECD) (2017a), *Background Brief: Inclusive Framework on BEPS* (Paris: OECD).

Organisation for Economic Co-operation and Development (OECD) (2017b), *Inclusive Framework on BEPS, Action 5: Harmful Tax Practices - 2017 Progress Report on Preferential Regimes* (Paris: OECD).

Sheehan, Jack and Jonathan Blaine (2017), "Thailand in International Planning", 23(3) *Asia-Pacific Tax Bulletin* online.

Swire, Mary (2017), "IMF Says Thailand Should Double VAT Rate", Tax-News, 8 June, https://www.tax-news.com/news/IMF_Says_Thailand_Should_Double_VAT_Rate____74432.html (accessed on 12 July 2018).

17 The Adoption of BEPS in the United Kingdom

Alice Pirlot* **and John Vella****

Abstract

This chapter discusses the United Kingdom's participation in and response to the Base Erosion and Profit Shifting project. It starts with a short introduction on the UK's economy, and its political and tax system (section 17.1). Second, this report provides an overview of the UK's proactive and leading role in the OECD/G20 project (section 17.2). Third, it analyses the UK's response to the BEPS project, including measures implementing BEPS minimum standards (section 17.3), measures in response to other BEPS actions (section 17.4) and some of the UK's unilateral "BEPS" measures (section 17.5). Generally, the UK has been an enthusiastic and early adopter of BEPS proposals. Fourth, this chapter discusses the role of the UK tax administration in international tax reform (section 17.6). Finally, this chapter sheds light on the opportunities and challenges that characterise the UK's international tax agenda (section 17.7).

17.1 Introduction

The UK is a developed country based on a constitutional monarchy. The UK is one of the original members of the Organisation for Economic Co-operation and Development (OECD) (since 1961) and it is also part of the G20. In 1973, the UK became a member of the European Union (EU). In June 2016, however, a majority (51.9 per cent) of UK citizens voted for the UK to leave the EU in the "Brexit" referendum. Negotiations with the EU started in 2017 after the UK government triggered article 50 of the Treaty on the European Union (TEU), which regulates the withdrawal of Member States from the EU. Until the UK leaves the EU (which is planned to take place on 29 March 2019, unless the European Council and the UK unanimously agree to extend the negotiation of the withdrawal agreement), the UK remains a member of the EU and maintains its obligation to apply and implement EU law.[1]

* Research Fellow in Law, Centre for Business Taxation, University of Oxford.

** Associate Professor of Taxation, Faculty of Law and Centre for Business Taxation, University of Oxford.

1 See, e.g., the Background Note in HM Treasury, Draft provisions for Finance Bill: Explanatory Notes, Clauses 1 to 40 (6 July 2018), p. 84. On the UK's tax system and Brexit, see also Freedman (2017).

Her Majesty's Revenue and Customs (HMRC) is the UK's tax, payments and customs authority. It is a non-ministerial department and is responsible for the collection of taxes.[2]

In 2017, the UK's GDP (at current prices) amounted to USD 2,625 billion,[3] which made up around 15 per cent of the EU's total GDP, ranking the UK second after Germany among EU Member States and fifth in the world.[4] GDP growth rate averaged 1.7 per cent between 2016 and 2017.[5]

In relation to UK trade:

a) in 2016, the current account deficit averaged 5.9 per cent of nominal GDP;[6]

b) the total trade deficit averaged 2.2 per cent of gross domestic product. Trade in goods was characterised by a deficit of around 6-7 per cent of GDP where trade in services was characterised by a surplus of around 4-5 per cent of GDP;[7]

c) the UK main trade partners were the United States (around 13 per cent of exports and 9 per cent of imports) and Germany (around 10-11 per cent of exports and 14 per cent of imports).[8] In 2017, the highest shares of exported goods included nuclear reactors, boilers, machinery (around USD 65 billion), vehicles other than railways, tramways (around USD 53 billion), pharmaceutical products (around USD 32-33 billion) and pearls, precious stones, metals, coins, etc. (around USD 29 billion). Similar sectors were amongst the most important on the import side: nuclear reactors, boilers, machinery (around USD 80 billion), vehicles other than railways, tramways (around USD 73 billion), pearls, precious stones, metals, coins, etc. (around USD 49 billion) and electrical, electronic equipment (around USD 60 billion);[9]

---

2 See HMRC, "Our governance", https://www.gov.uk/government/organisations/hm-revenue-customs/about/our-governance (accessed on 16 August 2018).

3 International Monetary Fund, "World Economic and Financial Surveys: World Economic Outlook Database, Report for Selected Countries and Subjects (the United Kingdom)" (2018).

4 See Eurostat, "Which Member States have the largest share of EU's GDP?", http://ec.europa.eu/eurostat/web/products-eurostat-news/-/DDN-20180511-1?inheritRedirect=true (accessed on 31 July 2018).

5 Office for National Statistics, "Statistical bulletin: Quarterly national accounts: January to March 2018" (29 June 2018), https://www.ons.gov.uk/economy/grossdomesticproductgdp/bulletins/quarterlynationalaccounts/januarytomarch2018 (accessed on 25 July 2018).

6 Office for National Statistics, "UK Balance of Payments, The Pink Book: 2017" (31 October 2017), www.ons.gov.uk/economy/nationalaccounts/balanceofpayments/bulletins/unitedkingdom balanceofpaymentsthepinkbook/2017 (accessed on 25 July 2018).

7 Ibid.

8 United Nations, World Statistics Pocket Book 2017 (Series V, No. 41), p. 241, https://unstats.un.org/unsd/publications/pocketbook/files/world-stats-pocketbook-2017.pdf (accessed 3 September 2018).

9 UN Comtrade, "International trade in goods and services based on UN Comtrade data", https://comtrade.un.org/labs/dit-trade-vis/?reporter=826&type=C&year=2017&flow=2 (accessed on 25 July 2018).

d) regarding services, the financial services sector contributed to a large share of UK exports of services in 2016 (around GBP 61 billion).[10] Exported services also included other business related services, such as services between related enterprises, business management and management consulting services, telecommunications and computer services.[11] On the import side, travel services were the largest imported service.[12]

17.2 The UK's Role in Countering Base Erosion and Profit Shifting and its Response to the G20/OECD BEPS Program of Tax Reform

17.2.1 The UK's Role in Fighting BEPS Before the OECD/G20 BEPS Package

The UK had measures in place to counter base erosion and profit shifting before the advent of the BEPS project (Economic Affairs Committee, 2013, sections 39ff). They included: anti-tax arbitrage provisions, Controlled Foreign Company (CFC) rules, and thin capitalisation rules. Moreover, provisions that deny treaty benefits when the main purpose or one of the main purposes of a transaction is to obtain those benefits were added in many double tax treaties (DTTs) (Baker, 2017, p. 283). The UK also had a broad array of domestically-focused anti-avoidance legislation, including a disclosure of tax avoidance schemes regime and a General Anti-Abuse Rule.

17.2.1.1 *Anti-Tax Arbitrage*

In 2005, the UK put in place anti-tax arbitrage provisions (*Finance (No. 2) Act 2005*, Part 2, chapter 4) (Boyle, 2005). Moreover, as of 2009, the UK adopted rules to prevent situations of double non-taxation arising from mismatches in the tax treatment of profit distributions (*Corporation Tax Act 2009*, ss 931B(c) and 931D(c) introduced by *Finance Act 2009*, s. 34 and Sch 14, part 1). These rules anticipated the inclusion of an anti-hybrid provision in the EU Parent-Subsidiary Directive in 2014 (Council Directive 2014/86/EU).

17.2.1.2 *CFC Rules*

The UK has had CFC rules since 1984 (*Finance Act 1984*, ss 82-108). These rules were later amended and, in 2012, relaxed in the context of broader reforms towards a territorial system of taxation (*Finance Act 2012*, s 180 and Sch 20). These reforms were undertaken with an eye towards competitiveness but also because of a series of decisions handed down by the Court of Justice of the European Union (CJEU)

10 Office for National Statistics, "UK Balance of Payments, The Pink Book: 2017", above n. 6.

11 Office for National Statistics, "Statistical bulletin: International trade in services, UK: 2016" (31 January 2018), https://www.ons.gov.uk/businessindustryandtrade/internationaltrade/bulletins/internationaltradeinservices/2016 (accessed on 31 July 2018).

12 Office for National Statistics, "UK Balance of Payments, The Pink Book: 2017", above n. 6.

(HM Treasury and HMRC, 2011, para. 1.12).[13]

17.2.1.3 Thin Capitalisation Rules

Thin cap rules have been in force in the UK for a long time (*Taxes Act 1988*, s. 209). These rules were integrated into UK transfer pricing (TP) legislation in 2004 (*Finance Act 2004*, ss 34-36). Moreover, as of 2010, a worldwide debt cap was introduced so as to limit the deduction of groups' interest expense in the UK (*Finance Act 2009*, s. 35 and Sch 15).[14]

17.2.1.4 Rules on the Disclosure of Tax Avoidance

The UK adopted provisions on the disclosures of tax avoidance schemes in 2004 (*Finance Act 2004*, s 19 and Sch 2; ss 306 to 319). The disclosure of tax avoidance schemes regime (DOTAS) applies to direct taxes and national insurance contributions (*Finance Act 2004*, ss 316ff).[15] The Disclosure of Tax Avoidance Schemes: VAT and Other Indirect Taxes (DASVOIT) applies to value added tax (VAT), customs duties, the climate change levy, hydrocarbon oils duty and other indirect taxes (*Finance (No. 2) Act 2017*, s. 66 and Sch 17).[16]

17.2.1.5 General Anti-Abuse Rule

The UK introduced a statutory GAAR in 2013 (*Finance Act 2013*, part 5). Although the timing of the introduction of this measure coincided with the publication of the first BEPS report, discussions on the need for a UK GAAR started well before the BEPS project (Freedman, 2016, p. 743). The UK GAAR is a domestic measure which was never intended to solve the specific challenges that were identified by the OECD/G20 (Freedman, 2016, pp. 743 and 759).

17.2.2 The UK's Role in the Development of the G20/OECD BEPS Package

The UK played a proactive and leading role in setting the G20/OECD agenda for addressing base erosion and profit shifting (Osborne, 2012), which can be partly explained by the UK's public and political disquiet over the tax affairs of multinational companies in the years preceding the start of the BEPS project.[17]

National newspapers from different sides of the political spectrum ran articles highlighting the tax practices of multinational companies, thus raising the public interest in this issue. In 2012, the Committee of Public Accounts started to investi-

13 In *Cadbury Schweppes plc v IRC* (C-196/04) [2006] E.C.R. I-1995 (ECJ Grand Chamber) the CJEU cast doubt on the compatibility of the UK's then existing CFC regime with EU law.

14 These rules have been subsequently modified (*Taxation (International and Other Provisions) Act 2010*, ss 260 et seq) and further amended by the *Finance (No. 2) Act 2017* and *Finance Act 2018* (see further below, section 17.4.4).

15 The regime has been strengthened in 2015 (see the amendments made by *Finance Act 2015*, s. 117 and Sch. 17).

16 This regime has replaced the VAT disclosure regime (VADR) (*Finance Act 2004*, Sch. 17).

17 On the history of the BEPS project, see Hernández González-Barreda (2018, esp. p. 293).

gate the tax paid by multinational companies, including Google, Amazon and Starbucks and issued a list of recommendations in order to restore public confidence in the tax system. Some of the recommendations proposed by the Committee pursued similar objectives as the ones underlying the BEPS project. For example, the Committee suggested that the HMRC should be "much more effective in challenging the artificial corporate structures created by multinationals with no other purpose than to avoid tax" (Committee of Public Accounts, 2013, para. 2). The Committee also recommended that HMRC and HM Treasury "push for an international commitment to improve tax transparency, including by developing specific proposals to improve the quality and credibility of public information about companies' tax affairs, and use that information to collect a fair share of tax from profits generated in each country" (Committee of Public Accounts, 2013, para. 3).

In 2013, the Economic Affairs Committee (2013) issued a report on corporate tax avoidance. In this report, the Committee recognised that "fundamental reform of the international tax framework should be pursued in the OECD" (Economic Affairs Committee, 2013, para. 93). The Committee underlined that the UK should play an active role in the OECD BEPS project while remaining open to "more radical alternative approaches to corporate tax", such as the unilateral adoption of a destination-based cash flow tax (Economic Affairs Committee, 2013, paras 93 and 111). In response to the Committee's report, the UK Government (2013) emphasised its leadership role within the G20 in order to reform international tax rules and fight against BEPS. Moreover, the Government referred to the contribution of EUR 400,000 it made to the OECD in July 2013 as a way to illustrate its commitment to finding a multilateral solution against base erosion and profit shifting (UK Government, 2013).

The UK, together with Germany, played a key role in the definition of the modified nexus approach. In November 2014, the two countries issued a joint statement proposing new rules on preferential IP regimes in the context of the modified nexus approach under BEPS Action 5 (Germany and United Kingdom, 2014).

17.3 The UK's Compliance with the BEPS Inclusive Framework (4 Minimum Standards)

Overall, the UK has been an early and enthusiastic adopter of BEPS measures.

The UK is a member of the BEPS Inclusive Framework, which – at the time of writing – comprises 117 countries. With 22 other countries, the UK is also part of the steering group of the inclusive framework.[18] The UK has taken steps to comply with all four BEPS minimum standards (Actions 5, 6, 13 and 14).

18 OECD Steering Group, "Steering Group of the Inclusive Framework on BEPS, Members", www.oecd.org/tax/beps/steering-group-of-the-inclusive-framework-on-beps.pdf (accessed on 25 July 2018). The UK is represented by Mr. Mike Williams who serves as deputy chair.

17.3.1 Action 5: Peer Review and Monitoring

In the 2015 BEPS Action 5 report, the UK's patent box regime was considered inconsistent with the nexus approach (OECD, 2015b, p. 63, para. 148, table 6.1). The UK amended its regime in 2016 in order to comply with the OECD recommendations, which, as seen above, it had played a leading role in developing (*Finance Act 2016*, s. 64). The new regime applies the modified nexus approach for the determination of the relevant IP profits of a trade of a company that are eligible to be taxed at reduced rates (*Corporate Tax Act 2010*, ss 357BFff). In 2017, additional amendments were introduced regarding companies undertaking research and development activities under a cost-sharing agreement (*Finance (No. 2) Act 2017*, s. 23). The 2017 OECD Progress Report on Preferential Regimes highlights that the new regime is no longer considered harmful (OECD, 2017c, pp. 15-16).

Action 5 also addresses the compulsory spontaneous exchange of information on tax rulings. In December 2017 the OECD published peer review reports on the status of implementation in 44 jurisdictions, including the UK. The report indicates that the UK has fulfilled all the criteria evaluated under this peer review process, except for the collection and exchange of information on new assets of existing taxpayers who benefit from the grandfathered IP regime. This specific information was only available (and exchanged) in the case of a formal investigation. Consequently, the report recommends that the UK exchange this information if it becomes available in the future (OECD, 2017d, pp. 15 and 285ff).

17.3.2 Action 6: Preventing Treaty Abuse

Recent double tax treaties (DTTs) concluded by the UK follow the recommendations of the BEPS Action 6 report. The preambles of these treaties include an express statement of the intention of the parties not to create opportunities for non-taxation or reduced taxation through evasion or avoidance. Moreover, in line with past UK tax treaty practice, these treaties include a principal purpose test (PPT) clause as recommended by the BEPS Action 6 report (OECD, 2015c, para. 26). This is not surprising, as the UK's treaty negotiators were the ones to push for the inclusion of a generalised PPT (Baker, 2017, p. 283). As with most DTTs concluded by the US, the UK/US DTT nevertheless includes a limitation of benefits (LOB) clause (art. 23).

The UK's preference for the PPT clause was confirmed in the framework of the Multilateral Convention to Implement Tax Treaty Related Measures to Prevent BEPS (MLI). The UK has also chosen to apply Article 7(4) of the Multilateral Instrument, which requires the competent authority of the relevant jurisdiction to grant treaty benefits (that would otherwise be denied on the basis of the PPT clause) to a person when "such benefits would have been granted to that person in the absence of the transaction or arrangement".[19]

---

19 The list of reservations and notifications made by the United Kingdom of Great Britain and Northern Ireland upon deposit for the instrument of ratification, acceptance or approval pursuant to Article 28(5) and 29(1) of the Multilateral Convention to implement tax treaty

Beyond the BEPS minimum standards, the UK has also modified its withholding regime on intellectual property royalty payments in order to prevent the abuse of DTTs (*Finance Act 2016*, s. 41).[20] The new targeted anti-tax avoidance rule (TAAR) applies to counter arrangements the purpose (or one of the main purposes) of which was to obtain a tax advantage by virtue of any provisions of a double taxation arrangement, while obtaining that tax advantage is contrary to the object and purpose of those provisions (*Income Tax Act 2007*, s. 917A(1)c and (4)). Under these conditions, the new provisions require payers of royalties to deduct income tax from the payments made to connected persons, regardless of any double taxation arrangements.

17.3.3 Action 13: Country-by-Country Reporting

The first OECD annual peer review process for BEPS Action 13 indicates that a legal and administrative framework has been put in place in the UK to implement country-by-country reporting (CbCR) (OECD, 2018b, p. 723ff). The UK signed the Multilateral Competent Authority Agreement for Exchange of CbC reports (CbC MCAA) on 27 January 2016. In February 2016 the Treasury introduced CbC Reporting Regulations (Statutory Instrument (SI) 2016/237). They came into force on 18 March 2016 and were amended in 2017 (SI 2017/497) to comply with subsequent developments that took place in the OECD (the inclusion of partnerships as reporting entities) and the EU (in particular, Council Directive 2011/16/EU as amended by Council Directive 2016/881/EU on CbCR).

The peer review report contains only one recommendation; it concerns UK provisions for calculating the annual consolidated revenue threshold in respect of MNE groups the ultimate parent entity of which is located in a jurisdiction other than the UK (OECD, 2018b, p. 723, paras 2 and 8). The report indicates that the calculation of this threshold may deviate from the OECD guidance on currency fluctuations, which could make the UK's local filing requirements inconsistent with BEPS recommendations.

17.3.4 Action 14: Tax Treaty Dispute Resolution

The first stage of the OECD peer review report on BEPS Action 14 highlights that the UK fulfils most requirements of the minimum standards. Most UK DTTs include a mutual agreement procedure (MAP) provision, which is similar to article 25 of the 2015 OECD Model Tax Convention (before the changes introduced by Action 14 final report), except for articles 25(1), second sentence; 25(2), second sentence and 25(3), second sentence of the OECD Model, which are absent from most UK DTTs (OECD, 2017b, p. 62, para. B.7). The large majority of UK DTTs include a provision

related measures to prevent base erosion and profit shifting (MLI) is to be found on the following website: https://www.gov.uk/government/publications/multilateral-convention-to-implement-tax-treaty-related-measures-to-prevent-base-erosion-and-profit-shifting (last updated 16 July 2018).

20 See also Greenfield (2016).

that requires correlative transfer pricing adjustment, as in Article 9(2) of the 2015 OECD Model.

Shortcomings in the MAP provisions found in UK DTTs will be addressed through the Multilateral Instrument, which the UK signed and ratified with no reservation as to the MAP provision (article 16) and the provision on corresponding adjustments (article 17). For the few treaties that will not be amended under the MLI, the UK will proceed through bilateral negotiations.

The OECD peer review report indicates that the MAP is accessible and efficient in the UK. Moreover, the report underlines that the UK runs an advance pricing agreement (APA) program (*Taxation (International and Other Provisions) Act 2010*, ss 218-230), which helps to prevent transfer pricing disputes from arising (OECD, 2017b, Part A, pp. 16-19). Roll-back of bilateral advance pricing agreements (APAs) is possible, which also contributes to the prevention of future disputes (OECD, 2017b, p. 18, paras. 9-11).

In addition to its action to meet the BEPS Action 14 minimum standard, the UK is committed to establishing mandatory binding MAP arbitration in its DTTs (G7, 2015; OECD, 2015e, pp. 10 and 41, para. 62). With regard to the type of arbitration process, the UK has opted in to apply Article 23(5) of the Multilateral Instrument, which requires the competent authorities to "ensure that each person that presented the case and their advisors agree in writing not to disclose to any other person any information received during the course of the arbitration proceedings from either competent authority or the arbitration panel".

Twenty-one of 129 DTTs concluded by the UK already include a provision on binding arbitration, which is identical to article 25(5) of the OECD Model Tax Convention. Moreover, the UK is a signatory of the EU Arbitration Convention (Convention 90/463/EEC) that can be relied upon by enterprises to solve cases of double taxation resulting from the application of transfer pricing rules or the attribution of profits to a permanent establishment. The draft Finance Bill published in July 2018 (clause 39) also proposes to give power to the Treasury to make regulations for implementing the new Directive (Council Directive EU 2017/1852) on tax dispute resolution mechanisms in the European Union, which has a much wider scope than the Arbitration Convention.

17.4 The UK's Responses to Other BEPS Actions

17.4.1 Action 1: Digital Economy

17.4.1.1 VAT

The UK's VAT rules, which are harmonised at the EU level, are largely in line with the recommendations of BEPS Action 1. As of 1 January 2015, the UK imposes VAT on the supply of telecommunications, broadcasting and electronic services to non-taxable persons located in an EU Member State (B2C) on the basis of the destination principle (namely where the non-taxable person is established, has their permanent address or usually resides).[21] VAT collection for the supply of these services is facilitated by a simplified compliance mechanism (commonly referred to as the VAT "Mini-One-Stop-Shop" (MOSS)), which allows suppliers not to register in each Member State of consumption.[22]

In the EU, the destination principle – and the MOSS - will be further extended to the supply of intra-Community distance sales of goods as of 1 January 2021 (Council Directive 2017/2455, Art. 2). Moreover, as of 1 January 2021, the exemption provision that applies to the importation of low value goods will be removed (Council Directive 2017/2455, Art. 3). These new rules are aimed at facilitating the collection of VAT for imports of low valued goods, which has been identified as one of the challenges raised by the digital economy in the OECD 2015 Action 1 Report (OECD, 2015a, pp. 120ff; OECD, 2018a, para. 304). They could apply to the UK, depending on the tax arrangements made on the UK's exit from the EU (European Scrutiny Committee, 2018).

17.4.1.2 *Corporation Tax*

In November 2017 HM Treasury issued a position paper (updated in March 2018) on the UK's approach to future changes that need to be made to adapt corporate tax rules to meet the challenges posed by the digital economy (HM Treasury, 2017; 2018).

The position paper considers three approaches to these challenges.[23] First, it argues for a long-term reform of international tax rules in order to give countries the right to tax profits that are generated from user participation, including in the absence of a traditional permanent establishment in the country of the user base (HM Treasury, 2017, para. 4.3). The 2018 updated position paper clarifies the meaning of "user participation" by defining it as "the process by which users can create value for certain types of digital businesses through their engagement and active contribution" (HM Treasury, 2018, para. 2.4) and distinguishing it from data collection (paras 2.33ff). The 2018 updated paper also indicates ways to modify articles 9, 5 and 7 of the OECD Model Tax Convention so as to recognise the value created

21 See *Finance Act 2014*, ss 103-106 and Sch. 22. These new rules transpose the amendments made to the EU VAT Directive (2006/12/EC) in 2008 (Council Directive 2008/8/EC). See also the amendments made by Council Directive 2017/2455 of 5 December 2017 so as to lower administrative burdens on micro-businesses. As of November 2017, the UK no longer distinguishes between telecommunication services supplied to UK consumers that are effectively used in the EU (subject to UK VAT) and those that are effectively used outside the EU (previously not subject to UK VAT) (SI 2017/778). These provisions are in line with the OECD VAT/GST Guidelines (2017) for determining the place of taxation for cross-border business-to-consumer (B2C) supplies of services and intangibles based on the destination principle (SI 2017/778, Explanatory Memorandum, s. 7).

22 Articles 369a et seq. of EU VAT Directive 2006/12/EC (as amended in 2008). On the MOSS in the UK, see de la Feria (2014).

23 For a critical evaluation of the UK's position as set out in the position paper see Devereux and Vella (2018).

by user participation and tax them accordingly (HM Treasury, 2018, paras 3.53ff). Second, the position paper supports interim solutions, along the lines proposed by the EU Commission (HM Treasury, 2017, paras 4.8ff). The preferred option of the UK government here is to tax revenues derived from digital services provided to the UK market (HM Treasury, 2017, para. 4.10). Third, the position paper sets out the government's intention to extend the scope of the UK's withholding tax regime to royalty payments between foreign related-parties for the exploitation of intellectual property rights that takes place in the UK (e.g., when the IP is used to sell products in the UK), regardless of the absence of taxable presence in the UK (absence of residence, permanent establishment (PE) or "avoided" PE) (HMRC and HM Treasury, 2017; HM Treasury, 2017, para. 4.18). This proposal is aimed at preventing under-taxation: the tax would apply when royalties are paid to an entity located in a low-tax country (HM Treasury, 2017, paras 4.17-4.18). This proposal is expected to mostly affect digitalised businesses (OECD, 2018b, p. 140, para. 357).

Finally, the introduction of the diverted profits tax (DPT) in 2015 can also be understood in the context of BEPS Action 1 as it was introduced partly to address some concerns arising from digitalisation (OECD, 2018a, pp. 148ff). Indeed, it was known as the "Google tax" when first proposed. The DPT is further analysed in section 17.5 below that discusses unilateral measures that were adopted in the context of the BEPS package.

17.4.2 Action 2: Hybrid Mismatch Arrangements

The UK's provisions on anti-tax arbitrage were modified in 2016 in order to comply with BEPS Action 2 (HMRC, 2016; *Finance Act 2016*, s. 66 and Sch 10; *Finance (No. 2) Act 2017*, s. 24).[24] The new legislation contains two direct references to the BEPS Action 2 Final Report. First, foreign provisions which it is reasonable to suppose are based on the BEPS report are deemed to be equivalent to the UK hybrid mismatch provisions (*Taxation (International and Other Provisions) Act 2010*, s. 259BA). Second, the BEPS report may be considered in the context of the anti-avoidance rule targeted at hybrid structures. Indeed, the BEPS Action 2 report may be used to assess whether the obtaining of a tax advantage can be deemed consistent with the principles and policy objectives of UK anti-hybrid rules (*Taxation (International and Other Provisions) Act 2010*, s. 259M(7)).

Additional minor amendments to the hybrid and other mismatch regime have been announced in the draft Finance Bill published on 6 July 2018. They aim at transposing the Anti-Tax Avoidance Directive II (ATAD II, Council Directive (EU) 2017/952), which broadens the scope of EU provisions to mismatches with third countries.[25] The proposed amendments include new provisions to counter mis-

24 See also Bhogal (2017).

25 HM Treasury, Draft provisions for Finance Bill 2018-19, Explanatory Notes, Clauses 1 to 40 (6 July 2018), p. 137, clause 38, para. 15, https://assets.publishing.service.gov.uk/government/uploads/system/uploads/attachment_data/file/723031/Explanatory_Notes_for_draft_Finance_Bill_provisions.pdf (accessed on 25 July 2018).

matches arising in relation to "disregarded" PEs, in line with the OECD 2017 BEPS recommendations on branch mismatch arrangements (OECD, 2017a).

17.4.3 Action 3: Controlled Foreign Companies

The UK considers that its CFC regime is in compliance with BEPS Action 3, despite the fact that these rules were amended in 2012 with a competitive goal in mind, which stands in contrast with the objectives of the BEPS project (Maffini and Collier, 2015, pp. 16-17). To a great extent, the UK regime also meets the requirements on CFC rules that are laid down in the EU ATAD (Council Directive (EU) 2016/1164).[26] Only two minor amendments will be made so as to ensure full compliance with the provisions of the directive that apply to CFC rules (articles 7 and 8). The notion of "control" will be amended so as to comply with the definition of the ATAD that requires "control" to be assessed by taking into account all associated enterprises, including non-resident associated and related parties.[27] Moreover, the rules on non-trade finance profits will be slightly modified in accordance with the ATAD provisions on the identification of CFC profits.[28]

17.4.4 Action 4: Interest Deductions and Other Financial Payments

Before the BEPS project, the UK's provisions on interest deductibility were largely unrestrictive and therefore perceived as "a competitive advantage" by businesses (HMRC and HM Treasury, 2010, para. 3.8). This situation has changed. New legislation was introduced in 2017 so as to put a cap on the deduction of corporate interest expenses (*Finance (No. 2) Act 2017*, Sch 5, introducing new part 10 of *Taxation (International and Other Provisions) Act 2010*).[29] These "corporate interest restriction (CRI)" rules are in line with BEPS Action 4 recommendations.[30] The UK applies a fixed ratio that limits the net deduction of interest to 30 per cent of EBITDA, which is in line with EU ATAD Directive Council Directive (EU) 2016/1164) and at the top of the corridor recommended by the BEPS Action 4 report. As underlined by Collier, Devereux and Lepoev (2017, pp. 64 and 70), HM Treasury did not give any explanation as to why the UK chose a 30 per cent ratio.

17.4.5 Action 7: Permanent Establishment Status

The UK will not implement BEPS Action 7 with the exception of the anti-fragmen-

26 HMRC, Guidance: Anti-Avoidance Directive about controlled foreign companies and EU Exit (6 July 2018), https://www.gov.uk/government/publications/anti-avoidance-directive-about-controlled-foreign-companies-and-eu-exit/anti-avoidance-directive-about-controlled-foreign-companies-and-eu-exit (accessed on 25 July 2018). On the UK and the ATAD, see Cédelle (2016).

27 HMRC, Guidance: Anti-Avoidance Directive, above n. 26.

28 Ibid.

29 See also Collier (2017).

30 HM Treasury, Finance Bill. Explanatory Notes (8 September 2017), pp. 156-160, https://assets.publishing.service.gov.uk/government/uploads/system/uploads/attachment_data/file/642806/finance_bill_september_2017_explanatory_notes.pdf (accessed on 25 July 2018).

tation rule. Indeed, the UK has opted out of the provision of the Multilateral Instrument aimed at preventing the artificial avoidance of PE status through commissionaire arrangements (article 12 of the MLI) and of the provision on the splitting-up of contracts (article 14 of the MLI). Similarly, the UK has opted out of the provision on artificial avoidance of PE status through the specific activity exemptions (article 13 of the MLI), except for article 13, para. 4 which addresses the fragmentation of activities between closely related parties.

Possible explanations for these choices include that the revenues expected from changing the current PE provisions would not justify the change and a desire to protect UK tax competitiveness (Watson, Palazzo-Corner and Haemmerle, 2017). Furthermore, the UK has unilaterally adopted the DPT, which, among other objectives, aims at preventing exploitation of PE provisions.[31]

Finally, it should be recalled that the UK favours reforming PE rules so as to allow jurisdictions to tax profits arising from the value created by user participation in the context of the digital economy (HM Treasury 2018, p. 14, paras 3.1-3.6).

17.4.6 Actions 8-10: Transfer Pricing

The UK tax system explicitly requires the interpretation of transfer pricing provisions in accordance with OECD principles. Transfer pricing provisions should be read "in such manner as best secures consistency" between the effect of UK domestic transfer pricing provisions and the effects to be given to DTTs that include in whole or in part the OECD model (*Taxation (International and Other Provisions) Act 2010*, s. 164(1)(b)). Consequently, OECD recommendations made in the BEPS Actions 8-10 reports were easily integrated into UK tax law. In 2016, an explicit reference to the BEPS Actions 8-10 reports was added in UK transfer pricing provisions (*Finance Act 2016*, s. 75). Moreover, on 2 February 2018, HM Treasury made a designation order to clarify that account should be taken of the latest 2017 version of the OECD transfer pricing guidelines (SI 2018/266). Questions arise as to whether the inclusion of the new OECD transfer pricing approach in UK domestic law has been sufficiently thought through. Indeed, the new OECD approach may not be easy to reconcile with UK domestic transfer pricing provisions, including the definition of the arm's length principle (Collier, 2016, pp. 591-592).

17.4.7 Action 12: Disclosure of Aggressive Tax Planning Practices

The UK's provisions on the disclosure of tax avoidance (DOTAS) are referred to in the BEPS Action 12 final report as a concrete example of disclosure rules (OECD 2015d, e.g., in paras 36 and Annex E). However, as noted by Baker, the UK DOTAS regime was initially designed as a "domestic scheme", which was aimed at "reduc[ing] the period of time between the invention of a marketed tax avoid-

31 HMRC, Diverted Profits Tax: Guidance (30 November 2015), p. 4, https://assets.publishing.service.gov.uk/government/uploads/system/uploads/attachment_data/file/480318/Diverted_Profits_Tax.pdf (accessed on 25 July 2018).

ance scheme and the point in time when HMRC became aware of the scheme ..." (Baker, 2015, p. 88). Its purpose was not to target international tax arrangements (Baker, 2015, p. 88).

New rules targeted at promoters of tax avoidance schemes and serial avoiders were added to these two regimes in 2014 and 2016. Under the provisions targeted at promoters of tax avoidance schemes, monitored promoters may be required to disclose information related to their products and clients to HMRC, along the same line as the DOTAS regime.[32] With regard to the Serial Tax Avoidance Regime (STAR), the objective is to sanction "serial avoiders", namely those who repeatedly enter into tax avoidance schemes that are defeated (*Finance Act 2016*, s 159 and Sch 18). Tax avoidance schemes covered by the STAR include the schemes that fall under UK GAAR provisions, the DOTAS and the Disclosure of Tax Avoidance Schemes: VAT and Other Indirect Taxes.[33]

In 2016, the UK also introduced new provisions requiring MNEs that meet the OECD turnover threshold for CbCR (namely a turnover over EUR 750 million) to publish their tax strategy on the internet (*Finance Act 2016*, s. 161 and Sch 19). The published information should include information as to the approach of the group to risk management, governance arrangements in relation to UK taxation and its dealings with HMRC; the attitude of the group to tax planning and the level of risk in relation to UK taxation that it is prepared to accept (*Finance Act 2016*, Sch 19, para. 17). Similar provisions apply to qualifying companies and subgroups for which a tax strategy has not been published at a higher level as well as to qualifying UK partnerships.[34] Penalties may apply in certain circumstances of non-compliance. Moreover, sanctions, including "naming and shaming", may be adopted against large businesses that are deemed to be "persistently unco-operative" (*Finance Act 2016*, Sch 19, Part 3). These sanctions, if used extensively, could undermine the dynamic of trust that underlies co-operative compliance regimes (Freedman and Vella, 2016). In the context of BEPS, it is interesting to note that this new regime entitles HM Treasury to adopt regulations requiring groups to publish their CbCR as part of their tax strategy (*Finance Act 2016*, Sch 19, para. 17(6)). The UK government has, however, made clear that it is in favour of public CbCR only under the condition that it is implemented on an international or multilateral basis (Committee of Public Accounts, 2016, p. 9, para. 7).

32 *Finance Act 2014*, ss 234-283; HMRC, Guidance on Part 5 and Schedules 34 to 36 of the Finance Act 2014, Promoters of tax avoidance schemes (2015), https://assets.publishing.service.gov.uk/government/uploads/system/uploads/attachment_data/file/454865/POTAS.pdf (accessed on 25 July 2018). See also Salter and Oats (2014).

33 HMRC, Technical Guidance on the Serial Tax Avoidance Regime (STAR) (12 January 2018), https://assets.publishing.service.gov.uk/government/uploads/system/uploads/attachment_data/file/671694/Serial_Tax_Avoidance_Regime__STAR__guidance.pdf (accessed on 26 July 2018).

34 HMRC, Guidance on Publish your large business tax strategy (last updated 22 June 2018), https://www.gov.uk/guidance/large-businesses-publish-your-tax-strategy_(accessed on 25 July 2018).

Regarding offshore structures, HMRC has announced that it plans to use Common Reporting Standard data to detect and impose new sanctions on undeclared offshore tax liabilities that have not been voluntarily disclosed and corrected on or before 30 September 2018.[35]

Finally, the draft Finance Bill published in July 2018 includes a clause allowing the Treasury to make regulations on disclosable arrangements so as to allow the UK to comply with the EU Directive on administrative cooperation (2011/16/EU) as amended by Council Directive 2018/822, which extends the scope of mandatory automatic exchange of information to reportable cross-border arrangements.[36] The Treasury will also rely on this clause to make regulation if the UK decides to adopt new OECD mandatory disclosure rules.[37]

17.4.8 Action 15: Multilateral Instrument

The UK has been actively involved in drafting the Multilateral Instrument. The ad hoc Working Party that completed the work under BEPS Action 15 was chaired by Mike Williams, Director Business and Tax at HM Treasury.

The UK signed the Multilateral Instrument on 7 June 2017 and deposited its instrument of ratification and final list of reservations and notifications on 29 June 2018. This implies that the MLI will enter into force on 1 October 2018, three calendar months after the ratification as required by article 34, para. 2 of the MLI.

17.5 The UK's Unilateral "BEPS" Measures

In addition to its active participation in the OECD/G20 BEPS project, in recent years the UK has undertaken further unilateral action to mitigate base erosion and profit shifting.

The DPT is a key unilateral anti-avoidance measure, which the UK government adopted while the BEPS project was still ongoing (*Finance Act 2015*, ss 77-116). The DPT imposes a 25 per cent charge on diverted profits from all business sectors, including digitalised businesses.[38] Two scenarios are covered. First, the DPT applies to situations where UK or non-UK companies use entities or transactions that lack economic substance. Second, it covers situations where a non-UK company avoids a UK taxable presence ("avoided PE rule"). Companies that poten-

35 HMRC, Guidance on Make a disclosure using the Worldwide Disclosure Facility (last updated 23 July 2018), https://www.gov.uk/guidance/worldwide-disclosure-facility-make-a-disclosure (accessed on 25 July 2018); *Finance (No. 2) Act 2017*, Sch 18 introducing the "requirement to correct" legislation.

36 HM Treasury, Draft provisions for Finance Bill 2018-19, Explanatory Notes, above n. 25, clause 40.

37 Ibid.

38 For the oil sector, the 25 per cent rate may be increased to 55 per cent plus true-up interest (if the taxable diverted profits are ring-fence or notional ring-fence profits): HMRC, Diverted Profits Tax: Guidance, above n. 31, p. 5.

tially fall within one of these two scenarios have a duty to notify an officer of the Revenue and Customs (*Finance Act 2015*, s. 92). According to HMRC Guidance on the DPT, this measure "is aimed at large groups (typically multi-national enterprises) that use contrived arrangements to circumvent rules on permanent establishment and transfer pricing".[39]

In the first report produced as part of the BEPS project, the OECD warned against unilateral action as it could undermine the "consensus-based framework for establishing jurisdiction to tax and addressing double taxation which exists today" (OECD, 2013, p. 48). However, HMRC has argued that the DPT's objective "is consistent with the aims of the OECD Base Erosion and Profit Shifting Project".[40] In its 2018 interim report on the digitalised economy, the OECD reiterated its views on the risks that such unilateral initiatives may generate, including economic distortions, double taxation, uncertainty, complexity and compliance costs for businesses (OECD, 2018a, p. 159 para. 368).

The DPT has come under significant criticism by academics and practitioners. It was proposed in the run up to a general election leading many to question the actual motivation behind it. Two leading practitioners expressed this broadly held view succinctly: "[i]t was clear (at least to us) that the main motivation for introducing the DPT was political: it was designed to take what had become a very muddled and hostile discussion about multinational taxation off the table during the election and it succeeded in that first objective" (Edge and Robertson, 2015).

The tax has also been criticised in its design, scope, application and effect. Another leading practitioner provided this scathing evaluation of the tax:

> I continue to be fascinated by the DPT. I still don't know what it's for. A "Google tax" that doesn't apply to Google? A tax aimed at foreign multinationals whose only public victim is Diageo? HMRC boasting to the press about how many companies it is attacking, but refusing to give any figures when asked in Freedom of Information Act requests? All very odd. It's a car crash of a tax, and will keep academics entertained and litigators well fed for many years.[41]

17.6 The UK's Tax Administration and its Role in International Tax Reform

At the domestic level, HMRC's role in countering abusive practices has been supported by additional resources (UK Government, 2013, para. 154). HRMC's capacity to challenge transfer pricing arrangements has been strengthened and the number of transfer pricing experts working for HMRC has been increased (Eden, 2017, p. 754).

39 HMRC, Diverted Profits Tax: Guidance, above n. 31, p. 4.

40 Ibid, pp. 4 and 76.

41 Neidle (2017). See also Neidle (2015).

At the international level, HRMC has played an active role in the BEPS project, not only in the framework of the OECD/G20 negotiations but also with helping developing countries in coping with BEPS (Harra, 2015). In 2013/2014, HMRC established a tax capacity building unit, aimed at providing advice and expertise to developing countries on G20/OECD tax priorities. Moreover, in 2015, HMRC set up a Tax Expert Unit that provides expertise on international tax technical issues, including transfer pricing and automatic exchange of information (OECD, 2016, p. 46, box 3.11).

HMRC participates in platforms that allow tax administrations to collaborate and exchange ideas on tax administration, the exchange of information and tax avoidance. The UK is part of the Forum on Tax Administration, which was chaired for three years by Sir Edward Troup, who served as HMRC's executive chairman until December 2017. The UK is an original member of the Joint International Taskforce on Shared Intelligence and Collaboration (JITSIC). Moreover, in 2013, HMRC joined the E6 project, which brings together jurisdictions that exchange information on how MNEs operate in the digital sector.

17.7 The Future of the UK's Agenda for International Tax Reform

Recent UK governments have had a clear, eye-catching, policy goal: "to create the most competitive corporate tax regime in the G20" (HMRC and HM Treasury, 2010). The most notable expression of this policy can be seen in the fall of the headline corporate tax rate from 30 per cent in 2007 to 17 per cent by 2020. But a closer look reveals a more nuanced policy that attempts to strike a delicate balance between competitiveness and clamping down on tax avoidance and aggressive tax planning (UK Government, 2013).

A recent official articulation of UK corporate tax policy emphasised this balancing act (HM Treasury, 2016 , pp. 3 and 11):

> Taxes should be low, but must be paid. There should be a level playing field, including between large businesses and small, and between different corporate structures. The system must encourage entrepreneurship and not reward aggressive tax planning… The government is committed to low business taxes – but these taxes must be paid. There cannot be an uneven system in which some businesses pay the tax due while competitors can avoid tax. That means clamping down on the artificial structures used to gain a tax advantage. Tackling evasion, avoidance, and aggressive tax planning also maintains the tax base.

The increased competitiveness of the system through rate cuts has thus been counterbalanced by measures such as the DPT and a (broadly) committed and early adoption of BEPS measures. Whether this balance has been struck in a satisfactory manner is open to debate.

There are reasons to believe that the UK will persevere with this broad policy, including the fundamentals of the UK economy, current political debate, public sensitivities and the influence of the media. However, when projecting into the future a number of factors immediately come to mind which could lead to some change – at least change in how the balance is currently struck between the two. One is Brexit and all the uncertainties and challenges (some might argue opportunities) it brings. A second is the possibility of a government that leans towards the hard left – or, at least, that leans further to the left than any recent government.

From a more technical perspective, in the March 2018 updated position paper on the digital economy (HM Treasury, 2018), the UK positioned itself among the group of countries that favours reforms targeted at certain highly digitalised businesses, but oppose reform of the existing corporate tax system as a whole.[42] In particular, it opposes reform that moves – even partially - towards a destination basis of taxation, i.e. reform that allocates some taxing rights over multinational companies' profit to market countries. The UK has thus taken a clear position on what could become a key battleground for future international corporate tax reform.

References

Baker, Philip (2015), "The BEPS Project: Disclosure of Aggressive Tax Planning Schemes", 43(1) *Intertax* 85-90.

Baker, Philip (2017), "The Multilateral Convention to Implement Tax Treaty Related Measures to Prevent Base Erosion and Profit Shifting", 3 *British Tax Review* 281-284.

Bhogal, Sandy (2017), "Finance (No. 2) Act 2017 Notes: Section 24: Hybrid and Other Mismatches", 5 *British Tax Review* 558-563.

Boyle, Mark (2005), "Cross-border Tax Arbitrage - Policy Choices and Political Motivations", 5 *British Tax Review* 527-543.

Cédelle, Anzhela (2016), "The EU Anti-Tax Avoidance Directive: A UK Perspective", 4 *British Tax Review* 490-507.

Collier, Richard (2016), "Finance Act 2016 Notes: Section 75: Transfer Pricing: Application of OECD Principles", 5 *British Tax Review* 590-592.

Collier, Richard (2017), "Finance (No. 2) Act 2017 Notes: Section 20 and Schedule 5: Corporate Interest Restriction", 5 *British Tax Review* 555-558.

Collier, Richard, Michael Devereux and Strahil Lepoev (2017), "Proposed UK Changes on the Tax Deductibility of Corporate Interest Expense", 1 *British Tax Review* 60-79.

Committee of Public Accounts, House of Commons (2013), "Tax Avoidance – Google", Ninth Report of Session 2013-14, 10 June, https://publications.parliament.uk/pa/cm201314/cmselect/cmpubacc/112/112.pdf.

Committee of Public Accounts, House of Commons (2016), "HMRC Revenue & Customs performance in 2015-16", Twenty-ninth Report of Session 2016-17, 28 November, https://publications.parliament.uk/pa/cm201617/cmselect/cmpubacc/712/712.pdf.

42 On the views held by three broad groups of countries on how to respond to the challenges posed by digitalisation, see OECD (2018a).

De la Feria, Rita (2014), "Finance Act 2014 Notes: Section 103: VAT: special schemes; Section 104: VAT: place of belonging; Section 105: VAT: place of supply orders: disapplication of transitional provision; Section 106: VAT: supply of services through agents; Section 107: VAT: refunds to health service bodies; Section 108: VAT: prompt payment discounts", 4 *British Tax Review* 428-433.

Devereux, Michael and John Vella (2018), "Taxing the Digitalised Economy: Targeted or System-Wide Reform?", 4 *British Tax Review* 387-406.

Economic Affairs Committee, House of Lords (2013), "Tackling corporate tax avoidance in a global economy: is a new approach needed?", First Report of Session 2013-2014, 23 July, https://publications.parliament.uk/pa/ld201314/ldselect/ldeconaf/48/4802.htm.

Eden, Sandra (2017), "United Kingdom", in Ana Paula Dourado (ed.), *Tax Avoidance Revisited in the EU BEPS Context* (Amsterdam: IBFD Publications), 737-778.

Edge, Steve and Dominic Robertson (2015), "Diverted Profits Tax – What happens next?", *Tax Journal*, 7 August.

European Scrutiny Committee, House of Commons (2018), "Value Added Tax: EU proposals for reform and the implications of Brexit", Twenty-third Report of Session 2017-19, Documents considered by the Committee on 28 March 2018, publications.parliament.uk/pa/cm201719/cmselect/cmeuleg/301-xxii/301-xxii.pdf.

Freedman, Judith (2016), "United Kingdom", in Michael Lang, Jeffrey Owens, Pasquale Pistone, Alexander Rust, Josef Schuch and Claus Staringer (eds.), *GAARs - A Key Element of Tax Systems in the Post-BEPS World* (Amsterdam: IBFD Publications), 741-764.

Freedman, Judith (2017), "Tax and Brexit", 33(1 Supp.) *Oxford Review of Economic Policy* S79-S90.

Freedman, Judith and John Vella (2016), "Finance Act 2016 Notes: Section 161 and Schedule 19: Large Businesses: Tax Strategies and Sanctions for Persistently Uncooperative Behaviour: Further Commentary", 5 *British Tax Review* 653-663.

G7 (2015), "Leaders' Declaration", G7 Summit, Schloss Elmau, 7-8 June, https://sustainabledevelopment.un.org/content/documents/7320LEADERS%20STATEMENT_FINAL_CLEAN.pdf.

Germany and United Kingdom (2014), "Germany-UK Joint Statement: Proposals for New Rules for Preferential IP Regimes", 11 November, https://www.gov.uk/government/publications/proposals-for-new-rules-for-preferential-ip-regimes-germany-uk-joint-statement.

Greenfield, Philip (2016), "Finance Act 2016 Notes: Section 41: Deduction of Income Tax at Source: Intellectual Property – Tax Avoidance", 5 *British Tax Review* 557-560.

Harra, Jim (2015), "BEPS and HMRC", 1283 *Tax Journal*, https://www.taxjournal.com/articles/beps-and-hmrc-29102015.

Hernández González-Barreda, Pablo A. (2018), "A Historical Analysis of the BEPS Action Plan: Old Acquaintances, New Friends and the Need for a New Approach", 46(4) *Intertax* 278-295.

HM Revenue and Customs (HMRC) and HM Treasury (2010), *Policy Paper: The Corporate Tax Road Map*, 29 November, https://www.gov.uk/government/publications/the-corporation-tax-road-map.

HM Revenue and Customs (HMRC) (2016), *Policy Paper: Corporation Tax, anti-hybrids rules*, 16 March, https://www.gov.uk/government/publications/corporation-tax-anti-hybrids-rules/corporation-tax-anti-hybrids-rules.

HM Revenue and Customs (HMRC) and HM Treasury (2017), *Royalties Withholding Tax, Consultation document*, 1 December, https://assets.publishing.service.gov.uk/government/uploads/system/uploads/attachment_data/file/663889/Royalties_Withholding_Tax_-_consultation.pdf.

HM Treasury (2016), *Policy Paper: Business Tax Roadmap*, 16 March, https://www.gov.uk/government/publications/business-tax-road-map.

HM Treasury (2017), *Corporate tax and the digital economy: position paper*, November, https://assets.publishing.service.gov.uk/government/uploads/system/uploads/attachment_data/file/661458/corporate_tax_and_the_digital_economy_position_paper.pdf.

HM Treasury (2018), *Corporate tax and the digital economy: position paper update*, March, https://assets.publishing.service.gov.uk/government/uploads/system/uploads/attachment_data/file/689240/corporate_tax_and_the_digital_economy_update_web.pdf.

HM Treasury and HM Revenue and Customs (HMRC) (2011), *Consultation on Controlled Foreign Companies (CFC) reform*, June, https://assets.publishing.service.gov.uk/government/uploads/system/uploads/attachment_data/file/81304/consult_cfc_detailed_proposals.pdf.

Maffini, Giorgia and Richard Collier (2015), "The UK International Tax Agenda for Business and the Impact of the OECD BEPS Project", Oxford University Centre for Business Taxation Working Paper Series 2015/13, August.

Neidle, Dan (2015), "The Diverted Profits Tax: Flawed by Design?", 2 *British Tax Review* 147-166.

Neidle, Dan (2017), "One minute with… Dan Neidle", 1358 *Tax Journal*, 15 June, https://www.taxjournal.com/articles/one-minute-dan-neidle-14062017.

Organisation for Economic Co-operation and Development (OECD) (2013), *Addressing Base Erosion and Profit Shifting* (Paris: OECD).

Organisation for Economic Co-operation and Development (OECD) (2015a), *Action 1 - 2015 Final Report: Addressing the Tax Challenges of the Digital Economy* (Paris: OECD).

Organisation for Economic Co-operation and Development (OECD) (2015b), *Action 5 - 2015 Final Report: Countering Harmful Tax Practices More Effectively, Taking into Account Transparency and Substance* (Paris: OECD).

Organisation for Economic Co-operation and Development (OECD) (2015c), *Action 6 - 2015 Final Report: Preventing the Granting of Treaty Benefits in Inappropriate Circumstances* (Paris: OECD).

Organisation for Economic Co-operation and Development (OECD) (2015d), *Action 12 - 2015 Final Report: Mandatory Disclosure Rules* (Paris: OECD).

Organisation for Economic Co-operation and Development (OECD) (2015e), *Action 14 - 2015 Final Report: Making Dispute Resolution Mechanisms More Effective* (Paris: OECD).

Organisation for Economic Co-operation and Development (OECD) (2016), *Tax Administrations and Capacity Building: A Collective Challenge* (Paris: OECD).

Organisation for Economic Co-operation and Development (OECD) (2017a), *Inclusive Framework on BEPS, Action 2: Neutralising the Effects of Branch Mismatch Arrangements,* July (Paris: OECD).

Organisation for Economic Co-operation and Development (OECD) (2017b), *Inclusive Framework on BEPS, Action 14: Making Dispute Resolution More Effective - MAP Peer Review Report, United Kingdom (Stage 1),* September (Paris: OECD).

Organisation for Economic Co-operation and Development (OECD) (2017c), *Inclusive Framework on BEPS: Action 5, Harmful Tax Practices – 2017: Progress Report on Preferential Regimes,* October (Paris: OECD).

Organisation for Economic Co-operation and Development (OECD) (2017d), *Inclusive Framework on BEPS: Action 5, Harmful Tax Practices - Peer Review Reports on the Exchange of Information on Tax Rulings,* December (Paris: OECD).

Organisation for Economic Co-operation and Development (OECD) (2018a), *Inclusive Framework on BEPS: Tax Challenges Arising from Digitalisation – Interim Report 2018,* March (Paris: OECD).

Organisation for Economic Co-operation and Development (OECD) (2018b), *Inclusive Framework on BEPS, Action 13: Country-by-Country Reporting – Compilation of Peer Review Reports (Phase 1),* May (Paris: OECD).

Osborne, Rt. Hon. George (Chancellor of the Exchequer) (2012), "Britain and Germany call for international action to strengthen tax standards, Joint Statement by the United Kingdom and Germany", 5 November, https://www.gov.uk/government/speeches/statement-by-the-chancellor-of-the-exchequer-rt-hon-george-osborne-mp-britain-germany-call-for-international-action-to-strengthen-tax-standards.

Salter, David and Lynne Oats (2014), "Finance Act 2014 Notes: Sections 234-283 and Schedules 34-36: Promoters of Tax Avoidance Schemes (High Risk Promoters)", 4 *British Tax Review* 454-463.

UK Government (2013), "Government response to House of Lords Select Committee on Economic Affairs 1st report of Session 2013-14: 'Tackling corporate tax avoidance in a global economy: is a new approach needed?'", 14 October,, SC/13-14/EA66, https://www.parliament.uk/documents/lords-committees/economic-affairs/Corporate-Taxation-April-2013/Government%20Response/EA66%20HMT%20Response%20to%20Corp%20Tax%20Report.pdf.

Watson, Sonia, Nick Palazzo-Corner and Stefan Haemmerle (2017), "UK View on Revised PE Standards in the Multilateral Instrument", 24(3) *International Transfer Pricing Journal* 181-187.

18 The Adoption of BEPS in the United States

Stewart Karlinsky* **and Thomas Phalen****

Abstract

The US as well as the rest of the world has struggled with how to tax foreign earnings by domestic corporations. In the case of the US, 1962 was a watershed moment with the imposition of Subpart F and the Controlled Foreign Corporation (CFC) rules. The OECD BEPS project initiated a few years ago and the 2017 US tax law's passage are two other significant watershed events that this chapter will discuss.

18.1 Uniqueness about the United States of America: Overview of Government and Tax System

The United States has both federal and subnational (state and local) tax systems which include income taxes imposed upon both individuals and corporations. Also, many states have a sales tax on goods and services, as well as property taxes. However, the US does not have a value added tax (VAT, also known as a goods and services tax or GST) nor a national sales tax.

The US has a bicameral legislature comprising the House of Representatives and Senate, an Executive Branch, and a historically strong independent judicial system. All of our income tax law as well as estate and gift taxation rules and related administrative provisions and definitions are currently included in the Internal Revenue Code of 1986. Thus, the Code covers domestic and international issues related to corporations, individuals, flow-through entities (partnerships, limited liability corporations (LLCs), limited liability partnerships (LLPs) and "S corporations"), trusts and estates. It does not include treaties. Prior to 1986, the tax law was codified in the Internal Revenue Code of 1954; before that in the 1939 Code, and so forth back to 25 February 1913 when the 16th Amendment of the US Constitution permitted a direct income tax on individuals pursuant to the Revenue Act of 1913.

To enact a tax law, a revenue measure must originate in the House of Representatives Ways and Means (W&M) Committee. It then goes to the House

* Emeritus Professor, San José State University, San José, California.

** Former corporate tax practitioner with over 50 years' experience in international taxation.

The authors would like to thank the Pacific Tax Policy Institute for their financial support for this important project.

of Representatives and if approved by a simple majority it proceeds to the Senate Finance Committee (SFC). They may approve the House bill or change it totally or to any extent in part. The Senate in the normal course will then vote on the SFC bill, but unless it is a reconciliation bill, it must have 60 senators approve it or else the filibuster rules may prevent its passage. If the House and Senate bills are different, the measure goes to a Joint Conference Committee (JCC) with members of the SFC and W&M committees from both sides of the aisle (Republicans and Democrats). It then goes back to the House and Senate to approve the JCC bill. If it passes both houses with a simple majority, the President can sign it, in which case it becomes law. Alternatively, if he vetoes it, the legislature has another "bite at the apple" but they need a supermajority to pass the bill.[1] Treaties are approved by the Senate and have the same level of authority as a tax law and, if they conflict, the later enacted provision will apply.

Within the Executive Branch is the Treasury Department and within that the Internal Revenue Service (IRS). Of the two, Treasury is more involved in tax policy, while the IRS is more heavily involved in administration and enforcement of the tax system often through regulations. There are three types of regulations that explain, interpret, enforce, or amplify the tax law passed by Congress.[2] Proposed regulations are trial balloons floated by Treasury to get various stakeholders' impressions, potential problems regarding implementation, etc. They do not have the authority of law but give guidance as to what the government is thinking about certain Code provisions. Often in conjunction with proposed regulations, Temporary Regulations are issued which are binding on government and taxpayers, but do sunset,[3] unless made final. Final Regulations are usually issued after a deliberation period and in the preamble they respond to various suggestions related to proposed regulations. Regulations are commercially available in a set of volumes that often exceed five books. The three types of regulations are also subdivided into legislative or interpretive. Interpretive regulations state what the law is with some explanation or examples. Legislative regulations are powers granted by Congress to the Secretary of the Treasury. For example, the consolidated regulations are over 300 pages long and have the force of law because in section 1502 of the Code[4] the legislature has deferred to the Treasury Department. Similarly, in section 337(d) the Treasury Department has been granted the power to assure that schemes and strategies to avoid the repeal of the General Utilities Doctrine[5] are not effective.

1 Exceptionally, the President may do neither and simply leave the bill unsigned (as in the case of the shortlived federal income tax Act of 1894 which preceded the 16th Amendment) in which case it in any event becomes law after 10 days provided that the Congress does not prevent return of the bill through adjournment during that period.

2 For further discussion of executive rule-making in the field of tax administration, see, e.g., Hickman (2011).

3 Internal Revenue Code, s 7805(e).

4 "The Secretary (of the Treasury) shall prescribe such regulations as he may deem necessary "

5 The *Tax Reform Act of 1986* repealed the General Utilities Doctrine so the tax law now requires the distribution of appreciated property (or in liquidation) to shareholders to be taxed at the corporate level as well as the shareholder level, in effect therefore being double taxed.

Besides regulations, the IRS issues numerous revenue rulings, revenue procedures, notices, information releases and private letter rulings.

In the case of the BEPS project, the Large Business & International (LB&I) division of the IRS has been assigned principal responsibility and currently these efforts are being spearheaded by Douglas O'Donnell, LB&I Commissioner, and his team. The US is a member of the OECD and the G20. As such it is somewhat impacted by the BEPS project, but some of the project's provisions were already in place as will be discussed below.

In the US court system disputes related to income taxes are primarily tried at the courts of original jurisdiction (Tax Court, District Court and US Court of Federal Claims). Court decisions may be appealed by either the government or the taxpayer to the Appeals level and if that does not produce a satisfactory verdict, the issue may be appealed to the US Supreme Court. However, that last appeal is rarely entertained[6] unless the case involves a constitutional issue or conflict among the courts or is of particular interest to some of the nine Supreme Court justices.

The BEPS project outcomes, officially released on 5 October 2015, are having some impact on US corporations doing business overseas and how they conduct business. However, concurrently with the implementation of BEPS worldwide, the US enacted a far-reaching income tax law on 22 December 2017 that makes a landmark change to the taxation of multinational domestic corporations in an attempt to make US corporations more attractive and competitive. We will first describe the US corporate tax regime before the impact of BEPS and the 2017 tax law changes (section 18.2), then discuss the new tax law changes (sections 18.3 and 18.4) and after that how the US is adapting to the BEPS changes (section 18.5). Section 18.6 concludes.

18.2 Former US Corporate Income Tax Regime

In Fiscal Year 2016 the US government spent USD 3.9 trillion on services provided and servicing of debt (Center on Budget and Policy Priorities, 2017). Revenue of USD 3.3 trillion was raised through taxes and USD 0.6 trillion was provided by Treasury borrowing. As noted in section 18.1, the US tax system is almost exclusively a direct tax system as there is no VAT, GST or national sales tax. Forty-seven per cent of Federal revenue is raised through individual income taxes, 34 per cent through employer and employee shares of social security and Medicare taxes, and 9 per cent through corporate income taxes. The remaining 10 per cent is raised through various excise taxes (tobacco, alcohol, petrol, tyres) and estate and gift taxes.

The US tax system had traditionally been a progressive tax system (especially for individuals) and was for the most part a cash basis system for small businesses and individuals. It has been moving to a consumption based tax system over the

6 Called granting a *writ of certiorari*.

last 30 years (see Karlinsky and Burton, 2004) and the latest tax law allows the immediate write-off of tangible personal property to the extent of taxpayer savings of USD 112 billion over ten years.

Historically, a domestic US corporation was technically taxed on its *worldwide* income as were US citizens and residents. However, if a domestic corporation (or individual for that matter) established a foreign corporation, that foreign income was not taxed to its shareholders, with a few exceptions, until it repatriated the funds back to the US in the form of dividends. As always in taxation, the devil is in the details and exceptions. The two main exceptions are Subpart F income and section 956 indirect repatriation of earnings and profits. Because profits were not taxed at the US statutory rate of 35 per cent (less foreign tax credits) until repatriated, there was the obvious tendency to keep the funds offshore. It also encourages shifting profits to a low tax country rather than the US. This then came under the scrutiny of section 482 transfer pricing regulations and in particular the "commensurate with income attributable to the intangible" provision.

Subpart F tries to deal with transactions that were set up for tax avoidance rather than good business or economic reasons. For example, if a US manufacturer of pharmaceuticals or computer chips set up a Cayman Island sales subsidiary that purchased products from the US parent corporation and then sold these products to South and Central America, the Cayman income would be taxable to the US parent corporation under the foreign base company sales provisions of Subpart F,[7] whether or not the profits were distributed to the US parent. On the other hand, if the US manufacturer produced scuba diving equipment and the Cayman corporation sold much of its inventory to Cayman Island dive shops, the income earned by the foreign subsidiary would not be taxable to the US parent until a dividend was paid or the shares were sold.[8] An obvious issue is the price that the US scuba diving manufacturer would charge the related party Cayman subsidiary. That is where transfer pricing rears its ugly head.

Section 956 deals with the foreign corporation investing in, or deemed to invest in, US property. This is aimed at the use of foreign funds in the US without declaring a formal dividend which would be taxed at the US statutory rate of 35 per cent.[9] For example, if the foreign corporation guaranteed a loan from an independent third party bank to the US shareholder, this would be taxable to the US shareholder to the extent of foreign earnings and profits. Similarly, if the foreign corporation bought real estate[10] in the US, that would be deemed to be taxable to the US shareholder.

7 Section 954(d).

8 Section 1248.

9 Net of any foreign taxes paid which would be creditable or taken as a deduction.

10 Section 956(c) defines property to include any US tangible property, stock of a domestic corporation, etc.

Because many US corporations have significant sales, service and use of intangibles overseas utilising foreign subsidiaries, there is estimated to be over USD 2.5 trillion in liquid assets "parked" overseas as of 31 December 2015, representing approximately 14 per cent of total US GDP (Cox, 2016, citing a report by forecaster Capital Economics). To tax the transfer of intangibles to foreign related parties, section 367(d) was enacted to tax the transfer as though it was a sale at fair market value. However, under this law as originally enacted, goodwill was not immediately taxed. One way to reduce the US tax burden was for the foreign affiliate to purchase existing intellectual property from the US parent (buy-in payment) early in the life cycle and enter into an R&D cost sharing agreement for ongoing R&D.[11] An agreement between the entities might also grant the foreign affiliate the right to license or manufacture and distribute the product in a designated territory outside the US.

Making the tax consequences of investing in overseas activities even more attractive, the financial accounting rules that impact effective tax rates[12] (ETRs) under US Accounting Principles Bulletin (APB) 23 allow "permanently reinvested" overseas income to be included in the denominator while the hypothetical US tax on the foreign income will not be in the numerator. This allowed some corporations to have an ETR in the low teens or even single digits.

To try to prevent earning stripping by a foreign related party lending money to its US affiliate, the Code included former section 163(j). The key factor in this provision was a thin capitalisation rule that if the payor's debt to equity ratio exceeded 1.5 to 1 and the payor's net interest expense exceeded 50 per cent of its adjusted taxable income, then the excess interest would be disallowed in the current period. It could then be carried forward for up to three years, after which it was permanently disallowed. One of the limitations of this provision was that a foreign parent corporation could have a worldwide borrowing relationship with an independent bank. The US corporation might borrow under this line of credit; so it was not borrowing from the parent corporation, and therefore was not subject to the interest deductibility limitation. The new section 163(j) (discussed in section 3 below) is not limited to a foreign parent nor to only related parties. Therefore, it is more encompassing and may impact venture capital, hedge and private equity funds as well as any business where debt is a significant funding mechanism.

Another important aspect of US international tax planning is the check the box (CTB) concept.[13] Originating in 1997, it is an integral part of many tax planning techniques. Essentially it allows a foreign or domestic entity's shareholder to choose whether they want a non-*per se* entity to be treated as a corporation or a flow through entity. It often is used to avoid the consequences of Subpart F on

11 Regulation 1.482-7.

12 The formula for the ETR is a numerator of foreign, domestic and state and local income taxes and the denominator is worldwide financial statement income.

13 Regulations 301.7701-2 and 3.

distributions between foreign entities as they would not be treated as a dividend but simply a transfer within the same tax entity. It is also how hybrid entities across countries often are created, which BEPS Action 2 is focused on. For example, for resident country purposes an entity may be recognised but for US tax purposes it may be treated as a disregarded entity or a flow-through partnership. *Per se* corporations are enumerated in Regulation 301.7701- 2(b)(8) as companies that are *not* eligible for this election. These include an Australian, UK, Hong Kong, Israel, Singapore, or Indian public limited company, a French or Belgian *société anonyme,* a Canadian corporation and company, EU *societas Europaea,* a German, Swiss or Liechtenstein *Aktiengesellschaft,* a New Zealand limited company or a US general corporation (Inc.).

18.3 US Tax Reform: The Tax Cuts and Jobs Act of 2017 Change to the US Corporate Regime

In a titanic shift in US tax policy, the 2017 tax act[14] permanently reduced the federal domestic corporate tax rate from the highest statutory tax rate of 35 per cent to a flat 21 per cent tax rate at a projected 10 year revenue loss of USD 1.35 trillion. This rate change became effective on 1 January 2018. Corporations that do not have a calendar year end will prorate the new and old tax rate to arrive at a blended tax rate[15] for the fiscal year ending after 1 January 2018. The Act also moved the corporate income tax from a progressive tax system, especially for small business, to a flat tax rate. These rules were designed to make the US more tax competitive with other OECD developed countries.

Unfortunately, non-corporate tax rates (sole proprietors, partnerships, LLCs, trusts, S corporations, and investment income) were not greatly reduced, with the exception of real estate and non-professional service businesses' receiving a 20 per cent tax rate cut.[16]

In order to limit the overall loss in projected total tax revenue over a ten year period to *only* USD 1.5 trillion, many longstanding corporate tax provisions were further restricted. For example, *net operating loss carryovers* arising after 2017 are limited to 80 per cent of the current year's taxable income and carryback of losses is no longer permitted, so generating USD 301 billion in revenue.

Business interest expense, which in the past had never been limited between unrelated parties, is now limited[17] to business interest income plus 30 per cent of adjusted taxable income. This is projected to increase tax revenue by USD 253 billion over ten years. Any excess is to be carried forward to be considered business interest in subsequent years. This provision applies to domestic lending as well as to cross-border lending and between unrelated as well as related parties.

14 Public Law 115-97, 131 Stat 2054, signed into law on 22 December 2017.
15 Section 15.
16 Section 199A.
17 Section 163(j).

Adjusted taxable income is the taxpayer's taxable income for the year without regard to:

a) income, gain, deductions or losses not properly allocable to a trade or business;
b) any business interest expense;
c) net operating loss (NOL) deduction;
d) depreciation, amortisation or depletion deduction for years prior to 2022;
e) other deductions prescribed by the Treasury; and
f) the 20 per cent artificial reduction in income.

As mentioned above, unlike our trading partners the US does not have any federal indirect taxes such as VAT, GST or national sales tax. Therefore, under World Trade Organization (WTO) rules the US may not subsidise exports through a direct tax exemption[18] system. This may be seen to put domestic producers at a competitive disadvantage that Congress has tried several times to alleviate.[19] In the 1970s and 1980s the US had a domestic international sales corporation (DISC) that exempted income on sales to foreign buyers. After almost ten years of litigation in the world courts, DISCs were held to violate GATT rules and were essentially repealed.[20] In 1984 Congress enacted another export subsidy, the foreign sales corporation (FSC) provisions which were also held to be non-compliant with international trade rules. These provisions were repealed in 2000 and replaced by extraterritorial taxed income (ETI) provisions which after two years were again held illegal. These provisions were primarily held to be illegal because they favoured sales to foreign buyers only. Finally, Congress passed a law (section 199) that did not discriminate between foreign buyers and domestic ones. Thus this Domestic Production Activity Deduction (DPAD) was viewed as WTO compliant. It was enacted to encourage domestic production and jobs. Ironically, it was repealed in the new tax law, involving an estimated revenue gain of USD 98 billion. As will be discussed further in section 18.4 below, the Foreign Derived Intangible Income (FDII) international tax provision of the new tax law may bring this US tax provisions again before the WTO. Some commentators have suggested that the rapidity at which the international trade organisations have ruled against discriminatory direct tax subsidies may damn this provision before it enters into full effect.[21]

18 See WTO Agreement on Subsidies and Countervailing Measures which allows indirect taxes to be border adjusted but not direct taxes.

19 For further discussion of the economic and legal issues and the debate in the US in the 1970s and early 1980s on this topic, see, e.g., Carlson, Hufbauer and Krauss (1976); Phillips (1976); Hufbauer (1983).

20 We still have an IC-DISC provision.

21 See Letter from Finance Ministers of Germany, France, the UK, Italy and Spain to US Treasury Secretary Mnuchin dated 11 December 2017, https://d500.epimg.net/descargables/2017/12/11/f155a6d45ee4aa21d61e70e55cd10040.pdf (accessed on 19 September 2018).

18.4 International Tax Reform

18.4.1 100 Per Cent Dividend Received Deduction from Certain Foreign Corporations

The International arena is where much of the new tax law change will impact multinational corporate taxpayers and intersect with BEPS. For dividends received after 31 December 2017 from specified 10 per cent or greater foreign companies, US corporations will be put on a Participation Exemption (territorial) tax system in the form of a 100 per cent dividend received deduction (DRD).[22] This is expected to save corporations USD 224 billion over the next ten years. None of the foreign taxes related to the tax free dividend will be creditable for US purposes. However, US citizens or residents are not eligible for this exemption. This 100 per cent DRD is not available to US corporations that are real estate investment trusts or regulated investment companies. Also, dividends from passive foreign investment companies (PFICs) and hybrid dividends, which are defined as dividends paid by a foreign corporation that receives a deduction or other type of tax benefit on the dividend payment, are not eligible for the 100 per cent DRD. If the foreign corporation receives a hybrid dividend from a lower tier controlled foreign corporation (CFC), then that dividend is automatically included in the income of the US shareholder.

18.4.2 Reduced Tax on Deferred Foreign Earnings[23]

To largely pay for the lower corporate tax rates and the move to a territorial system, the post-1986 "earnings and profits" sitting overseas will be taxed at 15.5 per cent for liquid assets and 8 per cent for other assets, whether these funds are repatriated or not. This is projected to generate USD 338 billion over the next eight years; however, the provisions are incredibly complex and, unlike similar 2004 repatriation provisions, are mandatory. The earnings and profits considered for this transition tax are the greater of net accumulated profits and losses of foreign affiliates as of 2 November 2017 or 31 December 2017 that have not been previously taxed in the US. Interestingly, in the short time over which the 2017 tax Act was discussed (roughly 50 days) it was suggested that the lower corporate tax rates and the repatriation of foreign earnings would create new jobs. In 2004, academic studies have shown that it primarily increased dividends, stock buybacks and C-suite salaries (Senate Permanent Subcommittee on Investigations, 2011; Pinson, 2011). In a recent media article (New York Times, 2018), it was pointed out that these three behaviours are already being exhibited. For example, nine pharmaceutical companies have announced USD 50 billion in stock buybacks since the tax law was passed. In another article it was pointed out that between 1 January 2018 and 20 February 2018 companies on the S&P 500 stock index announced USD 173 billion in stock buybacks (Brumley, 2018).

22 Section 245A.

23 Section 965 Transition Tax.

This tax can be reduced by foreign tax credits associated with the mandatory income inclusion provided the foreign taxes have been reduced by 55.7 per cent for income taxed at 15.5 per cent and 77.14 per cent for income taxed at the 8 per cent rate. The US multinational can also reduce the mandatory income inclusion by net operating losses carried forward into the 2017 tax year or elect not to use these losses.[24] An election can be made to pay this tax over eight years by paying 8 per cent in each of the first five years, 15 per cent in the sixth year, 20 per cent in the seventh year and 25 per cent in the eighth year. Interestingly, there is no interest charge on this potential eight-year deferral.

18.4.3 Valuation of IP Transfers

US tax law provides that if intellectual property (IP) is transferred to a related party outside the US, then it is deemed to be a sale at fair market value. Sections 936(h)(3)(B) and 367(d) have been tightened for transfers after 31 December 2017 to include goodwill, work in progress, going concern value and any similar item not attributable to tangible property or services. The new law has also granted the IRS under section 482 the right to value the transfer of intangibles on an aggregate basis which allows them to consider the holistic value. This new provision is meant to prevent base erosion on the transfer of IP overseas. It was largely prompted by several recent court cases including the *Veritas*[25] and *Amazon*[26] cases which affirmed that goodwill, going concern and workforce in place were not taxable when transferred overseas under the old law.

18.4.4 Global Intangible Low-Taxed Income

Another complex international tax provision, Global Intangible Low-Taxed Income[27] (GILTI), is expected to raise USD 112 billion. It functions as a minimum tax of 10.5 per cent. It presumes that above-normal foreign profits are attributable to intangibles and this extraordinary income will be taxed currently to the US shareholders. It requires US shareholders of controlled foreign corporations (CFC) to include in gross income their global intangible low taxed income for tax years beginning after 31 December 2017. Intangible income is defined as the adjusted net income of all low-taxed CFCs less an assumed 10 per cent reasonable return on the average tangible property[28] adjusted basis used in the trade or business. The shareholder basis in the CFC stock will be increased by the GILTI inclusion. The US shareholder is allowed a 50 per cent deduction of the pre-tax GILTI so the effective tax rate prior to any foreign tax credit is a 10.5 per cent minimum tax. In addition

24 Section 965(n).

25 *Veritas Software Corp. v. Commissioner* 133 TC 14 (Tax Court, 10 December 2009), non-acq IRB 2010-49 which affirmed that goodwill, going concern and workforce in place were not taxable when transferred overseas under the old law.

26 *Amazon.com Inc. v. Commissioner* 148 TC 8 (Tax Court, 23 March 2017).

27 Sections 951A and 250.

28 Defined as depreciable property, so land would not be counted.

to the 50 per cent deduction, this tax may be reduced by 80 per cent of foreign taxes paid or accrued on such income. The provision's stated intention is to discourage US corporations from operating abroad in low tax countries.

18.4.5 Foreign-Derived Intangible Income

Another complex new international tax provision is the Foreign-Derived Intangible Income (FDII) provision which resembles a patent box and results in an effective tax rate of 13.125 per cent on eligible income. However, unlike the typical patent box, this provision only favours income earned overseas by the US corporation. It is expected to save corporations USD 64 billion if, unlike DISCs, FSCs, ETI (discussed in section 18.3 above), it withstands international (WTO) scrutiny as to whether it is in legal terms a prohibited export subsidy. Interestingly, 11 days before tax law enactment (i.e., on 11 December 2017), the Finance Ministers from the five largest EU economies sent a joint letter to US Treasury Secretary Mnuchin outlining their concerns about FDII. They asserted that "the proposed incentive (FDII) would subsidize exports compared with domestic consumption. It could therefore face challenges as an illegal export subsidy under WTO Subsidies and Countervailing Measures Agreement rules". They also argued that this provision was not compliant with the BEPS consensus on accepted IP regimes. FDII has been scheduled to be discussed at the April 2018 OECD Forum on Harmful Tax Practices.

FDII-qualified income includes foreign sales, licenses, and leasing of US property and providing services to foreign related and unrelated parties for use outside the US. A sale to a foreign related person does not qualify unless ultimately sold to a foreign unrelated party. Services performed overseas to a related party will not qualify if substantially similar services are provided by the foreign related person in the US. There is also a carveout of a 10 per cent return on depreciable assets that would be taxed at the flat corporate rate of 21 per cent. The net income amount above the 10 per cent carveout receives a 37.5 per cent deduction which results in income of 62.5 per cent taxed at the new flat rate of 21 per cent or 13.125 per cent. These provisions are effective for tax years beginning after 31 December 2017, so companies are awaiting guidance on how to allocate costs toward this foreign income.

18.4.6 Base Erosion and Anti-Abuse Tax

The new tax law included a complex inbound Base Erosion and Anti-Abuse Tax[29] (BEAT) that is projected to raise USD 27 billion. It is characterised as a 10 per cent minimum tax on base erosion payments made to related foreign parties. The threshold for related parties is unusually low at 25 per cent. It will only apply to large corporations, as there is a threshold of USD 500 million in average gross receipts in the three immediately prior years and is effective for tax years beginning after 31 December 2017. Like the former and new section 163(j), discussed above,

29 Section 59A.

its purpose is to limit earnings stripping used to erode the US tax base. Assuming base erosion payments exceed 3 per cent of total consolidated deductions, this tax will kick in. It disallows interest, royalties, fees, services and other deductions between domestic and foreign related parties. It also covers acquisitions from foreign related parties of depreciable or amortisable property. This may limit transfers of IP from foreign to domestic related parties. Interestingly, it does not cover cost of goods sold items. Foreign tax credits may not be used to reduce this minimum tax.

The computation is essentially 10 per cent[30] of the corporation's modified taxable income which is taxable income including the disallowed BEAT payments. If the regular tax liability is lower than the BEAT, the higher minimum tax would be the tax liability for the year.

Another issue is that this provision might be contrary to the existing US model treaty[31] since a payment to a foreign related party would be treated differently than a payment to a domestic related party. Several trading partners have already raised this objection. For US purposes, a treaty and a tax law are viewed at the same authority level; however, if they conflict, then the latest provision (in this case the 2017 tax law) would prevail.

18.4.7 General Anti-Avoidance Rule (GAAR)

Many countries have a General Anti-Avoidance Rule (GAAR). The US does not. Instead it has section 7701(o) which looks at the economic substance of the transaction and the business purpose, and common law court cases such as *Gregory v Helvering*,[32] *Frank Lyon*,[33] etc. However, there have been a few cases recently where courts have been reluctant to apply these concepts.[34] In addition to the economic substance doctrine, US income tax treaties provide for limitation of benefits (LOB) to eliminate or reduce treaty benefits when the recipient of US source income is not the beneficial owner of the income. An example of this is the US-Barbados tax treaty and its protocols.

18.5 US Response to BEPS Program

As mentioned in section 18.1, the LB&I division of the IRS is tasked with implementing any BEPS changes as well as the new tax law. It serves corporations, S corporations and partnerships with more than USD 10 million of gross assets. This division is developing issue-based campaign areas of investigation where there is perceived to be higher risk of non-compliance that somewhat overlap with the spirit of the BEPS project. It first proposed on 31 January 2017, 13 such areas includ-

30 Five per cent in 2018.
31 Paragraph 24(4).
32 293 US 465 (1935).
33 435 US 561 (1978).
34 See, e.g., *Summa Holdings, Inc. v. Commissioner* (Sixth Circuit Court of Appeals, No. 16-1712, 16 February 2017).

ing Energy Credits, Section 199, Micro-Captive Insurance, Repatriation Campaign and Inbound Distributors and Form 1120-F non-filers.[35] On 3 November 2017 it proposed 11 additional campaigns most of which are in the International arena including Form 1120-F withholding compliance, Swiss Bank Program non-compliance, meeting the Section 911 requirements, Deferral of Cancellation of Indebtedness Income (CODI), Foreign Tax Credit Utilization, and Section 956 Avoidance.[36] This division is also heavily involved in Competent Authority, Treaty Analysis, Transfer Pricing, issues etc.

There are 15 action items which have been generated by the BEPS project and 2016 and 2017 were the years of implementation, although some countries had started implementing elements of this project before it had been finalised.

The 15 items are: Action 1, Digital Economy; Action 2, Hybrid Mismatch; Action 3, Strengthen Controlled Foreign Corporation (CFC) Rules; Action 4, Limit Interest Deductions; Action 5, Transparency and Substance; Action 6, Treaty Abuse; Action 7, Artificial Avoidance of Permanent Establishment (PE); Actions 8-10, Transfer Pricing; Action 11, Collect and Analyse Data; Action 12, Disclose Aggressive Tax Planning; Action 13, Country–by-Country (CbC) Reporting; Action 14, Improve Dispute Resolution within and between Countries; and Action 15, Multilateral Instrument.

Among the most contentious issues from the perspective of the US government and corporations are:

a) the fact that Action 2 is being implemented at the individual country level;

b) which model to use for PE status, i.e., the UN vs OECD Model, especially as to the rules governing Selling and Ancillary Services, Servers, and Commissionaires;

c) whether arms-length or profit split is the right model for Actions 8-10, Transfer Pricing;

d) serious concerns about Action 13, CbC Reporting, especially as to leakage to newspapers, competitors and the public and security of information in the face of hackers and loose government controls; and

e) different views on Action 14, Dispute Resolution, particularly Binding Arbitration, which the US, Canada and Singapore feel should be mandatory, while India worries for example about its loss of sovereignty and control.

35 IRS, "Large Business and International Launches Compliance Campaigns" (21 January 2017), https://www.irs.gov/businesses/large-business-and-international-launches-compliance-campaigns.

36 IRS, "Large Business and International Launches Compliance Campaigns" (3 November 2017), https://www.irs.gov/businesses/large-business-and-international-launches-compliance-campaigns-0.

18.5.1 Four Minimum Standards

Action 5, Transparency and Substance, involves issues that the US government had been working on for years prior to and during the BEPS implementation.

The same is true with Action 6, Treaty Abuse. For example, the US has long had a Limitation of Benefits (LOB) provision in its treaties. In February 2016, the Treasury Department released a revised US model income tax convention which makes the LOB provisions of future treaties even more restrictive.

In the area of Action 13, CbC Reporting, the US has issued regulatory guidance[37] to the US ultimate parent companies of a multinational business for tax years beginning on or after 20 June 2016, and in Revenue Procedure 2017-23 gave guidance regarding filing Form 8975 and Schedule A. It applies to US multinational enterprises with revenue of at least USD 850 million. The US competent authority has also established procedures to share this data with other countries. Essentially, the IRS will exchange Form 8975 information automatically with tax authorities where the US enters into a bilateral Competent Authority arrangement and the multinational has reported that it conducts business in the other country concerned. The IRS has indicated that it has been receiving the 2016 Country-by-Country Reports as requested by the BEPS Initiative.[38]

The US has been a leader in implementing Action 14. The LB&I have been working with many other developed countries to improve dispute resolution mechanisms between countries. The US is definitely committed to binding arbitration.[39]

18.5.2 Other BEPS Actions by the US

In relation to Action 1, Digital Economy, the US is not in agreement with the OECD interim report on the taxation of the digital economy. The US Treasury Secretary recently stated that "[t]he US firmly opposed proposals by any country to single out digital companies".[40] He went on to say that "I fully support international cooperation to address broader tax challenges arising from the modern economy and to put the international tax system on a more sustainable footing". The US continues to work with the OECD Working Group on the digital economy issues. Also, as noted the US does not have a VAT system nor are there any proposals to introduce one.

On Action 2, Neutralising the Effects of Hybrid Mismatch Arrangements, some of the US tax law changes[41] are aimed at general perceived abuses of the international tax system. Section 267A provides that a US interest or royalty tax deduction

37 TD 9773 1.6038-4.

38 Comment by Douglas O'Donnell, LB&I Commissioner, Eighth Annual Pacific Rim Tax Conference, Redwood City, CA, 8 March 2018.

39 US Model Income Tax Convention, Art. 25 (17 February 2016).

40 US Treasury, "Secretary Mnuchin Statement on OECD's Digital Economy Taxation Report", press release (16 March 2018), https://home.treasury.gov/news/press-releases/sm0316.

41 Specifically section 267A.

will be denied if the recipient is a related foreign hybrid entity, to the extent that such amount is not included in the counterparty's taxable income. Its application includes a situation where the income is not taxable in the foreign entity's country of residence or the foreign country gives a corresponding tax deduction relative to the income. A hybrid entity is defined as an entity that is fiscally transparent under US tax law, but not so treated as such under foreign tax law, or is treated as fiscally transparent under foreign law but not so treated under US law. Also, the US has dual consolidated loss rules that have predated Recommendations 6 and 7 of Part I.

Action 3, Strengthen CFC Rules, is largely met by the GILTI provisions discussed in section 18.4.4 above, and the existing CFC regime already incorporates many of its recommendations.

Action 4, Limit Interest Deduction and Income Stripping, has been addressed under new section 163(j) (discussed in section 18.3 above) in which interest expense between domestic or foreign related parties or unrelated parties is limited beginning in 2018.

Actions 8-10, Transfer Pricing, involves an area that the US government has been pursuing for many years, especially after the *Tax Reform Act of 1986* amended section 482 to include a "commensurate with income" provision that particularly impacts intangibles. The application of article 9 of US tax treaties is expected to be consistent with these Actions.

In the case of Action 11, Collect and Analyse Data, the IRS has been participating with many other parallel organisations in legally and appropriately sharing data and development of administrative effective practices, such as the Federation of Tax Administrators (FTA) and multilateral tax information exchanges (e.g., the Joint International Tax Shelter Information Centre, JITSIC).

In the area of Action 12, Disclosure of Aggressive Tax Planning, the US has statutory and regulatory disclosure rules for identifying and dealing with aggressive tax planning. Tax shelter identification has been ongoing for many years. However, the US does not have a GAAR nor a Diverted Profit Tax regime.

Finally, in the case of Action 15, Multilateral Instrument initiative (MLI), the US has not signed onto this instrument because it feels that the current US tax treaties are sufficient, although the US is pleased that the MLI includes mandatory binding arbitration which the US has long been a strong proponent of.

The US has agreements for exchange of information under Exchange of Information Request (EOIR).

The US was rated largely compliant (OECD, 2018, p. 31). It should be noted that the same report by the OECD (OECD, 2018, p. 5) commends the US for three specific tax law provisions: Interest Deductibility; Anti-Hybrid Rules; Minimum Tax on Certain Foreign Income.

Also, section 6038A deals with a US corporation that is 25 per cent foreign owned. Additional information is required that is directly related to transactions between the foreign and domestic entities to help enforce the new BEAT provisions. The penalties for not filing 5472 information reports have been increased from USD 10,000 to USD 25,000 by the new tax law.

18.6 Conclusion: Future of Tax Reform in the US

The future is always hard to predict, especially with the wild swings that have been occurring under the current Administration and the composition of the two branches of the legislature. In November 2018 the US will hold elections for all seats in the House of Representatives and one-third of the seats in the Senate. Depending on those results, the prognosis for tax law changes in general and in relation to international tax in particular may be very different from that prevailing at present. At a minimum, the WTO and EU challenges to the new FDII provisions discussed in section 18.4.5 above will need to be dealt with. The next year or two will probably involve digesting the massive and complex tax law changes and providing guidance and technical corrections to unintended consequences of those recently enacted changes.

Several countries and regions (e.g., the EU) have suggested or proposed tax law changes aimed at the digital economy, including a gross revenue tax or a rule which will somehow attribute generation of a permanent establishment to users. These actions however do not conform to BEPS. The reaction of the US to any such actions remains to be seen.

The US executive branch has proposed making the recently enacted individual tax rates permanent but legislative roadblocks and deficit increases may be insurmountable obstacles to this proposal right now.

References

Brumley, James (2018), "10 Companies Making Huge Stock Buybacks in 2018", *Kiplinger* (5 March), https://www.kiplinger.com/slideshow/investing/T052-S001-10-companies-making-huge-stock-buybacks-in-2018/index.html.

Carlson, G. N., G. C. Hufbauer and M. B. Krauss (1976), "Destination Principle Border Tax Adjustments for the Corporate Income Tax and Social Security Taxes", US Treasury Office of Tax Analysis Paper 20, November.

Center on Budget and Policy Priorities (2017), *Policy Basics: Where Do Our Federal Tax Dollars Go?*, Washington, DC, 4 October.

Cox, Jeff (2016), "US companies are hoarding $2.5 trillion in cash overseas", CNBC (20 September), https://www.cnbc.com/2016/09/20/us-companies-are-hoarding-2-and-a-half-trillion-dollars-in-cash-overseas.html.

Hickman, Kristin (2011), "The Promise and the Reality of US Tax Administration", in Chris Evans, Judith Freedman and Richard Krever (eds.), *The Delicate Balance: Tax, Discretion and the Rule of Law* (Amsterdam: IBFD Publications), 39-62.

Hufbauer, Gary Clyde (1983), "Subsidy Issues After the Tokyo Round", in William R. Cline (ed.), *Trade Policy in the 1980s* (Washington, DC: Institute for International Economics), 327-362.

Karlinsky, Stewart and Hughlene Burton (2004), "America's Inexorable Move to a Consumption-Based Tax System, or Why Warren Buffett is Winning the Class Tax War", 105 *Tax Notes* 699-710 (1 November).

New York Times (2018), "Well-Heeled Investors Reap the Republican Tax Cut Bonanza" (editorial), *New York Times* (25 February), https://www.nytimes.com/2018/02/25/opinion/investors-republican-tax-cut.html.

Organisation for Economic Co-operation and Development (OECD) (2018), *Secretary General's Interim Report to G20 Finance Ministers and Central Bank Governors*, March.

Phillips, J. C. (1976), "Border Tax Adjustments in International Trade", 9(2) *University of Queensland Law Journal* 151-166.

Pinson, M. Mendel (2011), "Effects of 2004 Int'l Tax Holiday: Recommendations Going Forward", Tax Analysts, 31 August, http://www.taxhistory.org/www/features.nsf/Articles/E7A958612953C1EF852578FD00607975?OpenDocument.

Senate Permanent Subcommittee on Investigations (2011), *Repatriating Offshore Funds: 2004 Tax Windfall for Select Multinationals*, Washington, DC, 11 October.

19 The Adoption of BEPS in Vietnam

Binh Tran-Nam*

Abstract

As a developing country, Vietnam has encountered some difficulties in collecting proper amounts of tax revenue from multinational enterprises. Thus, it has been closely and keenly monitoring the G20/OECD BEPS Program of tax reform since the publication of the BEPS final reports in 2015. Following its active role in promoting the implementation of BEPS Actions throughout the APEC member countries, Vietnam was admitted as the 100th member of the Inclusive Framework on BEPS in June 2017. This chapter examines Vietnam's implementation of the 15 Actions to date, particularly the minimum requirements involving Actions 5, 6, 13 and 14. It is apparent that, prior to becoming a member of the Inclusive Framework, Vietnam had introduced unilateral measures to protect its tax bases, particularly its corporate income tax base, with respect to multinational enterprises. A good example is the Decree 20/2017/ND-CP which contains a host of BEPS-related measures such as transfer pricing and country-by-country reporting. The chapter concludes that the implementation of BEPS would present both challenges and opportunities for Vietnam. The key challenge is the General Department of Taxation's lack of suitable human resources. In terms of opportunities, Vietnam could rapidly improve its tax legislative framework and tax administrative practices with reasonable costs within a short time frame.

19.1 Introduction

Located on the easternmost part of the Indochinese Peninsula in the Asia Pacific, Vietnam covers approximately 311,000 km^2 of land area (about the size of Poland).[1] Its population as of 1 July 2018 is about 96.5 million, making it the 15th most populous country in the world, and the 8th most populous in Asia.

Vietnam is one of the few remaining countries which still formally adhere to socialism. However, since the launch of the *Đổi Mới* (renovation) policy in the late 1980s, the country has made a gradual but steady transformation from having an inward looking, centrally planned economy to an outward looking, market-based

* Professor, School of Taxation and Business Law, UNSW Sydney and School of Business and Management, RMIT University Vietnam

1 Worldometers, "Countries in the World by Population" (2018), http://www.worldometers.info/world-population/population-by-country (accessed on 1 July 2018).

economy. After three decades of economic reform, it has achieved remarkable outcomes in terms of economic growth, poverty reduction and macroeconomic stability. Thanks to persistently high GDP growth rates, Vietnam has improved from being one of the 30 poorest countries in the world in the early 1990s to becoming a lower-end middle-income country by 2013.[2]

Vietnam's main economic sectors include food processing, clothing, footwear, farming and aquaculture. It depends crucially on trade with the rest of the world, particularly the US, China, Japan, South Korea, Germany and Singapore. In 2017, its exports were almost the same in value as its GDP while the value of its exports and imports combined were almost twice its GDP. Vietnam has also been the recipient of increasing foreign direct investment inflows (about 16 per cent of GDP in 2017), which contribute significantly to its economic growth and exports.[3]

In terms of trade grouping, Vietnam is a member of the Association of Southeast Asian Nations Economic Community (AEC) and Asia–Pacific Economic Cooperation (APEC). Most significantly, it became the 150th member of the World Trade Organization (WTO) in 2007. At the APEC summit in Da Nang in 2017, Vietnam reaffirmed its commitment to the Comprehensive and Progressive Trans-Pacific Partnership (CPTPP) without the US. In addition, Vietnam has also signed trade agreements with Australia, Chile, China, India, Japan, New Zealand, South Korea and the US, and completed negotiating a free trade agreement with the European Union (EU). With respect to the Organisation for Economic Co-operation and Development (OECD), Vietnam has an observer status.

The process of tax reform in Vietnam since *Doi Moi* has several noteworthy features. First, in the early stage, tax reform in Vietnam could be characterised by the formalisation of tax laws. Since 2003, Vietnam has undertaken a tax overhaul to meet ASEAN and WTO standards. Secondly, Vietnam's tax reform can be summarised by a structural shift from initial reliance on production taxes to increasing reliance on consumption and income taxes. Thirdly, in more recent times, Vietnam's tax reform can be described by the continuous fine-tuning of its main taxes together with the modernisation of its tax administration.

In Vietnam, there are currently 10 tax types and the three most important taxes in terms of revenue are value added tax (VAT), corporate income tax (CIT) and trade taxes. Vietnam's tax to GDP ratio is high by regional comparison. Tax laws are code based and enacted by the National Assembly with accompanying explanatory decrees from the Government and circulars from the Ministry of Finance (MoF), which controls tax policy. The General Department of Taxation (GDT), established in 1990, is within the MoF and responsible for administering all domestic revenue collection for the whole country.

---

2 World Bank, "Vietnam: Achieving Success as a Middle-income Country" (12 April 2013), http://www.worldbank.org/en/results/2013/04/12/vietnam-achieving-success-as-a-middle-income-country (accessed on 1 July 2018).

3 General Statistics Office of Vietnam, Statistics, https://www.gso.gov.vn/Default_en.aspx?tabid=766 (accessed on 1 July 2018).

19.2 The Vietnamese Government's Response to the G20/ OECD BEPS Program of Tax Reform

As an observer to the OECD trade and finance committees, Vietnam has been closely and keenly monitoring the G20/OECD BEPS Program of tax reform since the publication of the BEPS final reports in 2015. Based on the observed responses of the MoF and GDT, it seems plausible to suggest that the Vietnamese Government's initial attitude towards the BEPS project was one of cautious support. Since then, Vietnam has demonstrated a serious commitment to the BEPS project and a proactive approach to make it a reality in Vietnam. This can be illustrated by the following events:

a) in November 2015, the GDT invited Sean Foley, KPMG's global leader for transfer pricing, to share his insight in a workshop in Hanoi. The workshop covered many BEPS issues, particularly country-by-country (CbC) reporting and advance pricing agreement (APA) programs. The GDT expressed particular interest in the new CbC reporting regime and participation of the government-to-government sharing of tax information (Thuy, 2015);

b) in July 2016, the MoF and GDT jointly organised an international conference on the "BEPS Action Plan: International Practices and Vietnam's Perspectives" to promote awareness of the BEPS project in Vietnam. Following the conference, three working groups were established to study the best practices relating to the BEPS project (Nguyen and Du, 2017, p. 158);

c) in February 2017, the Vietnamese Government issued Decree No. 20/2017/ ND-CP on the tax administration of enterprises with related party transactions to take effect on 1 May 2017. The decree directly addresses several BEPS actions;

d) in the context of APEC, Vietnam has, as host and chair, also actively promoted the BEPS project during the APEC meetings during 2017. For example, during the APEC Finance and Central Bank Deputies meeting, the GDT held a side workshop on "BEPS Action Plan Deployment in APEC" in Nha Trang on 22 February 2017 (Tung, 2017). The BEPS action plan was further discussed at the APEC Finance Ministers' meeting held in Quang Nam on 20 October 2017 (Bon, 2017).

Vietnam's support for the BEPS project is not surprising. First, the government recognises that Vietnam is operating in a globally-integrated economic environment so it is imperative to join in global efforts against cross-border tax avoidance. Secondly, the GDT has been concerned with transfer pricing practices of multinationals operating in Vietnam, especially those companies which have declared losses continuously.[4] Thirdly, in view of its ongoing budget deficit, Vietnam has

4 For example, Coca Cola Vietnam began operating in the 1990s and for nearly 20 years it has continuously declared losses.

a great incentive to raise more tax revenue through improved tax legislation and administrative practices.

As argued, BEPS was a concern in Vietnam prior to the G20/OECD initiative. As a result, the country did already have some robust anti-avoidance regulations. Some examples of those regulations include:

a) Circulars 117/2006/TT-BTC and 66/2010/TT-BTC on transfer pricing issued by the MoF in 2006 and 2010 respectively. These Circulars provided guidance on the determination of market prices in related party transactions;

b) Circular 201/2013/TT-BTC issued by the MoF in 2013 with effect from 4 February 2014. This Circular provided guidance on the application of APAs in tax administration;

c) with Circulars 66 and 201, the legal regime relating to transfer pricing came to be based on a set of relatively comprehensive regulations;

d) treaty-shopping rule: based on the OECD's substance over form approach, tax treaty relief may be denied if the recipients are proven not to be the beneficial owners of the relevant payments;

e) interest deductibility: deductibility rules were set out governing interest payments on loans (see section 4 below for elaboration); and

f) there were neither explicit thin capitalisation nor CFC rules in Vietnam (Sheehan, 2017, p. 443). However, certain restrictions similar to thin capitalisation could be found in the regulations on foreign loans and CIT (i.e., permitted borrowing capacity and excessive interest rates). Further, as will be discussed in section 19.4.3, there have been regulations with similar effects to CFC rules.

19.3 Vietnam's Implementation of the Minimum BEPS Standards

Vietnam's proactive approaches, elaborated above, culminated in it becoming the 100th jurisdiction to join the Inclusive Framework on BEPS at the third plenary meeting of the Inclusive Framework on 21 June 2017, held at Noordwijks, the Netherlands. The admission of Vietnam as an Inclusive Framework member reflected in part the recognition of Vietnam's active leadership (as host and chair of various APEC committees) in promoting the consistent implementation of BEPS Actions throughout the APEC member countries. In addition to its Inclusive Framework membership, Vietnam also stated its commitment towards greater tax transparency by expressing its interest to join the Multilateral Convention on Mutual Administrative Assistance in Tax Matters (the Convention).

From a preliminary analysis of the 15 Actions, it seems most likely that, in the present situation, not all of the Actions will have an impact. However, some Actions will have a direct impact on businesses operating in Vietnam. For example, the changes proposed in Actions 8–10 on transfer pricing could potentially have a significant impact on companies having intra-group members in Vietnam (Mukherjee, 2016). This is because the "value creating" approach proposed in the BEPS Project is not the same as the margin approach employed by the Vietnamese tax authorities. It is interesting to note that, in implementing the BEPS Action Plan, it is conceivable that companies that have not engaged in transactions targeted by the BEPS rules may be affected by the BEPS-inspired legislation, e.g., new restrictions on interest deductibility (PwC Global, 2017).

As an Inclusive Framework member, Vietnam is committed to implementing the four minimum standards, namely Actions 5, 6, 13 and 14. Vietnam's action to date with respect to each of the minimum standards will be discussed in turn below.

19.3.1 Action 5 (Countering Harmful Tax Practices)

Action 5 consists of two components: preferential tax regimes and transparency of tax information.

In relation to the first component, like many neighbouring countries, Vietnam currently has various forms of tax incentives. These include both profit-based incentives such as reduced CIT rates or tax holidays, and cost-based incentives such as exemption/reduction of indirect taxes (VAT and import tax) or accelerated depreciation. Prior to 2004, Vietnam's tax incentive policies exhibited discriminatory treatment between domestic and foreign investments in that tax incentives (especially CIT and import tax reductions) granted to foreign investment were higher than those applied to domestic investment. Such discriminatory practices were gradually dismantled and by 2006, just before Vietnam's accession to the WTO, domestic and foreign invested enterprises were treated equally in terms of eligibility and level of tax incentives (Truong and Le, 2016, p. 22).

The policy objective of Vietnam's tax incentives is to promote strategic and inclusive growth so that tax incentives are granted on the basis of sector, region and scale of investment. Vietnam's 2014 Law of Investment identifies 13 broad types of sectors and three types of geographical locations that are eligible for investment incentives, and provides the government with the power in determining which particular sectors or regions are entitled to tax incentives (Truong & Le, 2016, p. 22).

The OECD has conducted a peer review of Vietnam's preferential tax regimes in connection with Action 5. The latest results, published in the May 2018 update of the Progress Report, are as follows (OECD, 2018):

a) out of scope: export processing zones and industry parks/zones (because they do not relate to geographically mobile income);

b) under review: economic zones, disadvantaged areas and intellectual property benefits.

It is unclear what the ultimate outcome will be of the peer review of Vietnam's policies on economic zones, disadvantage areas and intellectual property benefits. Nevertheless, it seems likely that the peer review process may result in reduced power of the Vietnamese government in making discretionary tax incentive decisions.

On the second component of Action 5 relating to transparency and exchange of information for tax purposes, Vietnam has committed to becoming a member of the Global Forum and/or have a satisfactory tax governance rating by 2019 (Council of the European Union, 2017, p. 14). In its 2017 report, the Council of the European Union concluded that Vietnam did not pass tax transparency standards but had made sufficient commitments to improvement.

19.3.2 Action 6 (Preventing Abuse of Tax Treaties)

As mentioned previously, Vietnam's domestic tax law contains provisions to prevent the abuse of tax treaty benefits. From 1997, the MoF issued a number of circulars guiding the implementation of treaties on avoidance of double taxation (DTAs) between Vietnam and other countries (e.g., Circulars 52/1997/TC-TCT, 59/1998/TT-BTC, 37/2000/TT-BTC and 133/2004/TT-BTC). In the early 2010s, there were efforts throughout the Asia Pacific region to prevent double non-taxation. Consistent with this trend, Vietnam began to modify its tax regulation on double taxation treaties to mitigate abusive tax treaty practices.

On 24 December 2013, the MoF issued Circular 205/2013/TT-BTC to amend Circular 133, with effect from 6 February 2014. While Circular 205 is largely consistent with Circular 133, it introduces for the first time: (i) anti-treaty-shopping rules on the basis of which the GDT could in certain cases deny DTA benefits, and (ii) the assertion and expansion of the beneficial ownership provisions. The Circular generally adopts the OECD Model Treaty's definitions of key terms and the OECD "substance over form" principle for the determination of a true beneficial owner of income, but also modifies explanations to reflect Vietnam's local conditions and tax policies.

Generally, a tax treaty benefit will be denied if the main purpose of a transaction or arrangement is tax abusive or if a treaty benefit claimant is not a true beneficial owner. In particular, beneficial ownership can be challenged if:

a) the applicant is due to distribute more than 50 per cent of its profit to an entity in a third country within 12 months from the receipt of such income;
b) the applicant has no or little business operations except the right to income from asset ownership;
c) income received by the applicant is disproportionately large for its assets, business scale or number of employees;
d) the applicant has no or low control, power or risk over assets, income or the right to future income;

e) the applicant has a back-to-back loan, licensing or technical service agreement with a third party;

f) the applicant is a resident of a jurisdiction with low (below 10 per cent) or no taxes; and

g) the applicant is an intermediary solely formed for obtaining treaty benefits.

Circular 205 also provides various examples to clarify applicability of the tax treaty benefit such as the determination of the permanent establishment (PE) and of profits attributable to the PE. Additionally, the Circular imposes a three-year deadline for companies to claim any benefits arising under the existing DTAs (no time limit in previous Circulars).

19.3.3 Action 13 (Transfer Pricing Documentation and Country-by-Country Reporting)

As mentioned in section 19.2 above, on 24 February 2017, the Vietnamese Government issued Decree 20 to replace Circular 66/2010/TT-BTC in prescribing the tax administration of enterprises engaging in transfer pricing. The new decree includes substantial changes to Circular 66, including a new transfer pricing documentation requirement and transfer pricing declaration form, with the aim of collecting more tax-related information on MNEs' business operations, using the approach set out in BEPS Action 13. Decree 20 has since been supplemented by Circular 41/2017/TT-BTC issued by the MoF in April 2017 with effect from 1 May 2017.

Some of the key features of Decree 20 relating to BEPS Action 13 are:

a) the three-tier transfer pricing documentation regime: Article 10(4) of Decree 20 stipulates that an MNE taxpayer is required to prepare and submit a local file, master file and CbC Report on prescribed forms;

b) CbC reporting requirement: a taxpayer must also submit a copy of its ultimate parent company's CbC Report if the ultimate parent company is obliged to submit such a document to its respective foreign tax authority, or if the taxpayer is a Vietnamese ultimate parent company with worldwide consolidated revenue in a fiscal year exceeding VND 18,000 billion (USD 781 million). If a taxpayer cannot provide such a CbC Report, the taxpayer shall provide a written explanation for the reason, the legal basis and reference to specific provisions from the law of the counterparty jurisdiction that prohibits the taxpayer from providing a copy of the CbC Report;

c) a new transfer pricing declaration form: the new form requires disclosure of more detailed information, including segmentation of profit and loss by related party and third-party transactions. Any gap between the margins earned on related and third-party transactions may increase the taxpayer's risk profile and trigger queries from the GDT. A taxpayer engaged in related party transactions solely with domestic related parties could be exempt from disclosing information on such transactions in the new transfer pricing declaration form under the condition that both parties have the same tax rate and neither party enjoys a tax incentive;

d) submission: the transfer pricing documentation package must be prepared before the submission date of the annual tax return, which gives taxpayers just 90 days (from the fiscal year end date) to complete the year's transfer pricing documentation package; and

e) exemption: a taxpayer is exempt from preparing its transfer pricing documentation package (but not any other aspect of Decree 20) if one of the following conditions is met:

   i) its turnover falls below VND 50 billion (USD 2.2 million) and the total value of related party transactions is below VND 30 billion (USD 1.3 million) in a tax period;

   ii) it has concluded an APA and submits annual APA report(s);

   iii) its turnover is below VND 200 billion (USD 8.7 million) and it performs simple functions and achieves at least the following ratios of earnings before interest and tax to revenue on its respective business: distribution (5 per cent), manufacturing (10 per cent) and processing (15 per cent).

19.3.4 Action 14 (Making Tax Dispute Resolution Mechanisms More Effective)

The anti-BEPS approach has the potential of creating more tax disputes, especially in the areas of tax incentives, tax treaty interpretations and transfer pricing adjustments. Action 14 is concerned with ensuring: (i) the mutual agreement procedure (MAP) is employed in good faith and a timely manner, (ii) timely administrative processes for averting treaty disputes and resolving tax disputes, and (iii) the rightful taxpayers are able to lodge MAP requests.

There are currently two avenues for resolving tax disputes in Vietnam: administrative tax appeal and litigation. Most tax disputes in Vietnam are resolved through administrative tax appeals whereas litigation is possible but less common. Alternative tax dispute resolution is not yet formally available under Vietnam's current tax administrative law.

The administrative tax appeal system provides in principle two levels of appeal: one at the local/provincial level and one at the higher level. In practice, further administrative appeals may still be possible, especially if the GDT perceives that the taxpayer has good grounds. At any stage during the administrative appeal process, the taxpayer may choose to exit and proceed to litigation at an administrative court. Once the taxpayer has started litigation proceedings against the GDT, the taxpayer cannot return to tax administrative appeal.

The system of Vietnam's People's courts, containing administrative courts, has three levels: district courts, provincial courts and the Supreme People's Court (under the administrative responsibility of the National Assembly of Vietnam). The mechanism for tax dispute resolution is neither comprehensive nor has yet become sufficiently strong although the framework of substantial tax laws has been greatly improved during the past 10 years. Further, local ambitions can sometimes prevail over centrally-formulated policies.

As a result of adopting the BEPS approach, there will be potentially more tax disputes between the GDT and business taxpayers. For example, Article 12 of Decree 20 provides that the GDT can use internal comparable data to impose transfer pricing adjustments in cases where a taxpayer is deemed non-compliant with the requirements of the Decree. This type of development could clearly give rise to increasingly lengthy disputes that may have to be settled through competent authority MAPs, and will likely also encourage increased use of APAs.

In principle, transfer pricing administrative appeals, litigation and MAPs are all available under Vietnam's current laws and bilateral tax treaties. In practice, the appeals process is often lengthy with mixed results, the litigation process is unpopular and MAP proceedings are not very productive (KPMG Vietnam, 2017, p. 4). Thus, Vietnam needs to demonstrate a firm commitment and a clear plan of reform in order to implement Action 14. To this end, it is necessary to await the final report and recommendations relating to Action 14 of the GDT Working Group on International Tax and Tax Treaties.

19.4 Vietnam's Implementation of Other BEPS Actions

Vietnam's implementation of the other BEPS Actions to date is summarised below.

19.4.1 Action 1: Addressing Tax Challenges of the Digital Economy

It has long been recognised that while Vietnam's tax laws are quite comprehensive in dealing with traditional tax matters, they have so far been unable to adequately cope with e-commerce or, more generally, the digital economy, as highlighted by unfounded allegations of tax evasion by the online advertising arms of Google and Facebook in Vietnam in 2012 (Vietnamnet, 2012; Bách, 2012). The Vietnamese Government has indicated the development of tax rules to deal with income derived from Vietnam by the digital companies is at the top of its agenda. The government's intention is to require all foreign digital companies to register, declare and pay tax in Vietnam. The GDT has recently affirmed that all kinds of e-commerce companies, including those conducting both business-to-customer and customer-to-customer transactions, will be obliged to declare and pay tax on their income arising from Vietnam.

Vietnam has chosen to formally deal with tax challenges of the digital economy through amending its law on tax administration. The proposed new law has been submitted to the National Assembly for consideration in 2018 and 2019. The new tax administration law is expected to become effective on 1 January or 1 July 2020. Below are some key points relating to the digital economy in the draft law (PwC Vietnam, 2017):

a) e-commerce is formally recognised as a specialised industry that requires special treatment;
b) foreign e-commerce enterprises will be required to establish a representative office in Vietnam;
c) payments for cross-border transactions are required to be processed through a domestic channel (i.e., the National Payment Corporation of Vietnam (NAPAS)). The tax authorities thereby aim to manage revenue from such transactions to tax foreign e-commerce enterprises.

In the meantime, Vietnam has sought to reinforce its current Foreign Contractor Tax (FCT) regime to protect its taxing right on Vietnam-sourced income derived by certain e-commerce businesses. Specifically, the MoF in January 2017 issued Official Letter 848/BTC-TCT to clarify the FCT declaration and payment obligations with respect to commission income of foreign digital companies, conducting business in online room booking services in Vietnam. Similarly, Official Letter 11828/BTC-CST by the MoF requires Uber Vietnam or entities delegated by Uber in the Netherlands to declare and pay FCT on behalf of Uber in the Netherlands.

19.4.2 Action 2: Neutralising the Effects of Hybrid Mismatch Arrangements

Vietnam has not yet taken any specific and formal steps to implement this Action although it is clearly in its interest to design domestic rules to neutralise the effects of hybrid instruments and entities (e.g., double non-taxation, double deduction, long-term deferral).

19.4.3 Action 3: Designing Effective CFC Rules

Vietnam has neither specific CFC rules nor an alternative regime. However, if a Vietnamese enterprise derives income from an investment project in a foreign country, it must declare and pay corporate income tax (CIT) in respect of the foreign income to the GDT, including in the case in which it enjoys tax reduction or exemption under the tax law of the foreign country. The foreign-derived income will be taxed at Vietnam's prevailing standard CIT rate, even if the Vietnamese enterprise enjoys an exemption or a reduced tax rate in accordance with the current CIT law. In principle, the Vietnamese enterprise may claim a foreign tax credit up to the equivalent of the tax payable under Vietnam's CIT law provided that the foreign income has been subject to any foreign tax, which is similar to Vietnam's CIT.

At this stage, it is unclear how Vietnam would consider introducing formal CFC rules or an alternate regime.

19.4.4 Action 4: Limiting Interest Deductions

Decree 20, effective from 1 May 2017, has introduced new restrictions on interest deductibility. Broadly speaking, the restriction takes the form of a fixed-ratio rule, which limits tax relief for a company's total interest costs to 20 per cent of its earnings before interest, tax, depreciation and amortisation (EBITDA). This rule, which applies uniformly across all industry sectors and without regard to the financing position of the wider group, represented a departure from the OECD's recommendations. The OECD approach seeks to address the problem of excessive interest deductibility through a group-ratio rule along with the fixed-ratio rule, allowing 'enhanced' interest deductions based on the ratio of the group interest to EBITDA. While the rules appear targeted solely at related party interest, ambiguity in the drafting of Decree 20 has created an uncertainty in applying the rule in cases where a company has both third-party and related party interest costs (PwC Global, 2017).

Related to interest deductibility rules are thin capitalisation rules. In August 2017, the MoF announced many tax reform proposals, which have been expected to be enacted by the National Assembly in 2018 with effect from 1 January 2019. Among the proposed CIT amendments is the introduction of thin capitalisation rules to limit deductibility of interest expense to specific debt to equity ratios of 5:1 for manufacturing, 12:1 for banking and 4:1 for all other sectors (EY, 2017). Industry sectors that are subject to minimum legal capital requirements are not affected by the thin capitalisation proposal.

19.4.5 Action 7: Preventing the Artificial Avoidance of Permanent Establishment Status

Vietnam has taken steps to implement Action 7 mainly in connection with the digital economy. For example, as discussed in section 19.4.1 above in relation to Action 1, the proposed revision of the law on tax administration requires foreign e-commerce enterprises to establish representative offices in Vietnam. Further, the Vietnamese tax authorities have brought some expanded PE concepts into effect under the current interpretive guidance on Vietnam's tax treaties such as GDT's Official Letter 2826/TCT-DNL. This letter stipulates that the involvement in the negotiation or performance of contracts by staff of a foreign company's representative office in Vietnam would constitute a PE for the foreign company in Vietnam.

19.4.6 Actions 8-10: Aligning Transfer Pricing Outcomes with Value Creation

Vietnam has also taken steps to update and expand its transfer pricing rules and other tax regulations to better align transfer pricing outcomes with value creation. This is best illustrated by such initiatives as Decree 20 on transfer pricing and the proposed new tax administration law regarding the digital economy. In particular, the draft new law of tax administration seeks to align profit outcomes with substantive economic activities and value created, and to implement the destination principle of indirect taxation.

19.4.7 Action 11: Measuring and Monitoring BEPS

As mentioned in section 19.2, following an international conference on BEPS in July 2016, the GDT announced the establishment of a BEPS Working Group within the GDT in accordance with Decision 1286/QD-TCT. This Working Group, led by the GDT General Director, is responsible for preparing and overseeing the implementation of the BEPS Action Plan. The GDT's BEPS Working Group consists of three sub-groups:

a) International Tax and Tax Treaty: Actions 6, 7, 14 and 15;

b) Transfer Pricing: Actions 8-10 and 13;

c) Other BEPS Action Plan: Actions 1, 2, 3, 4, 5, 11 and 12.

In fulfilling its aims and duties, the Working Group also plays the role of measuring and monitoring the implementation of the BEPS Action Plan in Vietnam.

19.4.8 Action 12: Mandatory Disclosure Rules

Action 12 contains recommendations regarding the design of mandatory disclosure rules for aggressive tax planning schemes, taking into consideration the administrative costs of tax administration and compliance costs of business taxpayers. Vietnam does not currently have any mandatory disclosure rules for aggressive tax planning and it is unlikely to introduce such rules in the near future. The primary reason for this policy stance is the perception that the tax system in Vietnam is comparatively too complex to businesses. The GDT is very concerned about Vietnam's poor international ranking in terms of the average time spent on business tax affairs (see PwC and World Bank Group, 2018). Since the GDT is actively trying to improve Vietnam's *Paying Taxes* ranking, it is most unlikely that the MoF or GDT will introduce a new measure that can potentially add to business tax compliance costs.

19.4.9 Action 15: Developing the Multilateral Instrument

The application of BEPS requires some adjustments to the existing model tax convention and bilateral tax treaties. As an overarching framework for tackling BEPS while respecting jurisdictional sovereignty, the Multilateral Instrument (MLI) can enhance bilateral tax treaties by incorporating Actions 2, 6, 7 and 14 into such treaties.

While Vietnam has expressed its interest in joining the Multilateral Instrument, it has not yet signed it. At present Vietnam has about 70 bilateral tax treaties. The GDT is still in the process of studying the MLI and the experience of the MLI signatory countries, as well as reviewing Vietnam's existing tax treaties. The GDT is expected to announce its final position by the end of 2018 (PwC Vietnam, 2018). Given the significant impact the MLI may have on Vietnam's existing tax treaties, the MoF will then further seek consultation from relevant ministries. If Vietnam eventually adopts the MLI, it is estimated that about 50 per cent of its existing tax treaties would be affected and those treaties could be amended accordingly (PwC Vietnam, 2018).

19.5 Vietnam's Adoption of Unilateral BEPS Measures

As discussed in previous sections, prior to becoming a member of the Inclusive Framework, Vietnam had already adopted many unilateral BEPS measures to protect its tax bases, particularly its CIT base with respect to MNEs. A good example is the Decree 20 which contains a host of BEPS-related measures. In terms of general anti-avoidance rules and diverted profit tax, Vietnam neither has such measures nor intends to introduce them in the near future. Nevertheless there are other measures that have played similar roles to a diverted profits tax or general anti-avoidance rules. Some of these measures are briefly discussed in the remainder of this section.

19.5.1 Diverted Profits Tax

There is no formal diverted profits tax in Vietnam. In particular, dividends paid to non-resident corporate investors are not subject to withholding tax. However, there are withholding tax measures which ensure that the tax paid by MNEs properly reflects the economic substance of their activities in Vietnam.

A withholding tax of 5 per cent is applicable to interest and any other amounts charged by the offshore lender in connection with the loan agreement. An offshore loan provided by a particular government or a semi-government institution may be eligible for an exemption where a tax treaty applies.

Royalties paid to a foreign party for the right to use or licence of patents, inventions, industrial property, designs, trademarks, copyright, and technical knowhow (broadly referred to as transfer of technology) are subject to withholding tax of 10 per cent. Where a tax treaty provides for a lower rate and conditions are met, the tax treaty rate should apply.

Vietnam's FCT regime covers the taxation of outbound, cross-border remittance of contract payments by a resident entity (including foreign-invested enterprises incorporated in Vietnam) to a foreign party that does not have a licenced presence in Vietnam, irrespective of whether the services are provided in Vietnam or overseas. This FCT generally applies to payments derived from Vietnam, except for the pure supply of goods, services performed and consumed outside Vietnam, and various other services performed wholly outside Vietnam (e.g., certain repairs, training, advertising, promotion). For direct (non-deduction-method) foreign contractors, VAT and CIT will be withheld by the contracting party at deemed rates. Various rates are specified according to the nature of the contract performed. For CIT, the FCT rate varies from 0.1 per cent to 10 per cent.

19.5.2 Tightening of General Anti-Avoidance Rules

Vietnam does not have any explicit, comprehensive general anti-avoidance rules. There is no indication that Vietnam will consider introducing such rules soon. However, Vietnam has sought to address the issue of tax avoidance through a combination of separate tax rules. The main approaches are briefly discussed below.

First, the Tax Administration Law in Vietnam contains a provision which generally requires all commercial transactions to be conducted in line with market rates.[5] Otherwise, the GDT will have the right to reassess for taxation purposes.

Secondly, as discussed previously, Decree 20 contains a host of revised and expanded transfer pricing rules which generally follow the OECD guidelines. Thirdly, there are some general anti-avoidance rules concerning beneficial ownership requirements for the purposes of claiming a tax treaty benefit. These regulations act to discourage business tax avoidance practices, especially those by MNEs operating in Vietnam.

Fourthly, in the area of special consumption tax (excise), there are various anti-avoidance rules which specify the minimum prices for excise purposes. For example, for certain manufactured or imported goods which are subsequently sold by a trading entity, the excise taxable price cannot be less than 93 per cent of the average selling price of the trading entity (PwC, 2016).

19.5.3 Automatic Exchange of Information

Prior to becoming a member of the Inclusive Framework, Vietnam did not formally commit to any automatic exchange information with other tax jurisdictions.

19.5.4 Voluntary Transparency Measures

Vietnam had not imposed a voluntary tax transparency code before joining the Inclusive Framework in June 2017. However, it had formally required information disclosure from businesses in the securities market. In particular, on 6 October 2015, the MoF issued Circular 155/2015/TT-BTC, superseding Circular 52/2012/TT-BTC regarding information disclosure in the securities market. Broadly speaking, Circular 155 requires businesses/investors in the securities market in Vietnam to disclose adequate and accurate information (especially information affecting security prices) in a timely manner.

19.6 Vietnam's International Tax Policy and Administrative Reforms Apart from BEPS

As far as CIT and VAT are concerned, the MoF and GDT are planning to submit to the Government and National Assembly proposals for amending and supplement-

5 See *Law on Tax Administration 2006*, Ch. III, http://moj.gov.vn/vbpq/en/lists/vn%20bn%20php%20lut/view_detail.aspx?itemid=3716 (accessed on 12 July 2018).

ing these tax laws. There are many proposed modifications, which are essentially to overcome the problems associated with the inadequacy of the current tax regulations. Most modifications are related to foreign companies such as taxation on capital transfer/project transfer, taxation of companies with related party transactions, or taxation on e-commerce, digital transactions and digital currency. Many of these issues are thus within the scope of the BEPS Action Plan, and are currently dealt with by government decrees rather than laws enacted by the National Assembly.

Similarly, the current law of tax administration in Vietnam has been amended and supplemented in response to the changing global economic and tax environments. Many of these changes are related to international taxation and BEPS (e.g., the proposed regulation on the digital economy) although some other changes are applicable to all business taxpayers. The revised draft law on tax administration is expected to be submitted to the National Assembly at the end of 2018 for approval in the beginning of 2019.

There are recent broader economic reform policies that have direct implications for international tax policy and administration. In particular, the Vietnamese Government has proposed a new policy on special economic zones (SEZs) in an attempt to accelerate the country's seemingly unsatisfactory economic growth rates in recent years. Vietnam's Ministry of Planning and Investment (MPI) has been drafting the law to open three SEZs that offer investors greater incentives and fewer restrictions than available to date in the country. The three SEZs are located in the coastal districts of Van Don (in the northern province Quang Ninh) and Bac Van Phong (in the central district of Khanh Hoa), and Phu Quoc Island in the south. The draft SEZ law was discussed by the National Assembly in early 2018 and planned to be voted on in June 2018. However, due to strong public opposition to the 99-year land lease as part of the proposed SEZ law, the Government has decided to delay voting on the draft law until the end of 2018.

A main feature of the proposed SEZs is the availability of a range of tax incentives, including exemption of trade taxes to businesses and individuals, tax holiday, reduced CIT rates, and VAT and excise free status (Government of Vietnam, 2018). The proposed tax incentives will be administered locally and potentially impose additional burdens on local tax offices. More important, it is unclear whether the spirit of such preferential tax regimes is consistent with Action 5. If the SEZ law is passed by the National Assembly in late 2018, one could plausibly expect the resulting tax preferential regimes to come under the review and scrutiny of the OECD's Harmful Tax Practices Committee. This would certainly impede the progress of the implementation of the BEPS Plan in Vietnam.

19.7 Concluding Remarks: Future of International Tax Reform in Vietnam

To move forward, Vietnam needs to develop a flexible and competitive economy that can effectively respond to rapid changes in the global economy. A viable and growing tax system is an integral part of such an economy. Given the significant role played by FDI and foreign-invested enterprises in driving economic development in Vietnam, international taxation is of critical importance to its tax system. In this concluding section, some of the key challenges and opportunities in the future of international tax reform in Vietnam are discussed as set out below.

19.7.1 Challenges

As in all developing countries, the demands for publicly provided goods and services in Vietnam have steadily grown over time. At the same time, traditional sources of public revenue such as oil and trade taxes have been declining. This puts pressure on VAT and CIT to grow continuously to avoid recurrent budget deficits. Due to the 2017 US tax cut, there is downward pressure on the company tax rate in Vietnam (and elsewhere). Thus, maintaining the integrity of the VAT and CIT bases remains the most fundamental challenge to the Vietnamese tax authorities.

Despite a comprehensive tax legislative framework and the government's commitments, the ability of the MoF and GDT to effectively implement international tax reforms remains limited. Generally, the staff of the MoF and GDT lack the technical expertise and experience to handle difficult international tax cases. It is more than just a question of financial resources. It is difficult for the MoF and GDT to recruit a sufficient number of employees having appropriate skills, knowledge and experiences to administer international taxation. The domestic university system is not yet geared toward producing such graduates. The use of private sector consultants from large accounting firms to train MoF and GDT staff may give rise to conflicts of interest because those consultants many also advise business taxpayers.

Vietnam's ability to attract FDI inflows is essential to its economic development. Yet the tax system in Vietnam is perceived as complex, especially in terms of time spent on complying with tax requirements. According to *Paying Taxes 2018* (PwC and World Bank Group, 2018), a mid-size company in Vietnam spends on average 498 hours annually on tax-related matters, which is far more than in any other member countries of the AEC. It is unclear whether international tax reforms will help or hinder Vietnam's tax simplification efforts.

19.7.2 Opportunities

As an Inclusive Framework member, Vietnam could rapidly improve its tax legislative framework and tax administrative practices with reasonable costs. If Vietnam is left to its own devices, under the principle of gradualism, international tax reforms in Vietnam would proceed at a much slower pace and in a more circuitous and costly manner. Thus, the externally imposed BEPS Action Plan can be viewed as a blessing in disguise.

Admittedly the BEPS Actions are not ones of Vietnam's own choosing but the BEPS Project has not been driven exclusively by the more technically advanced and internationally active countries. The Project has explicitly recognised the needs of developing countries, including members of the AEC such as Vietnam. After all, prior to becoming an Inclusive Framework member, Vietnam had already introduced legislation that specifically addressed BEPS-type issues. Further, being an Inclusive Framework member does not necessarily rule out Vietnam's ability to adapt BEPS Actions to local conditions and national aspirations (Walpole, 2017, p. 653).

There are other benefits to Vietnam. International tax reforms brought about by the BEPS Project would assist in enhancing the sophistication of the GDT that has few resources and little expertise at its disposal. The BEPS peer review process will provide Vietnam with much needed support. In addition, through the exchange of information between jurisdictions, there will be greater international collaboration and cooperation that will benefit Vietnam in the long run.

References

Bách, Xuân (2012), "Google, Facebook Không Trốn Thuế tại Việt Nam", *ICT News*, 10 April, http://ictnews.vn/internet/google-facebook-khong-tron-thue-tai-viet-nam-101814.ict (accessed on 12 July 2018).

Bon, Manh (2017), "Finance Ministers Scrutinise Tax Base Erosion in APEC Economies", *Vietnam Investment Review*, 14 October, http://www.vir.com.vn/finance-ministers-scrutinise-tax-base-erosion-in-apec-economies-52958.html (accessed on 17 August 2018).

Council of the European Union (2017), *Outcome of Proceedings: The EU List of Non-Cooperative Jurisdictions for Tax Purposes*, Brussels, 5 December, http://www.consilium.europa.eu/media/31945/st15429en17.pdf (accessed on 12 July 2018).

EY (2017), "Vietnam Announces Tax Reform Proposals", *Global Tax Alert*, 8 September, https://taxinsights.ey.com/archive/archive-news/vietnam-announces-tax-reform-proposals.aspx (accessed on 12 July 2018).

KPMG Vietnam (2017), *Integrated International Tax - Transfer Pricing*, Hanoi, https://home.kpmg.com/content/dam/kpmg/xx/pdf/2017/03/tnf-tp-vietnam-mar7-2017.pdf (accessed on 12 July 2018).

Mukherjee, Joy (2016), "BEPS – What Does It Mean for Vietnam?", *Vietnam Economic Times*, 14 October, http://www.vneconomictimes.com/article/consultant-s-corner/beps-what-does-it-mean-for-vietnam (accessed on 17 August 2018).

Nguyen, Phat Tan and Bich Ngoc Du (2017), "Draft Decree on Transfer Pricing and Direct Tax Administration of Related-Party Transactions", 24(2) *International Transfer Pricing Journal* 158-166.

Organisation for Economic Co-operation and Development (OECD) (2018), *Harmful Tax Practices – 2017 Progress Report on Preferential Tax Regimes, Update as of 9 May 2018* (Paris: OECD).

PwC (2016), *Vietnam Pocket Tax Book,* https://www.pwc.com.au/asia-practice/assets/vietnam-pocket-tax-book-2016.pdf (accessed on 12 July 2018).

PwC Global (2017), "Vietnam Introduces New Restrictions on Interest Deductibility", *Tax Insights,* 2 June,https://www.pwc.com/gx/en/services/tax/publications/pricing-knowledge-network.html.

PwC Vietnam (2017), "The government has issued a draft law to replace the current law on Tax Administration", *Vietnam NewsBrief,* 29 November, https://www.pwc.com/vn/en/publications/2017/20171129-pwc-vietnam-newsbrief-tax-admin-law-en.pdf (accessed on 12 July 2018).

PwC Vietnam (2018), "Multilateral Convention to Implement Tax Treaty Related Measures to Prevent Base Erosion and Profit Shifting ('BEPS') coming into force soon", *Vietnam NewsBrief,* 4 June, https://www.pwc.com/vn/en/publications/2018/20180604-pwc-newsbrief-mli-en.pdf (accessed on 12 July 2018).

PwC and World Bank Group (2018), *Paying Taxes 2018,* https://www.pwc.com/gx/en/paying-taxes/pdf/pwc_paying_taxes_2018_full_report.pdf (accessed on 12 July 2018).

Sheehan, Jack (2017), "The Mekong Region: Cambodia, Laos, Myanmar, Thailand and Vietnam", in Sam Sim and Mei-June Soo (eds.), *Asian Voices: BEPS and Beyond* (Amsterdam: IFBD Publications), 443-458.

Thuy, Mai (2015), "KPMG Leader Visit Highlights BEPS Initiative", *Vietnam Investment Review,* 16 November, http://www.vir.com.vn/kpmg-leader-visit-highlights-beps-initiative-38524.html (accessed on 17 August 2018).

Tung, Thanh (2017), "BEPS Action Plan in APEC To Be Deployed", *Vietnam Investment Review,* 23 February, http://www.vir.com.vn/beps-action-plan-in-apec-to-be-deployed-47613.html (accessed on 17 August 2018).

Truong, Ba Tuan and Quang Thuan Le (2016), *Assessing Vietnam's Tax Incentive Policies* (Hanoi: Oxfam and UN Women), https://vietnam.oxfam.org/sites/vietnam.oxfam.org/files/file_attachments/Oxfam%20Tax%20incentive%20report%20ENG.pdf (accessed on 12 July 2018).

Vietnamnet (2012), "Facebook's, Google's Agents Suspected of Evading Tax in Vietnam", 9 March, http://english.vietnamnet.vn/fms/business/19568/facebook-s--google-s-agents-suspected-of-evading-tax-in-vietnam.html (accessed on 12 July 2018).

Walpole, Michael (2017), "Conclusion and What the Future Portends", in Sam Sim and Mei-June Soo (eds.), *Asian Voices: BEPS and Beyond* (Amsterdam: IFBD Publications), 653-662.

Lightning Source UK Ltd.
Milton Keynes UK
UKHW032302220223
417462UK00010B/130

9 781906 201487